Restorative Justice, Reconciliation, and Peacebuilding

STUDIES IN STRATEGIC PEACEBUILDING

Series Editors
R. Scott Appleby, John Paul Lederach, and Daniel Philpott
The Joan B. Kroc Institute for International Peace Studies
University of Notre Dame

Strategies of Peace
Edited by Daniel Philpott and Gerard F. Powers

Unionists, Loyalists, and Conflict Transformation in Northern Ireland
Lee A. Smithey

Just and Unjust Peace
An Ethic of Political Reconciliation
Daniel Philpott

Counting Civilian Casualties
An Introduction to Recording and Estimating Nonmilitary Deaths in Conflict
Edited by Taylor B. Seybolt, Jay D. Aronson, and Baruch Fischhoff

Restorative Justice, Reconciliation, and Peacebuilding
Edited by Jennifer J. Llewellyn and Daniel Philpott

Restorative Justice, Reconciliation, and Peacebuilding

EDITED BY JENNIFER J. LLEWELLYN
and
DANIEL PHILPOTT

OXFORD
UNIVERSITY PRESS

OXFORD
UNIVERSITY PRESS

Oxford University Press is a department of the University of Oxford.
It furthers the University's objective of excellence in research, scholarship,
and education by publishing worldwide.

Oxford New York
Auckland Cape Town Dar es Salaam Hong Kong Karachi
Kuala Lumpur Madrid Melbourne Mexico City Nairobi
New Delhi Shanghai Taipei Toronto

With offices in
Argentina Austria Brazil Chile Czech Republic France Greece
Guatemala Hungary Italy Japan Poland Portugal Singapore
South Korea Switzerland Thailand Turkey Ukraine Vietnam

Oxford is a registered trade mark of Oxford University Press
in the UK and certain other countries.

Published in the United States of America by
Oxford University Press
198 Madison Avenue, New York, NY 10016

© Oxford University Press 2014

All rights reserved. No part of this publication may be reproduced,
stored in a retrieval system, or transmitted, in any form or by any means,
without the prior permission in writing of Oxford University Press,
or as expressly permitted by law, by license, or under terms agreed with the
appropriate reproduction rights organization. Inquiries concerning reproduction
outside the scope of the above should be sent to the Rights Department,
Oxford University Press, at the address above.

You must not circulate this work in any other form
and you must impose this same condition on any acquirer.

Cataloging-in-Publication data is on file with the Library of Congress

9780199364862 (hbk.)
9780199364879 (pbk.)

9 8 7 6 5 4 3 2 1

Printed in the United States of America on acid-free paper

Dedicated to:

Blake Brown, Owen and Elliott Llewellyn-Brown
And to Diana, Angela, James, and Peter Philpott

The relationships that sustain us.

CONTENTS

Acknowledgments ix
Biographies of the Contributors xi

CHAPTER 1. Introduction 1
JENNIFER J. LLEWELLYN AND DANIEL PHILPOTT

CHAPTER 2. Restorative Justice and Reconciliation:
Twin Frameworks for Peacebuilding 14
JENNIFER J. LLEWELLYN AND DANIEL PHILPOTT

CHAPTER 3. Charting the Path of Justice in Peacebuilding 37
AARON P. BOESENECKER AND LESLIE VINJAMURI

CHAPTER 4. Reconciliation as Heterodoxy 77
JONATHAN VANANTWERPEN

CHAPTER 5. Accountability 118
DANIEL W. VAN NESS

CHAPTER 6. Amnesties in the Pursuit of Reconciliation,
Peacebuilding, and Restorative Justice 138
LOUISE MALLINDER

CHAPTER 7. The Role of Forgiveness in Reconciliation
and Restorative Justice: A Christian Theological
Perspective 174
STEPHEN J. POPE

CHAPTER 8. Pursuing Inclusive Reparations: Living between
Promise and Non-Delivery 197
CHARLES VILLA-VICENCIO

CHAPTER 9. Traditional Justice 214
JOHN BRAITHWAITE

CHAPTER 10. Doing Justice Differently: From Revolution
to Transformation in Restorative Justice
and Political Reconciliation 240
JASON A. SPRINGS

Index 259

ACKNOWLEDGMENTS

This volume pairs restorative justice and reconciliation as a conceptual framework for peacebuilding grounded in a relational approach that is contextual, comprehensive, integrative, and holistic. The collaboration behind the volume bears these same attributes. It involved leading scholars in political science, law, criminology, sociology, theology, and religious studies and has benefited from their diversity of scholarly contexts and practical experience. The authors accepted with enthusiasm the invitation to work together in developing a conceptual framework for peacebuilding. Their embrace of this mission and their cooperation with one another resulted in an integrated volume whose whole is greater than the sum of the individual contributions. We are grateful for each author's wisdom, knowledge, and intellectual passion.

The Program on Religion and Reconciliation at the Joan B. Kroc Institute for International Peace Studies at the University of Notre Dame served as an important home for our endeavors. The Kroc Institute provided a vibrant intellectual environment for the project, whose themes manifest deeply Kroc's own stress on "strategic peacebuilding." Kroc also provided critical funding both for an authors' workshop in September 2010 and for an international symposium and public panel discussion in New York City in November 2011, both organized to reflect our project's themes and participants. We thank Kroc's Director, Scott Appleby, for his indispensable support from beginning to end. We thank also Kroc's event planners Kathy Smarella and Anne Riordan, its Communication Director, Joan Fallon, its Executive Director, Hal Culbertson, and Faculty Assistant Cathy Laake. We thank also the many faculty at Kroc and elsewhere at the University of Notre Dame who served as interlocutors and participants at the authors' workshop.

The project was also supported by the Nova Scotia Restorative Justice Community University Research Alliance (NSRJ-CURA) at the Schulich School of Law, Dalhousie University. The NSRJ-CURA was funded in this work by the

Social Science Humanities Research Council of Canada. We are grateful to the Project Manager Chrystal Gray for her assistance throughout the project.

The project drew early inspiration and support from the Restorative Peacebuilding Project of the Alliance of NGOs on Criminal Justice and Crime Prevention's Working Party on Restorative Justice. Members of the project contributed to this volume and in doing so to the project's goal of expanding the scholarly foundation for a restorative approach to peacebuilding.

This volume was the subject of an international symposium as well as a public panel discussion, "Paradigms for Peacebuilding," held in New York City in 2011. We are grateful to the many leading scholars and practitioners who provided their insights and reflections as part of these events. We also owe a debt of thanks to our partners and hosts for these events: the Institute for International Law and Justice and the Center for Human Rights and Global Justice at New York University Law School, the New York Law School, the Kroc Institute, the Nova Scotia Restorative Justice Community University Research Alliance, and the Schulich School of Law at Dalhousie University. In particular, we were fortunate to collaborate with Robert Howse, Angelina Fisher, and Ruti Teitel on these events.

We are pleased and honored to have this volume appear in Oxford University Press' series on strategic peacebuilding, edited by Scott Appleby, John Paul Lederach, and Daniel Philpott, and are grateful to our editors at Oxford for their careful and thorough attention.

In short, in a project aimed at developing a relational approach to peacebuilding, we are grateful for the many relationships on which we have been critically dependent. It is our hope that the enterprise of building peace will be strengthened by these efforts.

Jennifer J. Llewellyn, Halifax, Nova Scotia
Daniel Philpott, Notre Dame, Indiana
October 15, 2013

BIOGRAPHIES OF THE CONTRIBUTORS

Aaron P. Boesenecker is an Assistant Professor in the International Politics Program at the School of International Service, American University, where he also serves as the School's Undergraduate Research Coordinator. His research interests include European politics, comparative political economy, social policy, the intersection of religion and politics, the politics of transitional justice, and research methods and methodology. His current research focuses on social policy development and reform in Europe and the United States. He is also engaged in an ongoing collaborative research project concerning the role of religion and the transmission of norms in post-conflict and transitional justice settings. Boesenecker received his BA in International and Comparative Politics, Comparative Religion, and German from Western Michigan University; his MA from Georgetown University's BMW Center for German and European Studies; and his PhD from Georgetown University's Department of Government.

John Braithwaite is a Professor at the Australian National University. He leads a project there called Peacebuilding Compared. It seeks to code more than 600 variables about the most significant 50 armed conflicts since 1990. Recent books from the project, available as free downloads, are *Networked Governance of Freedom and Tyranny: Peace in Timor-Leste* (with Charlesworth and Soares); *Anomie and Violence: Non-Truth and Reconciliation in Indonesian Peacebuilding* (with Cookson, V. Braithwaite, and Dunn); *Reconciliation and Architectures of Commitment: Sequencing Peace in Bougainville* (with Charlesworth, Reddy, and Dunn), and *Pillars and Shadows: Statebuilding as Peacebuilding in Solomon Islands* (with Dinnen, Allen, V. Braithwaite, and Charlesworth).

Louise Mallinder is a reader in human rights and international law at the Transitional Justice Institute (TJI), University of Ulster. Her research focuses on amnesty laws and transitional justice. As part of this research, she has worked with colleagues on an interdisciplinary, comparative study of amnesty laws in Argentina, Bosnia-Herzegovina, South Africa, Uganda, and Uruguay, including fieldwork in these jurisdictions. She has also written extensively on amnesties and has developed the Amnesty Law Database, which currently contains information on over 520 amnesty laws in 138 countries since the end of World War II. In addition to her scholarly work, she is Vice-Chair of the Committee on the Administration of Justice, a leading human rights organization in Northern Ireland. She has also advised a range of policymakers and activists on transitional justice and rule of law internationally and in a number of countries.

Daniel Philpott is Professor of Political Science and Peace Studies at the University of Notre Dame. He is on the faculty of the Joan B. Kroc Institute for International Peace Studies, where he directed the Program on Religion and Reconciliation. His most recent books are *Just and Unjust Peace: An Ethic of Political Reconciliation* (Oxford, 2012) and, coauthored with Monica Duffy Toft and Timothy Samuel Shah, *God's Century: Resurgent Religion and Global Politics* (Norton, 2011). He has also promoted reconciliation as an activist—in Kashmir from 2000 to 2006 as Senior Associate of the International Center for Religion and Diplomacy; and in the Great Lakes Region of Africa from 2009 to the present, as part of the Catholic Peacebuilding Network.

Stephen J. Pope is a Professor in the Theology Department at Boston College, where he teaches courses on social ethics and the intersection of science and theology. He received his PhD from the University of Chicago. His publications include *The Evolution of Altruism and the Ordering of Love* (Georgetown University Press, 1994), *Human Evolution and Christian Ethics* (New York: Cambridge University Press, 2007), and *Hope and Solidarity: Jon Sobrino's Challenge to Christian Theology*, editor (Maryknoll, NY: Orbis Press, 2008), and "Restorative Justice as a Prophetic Path to Peace," *Catholic Theological Society of America Proceedings* 65 (2010):19–34. He has worked for five years as a volunteer for Catholic chaplaincies in several Massachusetts prisons and served on a variety of workshops focused on the contribution of religion to political reconciliation for Catholic Relief Services and the Jesuit Refugee Service.

Jason A. Springs is Assistant Professor of Religion, Ethics, and Peace Studies at the Kroc Institute for International Peace Studies at the University of Notre Dame, where he also holds an appointment as faculty fellow in the Center for the Study of Religion and Society, Department of Sociology. His research and teaching focus on ethical perspectives on restorative justice, conceptions of religious toleration and the challenges posed by oppositional forms of moral and religious pluralism for transforming conflict in European and North American contexts, religious nationalism, and lenses of structural and cultural violence for peacebuilding. His articles addressing the role of religion and conflict in modern public life appear in *Journal of Religion*, *Journal of Religious Ethics*, *Modern Theology*, *Journal of the American Academy of Religion*, *Contemporary Pragmatism*, and *Soundings: An Interdisciplinary Journal*. His broader interests include the ethical and political dimensions of American pragmatist thought and postliberal theology. He is the author of *Toward a Generous Orthodoxy: Prospects for Hans Frei's Postliberal Theology* (Oxford University Press, 2010), and co-author (with Atalia Omer) of *Religious Nationalism* (ABC: Clio, 2013).

Jonathan VanAntwerpen is Director of the program on religion and the public sphere at the Social Science Research Council and editor of *The Immanent Frame*. Originally trained as a philosopher, he received his doctorate in sociology from the University of California, Berkeley. He is co-editor of a series of books on secularism and religion, including *Habermas and Religion* (Polity, 2013), *Rethinking Secularism* (Oxford University Press, 2011), *The Post-Secular in Question* (NYU Press, 2012), *The Power of Religion in the Public Sphere* (Columbia University Press, 2011), and *Varieties of Secularism in a Secular Age* (Harvard University Press, 2010).

Daniel W. Van Ness is Executive Director of the Centre for Justice and Reconciliation at Prison Fellowship International (PFI). Restorative justice has been Van Ness's major professional interest for over 30 years. He has explored and promoted it as a public policy advocate, a program designer, a writer and a teacher. He is the general editor of PFI's highly regarded website, www.restorativejustice.org. Van Ness was intimately involved in the development of the UN Declaration of Basic Principles on the Use of Restorative Justice Programmes in Criminal Matters, which was endorsed by the Economic and Social Council in 2002. Van Ness led the design effort for the Sycamore Tree Project®, a program that brings groups of victims into prison for conversations with unrelated prisoners, over an eight-week period. The program is now used in 29 countries. It was adapted for use in Rwanda to prepare genocide victims and perpetrators for the Gacaca hearings, and in the Solomon Islands to help that nation pursue reconciliation in the aftermath of civil war.

Charles Villa-Vicencio is a Visiting Professor in the Conflict Resolution Program at Georgetown University and a Senior Research Fellow at the Institute for Justice and Reconciliation, Cape Town, South Africa. Prior to that, he served as the National Research Director in the South African Truth and Reconciliation Commission and as Professor of Religion and Society at the University of Cape Town. Villa-Vicencio works largely in the area of transitional justice and social transformation in South Africa. He works on transitional mechanisms and peacebuilding initiatives in Africa and the Middle East.

Leslie Vinjamuri is Co-director of the Centre for the International Politics of Conflict, Rights and Justice and is a Senior Lecturer (Associate Professor) in the Department of Politics and International Studies at the School of Oriental and African Studies, University of London. She is also co-editor of *openGlobalRights*, and founded and co-chairs the London Transitional Justice Network. Vinjamuri speaks and writes on the politics of the International Criminal Court and international justice, international institutions and global governance, transatlantic relations, and human rights in the global south. Her publications have appeared in journals such as *International Security, Ethics and International Affairs, Survival, International Theory,* and the *Annual Review of Political Science.* Vinjamuri has taught at Georgetown University and was a Fellow at the John M. Olin Institute at Harvard University and at the London School of Economics. Previously, she worked at the United States Agency for International Development, and in the Foreign Affairs Division at Congressional Research Service. She received her PhD from Columbia University.

CHAPTER 1

Introduction

Jennifer J. Llewellyn and Daniel Philpott

The past generation has seen a global outburst of efforts to build peace in sites of massive injustice: genocide, civil war, dictatorships, and other large-scale violations of human rights such as slavery or the abuse of native peoples. Truth commissions, international tribunals, UN peace operations, and multiple other institutions and practices have exploded in the past three decades, so much so that our era might be called "the age of peacebuilding." Attending all of these activities are vociferous and still unresolved debates. To offer but a few examples:

- A public argument has roiled in Uganda, the site of a vast civil war since 1987, between the Acholi Religious Leaders Peace Initiative (ARLPI) and the International Criminal Court (ICC) and its allies. The ARLPI, a coalition of Catholic, Anglican, Muslim, and traditional tribal leaders, was the prime mover behind the Amnesty Act of 2000, part of an approach to re-integrating thousands of soldiers into their villages, a process the ARLPI envisions as accompanied by traditional rituals like *mato oput* that combine apology, forgiveness, and reintegration ceremonies. The ICC, by contrast, handed down the first indictments in its history to five leaders of the opposition Lord's Resistance Army, arguing that accountability, not amnesty, is essential for peace.
- A parallel debate has taken place in Timor-Leste in the aftermath of a quarter century of occupation by Indonesia and a violent referendum in 1999 in which the Timorese gained their independence. Decrying impunity, human rights advocates both within and outside Timor-Leste call for trials of major human rights violators, including Indonesian generals sheltered by the Indonesian government. Other prominent voices, including Timor-Leste's president and foreign minister, have called for an approach based on forgiveness and reconciliation. The upshot has been a combination of

reintegrative Community Reconciliation Panels at the local level and the Special Panel for Serious Crimes, a hybrid United Nations–national tribunal for murder, rape, and torture suspects at the national level. The tribunal has tried mostly low-level defendants and few "big fish."
- Prior to one hearing in the South African Truth and Reconciliation Commission (TRC), officials complained to the commission's chair, Archbishop Desmond Tutu, that his conduct of the hearings had been too religious. Tutu at first reluctantly assented to their concerns but then found that he could not resist opening the next hearing—and all subsequent hearings—with a prayer.[1] The role of religion in South Africa's transition was debated in South Africa but not nearly as hotly as it was debated in North America and Europe, which are far more secular settings.
- A school of critics takes to task transitions away from dictatorship and democracy around the globe for focusing on individual human rights violations while ignoring structural economic and gender inequalities. Such inequalities, these critics argue, are not only intrinsically unjust but also contribute to the civil wars and dictatorships that spawn the human rights violations.
- When, during the 1990s, the German government sought to negotiate a reparations settlement with victims of forced labor during the Holocaust, many of these victims objected to such reparations as "blood money." It was not until the German government agreed to pronounce a public apology and to teach this episode of injustice in its public school history textbooks that the deal went forward.
- In response to thousands of legal claims brought by survivors of abuse within Indian Residential Schools, the Canadian government reached a court-sanctioned settlement agreement for compensation and a truth and reconciliation process. The compensation was limited to survivors and did not relate to harm resulting from the schools to communities, language, culture, and the next generation impacted by the cycles of abuse. It was clear that such compensation was not enough and that the work of the Commission was to bring a more holistic response. The delinking of compensation from the work of the Commission and the lack of any mandate for further compensation is a challenge for its work toward reconciliation.

Strikingly, all of these debates are about justice. They are not simply about the consequences of policies, the pluses and minuses of programs and institutions, or instrumental logic. They cannot be reduced to power, position, or interest. No, in good part the controversies are about ends. Even in the aftermath of colossal bloodshed and systematic political crimes, citizens argue passionately about the meaning and requirements of justice.

But what ought we to make of the fierce disagreement? It is not altogether lamentable. Vigorous argument about justice is a sign of healthy democracy. Theorists of transition commonly argue that in the aftermath of civil war and dictatorship restoring civil disagreement is a priceless achievement.[2] We agree. In no way do we want to quell or dampen democratic deliberation.

But there are also good reasons to hope for progress toward overcoming some of the sharp antinomies. Each side in these conflicts, after all, believes that it grasps and the other side misapprehends a morally crucial dimension of peacebuilding. If there is merit in either side's views then it ought to be incorporated into the concept of justice that is brought to peacebuilding. Justice is a matter of substance and not only of democratic procedure.

Further, both sides of many of these controversies may well have valid claims about justice. To synthesize these insights is thus to expand justice itself. Conversely, when these debates come to an impasse, what results is not healthy deliberation but rather the defeat of a coherent and practicable program of peacebuilding that brings desperately needed repair to societies. When notions of justice are at cross-purposes they may well end up stymieing each purpose.

Indeed, it is our view that both sides of most of the antinomies have something important to say about justice. While we seek to avoid eliding irreducible differences, we nevertheless believe that syntheses, regions of overlap, and common ground are to be found. Were these synergies to be developed, the enterprise of social repair would profit greatly.

Finding and developing these synergies is the project of this volume. Our aim is to develop a way of thinking about justice that integrates the various and often competing goals involved in peacebuilding into a holistic framework for normative assessment and guidance. Such a framework applies not only to the limited set of activities that often go under the name "justice"—prosecution, vetting, and other judicial procedures—but also to the broad work of peacebuilding. Where might we find such a notion of justice? In the explosion of practices that make up the age of peacebuilding, there have arisen two concepts for framing these practices that we believe qualify as candidates for the holistic, integrated approach to justice that we seek: restorative justice and reconciliation. These concepts are close enough in meaning that they form twin concepts, partner principles providing frameworks for peacebuilding.

As we describe in the next chapter, both restorative justice and reconciliation are relational approaches. They conceive of human persons not as isolated individuals or as mere bearers of utility but rather as beings who are fundamentally connected and defined in and through their relationship with others. Peacebuilding at the level of the nation-state, then, seeks not only to restore rights and the rule of law but also to address the range of harms that violence causes to human relationships, to restore relationships out of these variegated harms, and to elicit the participation of a wider range of parties involved in understanding and responding to these harms. The holistic and multidimensional character of relationality, we believe, can integrate what is right on both sides of various controversies. Relational theories, though, are more than an amalgamation of diverse insights. As we shall describe, both restorative justice and reconciliation contain distinctive core commitments.

The Context: Global Peacebuilding

Four features of global debates about peacebuilding elaborate the case for a holistic, integrative concept of justice. First, to repeat, a global explosion of peacebuilding efforts has taken place over the past generation. By peacebuilding we simply mean activities that aim to build sustainable, just, and peaceful relationships in the wake of war or other systemic human rights violations. More civil wars ended through negotiations between 1989 and 2004 than in the previous two centuries.[3] Many of these negotiations were conducted under UN auspices or led to UN operations. Between 1989 and 1999, the UN undertook 33 peace operations, more than twice the 15 missions that it had sent out during the previous 40 years.[4] Between 1989 and 2005, it launched 22 "post-conflict peacebuilding operations"—the most ambitious kind in administrative terms.[5] Peacebuilding might also include humanitarian relief, refugee resettlement, the demobilization and reintegration of ex-combatants, security-sector reform, election monitoring, judicial reform, social and economic development, and other activities. Peacebuilding involves explicit efforts to address past injustices as well. One of the recent innovations in global politics is the truth commission, an officially sanctioned body that is tasked with investigating the injustices of a specified place and period of time. Since the late 1970s some 40 truth commissions have taken place.[6] Another recent trend is the rise of internationally sanctioned tribunals for trying and punishing individual human rights violators, an institution that emerged through the Nuremberg and Tokyo Tribunals after World War II but was then placed on ice during the Cold War. Two ad hoc international criminal tribunals, one for Yugoslavia and one for Rwanda, arose in the 1990s and were followed by the establishment of the permanent International Criminal Court through the Treaty of Rome in 1998. International-domestic hybrid courts have been created in Sierra Leone, Timor-Leste, Cambodia, and Kosovo. Reparations have also become a common practice in global politics and have been endorsed and elaborated by the United Nations. A wave of public apologies has taken place as well.[7] Forgiveness has appeared on the scene as a relatively novel practice in the politics of the nation-state, practiced by victims in sites as diverse as Uganda, South Africa, Northern Ireland, and Timor-Leste. Traditional rituals of integration, usually derived from tribal traditions, have been employed in the wake of massive violence in Rwanda, Mozambique, Uganda, Timor-Leste, and other countries. Memorials, monuments, rituals of remembrance, and the revision of school textbooks also add to the array of practices.

If we live in an age of peacebuilding, though, we do not live in an age of peace. A second feature of the contemporary world that informs debates about peacebuilding is the persistence of war. At the time of this writing, large-scale violence roils in Iraq, Afghanistan, Libya, Syria, Sudan, Congo, and many other locales. A survey of studies conducted by researchers Charles T. Call and Elizabeth M. Cousens shows that one-fifth to one-third of all settled conflicts regress back into war within five years.[8] Researcher Andrew Mack's 2007 report showed, too, that armed conflicts settled through negotiation revert to war at a rate of 43 percent within five years.[9] The most troubling chapters in the annals of peacebuilding are wars that have taken place in the imminent aftermath of UN peace operations: for instance, Angola in 1993, which took 350,000 lives, and Rwanda in 1994, which left roughly 1,000,000 dead. Our claim is not that peacebuilding is futile. Mack has also charted a steady decline in armed conflict since 1992 and attributes it in part to peacebuilding efforts.[10] We claim only that violent conflict and large-scale injustices are still common, that efforts to build and sustain peace have achieved mixed success, and that this mixed success is a reason to seek out notions of justice that take a more holistic view of peacebuilding.[11]

The difficulty of peacebuilding, though, does not arise simply from the frequency and intractability of violence and armed conflict around the world. A third feature of the age of peacebuilding, to elaborate a point that we have been alluding to and exemplifying, is the presence of conceptual antimonies and antagonistic paradigms. The most encompassing paradigm war is one that pits punishment against reconciliation or restorative justice. *Nunca mas!* Overcome impunity! These are the cries of international lawyers and human rights activists, whose program for justice gives pride of place to the judicial punishment of arch human rights violators. By contrast, proponents of reconciliation and restorative justice often advocate the restoration of right relationship through a family of restorative measures among which accountability is one of several siblings. This grand controversy has characterized public arguments in South Africa, Uganda, post-unification Germany, Timor-Leste, El Salvador, Guatemala, and many other countries. In this antinomy, of course, reconciliation and restorative justice, the concepts that we believe can overcome polarities, pose as one side of a polarity. One of our aims is to show how the best aspirations of proponents of accountability can be accommodated within reconciliation and restorative justice.

Other related antinomies abound across the globe. A more particularized version of the grand controversy is what might be called peace versus justice, in which one side insists on prosecution and the other counters that prosecution prevents a peace agreement from being signed. A further tension, one between the religious and the secular, can be found in several countries, as well as in debates about peacebuilding in the west. Secular actors often either underestimate the importance of religious actors, who have exercised a strong shaping influence on peace in South Africa, Chile, Guatemala, El Salvador, Northern Ireland, post-unification Germany, Liberia, Sierra Leone, and Timor-Leste, or else object to the character of religious influence. Reciprocally, religious actors sometimes speak and act in ways that leave little room for conversation with the secular. Still another tension, one found especially in African countries, is one between traditional rituals and a westernized, formal legal approach to addressing past wrongs. Then, a common controversy arises from the criticism that trials, truth commissions, and other measures that focus on individual human rights violations ignore deeper inequalities in wealth, social power, and gender relations.[12] In a separate, also frequently heard debate, victims criticize public officials' apologies as being empty words if these apologies are not accompanied by reparations. Sometimes, though, victims also charge that reparations amount to blood money if they are not accompanied by apologies and enduring efforts to sustain public memories of crimes. These and other arguments continue on, all over the globe.

A fourth and final feature of efforts to address large-scale injustices around the globe is the pervasiveness of justice claims in all of these antinomies. Rights, entitlement, deserts, due process, just distribution, restitution, the rule of law, and sometimes dimensions of restorative justice and reconciliation find their way into debates about peacebuilding. Justice is debated in two contexts. The first concerns the past: How ought societies to address the wrongs committed during the previous war, dictatorship, or other episode of wrongdoing? Through punishment? Amnesty, conditional or otherwise? Truth-telling? Apology? Reparations? Forgiveness? Rituals for re-integration? Over the past decade and a half or so, these questions have come to be known widely as ones of "transitional justice."[13] While our concepts intersect with transitional justice, we prefer a wider concept, that of peacebuilding. In part this is because not all of the episodes that have recently received redress occur in transitions. Australia, New Zealand, Canada, and the United States, for instance, have all come to grapple with their governments' past abuses of native peoples within the context of stable democracies, not amidst a transition. Transitional justice has also come to be associated with certain designated processes, judicial punishment first among these, but also truth commissions, restitution, vetting, and building the rule of law. Again, peacebuilding encompasses these endeavors but involves a wider range of activities and actors, reflecting our stress on holistic right relationship. The second context for debates about justice concerns the future: Which institutions and laws ought societies to construct? Which ones will best sustain peace and justice? These, too, are questions that concern peacebuilding, the context for our own approach to justice.

Restorative Justice and Reconciliation

Both restorative justice and reconciliation have expanded in their prestige and application in a wide variety of contexts in the past generation. They are reflected in the approach and the names of many institutional models and processes aimed at making the transition from pasts marred by conflict, violence, and oppression to ones founded on peace and justice. The South African TRC stands out as perhaps the most prominent example. It proffered reconciliation not only in its name but as its ultimate goal, reflected in its slogan "truth: the road to reconciliation." The Commission also named this work as restorative justice in its final report, as did the Commission's chair, Archbishop Desmond Tutu, in his book, *No Future Without Forgiveness*.[14] The word reconciliation has also appeared in the title of commissions in Chile, Peru, Ghana, East Timor, Solomon Islands, Sierra Leone, Liberia, and Morocco.[15] These approaches have not been limited to the nation-state level or to times of transition but have also been undertaken at the local and community level, sometimes as a precursor or supplement to national efforts or to address needs that national efforts do not meet. Established and stable democracies have appealed to the same concepts in dealing with their legacies of historic and systemic wrongs, including Australia, Canada, and the United States with respect to their treatment of aboriginal peoples, and the United States with respect to its history of slavery and civil rights abuses.

Despite the widespread deployment of these ideas and approaches, both the merit and the meaning of restorative justice and reconciliation are attended by cacophony and contestation. Some have heralded these ideas and approaches for their holistic and integrative potential. Others have claimed that such ideas and efforts represent, at best, one aspect of a disaggregated array of elements and activities required for peacebuilding, an array that includes security, development, and justice. At worst, they are criticized for being a sellout or compromise of justice for the sake of peace. Reconciliation has been conceived variously as a second-best alternative to retribution, one item in an array of peacebuilding practices, an end state of embrace, and as an intimate and personal phenomenon. Restorative justice gained prominence beginning in the 1970s as an approach to criminal justice, but its significance as a general concept of justice for nations and communities has not been fully realized. Finally, although these terms are often invoked in the same contexts and sometimes used interchangeably, there has been remarkably little engagement between scholars of reconciliation and scholars of restorative justice. In part this may be explained by a divide between secular and religious scholars, with reconciliation garnering more attention from religious scholars and restorative justice more often associated with domestic and secular criminal justice. But this is a partial explanation at best since restorative justice has important religious roots and reconciliation has found secular articulation as well.

To be sure, the notions of restorative justice and of reconciliation that we adopt and develop are particular instances of a wide array of meanings and usages of each term. But we construct our particular definitions with a purpose: to develop restorative justice and reconciliation as holistic, integrated concepts of justice that can be applied to the problem of peacebuilding on the level of the nation-state and the community. As we shall explain, a key common feature of these two notions is that they both can be rooted in a relational understanding of persons, societies, and the values and practices that connect them. Each concept aspires to integrate the competing goods found in the various antinomies. Each concept, we propose further, can also be understood both from religious and secular perspectives and can facilitate and promote communication and collaboration among these spheres.

An Outline of the Volume

Our central task in this volume is one of theory. But it is theory oriented to practice—that is, concerned with application to the world. In the conceptual chapter that follows, we explain in more depth what we mean by restorative justice and reconciliation as concepts of justice. We aspire to set forth core ideas from which more proximate principles, and in turn, institutions and policies, can be developed. Many of these principles, and to some degree, institutions and policies, are proposed and developed in more detail in the chapters that follow, which explore the elements and implications of restorative justice and reconciliation more specifically. On the whole, though, the volume tilts toward theory, reflecting our claim that the dilemmas and antinomies of peacebuilding require something deeper than new procedures and forms of politics, namely new thinking about justice and its application to peacebuilding. Mirroring the holistic character of restorative justice and reconciliation, the authors of the volume are diverse in their backgrounds. They include legal scholars, political scientists, sociologists, criminologists, and theologians. Several of them are also activists, having pursued restorative justice or reconciliation in the context of government, a non-governmental organization (NGO), or a religious body, and in some cases in globally diverse settings. Some of them involve religion in their reflection; others argue in wholly secular terms. That the authors' chapters converge on a common notion of justice from so many angles itself helps to make the case for the integrated, interdependent character of the volume's approach to peacebuilding.

The centrality of justice in debates about peacebuilding around the globe, as well as a sharp divergence in concepts of justice, are key themes in the empirical chart of actors that political scientists Aaron P. Boesenecker and Leslie Vinjamuri present in their chapter. Their comprehensive map situates restorative justice and reconciliation. It confirms, for instance, that international organizations and transnational networks such as the human rights community and the international legal community have converged around a "dominant normative framework" that stresses legalism, individualism, and accountability through judicial trials. Yet Boesenecker and Vinjamuri also wish to "challenge any lingering assumption" that a consensus has been attained on this framework and that debates have disappeared. Faith-based organizations and indigenous local organizations, among others, for instance, have embraced a "radically different" concept of justice, whose axial idea is the repair and restoration of relationships. Boesenecker and Vinjamuri then build their essay around a sophisticated and thorough typology that categorizes peacebuilding actors according to whether they are "universalist" or "identity-based," "local" or "transnational," and oriented toward "reconciliation" or "retribution" in their conception of justice. What emerges at the various intersections of these categories are three kinds of actors: "pragmatic restorers," "legalists," and "capacity-builders." They derive these distinctions through their willingness to direct their searchlight beyond the west, the secular, and the halls of international organizations to the local, the religious, and the truly global.

Like Boesenecker and Vinjamuri, sociologist Jonathan VanAntwerpen identifies the views of a "transitional justice mafia" of international lawyers and human rights activists as the "orthodoxy" in global approaches to past injustices, while characterizing "reconciliation," often inflected by religion, as a contending "heterodoxy." Restorative justice, he notes, has become increasingly linked with reconciliation. Complementing Boesenecker and Vinjamuri's empirical map, his chapter is an interpretive narrative of the debate over justice that has surrounded the transitional justice community in the past decade and a half. His story begins with South Africa's TRC, whose chair, Desmond Tutu, gave prestige to reconciliation and its important component theme, forgiveness. But then, when reconciliation traveled across the Atlantic and into the conversations of influential transitional justice voices in New York, it met with controversy, which VanAntwerpen documents through the internal debates of the International Center for Transitional Justice (ICTJ), an important NGO for transitional justice. Though some at the ICTJ sought to synthesize the best insights of reconciliation and the more legalist orthodoxy, deep tensions remain, he argues.

Next comes a succession of chapters on more particular aspects of restorative justice and reconciliation in the context of peacebuilding. Probably the most hotly contested issue in the past generation's politics of peacebuilding is punishment. Whether top criminals and human rights violators are brought into the dock is the critical test of a just peace for many transitional justice activists. Proponents of restorative justice and reconciliation, by contrast, do not reject accountability but pursue forms of it that address the harms and the responsibility of the wide web of victims, offenders, citizens, and state officials who committed or were affected by the crime. So argues Daniel W. Van Ness, a leading scholar of restorative justice. In his essay he explains how accountability can be understood and practiced so as to promote broad peacebuilding in the political contexts of wars and dictatorships. His approach reflects the holism of restorative justice, adopting a broad understanding of who the victims and offenders are and how the state and the community are involved. In numerous ways, he finds support for his holistic approach in international law and thus charts a pathway for integrating restorative justice into global norms and institutions.

But might restorative justice and reconciliation be realized even through settlements that provide for no judicial punishment at all—that is, ones that include amnesty? Just as the orthodoxy that VanAntwerpen describes proclaims combating impunity as its exemplary virtue, so, too, it identifies amnesty as its cardinal sin. International lawyers and human rights activists have sought determinedly to build international norms against amnesty in the past couple of decades. But as legal scholar Louise Mallinder points out in her chapter, historically amnesties have been common, even since the end of the Cold War, the period of their greatest controversy. More importantly, blanket amnesty and punishment are not exhaustive options. What has emerged in countries like Uganda, Timor-Leste, and South Africa are restorative amnesties, which are accompanied by truth-telling, reparations, and local forums for accountability, forums that are indeed modeled on restorative justice. Mallinder devotes the bulk of her chapter to a forceful defense of restorative amnesty.

Every bit as controversial as amnesty is forgiveness, the subject of theologian Stephen J. Pope's chapter. Forgiveness was a major theme in the reconciliation that Tutu and other South Africans touted and that was criticized by other South

Africans, and even more so overseas, for short-circuiting justice, subverting deserved punishment, and being an imposition on victims. Mindful of these criticisms, Pope lays out the case for the practice of forgiveness in the politics of peacebuilding. If justice means restorative justice and reconciliation, he argues, then forgiveness and justice are complementary and not at odds. It is in Pope's chapter that religion's contribution shines especially brightly. Restorative justice and reconciliation find a natural home in Christian theology, he shows, as does forgiveness. If he is right, then these concepts of justice are ones around which religious and secular people can come together.

Reparations, the subject of Charles Villa-Vicencio's chapter, are less hotly disputed. Both the legalist orthodoxy and relational theories generally endorse them. Reparations play an important role in both Van Ness's and Mallinder's arguments for restorative approaches to the issue of accountability, for instance. But as Villa-Vicencio, formerly an important official in South Africa's TRC, shows, relational theories offer a distinctive account of reparations and envision their contribution to justice as holistic. Their function is not simply to provide restitution that is equivalent to what victims lost but is more deeply symbolic, communicating recognition and helping to build community ties. Reparations, that is, are part and parcel of restoring relationships.

But even if restorative justice and reconciliation succeed in offering holistic, integrative, relational concepts of justice, we should refrain from using them as universal categories to describe local and community mechanisms of justice across the globe, cautions John Braithwaite, himself one of the leading theorists of restorative justice. Rather, there are *gacaca* courts in Rwanda, *gotong royong* in Indonesia, and the like. These might be called traditional justice, though even this term Braithwaite is reluctant to use. But in many traditional mechanisms, principles much like those of restorative justice and reconciliation, along with the separation of powers, women's rights, and freedom as nondomination, may be discovered and lauded for their ability to secure popular legitimacy, ownership, and participation.

In his conclusion, scholar of religious studies Jason Springs synthesizes the essays into his own interpretation of the project. He proposes transformation as the volume's central idea. As the intellectual godfather of the modern liberal peace, Springs identifies Immanuel Kant, who of course achieved his own Copernican revolution in philosophy. Restorative justice and reconciliation, Springs avers, do not so much replace the Kantian liberal peace with another paradigm shift but rather transform it—that is, incorporate some its commitments into an alternative concept of justice that is wider, broader, and deeper. Such a transformation in theory then results in a justice that is transformative in practice, aiming to repair relationships in the broad array of dimensions in which violence rents them apart.

Springs concludes by writing, "[s]uch a process of transformation should not cease to expect its own further enrichment and further transformation." It is our hope that the chapters that follow, through their efforts to overcome pervasive antinomies in thought and practice, will bring a new synthesis to the global dialogue on peacebuilding.

Notes

1. Piet Meiring, *Chronicle of the Truth Commission* (Vanderbylpark, South Africa: Carpe Diem, 1999), 30.
2. Reasoning along these lines are Amy Gutmann and Dennis Thompson, "The Moral Foundations of Truth Commissions," in *Truth v. Justice: The Morality of Truth Commissions*, ed. Robert I. Rotberg and Dennis Thompson (Princeton, NJ: Princeton University Press, 2000); Andrew Schaap, *Political Reconciliation* (New York: Routledge, Taylor and Francis Group, 2005); and Leigh Payne, *Unsettling Accounts* (Durham, NC: Duke University Press, 2008).
3. "A More Secure World: Our Shared Responsibility: Report of the High-Level Panel on Threats, Challenges, and Change," (New York, NY: The United Nations, 2004), 33–34.
4. Roland Paris, *At War's End: Building Peace After Civil Conflict* (Cambridge, UK: Cambridge University Press, 2004), 17.
5. Roland Paris, "Bringing the Leviathan Back In: Classical Versus Contemporary Studies of the Liberal Peace," *International Studies Review* 8 (2006), 433.
6. Depending on exactly how truth commission is defined, at least 40 have taken place in the last 40 years. Even on a restricted definition, some 30 have taken place. Of course this estimate is also a current one; more truth commissions are likely to be formed in subsequent years. The full list of commissions on an expanded definition is: Uganda (1974); United States (War Time Relocation and Internment of Civilians) (1981–1982); Bolivia (1982–1984); Argentina (1983–1984); Uruguay (1985); Zimbabwe (1985); Philippines (1986); Uganda (1986–1995); Nepal (1990–1991); Chile (1990–1991); Chad (1991–1992); Canada (Aboriginal Peoples) (1991–1996); South Africa (ANC) (1992, 1993); Germany (1992–1994); El Salvador (1992–1993); United States (human radiation experiments) (1994–1995); Sri Lanka (1994–1997); Haiti (1995–1996); Burundi (1995–1996); South Africa (TRC) (1995–2000); Australia (1996–1997); Ecuador (1996–1997); Guatemala (1997–1999); Nigeria (1999–2000); Sierra Leone (2000–2001); Uruguay (2000); South Korea (2000–2002); Peru (2001–2003); Panama (2001); Serbia and Montenegro (2002); Ghana (2002); Timor-Leste (2002–2005); Morocco (2004–2006); Colombia (2005); United States (Greensboro) (2005); South Korea (2005); Liberia (2005); Solomon Islands (2009); Kenya: Truth, Justice, and Reconciliation Commission (2009–present); Truth and Reconciliation Commission of Canada (2008–present).
7. "The Age of Apology," legal scholar Roy L. Brooks calls our time. Psychiatrist Aaron Lazare locates the outbreak of apologies in the 1990s and finds a sharp increase in them over the course of the decade. See Roy L. Brooks, ed., *When Sorry Isn't Enough: The Controversy Over Apologies and Reparations for Human Injustice* (New York: New York University Press, 1999); Aaron Lazare, *On Apology* (Oxford, UK: Oxford University Press, 2004).
8. Charles T. Call and Elizabeth M. Cousens, "Ending Wars and Building Peace: International Responses to War-Torn Societies," *International Studies Perspectives* 9 (2008), 1–21.
9. Andrew Mack, *Global Patterns of Political Violence* (New York, NY: International Peace Academy, 2007); cited in Call and Cousens, "Ending Wars and Building Peace," 5.
10. Andrew Mack, *Human Security Report 2005: War and Peace in the 21st Century* (Oxford, UK: Oxford University Press, 2005), 18; see also Joshua S. Goldstein, *Winning the War on War: The Decline of Armed Conflict Worldwide* (New York, NY: Penguin, 2011).

11. For scholarly assessments of the success of peacebuilding, see Daniel Philpott, "Introduction: Searching for Strategy in an Age of Peacebuilding," in *Strategies of Peace* (Oxford, UK: Oxford University Press, 2010), 3–18.
12. For the economic dimension of these criticisms, see Ismael Muvingi, "Sitting on Powder Kegs: Socioeconomic Rights in Transitional Societies," *The International Journal of Transitional Justice* 3, no. 2 (2009), 163–182; Lisa J. LaPlante, "Transitional Justice and Peace Building: Diagnosing and Addressing the Socioeconomic Roots of Violence through a Human Rights Framework," *The International Journal of Transitional Justice* 2, no. 3 (2008), 331–335; Roger Duthie, "Toward a Development-Sensitive Approach to Transitional Justice," *The International Journal of Transitional Justice* 2, no. 3 (2008), 292–309; Zinaida Miller, "Effects of Invisibility: In Search of the 'Economic' in Transitional Justice," *The International Journal of Transitional Justice* 2, no. 3 (2008), 266–291, as well as a piece by perhaps the most prominent of these critics, Mamdani, *Reconciliation without Justice*. For the gender dimension, see Daniel Aguirre and Irene Pietropaoli, "Gender Equality, Development and Transitional Justice: The Case of Nepal," *The International Journal of Transitional Justice* 2, no. 3 (2008), 356–377; Fionnuala Ní Aoláin and Eilish Rooney, "Underenforcement and Intersectionality: Gendered Aspects of Transition for Women," *The International Journal of Transitional Justice* 1, no. 3 (2007), 338–354.
13. Paige Arthur, "How 'Transitions' Reshaped Human Rights: A Conceptual History of Transitional Justice," *Human Rights Quarterly* 31 (2009), 321–367; Ruti G. Teitel, "Transitional Justice Genealogy," *Harvard Human Rights Journal* 16 (2003), 69–94. Also see for a helpful definition: *The Rule of Law and Transitional Justice in Conflict and Post-Conflict Societies, Report of the Secretary-General*, para. 8, U.N. Doc. S/2004/616 (August 23, 2004).
14. Desmond M. Tutu, *No Future without Forgiveness* (New York: Doubleday, 1999), see esp. 47–67.
15. Morocco was in name an "*Equity* and Reconciliation Commission."

CHAPTER 2

Restorative Justice and Reconciliation: Twin Frameworks for Peacebuilding

Jennifer J. Llewellyn and Daniel Philpott

The United Nations Peacebuilding Commission was created in 2005 to address a gap in the United Nations' mechanisms for building and maintaining peace in post-conflict contexts. The commission was designed to coordinate and integrate peacebuilding efforts around the world. Five years later, the mandated review of the Commission concluded these efforts have been disappointing at best.[1]

> [D]espite committed and dedicated efforts, the hopes that accompanied the founding resolutions have yet to be realized. We are now at a crossroads: either there is a conscious recommitment to peacebuilding at the very heart of the work of the United Nations, or the Peacebuilding Commission settles into the limited role that has developed so far.[2]

These findings, we suggest, are revealing. They do not call into question the insight animating the creation of the Commission itself, that peacebuilding requires an integrated and holistic approach, but suggest rather that such an approach needs more than logistical attention. The review of the Commission also identifies the need for something more than the approach taken thus far.

> However, something more is required if the vision and ambition of 2005 are to be restored. The Organization is still not rising to the peacebuilding challenge. A new level of attention and resolve on the part of Member States and the top echelons of the Secretariat is required.[3]

Even though the co-facilitators of the review recognize that "more is required," they seem conflicted about the nature of the problem. "The existence of a single strategic document does not guarantee that all actors will act in accordance with its priorities," they acknowledge.[4] What coordination will require is enhanced support for the Commission and increased enforcement on the part of the Commission. "The Commission must use its political weight to seek to align the various actors behind the same overarching objectives," the report argues.[5] However, there is some hint in the review that more than political power and will may be needed to achieve the goals of the Commission. "[W]e emphasize that the exercise will not succeed unless it is infused with a renewed commitment and a strengthened sense of engagement. Change must be psychological as well as institutional."[6] Such psychological change, we argue, requires more than a renewed commitment to practical solutions but also new ways of thinking about peacebuilding and its requirements. This volume advances just such a conceptual framing for peacebuilding, one that is needed to support the architectural vision and ambition for a holistic and integrated approach to building lasting peace.

The Peacebuilding Commission is not alone in seeing the need for coordination and integration. Others, too, have proposed institutions and policies that involve integration and coordination. In a recent edited volume on transitional justice, for instance, legal scholars Naomi Roht-Arriaza and Javier Mariezcurrena propose to overcome previous antinomies in transitional justice—trials vs. truth commissions; local vs. national and international institutions—with coordination and complementarity among the institutions and procedures.

But while coordination and complementarity are valuable, we argue, something more is needed than adding new mechanisms, processes, policies or institutions to the existing "toolbox" of peacebuilding. Our focus is more fundamental. It is about the nature of the work of restoration and not merely about the tools that are needed or even the order or combination in which they might be used. What is needed, we argue, is a new concept of peacebuilding founded on an overarching and operational concept of justice. Where might such a concept be found? This volume proposes that a relational concept of justice serves to integrate the various and often competing goals involved in peacebuilding into a holistic framework for normative assessment and practical guidance.

Restorative Justice and Reconciliation

As we argued in the introduction, in the explosion of practices that make up the age of peacebuilding there have arisen to prominence two concepts for framing these practices that we believe qualify as candidates for a holistic, integrated approach to justice: restorative justice and reconciliation. These ideas are close enough in meaning that they form twin concepts, partner principles that provide twin frameworks for peacebuilding. The twins are fraternal—not identical in their genetic codes, yet sharing a strong common parentage.

Both restorative justice and reconciliation are relational conceptions of justice. At their core, relational approaches to justice are not simply concerned with responding to wrongs but rather with the harm and effects of wrongs on relationships at all levels: individual, group, community, national, and international. The focus of justice so conceived is on what is required to address these harms in order to establish and maintain peaceful (read variously as: restored, reconciled, or right) relationships, thus ensuring that the conditions for wrongdoing are not replicated. In both accounts, then, the aspiration or goal of justice is the creation and protection of restored or reconciled relationships in the present and future. As relational conceptions, reconciliation and restorative justice can provide frameworks for peacebuilding with the potential to overcome its antinomies. In the chapters that follow, far more detailed development of this potential will take place. In this chapter, we sketch how a common relational framework can ground and integrate a wide array of measures that perform a wide array of tasks within peacebuilding.

What difference do these relational frameworks make for the practice of peacebuilding? Restorative justice and reconciliation are distinct in their assumptions from currently favored conceptions of justice and approaches to peacebuilding.[7] For the most part, the conceptions of justice and peace that lay beneath the approach to peacebuilding pursued by the international community—namely, United Nations officials, western diplomats, the human rights community, and the international lawyers—reflect liberal individualism. A stress on the individual and his autonomy, understood as freedom from the interference of others, rests at the core of these conceptions. Such an individualist orientation has profoundly shaped ideas of justice and peace and the processes and institutions through which they are pursued. These ideas find expression in the focus of identifying individual offenders to blame and isolate through punishment and on seeking protection though separation from others; in the logic of corrective justice and its reliance on material transfers from wrongdoer to victim in order to return the victim (as close as possible) to her position before the wrong; in the use of rights as shields or swords protecting individuals from the interference of others; and in the strong bifurcation of personal and public reconciliation. These ideas have shaped processes and institutions of peacebuilding as well. They can be seen in the overriding priority that human rights groups and international lawyers have given to international courts and in UN documents on transitional justice that stress rights and the rule of law almost exclusively. The result is a thin, legalistic notion of positive peace.

By contrast, restorative justice and reconciliation begin from a relational conception of people and the world they inhabit. Connection and not separation orient the work of justice and peace. Justice and peace are sought not in the assurance of our separation and in non-interference but rather in good relationships with one another. These accounts seek and demand relationships in and through which individuals can flourish and succeed in realizing their goals and ends. Individuals cannot achieve these goals irrespective of or apart from others but rather require right relations with others to do so. On a relational understanding we are not independent from one another and our autonomy and freedom is not found in separation from one another. We are instead interdependent and our freedom relies on mutual construction and the support of others. Wrong is understood in relational terms as well—as that which results in harm to individuals and the relationships in and through which they live. Understanding and addressing wrongs (the work of justice), then, requires attention to these relationships and how they might be restored.

Restorative justice and reconciliation, then, each offer a distinct starting point for framing justice and peace and their relationship. In the following sections we elaborate restorative justice and reconciliation. The advantage of these twinned conceptual frameworks for peacebuilding is to be found both in their identity and their differences. Through their different origins, influences, and character these concepts are able to bring into dialogue different actors, traditions, orientations, and disciplines, including secular and non-secular, western legalist and traditional, international officials and civil society. Examples of the unifying, connecting capacity of these twinned concepts emerge throughout the chapters in the volume.

Restorative Justice: A Relational Theory of Justice

Restorative justice has rapidly gained attention in countries throughout the world as an alternative that offers new justice processes and institutions. Restorative justice theory and practice have been developed most with regard to domestic criminal justice reform. The United Nations' Economic and Social Council reflected the increasing importance placed upon restorative justice in this sphere with the adoption of the "Basic Principles on the Use of Restorative Justice Programmes in Criminal Matters."[8] These principles encourage member states to implement restorative justice in the operation of their domestic criminal justice systems. The United Nations Office on Drugs and Crime also produced a *Handbook on Restorative Justice Programmes* to guide member states in establishing and developing restorative justice programs involving criminal matters.[9]

Restorative justice is, however, rapidly expanding beyond criminal justice and into other contexts like civil justice, education, employment, and health. The application of restorative justice theory and practice to transitional contexts and peacebuilding has also begun to receive significant attention.

Restorative justice is thus currently in favor among academics, policymakers, and justice professionals in many places throughout the world. The proliferation of restorative justice practice has not, however, always been based on sound understandings of its underlying theory, principles, and goals. As a result, users of the term sometimes apply it loosely to practices that do not fully reflect restorative principles and values. For instance, they often view restorative justice as an alternative *process* for doing justice, particularly in the criminal realm, but increasingly in other domains as well. Restorative justice, though, offers far more than alternative processes or a new path to the same destinations sought by predominant justice systems. While ours is not the only account of restorative justice, we propose it as an alternative theory of justice—a relational theory of justice.

Relational scholars (most notably, although not exclusively, feminist theorists) have challenged the traditional image of the individualistic human self that rests at the core of much of liberal social and political theory.[10] In place of the liberal individualist vision of the self, relational theorists have offered an account of the self that takes connection (relationship) over separation from others as central. The insights generated out of this secular relational account also resonate with religious and spiritual traditions (examples abound, including Aboriginal spirituality, Christianity, and others).[11] Relational theory provides a different starting point from which to understand the world. It compels us to take the fact of relationship, of our connectedness, as our starting assumption. As such, relationality must inform the ideas, principles, and conceptions that shape our interactions and social life. Liberal-inspired assumptions about the nature of the self and its interactions with others have shaped social, political, and legal ideas and institutions both in the West and at the international level.

As a relational theory of justice, restorative justice challenges individualist-based notions of justice, including retributive, corrective, restitutive, distributive, and social. Restorative justice takes the fact of human connection—of human beings as relational—as its starting point for thinking about what justice means and what is required to do justice. Viewing the world relationally reveals the inevitability and importance of our connection to others. From this perspective we can see that our protection lies not in isolation or separation but through the right conditions and character of relationships between individuals, communities, and nations. Attention to the multiple and intersecting relationships in which we live makes clear the ways in which wrongdoing causes harm not only to the individuals involved but also to the connections and relationships (not necessarily or not only personal or intimate) among those involved. A relational approach also draws attention to the ways in which harms related to wrongdoing extend from the individual victim(s) and wrongdoer(s) to affect those connected with them, including their immediate communities of care and support, broader communities to which they belong, and ultimately the social fabric of their society. This is true, on a restorative account, not only for the wrongs that we class as criminal in our current systems but also private wrongs.

Through its focus on harm to relationships, a relational approach to justice indeed challenges the dichotomy of public and private spheres at the core of western legal systems. From this view the effect of wrongdoing always extends beyond private relationships between two parties and involves wider sets of relationships. Wrongs, then, are always "public" on a restorative approach. It is still important, though, to recognize that harms will differ in the scope of their effects. It may thus be appropriate to differentiate wrongs from one another in terms of the breadth of their effects but not according to the more simplistic dichotomy of public and private. A relational approach holds that justice must be concerned with responding to the harms to relationships that result from wrongdoing and takes healthy or peaceful relationships as its goal or ideal. This truth is perhaps nowhere as evident as in times of transition from conflict. Indeed, it is because the harm from wrongdoing extends beyond the individual victim(s) that the necessity of dealing with the past is felt so strongly, even by those not directly victimized by wrongdoing. That justice requires restoration of relationships is a fact easily grasped in transitional contexts, but it is no less true in the period after a transition or in stable, established societies.

In response to a wrong, justice on a restorative (relational) account seeks relationships in which all parties involved enjoy equality in the character and terms of relationship with one another. The equality that is sought is equality in the basic elements required for peaceful and productive human relationships—namely, equality of respect, dignity, and mutual concern for one another. These elements reflect the building blocks of peaceful coexistence and human flourishing. The equality sought by justice on this account is relational equality. It is thus not concerned with equality measured by either opportunity or outcome but rather with equality within relationship. Figuring out what this requires cannot be achieved by a measure of treatment or result alone. Rather, as Christine Koggel in her foundational work on the idea, explains:

> [w]e need people with all of their encumbrances and in all their embeddedness in social and political contexts engaged in critical thinking about difference and perspective to know what equality requires. Impartiality, in the sense of the ability to treat each person with equal concern and respect, is achieved not through the monological thinking of a solitary and isolated moral reasoner but through a communicative process of an ongoing dialogue among different points of view.[12]

From this process, for Koggel, emerges two principles that mark a relational approach to equality: (1) that we ought to treat people with equal concern and respect; and (2) that human diversity and ways of being should be respected. These two principles reflect the formulation of the core commitment of restorative justice to relationships of equality in which parties enjoy equal respect, concern, and dignity.

In recasting the familiar liberal-inspired commitment to concern and respect as a commitment to equal concern, respect, and dignity, this formula should be understood not as a rejection of a liberal commitment to equality but rather as an attempt to make meaningful and realize equality for relational beings. The equality sought by restorative justice shares the fundamental commitment to equal respect and concern that animates liberal notions of equality, but unlike the liberal commitment it is not abstract in nature. Rather, relational justice takes equality *of relationship* as its goal.[13] Equality of relationship requires more than simple comparison at an abstract level. It is concerned with equality as it is realized in actual relationships between people. It is contextual and grounded. Achieving this equality thus requires attention to the particular contexts, the parties involved, and to what will be required to ensure respect, concern, and dignity in the relations between and among parties. The contextual and concrete nature of a relational approach resists generalized and universal practice in pursuit of its principled commitments. Such a relational approach to these commitments contrasts with the notion of these commitments at work in many liberal accounts.

Respect, on a relational conception, denotes the importance of recognizing, not violating or interfering with, the rights and needs of others. This respect, however, is not founded upon disinterest or self-interest as it is in many liberal approaches.[14] It is not respect achieved simply by recognition or negatively by non-interference but, rather, respect must be reconciled with (and understood in the context of) *concern* for others.

Concern makes clear that knowledge of and interest in others and their well-being is to serve as an animating and motivating factor. The inclusion of concern in this formulation of the aim of justice reflects insights gained from care feminists and some communitarian critiques of liberal justice and is incorporated into some liberal accounts.[15] They point out that the connections we have and want with others cannot be fully explained or accounted for in individualistic and self-interested terms. We are not only concerned for others because it is in our interests as rational agents to be so (so that others will have similar concern for us or because it is rational to do so). Rather, we have concern for others because as relational and connected selves we cannot respect self or others without such concern and interest.

Finally, the inclusion of dignity requires attention and respect for the diversity and ways of being that become clear when one approaches individuals in all their embedded and relational complexity. The inclusion of *dignity* also makes clear that this equality cannot be satisfied through process alone but is substantive in nature. Dignity requires that attention be paid to the needs and interests that give fundamental meaning to those involved in relationships and that their satisfaction be an animating concern for justice. But here again dignity conceived of relationally is different than the dignity reflected in liberal justice. Dignity does not refer to the inherent value of the individual simply qua *rational* agent. Dignity is not something that resides in the individual alone. Rather it marks the relationship between and among parties. Dignity refers here to the way in which we are connected with others—that such connections must reflect their value. Others cannot, on this account, simply serve as means to ends but must be accorded value in and of themselves and this must be reflected in the nature of relationships. The meaning of treating others as having value can only become clear in the context of relationships or connections between people and not through definitions that are universal and abstract.

The focus on relationships as the central concern of justice has implications for the "doing" of justice. Justice will be best served, on a restorative account, by including those involved or affected and empowering these parties to identify the related harms and what will be required to address them toward establishing conditions for just relationships in the future. Restorative justice practices and institutions are thus fundamentally shaped by context. One must understand the particular harms at issue, the relationships affected, the needs of the parties involved, and the appropriate means and modes of responding to the harms and restoring the relationships at stake. As a result of this commitment to contextually restorative processes, practices and institutions defy singular and uniform models. While this may frustrate those who seek ready-made and simple restorative answers, a strength of restorative justice, in our view, is its adaptability to context. This strength can become a significant weakness, however, if it inhibits the development of standards for identifying or evaluating what is restorative. A restorative theory of justice offers values and principles that define, guide, and ground its practice.

The values and principles are not, then, a recipe so much as a guide to the essentials of cooking. The principles do not dictate certain practices but inform the development and choice of practices in a given context. Restorative processes are focused on addressing harm to relationships or unjust relationships in order to restore relationships. In this way, restorative justice is forward looking and future oriented. The objective is to look at the outcome or implications of a wrong for the future. This contrasts with retributive justice, the conception of justice underlying most mainstream western criminal justice systems, which is animated by exacting payment from the offender for past actions.[16] The past is also not a reference point for restorative justice in terms of what restored relationships will look like. Restorative justice does not aim literally to "restore" relationships to some prior existing state. The commitment to restoration in restorative justice aspires to the conditions of human relationship that are needed for peaceful coexistence and within which individuals can flourish. The term "restore" references the sense in which these qualities of human relationship are inherently possible and desirable by virtue of our relational nature. It is in relationships of this character that our inherent human worth and potential can be recognized and respected.[17]

Another principle of restorative justice is its commitment and orientation to reintegration over isolation. While individual wrongdoers must bear much of the burden of repairing the harm caused by their actions, other parties involved in the process share some responsibility to contribute to the restoration of relationships. For example, the community must work to create reintegrative opportunities for the wrongdoer and for the victim. It is not possible to restore relationships if one party is isolated from the relationship altogether (i.e., through isolating forms of punishment). Restorative justice identifies one of the relationships harmed by wrongdoing as that between the wrongdoer and his or her community. Addressing the harms to these relationships often requires reintegration of the offender into the community.[18] Doing this work of restoration of relationships might involve a range of approaches and practices.

Another central commitment of a restorative approach is the recognition that the community plays an integral part in the creation and solution of social conflict. It is crucial for restorative justice that the community be recognized as a party and be included in restorative justice processes. Restorative approaches also make clear that wrongdoing causes harm not only to the immediate victim(s) but also to the relationships in which the victim(s) and the wrongdoer(s) exist. By virtue of relationships, harms affect all parties who are involved in them, ultimately including communities and sometimes entire societies.

It is crucial to understand, though, that while restorative justice requires attention to the harms suffered by particular parties in the process, including the victim(s), wrongdoer(s), and community(ies), the focus is broader than these individual units.[19] The focus is on the *relationships* between and among these parties and what will be required to restore them. This focus on relationships requires not only the inclusion but the meaningful participation of all those with a stake in the outcome of the situation and the development of a just future. This includes the victim(s) and wrongdoer(s) and the relevant community(ies).[20] Restorative justice is thus not simply justice for victims or for communities, as some critics (and even some advocates) have sometimes portrayed it. Rather it responds to the justice needs and requirements of victims, communities, and wrongdoers. Further, it takes an inclusive approach to who counts as parties within each of these categories.

As a relational theory of justice, then, restorative justice offers fundamental principles to guide practice. It is relationship-focused, holistic, integrative, inclusive, participatory, democratic, and committed to subsidiarity. These principles entail practices that are flexible and contextual; based on dialogue and encounter; non-adversarial, multi-party, and future-focused.[21]

Reconciliation: The Justice of Right Relationships

Reconciliation, too, can be understood as a concept of justice that is holistic, relational, and encompassing a wide array of practices involved in peacebuilding, including ones that are often in tension or thought to be at odds. Reconciliation as a concept of justice? That idea will ring strange to westerners, for whom reconciliation is more familiarly an overcoming of enmity, a state of embrace, or perhaps a personal and intimate matter. It is in fact in ancient religions, their texts and their traditions, that the idea of reconciliation as a concept of justice can be found. Here, we focus on Judaism, Christianity, and Islam. In these traditions (though perhaps not in every theological interpretation of them) the meaning of reconciliation indeed converges strongly with the meaning of justice as well as with the meaning of peace and mercy. Reconciliation is not an exclusively religious concept and can be articulated in secular terms and concepts, too. The very similarity between reconciliation as articulated here and restorative justice as articulated in the last section helps to demonstrate this. Religious meanings of reconciliation also require development as principles of peacebuilding, a project that prominent figures like Desmond Tutu and Pope John Paul II, along with several theologians, have begun to undertake in the past generation.[22] Our task here is to briefly set forth the meaning of reconciliation as it arises from religious traditions and to suggest how it can be adapted to modern political communities building peace. As we pointed out in the introduction, this particular concept of reconciliation is one of many that circulate in contemporary debates. But it is one that complements restorative justice, thus building a conceptual bridge between religious and secular concepts of peacebuilding and giving our approach to justice a wider global reach. The three religious traditions at hand, after all, make up about half of the world's population.

In the scriptures of Judaism, Christianity, and Islam, justice commonly translates to something very much like "righteousness," meaning the demands of right relationship among the members of a community in all of their roles—economic, political, familial, cultic—and with respect to God. Both the Hebrew word *sedeq* (or *sedeqah*), which appears numerous times in the Tanakh (or Old Testament), and the array of Greek words in the New Testament that begin with the *dik-* stem (for example, *dikaioō and dikaiosunē*) are rendered into English as both "justice" and "righteousness."[23] Arguably, the Arabic *"adl"* can also be translated dually into justice and righteousness. These notions of justice, as with justice in most traditions, have two valences in the sense that they can mean both a state of right relationship and a process of restoring right relationship after it has been broken. The Tanakh, for instance, means by justice a process of restoration when it uses the term in Second Isaiah, where it equates justice with salvation and connotes a wide set of reparative measures. These religions' actual terms for reconciliation likewise denote both a process of restoring right relationship and a state or condition of restoration, including the Greek words *katallage* and *katallosso* as found in the New Testament, the Arabic word *musalaha* as found in the Quran, the Hebrew word *teshuva*, a close but not exact cognate that appears in the Tanakh, and *tikkun olam*, found in the later Jewish tradition.[24] Reconciliation, then, converges closely with the meaning of justice as right relationship in the scriptures of these three traditions.

The same scriptures also manifest a convergence between reconciliation and peace—more specifically, between the valence of reconciliation that involves a state of right relationship and peace. Peace, then, is the comprehensive right relationship, or state of justice, that results from processes of restoration. The Hebrew term for peace, *shalom*, and the Greek word found in the New Testament, *eirene*, both mean a thorough condition of right relationship in a community. The same goes for the Arabic *salaam*, found in the Quran, which is obviously linguistically similar to *shalom*.[25]

If peace corresponds to the state of right relationship that is one valence of reconciliation and of justice, the concept of mercy corresponds to the other valence of reconciliation and justice, the sense in which these are processes of restoring right relationship. Mercy is reconciliation's animating virtue. Again, this will seem strange to modern western ears, trained since the Enlightenment to think of mercy as a departure or exception to the justice of retribution. But in the scriptures of Judaism, Islam, and Christianity, where mercy is represented as *hesed* and *rahamin* in Hebrew, *rahma* in Arabic, and *eleos* in Greek, mercy is something far more thoroughgoing, corresponding more closely to Pope John Paul II's definition of mercy as a virtue that is "manifested in its true and proper aspect when it restores to value, promotes and draws good from all the forms of evil existing in the world and in man."[26] For peacebuilding, mercy implies that every action and practice ought to be restorative in its aim.

The core ideas in an ethic of reconciliation—reconciliation, justice, peace, and mercy—are found not only in the language of the three traditions' scriptures but also in the three traditions' conceptions of action in response to wrongdoing. These conceptions can be found both in the traditions' scriptural accounts of God's response to evil as well as in communal practices that have developed within the traditions over centuries. In contrast to the Enlightenment tradition, which presented philosophical solutions to the problem of evil, the scriptures tell of a God who responds through action. The Tanakh portrays God restoring his covenant with the Jewish people variously through punishment, forgiveness, reparation, and restoration of justice for the poor and the dispossessed, and calls on kings and rulers to do the same—a many-orbed response, addressed toward an array of fractures in right relationship, carrying implications for political orders. In medieval Jewish communities, rituals of *teshuva*, a form of repentance involving restitution, remorse, confession, and the wrongdoer's commitment to change, practiced together by offender, victim, and community members, manifest the core ideas of holistic restoration of relationship in the context of community. In the New Testament, the same sort of justice is accomplished through the atoning sacrifice of God in Christ. To be sure, different theological understandings of atonement have arisen over the centuries. Among the most important of these differences is precisely the question of whether atonement is a holistic restoration or an acquittal pronounced upon sufficient payment. The holistic restoration model predominated in the early church of the first millennium; the juristic model arose in the late Middle Ages and the Reformation period. For the project at hand a positive development has been the re-emergence of the restoration model in the twentieth century among both Catholic and Protestant theologians—with an application to political and social affairs.[27] While an atoning sacrifice of God is not present in the Quran, God still performs restorative actions. Repeatedly, the Quran promises God's forgiveness for the repentant and exhorts believers to forgive in like manner. In later Muslim tradition, communal rituals of *musalaha*, much like Jewish communal rituals of *teshuva*, responded to crimes within the community through dialogue, repentance, reparations, forgiveness, and ceremonies for reintegrating the offender into the community.[28]

Justice understood as right relationship (in its two valences of restorative process and resulting state), along with peace, mercy, God's restorative response to evil, and communal rituals of reconciliation—these concepts and practices, derived from religious traditions, are the building blocks of reconciliation. To be sure, applying these concepts to peacebuilding in modern political orders requires adaptation, development, and grafting with modern concepts like democracy, constitutional rule of law, and international law. It also requires theological interpretation, arguments as to why certain narrative themes belong in the foreground and others in the background and why and how certain passages ought to be interpreted in light of others. There are strands of scripture in all three religions that admittedly are not restorative—for instance, episodes in which God punitively destroys entire communities or grants injunctions of the death penalty for a wide array of crimes. The religious traditions themselves have developed interpretations of these strands that help to reduce their tension with restorative justice and reconciliation. The traditions teach, for instance, that not all of God's actions or of scripture's laws carry direct implications for the norms of contemporary communities. In the case of the death penalty, by the second century c.e. Jewish rabbinic teaching placed such high procedural hurdles on its implementation that its practice became exceedingly rare in Jewish communities. Although tensions between the scriptures and restorative justice and reconciliation still remain, adaptation and development is possible.

The adaptation of reconciliation to modern political orders also takes place through filling out reconciliation's core concepts with greater content and specificity. Like restorative justice, the core concepts of reconciliation all involve the repair of actual harms to right relationship that injustices inflict. The justice of reconciliation restores right relationship by aiming to repair harms to persons and relationships. The peace of reconciliation is the condition of right relationship that results from this repair. Mercy is the virtue that wills the reparation of what is broken. These concepts attain content and specificity in two ways: (1) through identifying the specific harms, or wounds, to persons and relationships that injustices inflict; (2) through setting forth a set of political practices that bring repair to these harms.

A wound of political injustice can be defined as some respect in which a political injustice ruptures right relationship in or between political communities and diminishes the human flourishing of those who are involved in that injustice. This rupture and this diminishment take a variety of forms, each distinguished by the role that parties to these wounds play. All wounds that result from political injustices—that is, human rights violations and other crimes committed by agents of the state or of political opposition movements—are ruptures in right relationship since they are the result of actions that violate the terms of right relationship. This is true even of wounds that diminish primarily the flourishing of victims themselves such as death, lasting injury, trauma, psychological and emotional wounds, the death of loved ones, sexual violation, the loss of property, and the like. Other forms of wounds are more obviously relational, such as the failure of members of the surrounding political community to acknowledge the suffering of victims. Other examples of wounds are victims' ignorance of the source and circumstances of the political injustices; the "standing victory" of the political injustice that the perpetrator committed, that is, the sense in which it persists as an undiminished moral reality in the eyes of victims, members of the community, and even the perpetrator himself, at least as long as it is not met with a countering and nullifying communication; and finally, one that is familiar in the three faith traditions as well as in sources like Plato's *Gorgias*—that is, the wound that a crime inflicts in the soul of its perpetrator.

Wrought directly by political injustices, these wounds may be called primary wounds. Primary wounds may also lead to subsequent wounds through a chain of memories, emotions, and judgments that lead to further acts of injustice, in which case they may be called "secondary wounds." These are familiar in all of those places that have experienced cycles of violence, including Rwanda, Burundi, Bosnia, Kosovo, the Basque Country, Iraq, Israel and Palestine, and many, many other locales. Other wounds might be mentioned; some arise in the chapters that follow. Whatever exactly they are, the task of identifying wounds points us to the harms to which the justice of reparation is addressed.

If wounds identify the harms to which the justice of reconciliation brings repair, practices are the concrete activities that bring about this repair. Each practice redresses wounds to persons and relationships differently, involving victims, perpetrators, members of the community, and agents of the state in distinct ways. There are at least six of these practices, beginning with socially just institutions, both political and economic. A second is acknowledgment of the suffering of victims by members of the community through official political processes. The work of truth commissions is an example, as are museums, monuments, and rituals of remembrance. A third is reparations, which deliver material compensation to victims. They may partially alleviate at least some forms of loss but more importantly serve as a material fortification of public recognition of victims' suffering. Fourth is accountability, through which perpetrators acknowledge and make reparation for their political injustices. Fifth is apology, which perpetrators express for their own misdeeds and which public officials sometimes express for injustices committed in the name of the political order. Finally, forgiveness is a practice through which victims will to forego anger and revenge and resolve to look upon a perpetrator as one against whom they no longer hold their crimes.

When acts of restoration directly address the wounds that political injustices inflict, they may be called "primary restorations." Just as primary wounds can beget secondary wounds, so, too, primary restorations can lead to "secondary restorations," in which citizens make new and positive judgments about their political order, national community, or relations with a previously hostile foreign state. As with wounds, other practices may also be envisioned. A full account of practices would explain which wounds each practice seeks to address, how each practice brings restoration to persons and relationships, by what criteria the practices perform this restoration well, and how the practices are linked together and interdependent.[29] We do not provide such an account here, but the chapters that follow say far more about how each practice enacts justice.

Together, the practices may be thought of as composing a holistic notion of political reconciliation. Each reflects reconciliation as a concept of justice, mercy, and peace. To think of the practices holistically, of course, is not to expect that all or most of them will take place in any situation or that any of them will occur to more than a partial degree. Still, the practices may be thought of as integrated and as parts of a whole. Because accountability and forgiveness are both justified in restorative fashion, for instance, they need not be at odds. Each aims to repair different sorts of wounds through different sorts of measures. Power realities, of course, will often prevent accountability from taking place, but these realities are situational and varying. To take another example, measures to bring about long-term structural economic change need not be at odds with shorter-term measures like truth commissions or reparations to victims. Here again, each measure performs different sorts of restorations to different sorts of wounds in a restorative division of labor. Finally, insofar as religiously based concepts of reconciliation resemble a secularly articulated restorative justice, the religious and the secular need not be at odds.

The Difference Relationships Make: Restorative Justice and Reconciliation as Relational Frameworks for Peacebuilding

Restorative justice and reconciliation share a common commitment to a relational conception of justice and within this conception, they ground conceptual frames for peacebuilding. These conceptual frames support a different view of justice and peace and their relationship. But, one might ask: Is this a distinction without a difference? Skeptics might charge that restorative justice and reconciliation offer a different way of thinking or talking about justice and peace but that in the end these frameworks really don't make much of an operational difference. How, for instance, are they different in content from positive peace or human rights?

Our claim is that relational theories indeed yield distinct implications for the work of peacebuilding on the ground and not just for debates in ivory towers or UN corridors. This distinctiveness cannot be easily shown, though, simply by describing or prescribing "right" or "restored" relationships. To those who would ask, "What do these relationships look like?" restorative justice and reconciliation answer "it depends." The centrality of embeddedness and contextuality in a relational approach means that much depends on the context, circumstances, and relationships at issue in a given situation.

This does not mean that we are relativists. Equal concern, respect, dignity, human rights, the rule of law, and other values function as universal criteria of justice in our frameworks. But these values accommodate great breadth for adaptation to local situations.

This commitment to context is indeed one significant difference that a relational framework makes. This very commitment implies a further commitment to certain concrete principles like subsidiarity, cooperation, and complementarity. The concept of *subsidiarity* finds its origins in the social thought of the Catholic Church during the first half of the twentieth century and has made its way into democratic theory, the discourses of European federalism, and debates about federalism elsewhere.[30] Subsidiarity plays a prominent role, for example, in the Maastricht Treaty that established the European Union in 1992. According to the European Commission, the subsidiarity principle "is intended to ensure that decisions are taken as closely as possible to the citizen and that constant checks are made as to whether action at [European] Community level is justified in the light of the possibilities available at national, regional or local level. Specifically, it is the principle whereby the [European] Union does not take action . . . unless it is more effective than action taken at national, regional or local level."[31] The UN Peacebuilding Commission reflects this commitment in the requirement that it work *cooperatively* with the member states involved in its cases. Relatedly, *complementarity* is the principle underpinning the jurisdiction of the International Criminal Court, whereby jurisdiction will only be exercised if a country is unwilling or unable to prosecute.[32]

In a relational framework, these principles reflect a commitment to contextuality. It is important that we involve those with intimate knowledge of the contexts and relationships at stake if we are to have the knowledge and capacities needed to address harms and build a foundation for a new and better future. These principles would profoundly improve peacebuilding by making clearer the role that international actors should play in such efforts and the necessity of ensuring participatory and inclusive processes in which local and national actors lead the way. Peacebuilding cannot, on this approach, be done *to* nations or communities; it must, rather, be done *with* them. This does not leave international actors (NGOs, transnational churches, aid agencies, the United Nations, etc.) with no role. In fact, within a relational framework, the status and role of such "outsiders" becomes clearer. Indeed, the relational approach allows more complexity than do approaches based on binary and adversarial choices such as outsider versus insider. A relational approach invites the participation of different parties in the work of peacebuilding according to their roles in the causes and solutions of conflict. It asks: how have these parties contributed to the wrongs (the harms to relationships) and how have they been affected by the wrongs? What contribution can they make to the restoration of affected relationships? This relational approach envisions a more constructive role for regional and international organizations than that of conveners, instructors, or enforcers.

A relational approach carries other distinct implications for peacebuilding, too. First, relational theories can and ought to incorporate human rights, both as standards for identifying injustices and as desiderata for restored constitutional orders and relations between states. But relational theories perform this incorporation in a way that is consonant with their moral and philosophical commitments. They stress, for instance, the sense in which rights structure complex and robust forms of relationship, involving particular claims and obligations among citizens, between citizens and the society as a whole, between citizens and their government, and between populations of separate states. Rights within a relational framework must be grounded in the relational nature of the self and the commitment to right or restored relationships. This is not a stark departure from the traditional notion of rights. It is significant that, contrary to the beliefs of many liberals, natural human rights find their origins (though they were not labeled as human rights) not in the writings of Enlightenment theorists like Hobbes and Locke but in sources that far predate them: the Jewish scriptures, medieval canon law, the arguments of the Spanish scholastics who defended the rights of people in the New World in the sixteenth and seventeenth centuries, and early modern Protestant thought.[33] In these sources, the rights of persons were grounded in a larger, transcendent moral order. Contemporary relational theory argues along similar lines, namely that rights find their strongest meaning and justification in the duties, virtues, and obligations that make for strong human relationships.[34] Notably, the core values of restored relationships—equality of respect, concern, and dignity—are foundations for international and domestic human rights norms. Such a commonality reinforces the potential possibilities for secular and religious perspectives to meet around common commitments in the context of relational theories.

If rights are embedded in a larger framework of right relationship and if peacebuilding is oriented around restoring right relationship, this carries an important implication for action—namely, that rights are not the sole or even dominant concept in play. It also reduces tensions with human rights advocates, who take a legalistic approach to rights that measures justice in terms of the vindication of rights. A relational approach to rights requires much more attention to the work rights are intended to do in the world, to the relationships they structure. While the liberal peace focuses on the restoration of institutions to provide democracy, free market, civil liberties, and judicial prosecution—through the mechanism of rights—a relational approach to rights considers what institutions and structures will best foster and protect right relationships.

Rights alone, however, are an inadequate vessel to hold all at which a relational approach aims. Even if understood relationally, rights are not sufficient to reflect fully the goals and ambitions of restorative justice and reconciliation. Consider, for instance, the good that can be achieved when a victim comes to have her suffering acknowledged before a national truth commission.[35] She may well see fulfilled what international law now posits as a "right to truth telling," but such a right hardly describes fully the good that she experiences. Further, rights themselves may well depend on other kinds of restorations if they are to be sustained. A common story in accounts of truth commissions from around the world is that of the victim who, once acknowledged by the commission, decides to forego revenge and to increase his commitment to a nascent democratic regime or peace agreement and thus to the rights that they protect. Rights require legitimacy, but legitimacy is generated through measures and relationships that far exceed the legal establishment of rights themselves. Indeed, one of the potential benefits of processes based on restorative justice and reconciliation is that they may serve as forums able to provide feedback to the democratic processes charged with the establishment and protection of rights. Restorative processes can thereby contribute to the legitimacy of law.

Second, relational theories seek to overcome any sharp dichotomy between the public and the private and the personal and the political. To be sure, any relational theory of peacebuilding for modern politics must recognize the limits and checks on state power prescribed by constitutional democracy and international human rights norms—basic civil liberties, due process protections, elections, and the like. But in contrast with liberal theory's stress on personal autonomy and non-interference, relational theories recognize the deep link between sustainable peace and the emotions, judgments, memories, and attitudes that citizens hold toward one another, their society, and other societies. In the wake of war, dictatorship, genocide, and other injustices, it is essential that these "internal," "private," and "personal" issues be addressed if the public, political order is to be stable, peaceful, and just. A relational approach also shifts our understanding of harm and reveals the interconnectedness of the seemingly personal and private to the public and political. This connectedness is readily evident in post-conflict and transitional contexts where the connection between personal and political harms often explains the strength and urgency of the commitment to deal with the past.

Third, while relational theories encompass accountability for wrongdoers, they justify and approach accountability in restorative terms. Consistent with these theories' commitment to contextuality, accountability will take different forms. Relational theories also reject an equation of accountability with punishment for its own sake or with prosecution, calling into question the exclusive focus on individual blame that such an equation implies. Accountability fashioned toward the end of assigning blame can take quite a different form if, as in a relational approach, it is oriented to future restoration of relationships. Accountability in some form is envisioned in virtually every notion of reconciliation or restorative justice, which always justifies accountability by its aim of restoring and reintegrating the wrongdoer, of redressing the wounds suffered by victims, and of repairing the harm that the injustices have done to the larger social order, insofar as this is possible.

Fourth, framing peacebuilding through restorative justice and reconciliation will have significant implications for the temporal scope and horizon of peacebuilding. Viewed relationally, peacebuilding must focus not only on the establishment but also on the maintenance of relationships of equal concern, respect, and dignity. A relational approach does not offer the static "end state" of justice done, delivered, or served up or of peace settled, achieved, or realized, as is sought by retributive justice or liberal peace. On a relational approach justice and peace are transformed into a way of being in relationship and thus less something one has "done" than something one is "doing." Because relationships are dynamic, contextual, and interactive, the work of justice must also be so. Peacebuilding on this account, then, is not bounded by a limited transitional period, say during the replacement of a dictatorship with a democracy or the negotiation of a peace agreement and its immediate thereafter. Understood relationally, peace is not to be seen as built and done but rather as nurtured and maintained.[36] It is this maintenance that has been so elusive and led to the development, for example, of the UN Peacebuilding Commission. Yet, it is elusive, at least in part, because the conceptual framework utilized for justice and peacebuilding does not demand ongoing attention. A relational view challenges this more limited focus on justice and peacebuilding in the transition and reveals the need equally for the development of right relationships and their ongoing maintenance.

Perhaps the most important and distinctive dimension of this relational framework, though, is its aspiration to integration and holism. It calls for integrating a range of activities and actors, some of which are typically in tension with each other but all of whom complement the others in building peace and thus demand connection and coordination. In some respects, relational theories overlap with other frameworks. This is not a redundancy but an advantage, for the aspiration of relational theories is to integrate insights rather than to replace rival paradigms. What makes relational theories distinctive is the wide array of actors and activities that they incorporate into their theoretical ambit, an overarching account of the moral logic of various peacebuilding activities, and a framework in which actors and activities are intentionally linked. On this approach the relationship of security, political transition, rights protection, accounting for past wrongs, and development to the cause of peacebuilding can be explained and integrated. Restorative justice and reconciliation, then, are not simply more tools in an expanded toolbox for peacebuilding or prescriptions for combining tools. Neither are they a recipe for the sequencing of activities, an endeavor that the Review of the Peacebuilding Commission calls illusory:

> There is acceptance in all quarters that sequencing does not work, that effective peacebuilding must not follow peacekeeping operations but accompany them from their inception. . . . Despite this acknowledgement, there is a widespread sense that the sequential approach remains the dominant one at the United Nations. Even if modest elements of peacebuilding are incorporated in mandates, the focus and mindset of operations is a peacekeeping one. Peacebuilding tends to be viewed as an add-on during the lifetime of the peacekeeping operation, expected to come into its own in the aftermath. Such a sequential approach neither gives adequate weight to peacebuilding nor responds to needs and realities on the ground.[37]

Restorative justice and reconciliation provide frameworks for the work of peacebuilding that challenge the logic of silos and sequencing and instead favor an integrative approach.

In this broad outline of relational theories—restorative justice and reconciliation—we seek to open up the space to consider their many elements and components and their implications for peacebuilding. This development will be pursued further throughout this volume. In a framework that aspires to ambitions like holism, integration, relationship, overcoming antinomies, and a peace informed by justice, it is also worth stressing that in any context in which societies are facing large-scale injustices in the past and seeking to move toward greater justice in the future, the achievement of these ends is always likely to be only partially achieved. What is possible will be dependent on the relative power of parties and factions, the presence or absence of international actors and institutions, the scale and nature of the injustices being addressed, and numerous other political factors. It is our hope, though, that by conceiving justice in relational terms and framing peacebuilding accordingly, those who are involved in peacebuilding, whether they be a Secretary General, a tribal leader, a president, a prelate, or an ordinary citizen, will realize greater possibilities for a just peace.

Notes

1. The founding resolution of the Peacebuilding Commission required a review by member states in 2010, which was released in July 2010. The Permanent Representatives of Ireland, Mexico, and South Africa, co-facilitators of the review process, presented their report entitled "Review of the United Nations peacebuilding architecture," United Nations A/64/868–S/2010/393 (July 2010) [hereinafter: *PBC Review*]. For general discussions and assessments of the work of the commission also see: "Issue Brief: Perspectives on the Peacebuilding Commission and Mutual Accountability," International Peace Institute (November 2009); "Consolidating The Peace: Views from Sierra Leone and Burundi on the United Nations Peacebuilding Commission," ActionAid, CAFOD, and CARE International; Rob Jenkins, "Organizational Change and Institutional Survival: The Case of the U.N. Peacebuilding Commission," 38 *Seton Hall Law Review* (2008): 1327.
2. *PBC Review*, Executive Summary.
3. PBC Review at para. 13.
4. PBC Review at para. 58.
5. PBC Review at para. 58.
6. PBC Review at para. 167.
7. The accounts of restorative justice and reconciliation in this essay are drawn from our previous scholarship. See for example: Jennifer J. Llewellyn, "Restorative Justice in Transitions and Beyond: The Justice Potential of Truth Telling Mechanisms for Post-Peace Accord Societies," in *Telling The Truths: Truth Telling and Peace Building in Post-Conflict Societies*, ed. T. Borer (Notre Dame Press, 2006), 83–114; Jennifer J. Llewellyn, "Truth Commissions and Restorative Justice," in *Handbook of Restorative Justice*, ed. G. Johnstone and D. Van Ness (Devon, UK: Willan Publishers, 2006), 351–371; and Daniel Philpott, *Just and Unjust Peace: An Ethic of Political Reconciliation* (New York, NY: Oxford University Press, 2012).
8. United Nations Economic and Social Council, E/CN.15/2002/5/Add.1.
9. United Nations Office on Drugs and Crime, *Handbook on Restorative Justice Programmes* (Vienna: United Nations, 2006).
10. For a recent exploration of relational theory and its practical implications see: Jocelyn Downie and Jennifer Llewellyn, eds., *Being Relational: Reflections on Relational Theory and Health Law* (Vancouver: UBC Press, 2011). Also see: Penny A. Weiss and Marilyn Friedman, eds., *Feminism and Community* (Philadelphia: Temple University Press, 1995); Diana Tietjens Meyers, ed., *Feminists Rethink the Self* (Boulder, Colorado: Westview Press, 1997); Catriona Mackenzie and Natalie Stoljar, eds., *Relational Autonomy: Feminist Perspectives on Autonomy, Agency, and the Social Self* (Oxford: Oxford University Press, 2000). Jennifer Nedelsky, "Reconceiving Autonomy: Sources, Thoughts and Possibilities," 1 *Yale J.L. and Feminism* (1989): 7; Susan Sherwin, "A Relational Approach to Autonomy in Health Care" in *The Politics of Women's Health: Exploring Agency and Autonomy*, ed. Susan Sherwin et al. (Philadelphia: Temple University Press, 1998); Christine M.

Koggel, *Perspectives on Equality: Constructing a Relational Theory* (Lanham, MD: Rowman and Littlefield, 1998).
11. See generally, Michael L. Hadley, ed., *The Spiritual Roots of Restorative Justice* (Albany, NY: State University of New York Press, 2001).
12. Christine M. Koggel, *Perspectives on Equality: Constructing a Relational Theory* (Lanham, Maryland: Rowman and Littlefield Publishers, 1998), 5.
13. Jennifer J. Llewellyn, "Restorative Justice: Thinking Relationally about Justice" in *Being Relational: Reflections on Relational Theory and Health Law*, ed. Jocelyn Downie and Jennifer Llewellyn (Vancouver: UBC Press, 2011).
14. For example: John Rawls, *A Theory of Justice* (Cambridge, MA: Harvard University Press, 1971).
15. Some liberal accounts use the formulation of respect and concern without moving substantially from the notion of respect described above. Others see it as requiring some positive actions to support others. See for example, Barbara Herman, "Mutual Aid and Respect for Persons," 94 *Ethics* (1984): 577. However, many of these accounts do not challenge the fundamental assumptions of liberal individualism as they connect concern for others to some version of self-interest, for example, in how we each wish to be treated.
16. John Braithwaite and Phillip Pettit, *Not Just Deserts: A Republican Theory of Criminal Justice* (Oxford, UK: Oxford University Press, 1990).
17. This is a point reflected in universal human rights norms. Restored relationships describe the conditions within which these fundamental rights can be realized. They are the conditions of relationship between citizens that make possible peaceful and lasting co-existence.
18. John Braithwaite, *Crime, Shame and Reintegration* (Cambridge University Press, 1989).
19. This is a point often misunderstood as a result of the common claim that restorative justice is "victim-centered." Such a claim is comparatively true if one juxtaposes restorative processes with current criminal justice processes, which are centrally concerned with the offender and the state, often excluding or marginalizing the victim. However, as a description of restorative processes in their own right, "victim-centered" is problematic if it creates the impression that restorative justice is focused on victims at the exclusion of the wrongdoer or community.
20. Paul McCold, "The Role of Community in Restorative Justice Practice and Theory," in *Critical Issues in Restorative Justice*, ed. H. Zehr and B. Toews (Monsey, NY: Criminal Justice Press, 2004), 155–171. Also see Howard Zehr, *The Little Book of Restorative Justice* (Intercourse, PA: Good Books, 2002).
21. John Braithwaite, Jennifer Llewellyn, Paul McCold, and Dan Van Ness, "An Introduction to Restorative Peacebuilding" (New York: Working Party on Restorative Justice, Alliance of NGO's on Crime Prevention and Criminal Justice, 2007).
22. Desmond Tutu, *No Future without Forgiveness* (New York: Doubleday, 1999); Pope John Paul II, *Dives in Misericordia*, encyclical letter, 1980; and Pope John Paul II's messages for the World Day of Peace, 1997 and 2002.
23. Christopher D. Marshall, *Beyond Retribution: A New Testament Vision For Justice, Crime and Punishment* (Grand Rapids, MI: Eerdmans, 2001), 38.
24. *Teshuva* more precisely means "repentance," but teshuva rituals as they developed over the centuries came to involve a rich set of practices that approach the more holistic righteousness of reconciliation. *Tikkun olam* usually means something much like "repair of the world."
25. See Ulrich Mauser, *The Gospel of Peace: A Scriptural Message For Today's World* (Louisville, KY: Westminster/John Knox, 1992); Perry Yoder, *Shalom: The Bible's Word for Salvation, Justice, and Peace* (Newton, KS: Faith and Life Press, 1987); A. Rashied Omar, "Between Compassion and Justice: Locating an Islamic Definition of Peace," *Peace Colloquy* issue no. 7 (2005), 9–10.
26. Pope John Paul II, *Dives in Misericordia*, para. 6.
27. Gustaf Aulén, *Christus Victor: An Historical Study of the Three Main Types of the Idea of Atonement* (New York: Macmillan Publishing Company, 1969); Colin Gunton, *The Actuality of Atonement* (New York, NY: T&T Clark LTD, 1988); Marshall, *Beyond Retribution*.
28. Mohammed Abu-Nimer, *Nonviolence and Peace Building in Islam* (Gainesville, FL: University Press of Florida, 2003); George E. Irani and Nathan C. Funk, "Rituals of Reconciliation: Arab-Islamic perspectives," *Arab Studies Quarterly* 20, no. 4 (1998): 53–73.

29. For a fuller account, see Philpott, *Just and Unjust Peace*.
30. See Pope Pius XI, *Quadregissimo Anno*, encyclical, 1931.
31. The European Commission offers this definition of subsidiarity as delineated in Article 5 of the Treaty on European Union. See: http://europa.eu/legislation_summaries/glossary/subsidiarity_en.htm.
32. See section 20 of Rome Statute.
33. Brian Tierney, *The Idea of Natural Rights: Studies on Natural Rights, Natural Law, and Church Law, 1150–1625* (Atlanta, GA: Scholars Press, 1997); John Witte, *The Reformation of Rights: Law, Religion and Human Rights in Early Modern Calvinism* (Cambridge, UK: Cambridge University Press, 2007); Nicholas Wolterstorff, *Justice: Rights and Wrongs* (Princeton, NJ: Princeton University Press, 2008).
34. For original articulations of this idea see: Jennifer Nedelsky, "Reconceiving Rights as Relationship," 1 *Review of Constitutional Studies/Revue d'etudes constitutionnel* (1993): 1; and Wolterstorff, *Justice*.
35. André Du Toit, "The Moral Foundations of the South African TRC: Truth as Acknowledgment and Justice as Recognition," in *Truth v. Justice: The Morality of Truth Commissions*, ed. Robert I. Rotberg and Dennis Thompson (Princeton, NJ: Princeton University Press, 2000), 133.
36. This is a central theme in the work of John Paul Lederach, who is one of the intellectual pioneers of a relational approach to peacebuilding and whose work has done much to inspire this project. See his *Building Peace: Sustainable Reconciliation in Divided Societies* (Washington, DC: United States Institute for Peace, 1997). Lederach has argued for a necessary shift in the conceptual paradigm and praxis of peacebuilding away from "the traditional framework and activities that make up statist diplomacy" with its "concern with the resolution of issues towards a frame of reference that focuses on the restoration and rebuilding of relationships." His work, too, stresses relationships, integration of a wide variety of actors and activities at all levels of society, holism, and a notion of peace that is informed by justice rather than in tension with it. In these many ways, the present volume aims to advance the line of thinking that he powerfully initiated.
37. PBC Review at paras. 20–22.

CHAPTER 3

Charting the Path of Justice in Peacebuilding

Aaron P. Boesenecker and Leslie Vinjamuri

Human Rights Watch, Amnesty International, the Coalition for the International Criminal Court, and numerous other human rights organizations have played a central role in pushing both Northern and Southern governments to embrace the new international gold standard of accountability: criminal prosecutions for individual perpetrators of mass atrocities. The advocacy of these powerful international nongovernmental organizations (NGOs) has sometimes lagged behind local NGOs mobilized to pressure their governments to put perpetrators of heinous civilian crimes and mass atrocities on trial. Elsewhere, local NGOs have shored up initiatives driven by international NGO advocates. More recently, the International Criminal Court's high profile indictments in Libya, Kenya, the Sudan, the Democratic Republic of the Congo, Uganda, and beyond, have captured the public imagination, appearing to offer testament to an emerging belief in the natural concurrence of justice and peace.[1]

This portrayal of a collective pursuit of peace and justice by transnational and local organizations committed to a definition of accountability defined by individual criminal justice masks the contestation that pervades the politics of justice during periods of violent conflict, and also in subsequent peacebuilding initiatives.[2] Contestation is sometimes the product of conflict between pragmatic or self-interested state leaders, spoilers that seek to impede peace, and committed advocates of justice.[3] But contestation is also the product of contending beliefs or conceptions about justice among actors that are motivated primarily by a principled commitment to peace and justice. Scholarship on human rights and transitional justice often assumes that these "civil society" actors hold similar beliefs about the role of justice in peacebuilding. And yet, many organizations, especially faith-based organizations (FBOs), have embraced strategies that are radically different from the gold standard that Jonathan VanAntwerpen refers to in this volume as the "secular orthodoxy" that has characterized the field of transitional justice.

Our chapter considers this second source of conflict, which we refer to as principled contestation, that emerges from the diverse conceptions of justice held by local civil society actors and transnational organizations. It draws on a series of carefully selected examples to illuminate the diversity of organizational beliefs held by non-state actors and the peacebuilding strategies that follow. Many of these strategies reject some basic tenets of the liberal peace. Contrary to popular impressions, organizational peacebuilding strategies are characterized by an *absence* of consensus on the appropriate strategies for dealing with the problem of justice and accountability. We develop a conceptual framework for understanding the organizational basis of this dissensus and then evaluate the implications of this for reconciliation, restorative justice, and peacebuilding through a series of illustrative cases.

The typology below presents three categories of actors that capture key differences among non-state actors engaged in the politics of reconciliation, accountability, and justice, especially in transitional and conflict states that have seen mass atrocities and serious crimes. "Legalists," "Restorers," and "Capacity-builders" each share beliefs about what constitutes justice and the appropriate strategies for pursuing it. These shared beliefs comprise an actor's conception of justice, that is, the principled and causal beliefs that actors hold about accountability, truth, justice, peace, and reconciliation. The sources of these beliefs vary. Some are derived from international legal precepts, others from religious doctrine, and still others from local traditions or social psychological understandings of conflict resolution. All of the actors we consider are organizations whose identity is defined by a basic commitment to justice.[4]

Empirically, we examine how these actors have worked to deliver accountability, truth, and (sometimes) reconciliation for mass atrocities. We pay special attention to the period beginning in the early 1990s, when the politics of international justice became increasingly visible, consequential, and contentious. Our research suggests that indeed many prominent organizations based in the United States and Europe do share a conception of justice that attributes responsibility to individual perpetrators. But organizations based in the global south, which we refer to as "local" in this chapter, are more differentiated and, ultimately, less conformist, despite external pressures from international human rights networks and international institutions to adopt transitional justice orthodoxy.[5]

Second, faith-based organizations such as the Catholic Church and the Mennonite Central Committee have played a prominent role, working at both the elite and grassroots level to mediate peace settlements, create alternative understandings of peace, reframe understandings of justice and reconciliation, reconstruct communities, and build local institutional capacity. Faith-based organizations are a diverse group, but many embrace ideas of restorative justice and reconciliation and a broader conception of peacebuilding, as discussed by Jennifer Llewellyn and Daniel Philpott in the introduction to this volume. Often this means that peacebuilding strategies require longer-term engagement, which in turn gives these FBOs a greater understanding of how local conditions might foster or impede normative change and so enhances their ability to adapt international norms to local contexts.[6] Many FBOs also have access to private funding.[7] This alternative source of finances places those that can sustain it in a privileged position, especially when compared to organizations that depend on government funding. Fiscal autonomy gives FBOs a greater ability to evade pressures to conform. Together, these two factors help safeguard the influence of FBOs, especially as organizations that embrace a heterodox approach that has come under pressure to accept transitional justice orthodoxy.

Third, we find that faith-based organizations engaged in peacebuilding do not universally prefer reconciliation.[8] Even prior to international pressures to conform to an emerging orthodoxy, some vocal FBOs had mobilized around a prosecutorial agenda.[9] In some cases, FBOs have embraced the orthodoxy of the international human rights movement at the global level, but supported local exceptions to this orthodoxy. Strong faith-based organizational support for trials challenges the conventional wisdom that FBOs more uniformly prefer reconciliation and forgiveness.

Conceptions of Justice

Beliefs and norms about the nature of justice and its relationship to peacebuilding have diverse origins. Faith doctrines, local cultural beliefs, and international human rights precepts all shape the organizational strategies of justice, accountability, and peacebuilding that actors adopt. These beliefs, which we refer to as a conception of justice, may change over time but tend to be deeply embedded in an organization's identity. At one end of the spectrum, we locate those who embrace individualist and retributive strategies and at the opposite end we identify actors that see justice as relational and that emphasize reconciliation or restorative justice.

Retributive justice combines punishment of a perpetrator with public acknowledgment of a wrongdoing through mechanisms such as trials, reparations, or restitution.[10] Restorative justice, as the name implies, is more concerned with restoring human relationships, both between victim and perpetrator as well as within a larger community or group. Its origins can be found in both indigenous justice and in faith traditions, including Christian ideals from the Sermon on the Mount and injunctions stressing the universality of human suffering and the power of forgiveness; ideas such as *shalom* (Hebrew) and *salaam* (Arabic, meaning "peace with justice"); Talmudic teachings on restitution and repair; and diverse local traditions and customs.[11] Strategies for achieving restorative justice include truth-telling, community reconciliation rituals, and specific local customs that both acknowledge transgressions and focus on relationships within the larger community. In addition, actors pursuing reconciliation and restorative justice are more attentive to deeper structures of inequality, discrimination, and oppression that are often at the root of conflicts. For faith-based organizations in particular, the messages of peace, forgiveness, humility, and understanding found in their religious doctrines, as well as the injunctions to care for the poor and oppressed, are at the root of their commitment to restorative justice.[12]

Organizational Attributes

Actors also differ on a range of organizational attributes. Universalists aspire to assist a community that is defined only by its common humanity. Identity-based actors are primarily concerned with protecting or defending members of a community with whom they share a collective identity. Some organizations are transnational, others local.

Universalists have not uniformly embraced (or rejected) individual or relational conceptions of justice. Secular universalists embrace norms and beliefs grounded in international law and a conception of justice that favors retributive justice. Beliefs in international human rights law and its enforcement are both principled and causal, that is, linked to a broader theory of how to reform behavior. Faith-based universalists believe in mercy, tolerance, and sympathy with the poor and oppressed (irrespective of their faith or affiliation) and are more likely to embrace restorative justice. In contrast, identity-based (self-regarding) actors embrace retributive strategies as a natural extension of their commitment to protecting a particular group against harm. The focus on injustices committed against the members of one's own identity group creates a bias toward victimhood rather than relationship as a dominant frame.

Both universalist and identity-based actors may be organized on a local/national or transnational basis. We find that local and national organizations have a unique vantage point. They lack the benefit of "distant strangers" and so pursue strategies that are shaped by their proximity—geographically, emotionally, socially, and culturally—to conflict.[13] When it comes to justice, we suggest that their investment in the future of these particular locales leads to a stronger preference for strategies of forgiveness, apology, and reconciliation over retributive justice. Why? Unlike actors whose footprint is temporary, local organizations are more likely to give priority to reconciliation among conflicting constituencies. The more limited an organization's transnational network is, the greater and more persistent this effect will be. In contrast, the comparatively superficial relationships that transnational actors have with local communities will typically diminish their commitment to restorative justice strategies that depend on long-term engagement.

Below, we investigate in more detail the claim that more extensive ties to local communities and actors, especially when combined with less extensive ties to the international level, will lead locally rooted organizations to support strategies that stress restoring relationships between communities rather than embracing strategies that emphasize individual accountability. For example, the Mennonite Central Committee or Quaker Peace and Social Witness deploy peacebuilding teams (often families) to live with local communities for a number of years, and often only engage in peacebuilding work after a lengthy period of observation, listening, and relationship-building. In contrast, Human Rights Watch and Amnesty International send individual researchers to the field. The International Center for Transitional Justice (ICTJ), which maintained the majority of its offices in the United States but also developed a series of permanent field offices as core to its organizational structure, may be more sensitive to local requirements and needs. Each of these actors struggles to match the sustained commitment of local peacebuilding organizations. The Roman Catholic Church (RCC) is unique in that different components of the organization span the local-transnational divide. Within the RCC, a highly formalized hierarchy of church offices and officials spans the globe and links even the most local of clergy to the Vatican. Despite this hierarchy, though, the RCC affords significant latitude to local bishops, clergy, and lay communities.[14]

Highly localized actors have often embraced mechanisms for accountability grounded in deeply rooted local practices while rejecting outside models that are viewed as unlikely to work at home.[15] Local custom, more than any framework derived from external actors or norms, may define understandings and practices for linking accountability to peace. Localized actors recognize an obligation to address both the needs of victims and the alleged crimes of perpetrators and often view justice as local, public, and interpersonal, and in many cases emphasize rituals of shame as well as public apology and forgiveness.[16] Local customs were central to justice and accountability efforts in East

Timor where traditional community justice ceremonies (*lisan*) were incorporated. In Uganda and Mozambique, local healing ceremonies have played an important role in coming to terms with past (and ongoing) atrocities. In general, these efforts toward restorative justice and reconciliation, often rooted at the local level, have been overlooked in international debates concerning peace, justice, and accountability. Paradoxically, though, local actors must forge connections to larger international or transnational actors in order to advance their particular vision of justice and accountability beyond the local level. In some cases, linkages to international networks may prove essential in shaping local practice. Linking up to these networks, though, has increasingly placed local actors under pressure to converge on global standards and practices.

Categorizing "The Doers": Legalists, Restorers, and Capacity-Builders

LEGALISTS

Legalists have embraced an understanding of conflict, justice, and accountability that is grounded in a commitment to individual accountability and rule-following and typically draws on international human rights standards. Accountability and justice are not only inherently valuable but are also seen as mechanisms for deterring future atrocities. Legalists tend to eschew strategies that are perceived to evade or conflict with the goal of criminal prosecution. Amnesty in particular is problematic. Truth-telling and broader notions of restorative justice are also problematic if they impede criminal accountability.

Legalists are neither exclusively secular nor faith-based, though secular legalists have been most prominent. Secular legalists engaged in peacebuilding look to the law, and increasingly to international human rights law, to shape their understandings about justice, and they seek to apply these standards indiscriminately. Faith-based legalists embrace understandings of justice that may draw on secular laws as well, but these organizations also draw on faith traditions (such as the emphasis on rule of law in some Evangelical circles). Some of these organizations, especially the World Jewish Congress and the American Jewish Conference, spearheaded efforts to lobby for prosecutions of Nazis responsible for holocaust crimes during the Second World War. More recently, FBOs have embraced legalism under the umbrella of the Faith and Ethics Network for the International Criminal Court.

Restorers

The "Restorers" are a second category of peacebuilder in our typology. Restorers, both faith-based and secular, maintain a general commitment to justice, reconciliation, and accountability, but place priority on the establishment of peace above any particular accountability strategy. Restorers often provide good offices for mediation in high-level negotiations among parties to a conflict, but are less likely to advocate for specific accountability or justice strategies. Even when restorers emphasize reconciliation, these actors are less likely to become involved in long-term, grassroots efforts, instead choosing to engage with elites in "conventional" lobbying or advocacy efforts.

For faith-based restorers, the emphasis on peace and conflict settlement is grounded in faith doctrines such as the dignity of human life. These actors typically weigh transitional justice strategies against the impact that the strategy may have on ending the immediate conflict. Below, we discuss a number of faith-based restorers, including the Roman Catholic Church, the Catholic lay community of Sant'Egidio, the Interreligious Council of Sierra Leone (IRCSL), Interfaith Action for Peace in Kenya, the Interreligious Council of Bosnia-Herzegovina, Women to Women (Bosnia-Herzegovina), the Wajir Peace and Development Committee (Kenya), and the Organization of the Islamic Conference. Secular restorers, such as the Red Cross/Red Crescent, adopt similar approaches to conflict settlement, though the source of their views generally is grounded in a pragmatic reading of international law and human rights norms.

Capacity-Builders

Capacity-builders embrace a comprehensive approach to accountability, justice, and reconciliation that takes them beyond the state to work closely with local communities to bring about deeper reconciliation. Capacity-builders embrace a full range of restorative justice strategies, including attention to immediate injustices and wrongdoings, but also to the underlying causes of conflict such as patterns of socio-economic inequality, discrimination, or oppression. The concepts of reconciliation, healing, and forgiveness underpin the preference for truth-telling and community building held by both faith-based and secular capacity-builders. In adopting an explicitly long-term, grassroots approach to restorative justice, capacity-builders do not approach a given situation with a set of prescriptions but rather develop strategies in the field by first building trust among all parties to a conflict and then eliciting their input.

Actors in this category draw their beliefs from religious doctrine, social-psychological understandings of conflict resolution, and local tradition. Many faith-based capacity-builders draw on the themes of forgiveness, mercy, and reconciliation found in many faith traditions and share the belief that strategies of reconciliation grounded in public forgiveness and truth-telling are critical to peace. For faith-based capacity-builders, these specifically *religious* injunctions are central to their preference for strategies of reconciliation and relationship building over retribution. Another fundamental element, drawn from faith, is the notion that judgment is not to be passed by humans in this world, but is reserved for a time (and a judge) after life on Earth has passed.[17] As such, restoring the relationship between perpetrator and victim, and within the larger community, is more fundamental to peace and reconciliation than the immediate urge for vengeance or vindication.[18]

Secular capacity-builders differ from their faith-based counterparts in the sources of their beliefs, but share a comprehensive approach to issues of justice and reconciliation. Secular capacity-builders draw on social-psychological understandings of peace, conflict, and reconciliation, as well as on local or traditional customs. For these actors, lasting peace is not possible without reconciliation, and reconciliation is seen as contingent on an emotional catharsis between victims and perpetrators. Truth-telling becomes an important strategy for accountability because it allows for a collective account of past atrocities, sometimes in a public forum that allows for an emotional exchange.

Both faith-based and secular capacity-builders embrace a theory of conflict resolution that grants importance not only to relations between individuals but also to intergroup dynamics. Unlike legalism, which assumes that conflict is defused by attributing guilt to individuals, capacity-builders assume that conflict is defused by creating shared understandings of past crimes that in turn create durable relationships of trust and reconciliation for the future. Capacity-building actors tend to view the adversarial process of criminal justice as a method that perpetuates antagonisms rather than one that helps to transcend the perpetrator-victim relationship that is necessary for full reconciliation.

Most of the strategies that follow from this logic engage individuals at the popular level and seek to foster public recognition of wrongdoing. Through this sharing of the truth, groups are able to reconcile and lay the foundation for a lasting, restorative peace. Comprehensive reconciliation that goes far beyond an elite pact is deemed essential. At the same time, such strategies often do not specifically address the dimension of elite leadership common to most trials involving mass atrocities.[19] Although establishing new relationships among victims, perpetrators, and the community is a difficult, long-term process (with no guarantee of success), capacity-builders favor these efforts over trials, which may achieve momentary "justice" but still leave a divide among the parties of a conflict.[20] Below we discuss the work of two universalist faith-based capacity-builders, the Mennonite Central Committee and the Acholi Religious Leaders Peace Initiative in Uganda.

A Typology of Actors

In the typology shown in Table 3.1, we organize secular and faith-based non-state actors according to the two dimensions discussed above—their conception of justice (preferences for retributive or restorative justice) and their organizational attributes, subdivided into their worldview (universalist or identity-based) and their scale (transnational or local). For each category, we identify a few representative actors. Some actors exhibit a consistent, strong preference for justice grounded in either reconciliation or retribution (the top and bottom of the x-axis). More pragmatic actors, located in the middle ranges of the y-axis, have been less rigid in their attachment to either reconciliation or retribution; they willingly alternate strategies in response to the context in which they operate. The typology is illustrative of the types of actors, rather than an exhaustive list. Actors have been placed in the typology according to their predominant characteristics and attributes in the contemporary politics of international justice.

In the following sections, we trace the role of representative Legalists, Restorers, and Capacity-Builders to demonstrate how each has pursued justice and peacebuilding in practice. The categories we identify are useful analytic constructs for understanding and identifying non-state actors engaged in peace, accountability, and justice efforts. We recognize, though, that in practice these actors often embrace understandings and strategies that sit within more than one of these categories. The historical specificity of actors' motivations is crucial and the examples below illustrate how actors' approaches to questions of peace, accountability, and justice have changed over time, through internal reflection and deliberation as well as through deliberation and contestation with other actors. In particular, discussions among faith-based organizations in the 1970s and 1980s laid the foundations for alternative conceptions that have challenged the dominant legalist strategies. We also find that in some cases, mid-level and locally embedded actors have played a crucial role in adapting international norms to fit with local practices.[21]

The case studies trace how organizational understandings of reconciliation, restoration, and justice change over time. They also highlight how organizational structure has shaped the development of a particular conception of justice and the strategies that emerge. As such, these case studies illustrate how

Table 3.1 Non-state Actors in International Justice

	Organizational Attributes			
	Identity-Based		Universalist	
Justice Conception	Local	Transnational	Transnational	Local
Reconciliation			Faith-based Capacity-builders (Mennonite Central Committee, Quaker Peace and Social Witness, Muslim Peace Fellowship)	Faith-based Capacity-builders (Acholi Religious Leaders Peace Initiative Uganda)
Pragmatic (Reconciliation)	Faith-based Restorers (African Independent Churches)	Faith-based Restorers (U.S. Conference of Catholic Bishops, Organization of the Islamic Conference, Islamic Community of Bosnia-Herzegovina)	Faith-based Restorers (Roman Catholic Church, Community of Sant'Egidio, American Friends Service Committee, Interfaith Action for Peace in Kenya, International Center for Religion and Diplomacy, Catholic Relief Services) Secular Restorers (Wajir Peace and Development Committee (Kenya))	Faith-based Restorers (Inter-Religious Council Bosnia and Herzegovina, Inter-Religious Council Sierra Leone, South African Conference of Churches, Sudanese Women Civil Society Network for Peace) Secular Restorers (Women to Women (Bosnia-Herzegovina) Campaign for Good Governance Sierra Leone)

Table 3.1 (continued)

	Organizational Attributes				
	Identity-Based		Universalist		
Justice Conception	Local	Transnational	Transnational		Local
Pragmatic (Retribution)			Secular Restorers (International Center for Transitional Justice) Secular Legalists (Centre for Humanitarian Dialogue, Red Cross/Red Crescent)		Secular Restorers (Alliance Against Impunity Guatemala)
Retribution	Faith-based Legalists (National Association of Evangelicals) Secular Legalists (Mothers of Srebrenica)	Faith-based Legalists (World Jewish Congress, Islamic Human Rights Commission, ETAN East Timor)	Secular Legalists (Human Rights Watch, Amnesty International, Institute for War and Peace Reporting)		Secular Legalists (LIPRODHOR Rwanda)

debates over the ideal strategies for securing peace, accountability, and justice are marked by diversity at the level of ideas, actors, and strategies. This diversity has been overlooked by accounts that focus solely on major international organizations, NGOs, and state actors.

Faith-Based Legalists

Faith-based legalists share understandings of accountability and peace with their secular counterparts. However, the sources of these understandings and the resulting strategies that they pursue are drawn from their faith commitments and not from principles of international law or notions of individual accountability and deterrence. Faith-based legalists tend to favor trials, and may specifically emphasize the importance of prosecuting individual perpetrators who have harmed members of their own faith community. In most cases, the pressure by faith-based (legalist) organizations to prosecute has been targeted at individuals who are outside of this shared identity. The general preference for retributive justice is shaped in part by religious precepts that emphasize the rule of law. Faith-based legalists stress accountability, justice, and peacebuilding strategies centered on elite-level engagement, with limited grassroots involvement.

During the Second World War, the lobbying efforts of the World Jewish Congress (WJC) were made on behalf of victims with a Jewish identity. The WJC stressed the victimhood of their particular constituency and pressured the War Crimes Commission for a specific definition of "war crimes."[22] The WJC objected to the distinction drawn by the British and American governments between "atrocities committed against Allied nationals and those directed against Axis citizens." It maintained "that the Jews 'form a special class of victims,' as the crimes against them were being committed only by reason of their connection with the Jewish faith and race."[23] Similarly, when Eastern European groups sought compensation for property damage after the war on the same grounds advanced by Jewish groups whose bank accounts had been looted, the claims were viewed as offensive by Jewish groups who maintained the privileged nature of *Jewish* victims as the intended target of the crimes.[24]

This tendency to support retributive justice is framed differently across FBOs but in each case draws on faith as a basis for supporting the rule of law. Christian organizations mobilized to support the ICC argued for the importance of the rule of law to protect rights because "God chose to give us value, and therefore, rights" and "People of faith accept that legal order is necessary."[25] The Commission on Social Action of Reform Judaism argued also in support of the ICC on the basis that "We, as Jews, believe in the process of forming and developing national and international standards of law and building institutional frameworks for their implementation ... Our tradition also teaches that there is no limit to the judgments for the wicked ... Failure to apprehend and prosecute war criminals sends a message that such actions are acceptable."[26]

The US-based National Association of Evangelicals (NAE), a faith-based legalist actor based solely in the United States, draws its conception of justice from a fairly literal interpretation of the Bible (Biblical realism) and a specific vision of Christian engagement in politics that focuses on the "legal" elements of Scripture and faith: "As Christian citizens, we believe it is our calling to help government live up to its divine mandate to render justice (Rom. 13:1-7; 1 Pet. 2:13-17) [...] Our goal in civic engagement is to bless our neighbors by making good laws."[27] Although the NAE is engaged in many of the poverty relief, HIV/AIDS prevention, and social justice efforts that are shared by capacity-builders and restorers, the NAE acts with reference to a juridical framework, and a vision of socio-economic justice based on equality of opportunity (not outcomes).[28] Discussions of human rights are grounded in international legal frameworks such as the Universal Declaration of Human Rights and a discourse of making sure that states are held to their legal obligations.[29] The NAE has been a strong and consistent supporter of the International Criminal Court, not just as a general principle, but also out of a conviction that the ICC is the appropriate instrument for handling situations such as the Darfur crisis.[30]

The articulation of this particular conception of justice within the NAE is a relatively recent development. Although the NAE first issued a Human Rights policy resolution in 1956, it wasn't until the 1986 Peace, Freedom, and Security Studies (PFSS) guidelines that the organization engaged with questions of peace and justice in systematic fashion.[31] The PFSS guidelines were grounded in concerns over U.S. foreign policy during the Cold War (particularly vis-à-vis the Soviet Union) and reflected an ongoing debate over the use of force and American power.[32] The document contained several strands of thought concerning peace and justice that were woven together into a more coherent position during the 1980s and 1990s. The PFSS guidelines reflect a conception of justice that drew on rule of law understandings of scripture and its application to questions of peace and justice.

Departing from a biblical theology that views "evil as the result of sin," the guidelines emphasize the particular task of Evangelicals to "restrain sin and promote justice" in a fallen world.[33] As such, legal and political institutions become the natural tools with which to address questions of peace and justice: "Law and political community may promote, in a fallen world, the best available means to meet the challenge of peace."[34] Moreover, the PFSS guidelines are explicit in advancing a legalist view of peace itself, "as the antonym of war, a peace between organized political communities, achieved because law and political processes make possible the non-violent resolution of conflict."[35] Finally, peace and justice together are defined with reference to the "eschatological meaning of Shalom" and the need for Evangelical engagement in the world on "this side" of the final judgment.[36]

Above all, the PFSS guidelines reflect the initial uncertainty concerning questions of peace and justice as the NAE first addressed these concepts.[37] The central focus on human failing (sin) leads to a rule-of-law conception of justice that is further developed in subsequent policy articulations, such as the 1987 Peace, Freedom, and Human Rights Declaration, and the 1996 and 2002 Statements on Religious Persecution.[38] The identity-based commitments of the NAE are registered in statements that emphasize the need to support fellow Evangelicals and advance the cause of religious freedom that, in turn, is linked to the missionary activities of the Evangelical community.[39]

In the 1980s, the NAE's perceived need to engage in world affairs, and in questions of peace and justice in particular, motivated the development of a more comprehensive conception of justice. The NAE's conception of justice tends to be "inward"-looking, focusing on the specific community in question and an internally coherent rule of law interpretation of key religious tenets. The NAE is in this sense emblematic of faith- and identity-based legalists.

Secular Legalists

Secular legalists have been more visibly engaged in advancing justice, accountability, and, more generally, international human rights law on a global basis than any other type of organization. Because they have garnered a great deal of attention in the literature on transitional justice, we deal with them only briefly here. These organizations have embraced an absolute standard for international criminal accountability and framed this as a central component of peace, alleging that without individual criminal accountability for the major international crimes, the likelihood of conflict recurring will be higher. Transnational secular legalists, like Human Rights Watch, Amnesty International, and the Coalition for the International Criminal Court (an umbrella organization of NGOs) have been engaged in a wide range of post-conflict situations, advocating consistently for strategies of accountability that stress criminal justice for international crimes. These groups have promoted alternative strategies, especially truth commissions, only as a complement to criminal accountability. In Northern Uganda, Human Rights Watch and Amnesty International objected to the Museveni government's proposal to grant amnesty to leaders of the Lord's Resistance Army (LRA) as a means of ending the fighting: "Justice cannot be sacrificed for impunity. Impunity comes back in worse cycles of violence, and there will be no lasting peace—as we have seen in many countries."[40] The conception of justice held by secular legalists sees trials not only as the appropriate response to mass atrocities, but also as an important tool in deterring future human rights violations.[41]

The East Timor and Indonesia Action Network (ETAN), founded in 1991, is a transnational secular actor based in the United States but engaged in justice and accountability efforts exclusively in East Timor and Indonesia. ETAN has been a consistent advocate of trials and retributive justice for human rights violations and other crimes committed during Indonesia's occupation of East Timor and during the 1975–2002 war for independence.[42] Although ETANs larger agenda encompasses issues of social justice and democracy promotion, these claims are made with reference to juridical authority and international law. Working within the existing international law framework, ETAN has criticized the community-based truth-telling and reconciliation process (the CAVR, or Commission on Reception, Truth and Reconciliation) for not achieving "genuine" justice and continues to call for additional legal proceedings.[43]

Faith-Based Restorers

Faith-based restorers are pragmatic peacebuilders; their interest is in securing peace. They do not have a tightly held position on justice and accountability.[44] They are pragmatic both in terms of the strategies they adopt, and the partners they choose. Faith-based organizations working pragmatically to build peace are numerous. The Interfaith Action for Peace in Kenya, the Interreligious Council of Bosnia-Herzegovina, the Organization of the Islamic Conference, the International Center for Religion and Diplomacy, and the Inter-Religious Council of Sierra Leone all are central actors in this category.

Among these, the most prominent is the Roman Catholic Church.[45] The RCC is far from monolithic. The sheer size of the RCC, the scope and geographical diversity of its activities, its rich history and complex development, and its incorporation of numerous smaller communities, including national churches, religious orders, lay movements, and other organized communities, make it impractical to talk of a single RCC.[46] Communities within the RCC do not always act in lockstep fashion with the Pope or the Magisterium. Although these discrete units embrace certain common understandings and practices, the size and organizational complexity of the RCC has increased its tendency to take local contextual factors into account in developing strategies for promoting peace and ultimately entrenched its pragmatic approach to facilitating peace initiatives.

The RCC's peacebuilding activity is rich and diverse, including direct engagement by individual clergy, lay individuals, national bishops, and organizations such as Sant'Egidio, Pax Christi, Catholic Relief Services, and the Catholic Peacebuilding Network. Peacebuilding activities became even more central to various elements within the RCC following the 1963 *Pacem in Terris* papal encyclical, the Second Vatican council (1962–1965), the growth of liberation theology, and renewed attention to the social dimensions of Catholic teaching—especially in light of the political and social conflicts of the 1970s and 1980s.[47] Debates about justice and accountability were grounded in a strong preference for peace and the dignity of human life as a fundamental value.[48] However, these basic aspects of Catholic social teaching did not translate naturally into a theory of conflict resolution or justice.[49] As one observer noted:

> The paradoxical result of a strong positive doctrine of peace and a less articulated doctrine of conflict resolution is that even as church leaders are thrown into the role of national conciliators because of the credibility that they have on the basis of their work for peace in the fields like human rights and development, they find themselves bereft of tools and support as they attempt to exercise their responsibilities in conflict resolution.[50]

Individual bishops, church organizations, and the laity have significant leeway in responding to local conditions, but often lack an overarching strategy for addressing issues of justice.[51] In practice, the application of Catholic social teaching to issues such as economic underdevelopment or the civil conflicts in Central and Latin America often resulted in an over-emphasis of (social) *justice* ideas without thorough reflection on what might be necessary to build a lasting peace.[52] These dilemmas prompted not only debate within the RCC but also prompted a dialogue between the RCC and faith-based capacity builders such as the Mennonite Central Committee. Together, these efforts have informed a more comprehensive conceptualization of peace, justice, and accountability that has since been institutionalized in groups such as Catholic Relief Services and the Catholic Peacebuilding Network.[53]

The RCC also oscillates between its proclivity to represent all of humankind and its tendency to look out for its own. Since the Second Vatican Council, the RCC has stressed all of humanity as its concern. Some groups within the RCC, such as the lay community of Sant'Egido or Catholic Relief Services have long embodied this universalist worldview.[54] Other voices, however, have reflected a more self-regarding position, as seen in some declarations from the U.S. Conference of Catholic Bishops in defense of Christians and Catholics on certain foreign policy questions (e.g., the ICC debate or Sudan and Darfur), or in the decision to defend the interests of the RCC in Indonesia through most of the East Timorese independence struggle (discussed below). At times, elements within the RCC have been extreme in their support of peace and stability at the expense of justice and reform: in Argentina, the bishops supported the right-wing authoritarian regime during the Dirty Wars of the late 1970s, and in Rwanda, the RCC sided with the genocidal regime.[55]

Three cases, in particular, underscore the pragmatic approach to peace and justice adopted by the RCC: the Central American civil wars of the 1980s, Indonesia and East Timor following decolonization, and contemporary Uganda. The settlements of the civil conflicts in Guatemala, El Salvador, and Nicaragua were all informed by the broader Central American Process and the resultant *Esquipulas II* Accord that, among other provisions, endorsed amnesty as a mechanism for ending the conflicts.[56] In all three conflicts, local clergy and lay communities assumed a central role in calling for reconciliation, mediating between combatant groups, and serving on national peace or reconciliation committees. Each of the three key actors, Archbishop Artuo Rivera y Damas (El Salvador), Bishop Rodolfo Quezado Toruno (Guatemala), and Cardinal Obando y Bravo (Nicaragua) not only exhibited a measure of autonomy, but also came into conflict with the Vatican hierarchy at times. In the end, each supported the amnesties that were central to the peace and reconciliation processes in Central America in the interest of moving beyond conflict. Together, these three cases highlight the complex dynamic of truth, justice, and forgiveness that characterized the evolving debate on these themes within the RCC in the 1980s.[57]

In El Salvador, Archbishop Rivera y Damas was the key intermediary between the Farabundo Martí National Liberation Front (FMLN) and the military government and also served, along with other religious leaders, on the National Reconciliation Commission established in 1987. Support from both Damas and the Church hierarchy for a small unilateral amnesty granted in 1987 was essential in bringing the FMLN to the negotiating table.[58] Damas characterized the subsequent 1987 general amnesty as the path toward reconciliation in a famous televised homily.[59] At the same time, Damas resisted calls for retributive justice (trials) alone in the run-up to the 1992 settlement, instead supporting trials for officers implicated in human rights revisions as well as (importantly) the subsequent pardon of these individuals—a position that put him at odds with other members of the Jesuit and larger Catholic communities.[60] Although the Salvadoran Jesuit order did not oppose the amnesty granted to officers convicted of the murder of six Jesuit priests, the decision was characterized as a move toward a new peace and justice in light of the extrajudicial confessions made by some of the alleged perpetrators.[61] These local dynamics stand in contrast to the Vatican's criticism of general amnesty plans on the grounds that "reconciliation requires 'justice' and forgiveness" and "reconciliation cannot be the fruit of a decree."[62] Taken together, these positions reflected a pragmatic response to the political situation rooted in an overarching focus on peace that is emblematic of faith-based restorers.

In Guatemala, both Bishop Toruno and the national church were supportive of the 1988 amnesty as well as the subsequent 1994 and 1996 limited amnesties that helped bring the Guatemalan National Revolutionary Unit (UNRG) to the negotiating table.[63] At the same time, Toruno emphasized human rights as an element central to the peace process—a stance that eventually prompted his replacement as the central mediator.[64] In a complementary yet distinct expression of justice and accountability, the Guatemalan national church emphasized truth as the central element to justice and reconciliation and the Archbishop leveraged the prospect of an independent investigation by the RCC Human Rights Office.[65] Although disjointed, these efforts culminated in the 1994 agreement between the government and UNRG for a Truth and Reconciliation Commission, with Bishop Toruno as its director. This step was immediately followed by an amnesty decree.[66]

Frustrated with the halting nature of the peace process, the RCC withdrew altogether in 1995.[67] In response to another limited amnesty in the 1996 Agreement on a Firm and Lasting Peace, the RCC emphasized the appropriateness of repentance and forgiveness rather than retribution, thus framing as justice what many saw as immunity.[68] The RCC, under the leadership of Bishop Juan Gerardi, also instituted and facilitated the Project for Recovering Historical Memory (*Recuperación de la Memoria Histórica*, or REMHI) to document human rights abuses in the war as a means to peace, first and foremost.[69] In this context, either opposing the amnesty *or* pressing for prosecution were seen as threatening the peace process. Instead, the RCC sought to secure justice through reconciliation and truth recovery rather than risk re-opening the conflict. Even this was dangerous. Two days after Gerardi delivered REMHI's final report in the Cathedral in Guatemala City in April 1998, military officers bludgeoned him to death in his garage.

In Nicaragua, amnesty was also a key element in the peace process even before the Esquipulas II Accord. Cardinal Obando y Bravo, an opponent of the Sandinista movement, consistently supported a "wide amnesty" to foster peace, in contradistinction to Daniel Ortega and the Sandinista movement.[70] Following a 1987 pardon of political prisoners in accordance with the Esquipulas agreement, Obando used his seat on the National Reconciliation Commission to press for a general amnesty.[71] The Nicaraguan Conference of

Bishops supported Obando's efforts: "Amnesty should not be seen only as an instrument to press for the surrender and disarming of those in rebellion, but as forgetting past offenses and hatreds."[72] The Vatican also took an active role in the Nicaraguan settlement, with a 1983 Papal visit and subsequent support for Obando, as well as a later meeting between President Ortega and Pope John Paul II in 1988.[73] Although the Vatican opposed the Sandinista movement even as local clergy and lay communities supported it, pressure from both Obando and the RCC yielded pardons for small groups of prisoners and Contra rebels in 1989 and then culminated in the 1990 Law for General Amnesty and National Reconciliation.[74] Throughout the process, Ortega pointed to the RCC as the central actor in pressing for both peace and for amnesty.[75]

In all three Central American cases, the lack of a cohesive doctrine concerning justice and accountability for past atrocities, together with a "decentralized hierarchy" that afforded local clergy significant autonomy, allowed actors leeway, and contributed to a pragmatic approach to securing peace. Similar tensions and debates were also evident in the RCC's engagement with the East Timorese independence struggle, where an undeveloped conception of justice combined with the opportunities afforded the RCC's complex organizational structure shaped the approach taken to justice and accountability. Following decolonization in 1975 and then invasion by Indonesia, the Vatican was torn between its official support for the Indonesian state as the legitimate authority and the calls from Bishop Carlos Ximenes Belo for East Timor's independence and for an international tribunal to prosecute alleged human rights abuses carried out by the Indonesian military and militias in East Timor.[76] These internal disagreements complicated the ability of the RCC to agree upon a position and ultimately the Church decided *not* to take a stance on East Timor until late in the conflict.[77] The official Vatican position reflected the conviction that the welfare of the Church in Indonesia and the region necessitated a cooperative rather than confrontational stance vis-à-vis the Indonesian government.[78] The transfer of Indonesian clergy and catechists to East Timor designed to respond to a shortage of Timorese clergy, as well as the Indonesian regime's attempts to use the Church as an instrument in the integration policy, complicated discussions of peace and accountability.[79]

In the early 1990s, the Vatican shifted from emphasizing the "transcendent mission" of the Church to engaging in the political and social difficulties of the conflict, in part due to greater sensitivity to local conditions and in part due to an ongoing dialogue concerning justice and accountability.[80] The Vatican expressed support for trials, a position that aligned in large part with calls from both Bishop Belo and the East Timorese secular human rights community for an international tribunal after the 1999 peace agreement. As Belo stated, "justice must not be restricted to a chosen few. It must be universal."[81]

Belo's approach actually represented a complex mixture of retributive and restorative justice that emphasized truth-telling and forgiveness as appropriate strategies for lesser violators even as he resisted impunity for those accused of major human rights violations.[82] Despite Belo's embrace of restorative justice for lesser violators, the limited amnesty law that allowed pardons for those convicted of non-violent crimes was criticized within the Vatican and the RCC hierarchy.

In contrast, the newly formed East Timorese government adopted a strategy of reconciliation and only reluctantly pursued the trial of Indonesian officials. As East Timorese Prime Minister Alkatiri argued, "Justice is still the bridge for reconciliation."[83] The resulting community-based reconciliation and reintegration strategy (CAVR) combined local and traditional justice measures (*lisan*) with elements from Catholic teaching and worship, yet was criticized by the Timorese Church as endorsing amnesty and impunity rather than justice.[84]

The Vatican's preference for retributive justice in East Timor, a preference that was shared by local church actors in East Timor, stands in contrast to the stance adopted by RCC actors in Central America. This contrast underscores the pragmatic and situational response to questions of accountability that ultimately defines the strategies of Restorers. The lack of an overarching conception of justice and accountability with regard to past atrocities in the Catholic Church is reinforced by the size and diversity of the organization itself. In both Central American and East Timor, the pragmatic choices of faith-based restorers were shaped by local political conditions and a developing doctrine of peace and justice.

The organizational structure of the Catholic Church also facilitated the entrenchment of diverse perspectives on justice and accountability that contributed to conflict between the Vatican and local Catholic organizations in Uganda. Although the Vatican formally supported the International Criminal Court's pursuit of LRA indictments, local Catholic organizations in Uganda opposed these indictments and embraced the government's amnesty process.[85] One of the key negotiators in the Northern Uganda peace process, Archbishop John Baptist Odama, expressed concern that the ICC was undermining efforts to win the confidence of the LRA and secure a peace agreement.[86] Throughout the peace process, local Catholic clergy have worked with the amnesty commissions set up through the 2000 Amnesty Act to receive former combatants and reintegrate them into Ugandan society.[87]

The well-known Catholic lay Community of Sant'Egidio is a classic example of a faith-based restorer. The Community's activities are grounded in a religious identity of prayer, service to the poor, and friendship.[88] These traits have been crucial to Sant'Egidio's ability to build trust among all sides of a conflict situation and establish an environment for reconciliation, as seen most notably in the Community's role in the Mozambican peace process. The 1994 General Peace Agreement, mediated by Sant'Egidio, reflected a desire for "integration without individual punishment for acts perpetrated during the war."[89] Sant'Egidio facilitated deep engagement (not just negotiations) and established a trust and understanding among all parties to the conflict. This approach was informed by the Community's history of providing aid to local communities, which allowed Sant'Egidio to access the underlying sentiments among the Mozambican population.[90] Although criticized by secular human rights groups, FBOs emphasizing forgiveness, reconciliation, and the restoration of relationships supported the amnesty adopted shortly after the 1994 peace agreement. In particular, the Catholic Church of Mozambique became an important promoter of reconciliation rituals after the peace agreement.

Faith-based restorers can also be found beyond the Christian faith. The conception of justice held by the Organization of the Islamic Conference (OIC) is grounded in Islamic traditions of tolerance.[91] However, the OIC's position on the Israeli-Palestinian conflict included calls for the prosecution of Israeli "war criminals" based on the principles of international law.[92] Guided by pragmatism, the OIC typically defends members of its own faith tradition. Similarly, the strategy of peace, reconciliation, and national reconstruction embraced by the South African Conference of Churches in the wake of apartheid was tempered by the recognition that these goals could be accomplished through various justice strategies.[93]

Inter-faith organizations have also worked to restore peace. The Inter-Religious Council of Sierra Leone (IRCSL), a locally organized faith-based restorer composed of local FBOs drawn from both Christian (Catholic and Protestant) and Muslim faiths, was founded in 1997. Viewed by the Revolutionary United Front (RUF) and the government as a neutral party, the IRCSL served as a central mediator, helping to negotiate the 1999 Lomé Agreement, which included an amnesty and power-sharing provisions that granted former rebel leaders a role in the new government. Paradoxically, the IRCSL then found itself in the position of promoting the agreement to a skeptical public upset over the recognition and power granted to the RUF.[94] The pragmatism of this inter-faith peace-oriented organization stood at odds with the official positions on international law and justice taken by some of its member organizations, especially the RCC.[95]

Overall, faith-based restorers, such as Interfaith Action for Peace in Kenya (engaged in dialogue among faith communities across Africa) or the International Center for Religion and Diplomacy (engaged in mediation, dialogue, and faith-based diplomacy in the Middle East and Southeast Asia) that exhibit the general characteristics described here have proliferated since the

1990s. The pragmatic approach to peace, justice, and accountability central to this category of actors is exhibited by many organizations in many different faith traditions, indicating that a pragmatic approach to questions of peace, justice, and accountability is not distinct to any single faith doctrine.[96] Faith-based restorers have been marked by diversity and pragmatism in questions of peace, accountability and justice. Many prefer some form of reconciliation. In certain cases, those where they are willing to trade off accountability for peace, this compromise has been grounded in the belief that justice will come in another life, or that forgiveness is essential to reconciliation.[97] Local political conditions and the organizational structures within which these actors are embedded play an important role in their choices. Those FBOs that have been more willing to "negotiate" accountability, rather than taking an exclusive stance on either reconciliation or retribution, have had increased opportunities for forming alliances both with secular and with other faith-based organizations.

Secular Restorers

Secular restorers have been engaged both locally and transnationally in peacebuilding. The Campaign for Good Governance in Sierra Leone and Women to Women in Bosnia-Herzegovina—both locally organized—are emblematic restorers that tend to stress reconciliation over retribution. The Wajir Peace and Development Committee, a transnational organization based in Kenya but active in mediation and dialogue activities in conflict regions across Africa, is also representative of this category of peacebuilder.[98] One of the most prominent non-state actors engaged in transitional justice, the International Center for Transitional Justice (ICTJ), was created by individuals who embraced the value of reconciliation and adopted a pragmatic approach to peacebuilding.

Created in 2001, the ICTJ grew out of a conversation between the Ford Foundation, Priscilla Hayner, and two South Africans, Alex Boraine and Paul van Zyl, who had participated in the formation and leadership of the South African Truth Commission. The ICTJ was founded on the commitment to pursue accountability for mass atrocities through a comprehensive strategy aimed at achieving widespread reconciliation; its strategy was both more comprehensive and more eclectic than either Human Rights Watch or Amnesty International. Unlike those two organizations, whose work was confined almost exclusively to advocacy and whose staff was committed to an organizational position, the ICTJ also engaged in longer-term strategy-building through a process of working collaboratively with country representatives; its staff sustained a wide diversity of views on issues of amnesty, prosecutions, and transitional justice more generally through, at least, the organization's first eight years.

As Jonathan VanAntwerpen suggests in this volume, the ICTJ's approach to justice and accountability converged, over the course of a decade, on a more orthodox and legalist agenda reflective of broader international trends in transitional justice advocacy.[99] Even with this change, though, the ICTJ, unlike its legalist counterparts, maintained a far more adaptive approach, broadening its strategies for accountability and recognizing that "judicial measures, including trials, are unlikely to suffice."[100] The ICTJ maintained its pragmatic commitment to working collaboratively with local officials and community representatives to develop optimal solutions for addressing unique crimes and specific historical wrongdoings. In Kenya, ICTJ responded to requests by local NGOs to work with them to develop support for a truth-telling process following the violence in January 2008. Throughout the process ICTJ's approach was one of engaged advisor rather than advocate, working extensively with civil society groups to create a Truth, Justice, and Reconciliation Commission.[101] Although its engagements were limited in duration when compared to capacity builders, they remained extensive by comparison to transnational secular legalists.

The ICTJ's approach to reconciliation stands apart from faith-based capacity-builders, many of which accept amnesty as an integral, or at least necessary, component of reconciliation. Its shift toward a more legalistic emphasis began around 2005, though it continued to adopt diverse strategies for peacebuilding and reconciliation. When South Africa's National Prosecution Authority attempted, in 2005, to extend a de facto amnesty offer for a second round but with little real commitment to making this conditional on truth-telling, ICTJ and two partner organizations protested by launching a formal court challenge. Its legal efforts were eventually successful in contributing to the High Court's decision to stop the renewed amnesty offer.[102]

In Uganda, the ICTJ refrained from advocating strongly for the ICC's pursuit of the LRA and instead engaged in what it recognized as "complex issues" in Northern Uganda related to the "tensions between peace, justice, and humanitarian considerations."[103] Rather than advocating a strict position, ICTJ worked to educate local civil society organizations about the options for dealing with issues of accountability. In its survey research in Uganda, ICTJ found that by 2005, "more people expressed a willingness to sacrifice formal justice for the sake of peace if it came down to deciding between the two."[104] Its approach was to "sensitize" local actors to justice and accountability issues, and to develop extensive local partnerships, while at the same time advising the ICC on how to communicate its message to the relevant populations.

Faith-Based Capacity-Builders

Faith-based capacity-builders have a highly distinctive view of reconciliation and a unique set of justice strategies. They take a long-term approach to peacebuilding and emphasize local engagement with affected populations.[105] Non-violence, local control of reconciliation processes, attention to social and economic inequality, and the building of relationships over time are central; for capacity-builders, healing human relationships *is* justice.[106] This comprehensive conception of restorative justice and belief in the cathartic power of healing and reconciliation between victims and perpetrators stems from deep-seated faith traditions. Although they have achieved significant and lasting results in the communities in which they operate, capacity-builders' insistence on local ownership of reconciliation processes has limited their influence on global discussions of justice and accountability for mass atrocities.

The Mennonite Central Committee (MCC) and Quaker Peace and Social Witness (QPSW) are classic examples of faith-based capacity-builders. Their faith traditions are built around humility, mercy, pacifism, and tolerance.[107] The MCC stresses the commitment of the peacemaker to peacemaking as well as to the community in question, based on the "conviction that to be a peacemaker is the most fundamental religious injunction."[108] The Mennonite shift from separatism to engagement in the world, specifically in peace and justice issues, stemmed from a realization in the 1960s that "Christians could no longer allow relief, development, and justice to be in tension because the Bible demanded a creative synthesis."[109] Subsequently, a small group of thinkers within the Mennonite community began a systematic reflection on questions of peace, justice, and accountability.[110] Some of these same individuals later were involved in the peace and justice discussions convened by the Roman Catholic Church that led to the formation of the Catholic Peacebuilding Network.

The MCC and QPSW are both universalists; their strategies of justice focused on comprehensive, long-term reconciliation among all parties, irrespective of faith tradition *or* position in the conflict. These organizations engaged at the grassroots level, emphasizing the empowerment of local actors over the imposition of outside solutions. Such strategies stress the need to move beyond a conflict, guided by a spirit of reconciliation and hope.[111] Justice is achieved not through punitive measures but through trust-building among former combatants, perpetrators, and victims, as well as through attention to deep-seated sources of conflict, such as socioeconomic differences. Their commitment to comprehensive reconciliation, inclusiveness, and long-term involvement define this type of peacebuilder whose inspiration originates in faith and religious doctrine.[112]

Faith-based capacity builders were actively involved in building peace, justice, and accountability in the former Federal Republic of Yugoslavia, Latin America, and Uganda. In postwar Bosnia, the MCC and QPSW worked with local actors to develop reconciliation strategies and, in the process, fostered credibility and trust and created a feeling among locals that these organizations would remain even as others departed due to time pressure, budgetary constraints, or violence.[113] By contrast, transnational actors like World Vision and Catholic Relief Services had not (yet) developed grassroots peacebuilding capacities and were criticized as out of touch with the needs of local populations, focusing instead on implementing formulaic programs and fulfilling abstract benchmarks.[114] In discussing the activities of major transnational actors, one activist from Banja Luka noted, "I had the impression that they were ordering us to reconcile. You do not do that on order."[115] In addition, "[O]rganizers recall that they directly avoided potentially dangerous discussions and feared confrontations between participants from different religious and ethnic communities."[116] In contrast, the MCC and QPSW worked with local actors to develop reconciliation strategies, fostering credibility and trust as well as building the basis for a long-term peacebuilding commitment.[117]

The MCC's commitment to long-term personal and spiritual engagement shaped its unique approach to reconciliation in Latin America as well. The MCC approach, embodied in the Central American Peace portfolio, was characterized by patience, listening, and the empowerment of local actors, all of which seek to build trust gradually.[118] In Nicaragua, MCC efforts brought together former combatants (Sandinistas and Contras) and also focused on reconciliation between combatants and victimized populations (rural farmers and indigenous Indian groups). By focusing on conflict transformation, as opposed to short-term justice issues, and seeking to transform the social relationships at the root of the conflict, especially historic patterns of socioeconomic inequality and oppression, the MCC worked to achieve the status of a trusted partner.[119] The first dialogue among combatants and victims in the *Neuva Guinea* region (an area particularly affected by the civil war) was conducted in 1988, and within a year the MCC had aided local partners in establishing 33 local peace commissions.[120]

Attention to social justice themes also underpinned the MCC's engagement in Colombia's civil conflict (*la violencia*). The MCC's emphasis on community, non-violence, and fundamental human rights represented an important alternative to the (violent) liberation theology prevalent in Colombia through the 1960s and 1970s.[121] Instead of imposing a solution, the MCC listened to local populations, drawing on the belief that "it is those who are immersed in a conflict who hold the keys to the ways through it, since it is they who know and understand the sociopolitical structures and dynamics."[122] The focus on economic development and education as part of the overall reconciliation efforts culminated in the establishment of a justice and peace commission in 1990 (*Justapaz*) and in a 1991 agreement (Law for the Decongestion of the Courts) granting community centers for conflict mediation the same status as formal judicial proceedings.[123]

The MCC was also active alongside the Catholic Church and local Catholic lay communities in the Latin American Peace Process that culminated in the 1987 "Esquipulas II" Peace Treaty, signed by five Central American heads of state in their efforts to end the civil conflicts plaguing the region. The accord contained a series of measures for national reconciliation, democratization, and refugee assistance and, importantly, called for amnesty for political opposition and insurgent groups across the region. While the accord served as the foundation for the subsequent peace agreement in Guatemala, Nicaragua, and El Salvador, the work of a range of FBOs on the ground was critical to the broader social acceptance of these agreements.[124] As Catholic bishops became the official (elite level) intermediaries between governments and insurgent groups in the peace negotiations, the MCC was working with local communities and small groups of former combatants on reconciliation and reintegration measures.[125]

Capacity builders are by no means exclusively international; many local actors fit best into this category. The Acholi Religious Leaders Peace Initiative (ARLPI) in Northern Uganda, founded in 1997 by core actors from several faith groups (including the Anglican Bishop of Northern Uganda, the Catholic Archbishop of the Gulu Diocese, the Anglican Bishop of Kitgum Diocese, the Muslim Chief of Kadhi of Kitgum, and the Muslim Chief Kadhi of Gulu), is viewed as both a religious and moral authority as well as a neutral actor among local communities in the Acholi region of Northern Uganda.[126] The ARLPIs activities are grounded in a view of justice and reconciliation similar to that held by the MCC and QPSW: healing local communities and repairing individual relationships are central to its approach to peace and justice. Forgiveness and reconciliation were values shared by all actors in the ARLPI, whose approach to peace placed a strong emphasis on post-conflict reconstruction, social justice, and economic development for the affected region.[127]

The ARLPI was central in lobbying the Museveni government for a *blanket* amnesty for LRA rebels in the pursuit of peace and reconciliation. It drew lessons from the successful example of the 1988 peace treaty with a separate rebel group (the UPDA) that included an amnesty provision. After the passage of the 1999 Amnesty Law, the ARLPI engaged with local communities to disseminate information and to encourage rebels to take advantage of the amnesty provision and related programs for disarmament and reintegration. Even after the ICC announced the indictment of five LRA leaders in 2005, the ARLPI continued to defend amnesty in the name of forgiveness and reconciliation. In response to ICC criticisms of a new 2006 amnesty offer, the Archbishop of Gulu remarked that "forgiveness is always a virtue and a value to be very much promoted nationwide and internationally."[128] The pro-amnesty stance of local Catholic actors working with the ARLPI was not consistent with the pro-ICC stance of the RCC, which gave considerable discretion to local officials.

Conclusions

Actors engaged in the practices and politics of justice and peacebuilding are diverse, exhibiting a pluralism both in the conceptions of justice that constitute their identity and the practices they pursue. We argue that this diversity reflects different conceptions of justice and organizational attributes. Despite pressures to converge on a secular legalist transitional justice orthodoxy, no single consensus has emerged on appropriate peace, justice, and accountability strategies. Our research reveals areas of tension and contestation among actors (e.g., between legalists and capacity-builders) as well as areas of collaboration and cooperation (e.g., between faith-based restorers and faith-based capacity builders, or between faith-based and secular legalists).

The empirical cases also provide support for our three main claims. First, many *secular* actors (and some FBOs) have converged on a legalist conception of justice. Second, FBOs are unique in the sources for their conceptions of justice (faith doctrines and traditions), but there is significant diversity in the strategies adopted by faith-based actors. Third, we find that actors embracing a *relational* conception of peacebuilding grounded in ideas of restorative justice and reconciliation sit outside the orthodoxy. As discussed by Jennifer Llewellyn and Dan Philpott in the introduction to this volume, further study of actors engaged in these activities is critical if we are to understand the full range of peacebuilding efforts in the world today—and especially the efforts that the presumed orthodoxy concerning peace, justice, and accountability.

Our research sheds new light on the ways in which non-state actors, both faith-based and secular, have engaged in contestation and negotiation over the most meaningful, appropriate, and effective strategies for bringing justice, peace, and accountability into peacebuilding processes. Despite the purported international dominance of a liberal-legal strategy, numerous organizations have embraced and promoted alternatives ranging from pragmatism to a principled rejection of legalist strategies. For many faith-based organizations in particular, debates about peace and engagement in the world have prompted deep thought about conceptions of justice that represent important alternative visions to legalistic or retributive approaches. Our research indicates that a key dimension in which non-state actors differ is concerning their conception of justice—the principled and causal beliefs that actors hold about peace, justice, truth, accountability, and reconciliation. Our research also suggests that local organizations, many of which embrace conceptions of justice and pursue strategies that do not line up with dominant international norms, play a central role in embedding these norms locally. Understanding the strategies that local actors advocate, as well as their capacity to influence outcomes, will be crucial to explaining when and how norms become embedded at the local level.

Notes

1. We would like to thank Jonathan VanAntwerpen, R. Scott Appleby, Paige Arthur, Thomas Banchoff, Tatiana Carayannis, Nicolas Guilhot, Stephen Hopgood, Peter Katzenstein, Katherine Marshall, Kathleen R. McNamara, Juan Méndez, Daniel Nexon, Michael Schmitz, Jack Snyder, the Social Science Research Council's Working Group on Religion, Reconciliation, and Transitional Justice, Dan Van Ness, and especially Dan Philpott and Jennifer Llewellyn for their comments on this and earlier versions of this paper.
2. The strongest statement of the role of civil society in embracing individual criminal justice is Kathryn Sikkink, *The Justice Cascade: How Human Rights Prosecutions are Changing World Politics* W. W. Norton & Co (2011).
3. Jack Snyder and Leslie Vinjamuri, "Trials and Errors: Principles and Pragmatism in Strategies of International Justice," *International Security* 28, no. 3 (2003–2004).
4. Our categories draw in part on the distinction made by March and Olsen between logics of appropriateness and logics of consequences: James G. March and Johan P. Olsen, *Rediscovering Institutions: The Organizational Basis of Politics* (New York: Free Press, 1989); Leslie Vinjamuri and Jack Snyder, "Advocacy and Scholarship in the Study of Transitional Justice and International War Crimes Tribunals," *Annual Review of Political Science* 7 (2004); Snyder and Vinjamuri, "Trials and Errors: Principles and Pragmatism in Strategies of International Justice."
5. Ruti Teitel, "Transitional Justice Genealogy," *Harvard Human Rights Journal* 16 (2003). Leslie Vinjamuri, "Deterrence, Democracy, and the Pursuit of International Justice," *Ethics and International Affairs* 24, no. 2 (2010).
6. For an excellent analysis of the study of religious actors in transitional justice, see Daniel Philpott, "When Faith Meets History: The Influence of Religion on Transitional Justice," in *The Religious in Response to Mass Atrocity: Interdisciplinary Perspectives*, ed. Thomas Brudholm and Thomas Cushman (Cambridge, MA: Cambridge University Press, 2009). See also Daniel Philpott, "Religion, Reconciliation, and Transitional Justice: The State of the Field." (Social Science Research Council, 2007).
7. On the importance of private funding for shaping organizational autonomy, see Stephen Hopgood and Leslie Vinjamuri, "Faith in Markets" in Michael Barnett and Janice Stein, *Sacred Aid*, (Oxford: Oxford University Press, 2012).
8. R. Scott Appleby, *The Ambivalence of the Sacred: Religion, Violence, and Reconciliation* (Lanham, MD: Rowman & Littlefield Publishers, Inc., 2000).
9. Daniel Philpott, "Has the Study of Global Politics Found Religion?," *Annual Review of Political Science* 12 (2009).
10. Martha Minow, *Between Vengeance and Forgiveness: Facing History and Genocide after Mass Violence* (Boston, MA: Beacon Press, 1998); Martha Minow, ed., *Breaking the Cycles of Hatred: Memory, Law, and Repair* (Princeton, NJ: Princeton University Press, 2001); Nancy L. Rosenblum, "Justice

and the Experience of Injustice," in *Breaking the Cycles of Hatred: Memory, Law, and Repair*, ed. Martha Minow (Princeton, NJ: Princeton University Press, 2002); Jon Elster, *Closing the Books: Transitional Justice in Historical Perspective* (Cambridge: Cambridge University Press, 2004), Charles Villa-Vicencio, "The Reek of Cruelty and the Quest for Healing: Where Retributive and Restorative Justice Meet," *Journal of Law and Religion* 14, no. 1 (1999–2000).

11. Minow, *Between Vengeance and Forgiveness: Facing History and Genocide after Mass Violence*; Peggy Hutchison and Harmon Wray, "What Is Restorative Justice?," *New World Outlook* 1999; Donald W. Shriver Jr., "Truth Commissions and Judicial Trials: Complementary or Antagonistic Servants of Public Justice?," *Journal of Law and Religion* 16, no. 1 (2001); Alex Boraine, *A Country Unmasked* (Oxford: Oxford University Press, 2000); Donald W. Shriver Jr., "Forgiveness: A Bridge across Abysses of Revenge," in *Forgiveness and Reconciliation: Religion, Public Policy, and Conflict Transformation*, ed. Raymond G. Helmick, S. J., and Rodney L. Petersen (Philadelphia, PA: Templeton Foundation Press, 2001).
12. Throughout this essay, we use the term "reconciliation" in this general sense, while "restorative justice" is reserved for the specific meaning detailed here.
13. On the idea of distant strangers and the attempt of universalist advocates to overcome this, see Stephen Hopgood, "Moral Authority, Modernity, and the Politics of the Sacred," *European Journal of International Relations* 15, no. 2 (2009).
14. David R. Smock, "Catholic Contributions to International Peace," (2001).
15. Rejection of external initiatives on the premise that local custom must take priority has undoubtedly been mobilized at times by pragmatic political actors seeking to capture and control pressures to integrate justice initiatives, but evidence of this dynamic does not negate the presence of local actors genuinely committed to alternative conceptions of justice.
16. Rituals emphasizing or resulting in shame for the perpetrator are neither explicitly restorative nor retributive in nature.
17. Shriver Jr., "Truth Commissions and Judicial Trials: Complementary or Antagonistic Servants of Public Justice?," 24–25; see also Minow, *Between Vengeance and Forgiveness: Facing History and Genocide after Mass Violence*. Although she does not refer to the logic of faith, Minow's argument that religion itself may influence outcomes toward particular types of transitional justice reinforces the points made here.
18. Shriver Jr., "Forgiveness: A Bridge across Abysses of Revenge."; Shriver Jr., "Truth Commissions and Judicial Trials: Complementary or Antagonistic Servants of Public Justice?"
19. Vinjamuri and Snyder, "Advocacy and Scholarship in the Study of Transitional Justice and International War Crimes Tribunals."
20. Rosenblum, "Justice and the Experience of Injustice," 10; Rosenblum notes that one of the constraining elements of retributive justice is that "rules of evidence and norms of accountability dictate which memories are considered worthy of public acknowledgement and which are considered inadmissible, discounted as subjective and unreliable" (Ibid., 80).
21. Aaron Boesenecker and Leslie Vinjamuri, "Lost in Translation? Civil Society, Faith-Based Organizations and the Negotiation of International Norms," *International Journal of Transitional Justice* 5, no. 3 (2011).
22. Arieh J. Kochavi, *Prelude to Nuremberg: Allied War Crimes Policy and the Question of Punishment* (Chapel Hill, NC: University of North Carolina Press, 1998).
23. A. L. Easterman of the WJC, quoted in Kochavi, *Prelude to Nuremberg*, 140.
24. Elster, Closing the Books: Transitional Justice in Historical Perspective, 171. Elster cites John Authers and Richard Wolffe, *The Victim's Fortune: Inside the Epic Battle over the Debts of the Holocaust* (New York: HarperCollins, 2002), 232.
25. Faith-Based Caucus for the International Criminal Court, "Faith-Based Brochure Series: Christian Concepts."
26. "Resolution on U.S. Support for the International Criminal Court, Adopted by the Commission on Social Action of Reform Judaism," (2002).
27. National Association of Evangelicals, "For the Health of the Nation: An Evangelical Call to Civic Responsibility," (2004).

28. "God's prophets call his people to create just and righteous societies (Isa. 10:1–4, 58:3–12; Jer. 5:26–29, 22:13–19; Amos 2:6–7; Amos 4:1–3, 5:10–15). The prophetic teaching insists on both a fair legal system (which does not favor either the rich or the poor) and a fair economic system (which does not tolerate perpetual poverty). Though the Bible does not call for economic equality, it condemns gross disparities in opportunity and outcome that cause suffering and perpetuate poverty, and it calls us to work toward equality of opportunity." Ibid., 9.
29. Ibid., 10. See also "Top UN Official Addresses NAE," *Insight* (Fall 2007).
30. "International Criminal Court Needs Support," *Insight* (October/November 2005).
31. The 1956 Declaration noted how human rights violations hinder the "propagation of the gospel" in many countries. National Association of Evangelicals, "Human Rights," (1956). Policy Resolution, available at: http://www.nae.net/government-affairs/policy-resolutions/188-human-rights-1956; National Association of Evangelicals, "Peace, Freedom and Security Studies," (1986), Policy Resolution, available at: http://www.nae.net/government-affairs/policy-resolutions/436-peace-freedom-a-security-studies (henceforth "NAE PFSS Policy Resolution, 1986").
32. NAE PFSS Policy Resolution, 1986. The document contains numerous criticisms of other American religious organizations' engagement in public affairs, noting the specific support of some for repressive governments in Latin America and the blind eye that others turned to the tyranny and repression in the Soviet Union. In noting the impossibility of perfecting the present world, the document also advances a tacit critique of the larger liberal human rights project that was developing in the late 1980s. Ibid., Section III: Biblical Foundations.
33. Ibid., Section II: Our Intentions. Also stated: "The persistence of conflict is the political meaning of the doctrine of original sin." Ibid.
34. Ibid., Section III: Biblical Foundations. Although the document notes the Biblical injunction for Christians to be peacemakers, and notes the role that reconciliation may play in this process, the term reconciliation is typically used in a legal sense (settling of disputes) rather than in reference to what we have termed restorative justice (above).
35. Ibid., Section VIII: Assessment Criteria. The guidelines discuss several conceptualizations of peace, but emphasize the role of Evangelicals in focusing on the notion of peace quoted here as central to their engagement in public affairs.
36. Ibid., Section III: Biblical Foundations.
37. In particular, the document notes alternate conceptions of peace and justice such as those held by the Mennonite community and the pacifist tradition on the one hand and the focus on "just war" on the other in seeking to define a particular conceptualization for Evangelicals.
38. The specific conception of justice might be more "corrective" than "retributive" in the sense that the Biblical realism underpinning NAE articulations here focus on correcting human failings more than outright punishment.
39. National Association of Evangelicals, "For the Health of the Nation: An Evangelical Call to Civic Responsibility." The 2004 statement on Judicial Usurpation, while focused on a domestic political issue, also reiterated the legalistic foundation in noting that "law is a moral teacher."
40. Richard Dicker, HRW International Program Director, quoted in Nora Boustany, "Ugandan Rebel Reaches out to International Court," *The Washington Post*, March 19, 2008.
41. In February of 2009 in Africa alone, Human Rights Watch has pressured states and the international community to act on ICC arrest warrants in the Democratic Republic of Congo, Sudan, and Uganda and continues to pressure Senegal to resume the trial of exiled former Chadian dictator Hissène Habré. See http://www.hrw.org/en/africa.
42. See www.etan.org.
43. In a December 5, 2008 press release, ETAN stated that "The CAVR (Commission on Reception, Truth and Reconciliation) has already looked for truth and facts about human rights violations during the 24-year Indonesian occupation, thinking to find truth, reconciliation and justice, but many victims and their families still suffer because CAVR did not achieve genuine justice." ETAN, "Anti," (2008), http://etan.org/news/2008/12anti.htm.
44. See, for example, the distinction among various types of peacebuilding activities (e.g., mediation, advocacy, intermediary activity) made by Sampson. We contend that faith-based restorers engage

in different aspects of peacebuilding than do other actors discussed here. See Cynthia Sampson, "Religion and Peacebuilding," in *Peacemaking in International Conflict: Methods and Techniques*, ed. William Zartman and Lewis Rasmussen (Washington, DC: United States Institute of Peace Press, 1997).

45. For a survey of Muslim actors engaged in peacebuilding activities, see Mohammed Abu-Nimer and S. Ayse Kadayifci-Orellana, "Muslim Peace-Building: Actors in Africa and the Balkan Context: Challenges and Needs," *Peace & Change* 33, no. 4 (2008).

46. Throughout this paper, we speak of the RCC as a single actor only when referring to the Pope or Magisterium (e.g., in the instance of Papal statements or encyclicals).

47. "Pacem in Terris," in *Encyclical of Pope John XXIII on Establishing Universal Peace in Truth, Justice, Charity, and Liberty* (1963). Indeed, one could examine the work of Pope John Paul II as an example of a Catholic peacebuilder. Our thanks to the editors of this volume for highlighting this point.

48. Maryann Cusimano Love, "Catholic Peacebuilding and Emerging International Norms and Practices of the UN and Other International and Governmental Bodies," (2008). The emphasis on humanity as a collective stands in contrast to the emphasis on individual failings and the dignity of the *individual* emphasized by faith-based legalists such as the NAE.

49. Drew Christiansen, S.J., "Peacebuilding in Catholic Social Teaching: A Response to Kenneth Himes," in *Catholic Peacebuilding Conference* (University of Notre Dame, Notre Dame, IN, 2008). See also Smock, "Catholic Contributions to International Peace" and William R. Healey, "Justice but Little Peace: Peace-Building as a New Catholic Social Action Agenda," *Peace & Change* 25, no. 4 (2000).

50. Smock, "Catholic Contributions to International Peace," 5.

51. Christiansen notes that "on issues like amnesty, truth commissions, and so on, judgments are more contingent and so prudential." Christiansen, "Peacebuilding in Catholic Social Teaching: A Response to Kenneth Himes." Christiansen also notes a debate within the Church as to whether peacebuilding doctrine should be established through the accumulation of practice on the ground or first clarified through official Church teaching and then disseminated to those in the field.

52. William R. Headly, C.S.P., "Justice but Little Peace: Peace-Building as a New Catholic Social Action Agenda," *Peace & Change* 25, no. 4 (October 2000): 483–484.

53. R. Scott Appleby, "Catholic Peacebuilding," *America: The National Catholic Weekly*, September 8, 2008. Appleby notes that Catholic Relief Services, the United States Conference of Catholic Bishops, the Center for Mission Research and Study at Maryknoll, Pax Christi, the Community of Sant'Egidio, and several Catholic colleges and universities are represented in the CPN.

54. For a recent discussion of this evolution, along with the peace and justice activities of other actors, see Monica Duffy Toft, Daniel Philpott, and Timothy Samuel Shah, *God's Century: Resurgent Religion and Global Politics* (New York: W.W. Norton & Company, 2011), Ch. 4, Ch. 7.

55. Timothy Longman, *Christianity and Genocide in Rwanda* (Cambridge: Cambridge University Press, 2010), 5–7 and Ch. 6.

56. The accord's recommendations, including measures intended to end hostilities, terminate assistance to irregular forces, promote national reconciliation, and foster democratization, informed the Oslo accords in Guatemala, the General Peace Agreement and Chapultepec Peace Accords in El Salvador, and the final peace accords in Nicaragua. For a complete treatment of the Central American Peace Process, see Johanna Oliver, "The Esquipulas Process: A Central American Paradigm for Resolving Regional Conflict," *Ethnic Studies Report* 17, no. 2 (1999). On the town of Esquipulas, see Ibid. 152, footnote xi.

57. For a detailed discussion of justice and forgiveness in El Salvador, see Stephen J. Pope, "The Convergence of Forgiveness and Justice: Lessons from El Salvador," *Theological Studies* 64 (2003).

58. President Duarte characterized the amnesty as an attempt to "humanize" the war even as others in the military *junta* and on the political right criticized the move. Douglas Farah, "Duarte to Announce Amnesty, Help to the Wounded," United Press International, May 19, 1987.

59. Douglas Farah, "Archbishop Warns of Return to Days of Death Squads," United Press International, November 15, 1987. Although the law covered crimes committed against civilians,

it was altered at the last minute, under pressure from the RCC, to exempt the killers of Archbishop Oscar Romero who was killed on March 24, 1980, while holding mass. The 1987 amnesty was also opposed by the military and the political right, even though the amnesty provisions covered crimes against civilians (and others) committed by the official forces. Lindsey Gruson, "Amnesty Law Passed in El Salvador," *The New York Times*, October 29, 1987.

60. "Rights Groups Protest Amnesty for Jailed Soldiers," *The Associated Press*, March 17, 1990.
61. Pope, "The Convergence of Forgiveness and Justice"; Shirley Christian, "Jesuits Won't Reject Amnesty in Salvador Killings," *The New York Times*, October 6, 1991; Christian, "Jesuits Won't Reject Amnesty in Salvador Killings."
62. First quotation from Salvadoran Bishop Rosa Chavez, "El Salvador: Human Rights Group Fears Whitewash of Violations," IPS-Inter Press Service, January 18, 1992. Second quotation, referring in particular to the 1992 amnesty for those named in the UN report, from Archbishop Arturo Rivera, Daniel Alder, "Archbishop Criticizes Salvadoran Amnesty Law," United Press International, March 22, 1993.
63. "Guatemala Amnesty Is Passed," *The New York Times*, October 30, 1987. The amnesty followed a 1986 general self-amnesty granted by military leaders as they departed from office. Although the civilian government vowed to overturn the amnesty and investigate human rights violations, resistance from the Army thwarted these efforts. Toruno was also appointed to the National Reconciliation Commission. "Amnesty International Reports Abuses in Guatemala," United Press International, May 10, 1987.
64. "Nobel Laureate Apparently Not Welcome at Guatemala Peace Talks," United Press International, November 11, 1992. By 1993, Toruno was the only individual recognized by both the government and the UNRG as a legitimate mediator, yet his insistence on human rights issues led the government to replace him with a UN mediator in 1994. Toruno's selection over Guatemala's Nobel Laureate, and then his subsequent exclusion from negotiations in late 1993, led to a brief breakdown in the peace process. He was later appointed as the head of an assembly charged with making recommendations to the government concerning human rights issues and the UN appointed Jean Arnault as the chief peace process mediator.
65. Fabiana Freyssinet, "Guatemala: Peace Talks to Exclude Truth Commission Issue," IPS-Inter Press Service, February 16, 1994.
66. Teleonce TV, "President Welcomes Agreement with URNG on Forming a Truth Commission," (BBC Summary of World Broadcasts 1994).
67. The RCC criticized the politicization of the process and admonished Bishop Toruno for allowing the peace efforts to distract him for his pastoral duties Alfonso Anzueto, "Catholic Church Withdraws from Guatemala Peace Process," The Associated Press, January 31, 1995.
68. Philpott, "When Faith Meets History: The Influence of Religion on Transitional Justice," 21. The 1996 limited amnesty did not cover torture, disappearances, and massacres.
69. Victoria Sanford, "The 'Grey Zone' of Justice: NGOs and the Rule of Law in Postwar Guatemala," *Journal of Human Rights* 2, no. 3 (2003). The Church also aided in similar truth-telling processes in Brazil, Uruguay, Paraguay, and Chile; see Philpott, "When Faith Meets History: The Influence of Religion on Transitional Justice." 22–23.
70. In an interview with *La Prensa* newspaper, Obando y Bravo stated: "A wide amnesty would avoid tensions and favor a peaceful climate that is so sought after and talked about today." William Branigan, "Seized Papers Said to Reveal Salvadoran Rebel Plan," *The Washington Post*, July 11, 1987.
71. Filadelfo Aleman, "Ortega Names Leading Critic President of Peace Commission," The Associated Press, September 2, 1987. Bravo's presence as an anti-Sandinista Cardinal helped lend legitimacy to the body as more than just a token government response to the peace accords. In addition to Bravo, the President of the Evangelical Committee for Development was also named to the NRC. Carl Manning, "Sandinistas Announce Reconciliation Commission," The Associated Press, August 25, 1987.

72. Stephen Kinzer, "Nicaragua: Peace Path Has Pitfalls," *The New York Times*, September 25, 1987. The Nicaraguan Permanent Commission on Human Rights and the Bar Association also supported a general amnesty. Kinzer, "Full Amnesty Seen as a Test for Managua," *The New York Times*, September 10, 1987.
73. Francisco Conde, "Ortega: Nicaragua Intent on Direct Negotiations," The Associated Press, January 27, 1988. Implicitly, this entailed Vatican support for Bravo's pro-amnesty stance. Bravo, a known critic of the Sandinista movement, briefed the Pope before the meeting with Ortega. Frances D'Emilio, "Sandinista Critic Briefs Pope before Ortega Meeting," The Associated Press, January 28, 1988.
74. Marjorie Miller, "Nicaragua OKs Amnesty for All Sandinista Aides," *Los Angeles Times*, March 11, 1990. The law also pardoned crimes committed by government soldiers and the US-backed Contras.
75. In a 1989 interview, Obando stated: "It is true that I have been insisting on amnesty, and I am happy to see that steps are being taken in that direction, because I believe that if we release from prison all these people who were jailed for political reasons, we would be taking a step towards fraternity and reconciliation." Daniel Ortega and Miguel Obando y Bravo, "Nicaragua President and Cardinal Discuss Church's Possible Involvement in Peace Process: Amnesty," (BBC Summary of World Broadcasts, 1989).
76. Philip Shenon, "Timorese Bishop Is Calling for a War Crimes Tribunal," *The New York Times*, September 13, 1999; Carey notes that the Church was torn between its responsibilities to five million Catholics in Indonesia and the plight of the people of East Timor. Peter Carey, "The Catholic Church, Religious Revival, and the Nationalist Movement in East Timor, 1975–98," *Indonesia and the Malay World* 27, no. 78 (1999): 82. See also Patrick Smythe, *The Heaviest Blow: The Catholic Church and the East Timor Issue* (Munster, Germany: Lit, 2004).
77. The official Vatican position throughout most of the conflict was that East Timor was a non-self-governing entity in the process of decolonization; East Timor had "freed itself from Portugal but had not yet joined Indonesia." Carey, "The Catholic Church, Religious Revival, and the Nationalist Movement in East Timor, 1975–98," 82.
78. Smythe, The Heaviest Blow: The Catholic Church and the East Timor Issue, 57.
79. Indonesian army helicopters were placed at the disposal of Indonesian clergy to "spread the good word about Indonesia and development, and to coax FRETILIN to give up the struggle." Ibid., 59.
80. Ibid., 186–187. This shift followed the visit of Pope John Paul II in 1989 and was accelerated by the Santa Cruz (Dili) Massacre of pro-independent demonstrators in 1991 and the 1996 awarding of the Nobel Peace Prize to Bishop Belo. Smythe, *The Heaviest Blow: The Catholic Church and the East Timor Issue*, 187.
81. "Nobel Laureate Appeals for Timor Tribunal," Associated Press Worldstream, April 23, 2001.
82. Aniceto Guterres, an East Timorese human rights lawyer, noted: "Justice must come before amnesty . . . there cannot be amnesty without truth." "Justice Must Come before Amnesty, Says East Timor Lawyer," Agence France Presse, August 29, 2001.
83. The law did not issue an automatic pardon, but required a court decision. The law also offered the prospect of pardon for those coerced into joining pro-Jakarta militias in the 1999 wave of violence following the independence vote. Joanna Jolly, "East Timor to Pass Amnesty Law for Anti-Independence Militiamen Convicted of Minor Crimes," Associated Press Worldstream, May 28, 2002.
84. Lindsay Murdoch, "Timor's Truth Time Bomb," *Sydney Morning Herald*, February 13, 2006.
85. "Respecting International Law," *America: The National Catholic Weekly*, January 19, 2004.; Joseph J. Fahey, "On Peace and War," *America: The National Catholic Weekly*, October 17, 2005. On the role of local Catholic groups in Northern Uganda, see Gilbert M. Khadiagala, "Greater Horn of Africa Peace Building Project: Case Study Two: The Role of the Acholi Religious Leaders Peace Initiative (ARLPI) in Peace Building in Northern Uganda," (Washington, DC: USAID and Management Systems International, 2001).

86. Institute for War and Peace Reporting, "Uganda: Amnesty Offer Blow for Rebel Chief Arrest Plans," (2006).
87. Barney Afako, "Reconciliation and Justice: 'Mato Output' and the Amnesty Act," in *Conciliation Resources* (2002).
88. Andrea Bartoli, "Forgiveness and Reconciliation in Mozambique," in *Forgiveness and Reconciliation: Religion, Public Policy, and Conflict Transformation*, ed. Raymond G. Helmick, S. J., and Rodney L. Petersen (Philadelphia, PA: Templeton Foundation Press, 2001), 369.
89. Ibid., 379. Bartoli also cites a political dynamic emphasizing the power of war as something that overwhelms individuals and communities: "Hence, it was war and not specific individuals or parties... to be blamed for the massacres, destruction, and suffering. Therefore, when war ends, so does the need for revenge." Ibid.
90. Ibid., 374.
91. Organization of the Islamic Conference, "Homepage," http://www.oic-oci.org.; Organization of the Islamic Conference, "Press Release: OIC Attends Inauguration of National Consultation Days in Mauritania," (2005). For a general discussion of Islamic and Muslim positions on the debates concerning universal human rights and justice, see Heiner Bielefeldt, "Muslim Voices in the Human Rights Debate," *Human Rights Quarterly* 17, no. 4 (1995).
92. Organization of the Islamic Conference, "Resolution No. 1/9-P (Is): On the Cause of Palestine and Arab Israeli Conflict," (9th Session of the Islamic Summit Conference2000).
93. The SACC home page notes: "As a National Council of Churches and Institutions, the SACC, acting on behalf of its member churches, is called by the Triune God to work for moral reconstruction in South Africa, focusing on issues of justice, reconciliation, integrity of creation and the eradication of poverty and contributing towards the empowerment of all who are spiritually, socially and economically marginalized." South African Council of Churches, "Homepage," http://www.sacc.org.za.
94. Peter Penfold, "Faith in Resolving Sierra Leone's Bloody Conflict," *The Round Table* 94, no. 382 (2005).
95. The IRCSL was also involved in the 2002 Peace Treaty and truth commission negotiations.
96. Importantly, though, Abu-Nimer's survey of Muslim Peacebuilding Organizations suggests that the preference for this type of pragmatic engagement on the part of Muslim peacebuilders may stem from important organizational characteristics, such as a shorter history of formal organizational engagement in peacebuilding. See Abu-Nimer and Kadayifci-Orellana, "Muslim Peace-Building," 563.
97. Minow, *Between Vengeance and Forgiveness: Facing History and Genocide after Mass Violence*, Ch. 2.
98. For a more detailed discussion, see Abu-Nimer and Kadayifci-Orellana, "Muslim Peace-Building."
99. This evolution in ICTJ's approach to justice and accountability is discussed by Jonathan VanAntwerpen in this volume as movement from a position of heterodoxy in which a range of solutions were deemed viable, to a more typical human rights focus on legalism.
100. International Center for Transitional Justice, "What Is Transitional Justice, a Holistic Approach," (2008).
101. Interview with Priscilla Hayner, International Center for Transitional Justice, February 2009.
102. International Center for Transitional Justice, "Press Release: South Africa: High Court Ruling for Victims," (2008).
103. International Center for Transitional Justice, "Uganda, IJTJ Activity," (2008).
104. Ibid.
105. Cynthia Sampson, "Local Assessments of Mennonite Peacebuilding," in *From the Ground up: Mennonite Contributions to International Peacebuilding*, ed. Cynthia Sampson and John Paul Lederach (Oxford: Oxford University Press, 2000).
106. Sally Engle Merry, "Mennonite Peacebuilding and Conflict Transformation: A Cultural Analysis," in *From the Ground up: Mennonite Contributions to International Peacebuilding*, ed. Cynthia Sampson and John Paul Lederach (Oxford: Oxford University Press, 2000).
107. See John Paul Lederach, *The Journey Towards Reconciliation* (Scottdale, PA: Herald Press, 1999); Lederach, "Five Qualities of Practice in Support of Reconciliation Processes," in *Forgiveness and*

Reconciliation: Religion, Public Policy, and Conflict Transformation, ed. Raymond G. Helmick, S. J., and Rodney L. Petersen (Philadelphia, PA: Templeton Foundation Press, 2001).
108. Smock, "Catholic Contributions to International Peace," 2.
109. Joseph S. Miller, "A History of the Mennonite Conciliation Service, International Conciliation Service, and Christian Peacemaker Teams," in *From the Ground up: Mennonite Contributions to International Peacebuilding*, ed. Cynthia Sampson and John Paul Lederach (Oxford: Oxford University Press, 2000), 7.
110. See, for example, Cynthia Sampson and John Paul Lederach, eds., *From the Ground up: Mennonite Contributions to International Peacebuilding* (Oxford: Oxford University Press, 2000).
111. Lederach, *The Journey Towards Reconciliation*, 66.
112. Sampson, "Local Assessments of Mennonite Peacebuilding"; Lederach, "Five Qualities of Practice in Support of Reconciliation Processes."
113. United States Institute of Peace, "Can Faith-Based NGOs Advance Interfaith Reconciliation? The Case of Bosnia and Herzegovina," USIP Special Report No. 103, March 2003.
114. Importantly, Catholic Relief Services has sought to build up a grassroots peacebuilding capacity since the late 1990s. See, for example, William R. Headly and Reina C. Neufeldt, "Catholic Relief Services: Catholic Peacebuilding in Practice," In *Peacebuilding: Catholic Theology, Ethics, and Praxis*, ed. Robert J. Schreiter, R. Scott Appleby, and Gerard F. Powers (Maryknoll, NY: Orbis Books, 2010).
115. Branka Peuraca, "Can Faith-Based NGOs Advance Interfaith Reconciliation: The Case of Bosnia and Herzegovina," (United States Institute of Peace, 2003), 6. In Bosnia and Herzegovina, an activist noted that international pressure to rebuild mosques in Bosnia's predominantly Serb cities such as Banja Luka led to disillusionment, riots, and death within the local communities. Subsequent interfaith dialogue and grassroots engagement pursued by religious actors proceeded relatively peacefully.
116. Ibid.
117. Ibid.
118. On listening, Chupp notes that "When I was present in significant encounters, I seldom spoke. My role as an observer served the commission members, who would later turn to me during our debriefing sessions." Mark Chupp, "Creating Space for Peace: The Central American Peace Portfolio," in *From the Ground up: Mennonite Contributions to International Peacebuilding*, ed. Cynthia Sampson and John Paul Lederach (Oxford: Oxford University Press, 2000), 114.
119. Ibid., 119. On conflict transformation more generally, see John Paul Lederach, *Preparing for Peace: Conflict Transformation across Cultures* (Syracuse, NY: Syracuse University Press, 1995), 14–15.
120. Chupp, "Creating Space for Peace: The Central American Peace Portfolio," 110–111.
121. Ricardo Esquiva and Paul Stucky, "Building Peace from below and inside: The Mennonite Experience in Colombia," in *From the Ground up: Mennonite Contributions to International Peacebuilding*, ed. Cynthia Sampson and John Paul Lederach (Oxford: Oxford University Press, 2000), 123.
122. Ibid., 135.
123. Ibid., 129–135.
124. Conciliation Resources, "Guatemala: Chronology of the Peace Talks," http://www.c-r.org/our-work/accord/guatemala/chronology.php.
125. Chupp, "Creating Space for Peace: The Central American Peace Portfolio," 104.
126. For a survey of the ARLPI's work, see Khadiagala, "Greater Horn of Africa Peace Building Project: Case Study Two: The Role of the Acholi Religious Leaders Peace Initiative (ARLPI) in Peace Building in Northern Uganda." Khadiagala notes that up to 90 percent of the Acholi belong to one of the three faiths represented in the ARLPI. Ibid., 3.
127. Khadiagala, "Greater Horn of Africa Peace Building Project: Case Study Two: The Role of the Acholi Religious Leaders Peace Initiative (ARLPI) in Peace Building in Northern Uganda."
128. "Uganda Rebel Chief 'Still Wanted,'" *BBC News Online* (2006), http://news.bbc.co.uk/2/hi/africa/5150292.stm.

References

Abu-Nimer, Mohammed, and S. Ayse Kadayifci-Orellana. "Muslim Peace-Building: Actors in Africa and the Balkan Context: Challenges and Needs." *Peace & Change* 33, no. 4 (2008): 549–581.

Afako, Barney. "Reconciliation and Justice: 'Mato Output' and the Amnesty Act." In *Conciliation Resources*, 2002, available at: http://www.c-r.org/accord-article/reconciliation-and-justice-%E2%80%98mato-oput%E2%80%99-and-amnesty-act-2002.

Alder, Daniel. "Archbishop Criticizes Salvadoran Amnesty Law." United Press International, March 22, 1993.

Aleman, Filadelfo. "Ortega Names Leading Critic President of Peace Commission." The Associated Press, September 2, 1987.

"Amnesty International Reports Abuses in Guatemala." United Press International, May 10, 1987.

Anzueto, Alfonso. "Catholic Church Withdraws from Guatemala Peace Process." The Associated Press, January 31, 1995.

Appleby, R. Scott. *The Ambivalence of the Sacred: Religion, Violence, and Reconciliation*. Lanham, MD: Rowman & Littlefield Publishers, Inc., 2000.

———. "Catholic Peacebuilding." *America: The National Catholic Weekly*, September 8, 2008.

Authers, John, and Richard Wolffe. *The Victim's Fortune: Inside the Epic Battle over the Debts of the Holocaust*. New York: HarperCollins, 2002.

Bartoli, Andrea. "Forgiveness and Reconciliation in Mozambique." In *Forgiveness and Reconciliation: Religion, Public Policy, and Conflict Transformation*, edited by Raymond G. Helmick, S. J., and Rodney L. Petersen, 361–382. Philadelphia, PA: Templeton Foundation Press, 2001.

Bielefeldt, Heiner. "Muslim Voices in the Human Rights Debate." *Human Rights Quarterly* 17, no. 4 (1995): 587–617.

Boraine, Alex. *A Country Unmasked*. Oxford: Oxford University Press, 2000.

Boustany, Nora. "Ugandan Rebel Reaches out to International Court." *The Washington Post*, March 19, 2008.

Branigan, William. "Seized Papers Said to Reveal Salvadoran Rebel Plan." *The Washington Post*, July 11, 1987.

Carey, Peter. "The Catholic Church, Religious Revival, and the Nationalist Movement in East Timor, 1975–98." *Indonesia and the Malay World* 27, no. 78 (1999): 77–95.

Christian, Shirley. "Jesuits Won't Reject Amnesty in Salvador Killings." *The New York Times*, October 6, 1991.

Christiansen, Drew, S.J. "Peacebuilding in Catholic Social Teaching: A Response to Kenneth Himes." In *Catholic Peacebuilding Conference*. Notre Dame, IN: University of Notre Dame, 2008, available at: http://cpn.nd.edu/assets/14657/christiansen.pdf.

Chupp, Mark. "Creating Space for Peace: The Central American Peace Portfolio." In *From the Ground up: Mennonite Contributions to International Peacebuilding*, edited by Cynthia Sampson and John Paul Lederach, 104–121. Oxford: Oxford University Press, 2000.

Clark, Phil, and Nicholas Waddell, eds. *Courting Conflict? Peace, Justice, and the ICC in Africa*. London: Royal African Society, 2008.

Conciliation Resources. "Guatemala: Chronology of the Peace Talks." http://www.c-r.org/our-work/accord/guatemala/chronology.php.

Conde, Francisco. "Ortega: Nicaragua Intent on Direct Negotiations." The Associated Press, January 27, 1988.

Court, Faith-Based Caucus for the International Criminal. "Faith-Based Brochure Series: Christian Concepts," available at: http://amicc.org/docs/brochure_FBC_christian.pdf.

D'Emilio, Frances. "Sandinista Critic Briefs Pope before Ortega Meeting." The Associated Press, January 28, 1988.

"El Salvador: Human Rights Group Fears Whitewash of Violations." IPS-Inter Press Service, January 18, 1992.

Elster, Jon. *Closing the Books: Transitional Justice in Historical Perspective*. Cambridge: Cambridge University Press, 2004.

Esquiva, Ricardo, and Paul Stucky. "Building Peace from Below and Inside: The Mennonite Experience in Colombia." In *From the Ground up: Mennonite Contributions to International Peacebuilding*, edited by Cynthia Sampson and John Paul Lederach, 122–140. Oxford: Oxford University Press, 2000.

ETAN. "Anti." http://etan.org/news/2008/12anti.htm.

Fahey, Joseph J. "On Peace and War." *America: The National Catholic Weekly*, October 17, 2005.

Farah, Douglas. "Duarte to Announce Amnesty, Help to the Wounded." United Press International, May 19, 1987.

———. "Archbishop Warns of Return to Days of Death Squads." United Press International, November 15, 1987.

Freyssinet, Fabiana. "Guatemala: Peace Talks to Exclude Truth Commission Issue." IPS-Inter Press Service, February 16, 1994.

Gruson, Lindsey. "Amnesty Law Passed in El Salvador." *The New York Times*, October 29, 1987.

Healey, William R. "Justice but Little Peace: Peace-Building as a New Catholic Social Action Agenda." *Peace & Change* 25, no. 4 (October 2000): 483–484.

Healey, William R. "Justice but Little Peace: Peace-Building as a New Catholic Social Action Agenda." *Peace & Change* 25, no. 4 (2000): 483–496.

Healey, William R., and Reina C. Neufeldt. "Catholic Relief Services: Catholic Peacebuilding in Practice." In *Peacebuilding: Catholic Theology, Ethics, and Praxis*, edited by Robert J. Schreiter, R. Scott Appleby, and Gerard F. Powers. Maryknoll, NY: Orbis Books, 2010.

Hopgood, Stephen. "Moral Authority, Modernity, and the Politics of the Sacred." *European Journal of International Relations* 15, no. 2 (2009): 229–255.

Hutchison, Peggy, and Harmon Wray. "What Is Restorative Justice?" *New World Outlook* 56, no. 9 (1999): 4–8.

Institute for War and Peace Reporting. "Uganda: Amnesty Offer Blow for Rebel Chief Arrest Plans." 2006.

International Center for Transitional Justice. "Press Release: South Africa: High Court Ruling for Victims." 2008.

———. "Uganda, IJTJ Activity." 2008.

———. "What Is Transitional Justice, a Holistic Approach." 2008.

National Association of Evangelicals, "International Criminal Court Needs Support." *Insight* (October/November 2005).

Jolly, Joanna. "East Timor to Pass Amnesty Law for Anti-Independence Militiamen Convicted of Minor Crimes." Associated Press Worldstream, May 28, 2002.

"Justice Must Come before Amnesty, Says East Timor Lawyer." Agence France Presse, August 29, 2001.

Khadiagala, Gilbert M. "Greater Horn of Africa Peace Building Project: Case Study Two: The Role of the Acholi Religious Leaders Peace Initiative (ARLPI) in Peace Building in Northern Uganda." Washington, DC: USAID and Management Systems International, 2001.

Kinzer, Stephen. "Full Amnesty Seen as a Test for Managua." *The New York Times*, September 10, 1987.

———. "Nicaragua: Peace Path Has Pitfalls." *The New York Times*, September 25, 1987.

Kochavi, Arieh J. *Prelude to Nuremberg: Allied War Crimes Policy and the Question of Punishment*. Chapel Hill, NC: University of North Carolina Press, 1998.

Lederach, John Paul. *Preparing for Peace: Conflict Transformation across Cultures*. Syracuse, NY: Syracuse University Press, 1995.

———. *The Journey Towards Reconciliation*. Scottdale, PA: Herald Press, 1999.

———. "Five Qualities of Practice in Support of Reconciliation Processes." In *Forgiveness and Reconciliation: Religion, Public Policy, and Conflict Transformation*, edited by

Raymond G. Helmick, S. J., and Rodney L. Petersen, 193–203. Philadelphia, PA: Templeton Foundation Press, 2001.

Longman, Timothy. *Christianity and Genocide in Rwanda*. Cambridge: Cambridge University Press, 2010.

Love, Maryann Cusimano. "Catholic Peacebuilding and Emerging International Norms and Practices of the UN and Other International and Governmental Bodies." Unpublished Paper Delivered at the United Nations, October 7, 2008.

Manning, Carl. "Sandinistas Announce Reconciliation Commission." The Associated Press, August 25, 1987.

March, James G., and Johan P. Olsen. *Rediscovering Institutions: The Organizational Basis of Politics*. New York: Free Press, 1989.

Merry, Sally Engle. "Mennonite Peacebuilding and Conflict Transformation: A Cultural Analysis." In *From the Ground up: Mennonite Contributions to International Peacebuilding*, edited by Cynthia Sampson and John Paul Lederach, 203–217. Oxford: Oxford University Press, 2000.

Miller, Joseph S. "A History of the Mennonite Conciliation Service, International Conciliation Service, and Christian Peacemaker Teams." In *From the Ground up: Mennonite Contributions to International Peacebuilding*, edited by Cynthia Sampson and John Paul Lederach, 3–29. Oxford: Oxford University Press, 2000.

Miller, Marjorie. "Nicaragua OKs Amnesty for All Sandinista Aides." *Los Angeles Times*, March 11, 1990.

Minow, Martha. *Between Vengeance and Forgiveness: Facing History and Genocide after Mass Violence*. Boston, MA: Beacon Press, 1998.

———, ed. *Breaking the Cycles of Hatred: Memory, Law, and Repair*. Princeton, NJ: Princeton University Press, 2001.

Murdoch, Lindsay. "Timor's Truth Time Bomb." *Sydney Morning Herald*, February 13, 2006.

National Association of Evangelicals. "Human Rights." 1956.

———. "Peace, Freedom and Security Studies." 1986.

———. "For the Health of the Nation: An Evangelical Call to Civic Responsibility." 2004.

"Nobel Laureate Apparently Not Welcome at Guatemala Peace Talks." United Press International, November 11, 1992.

"Nobel Laureate Appeals for Timor Tribunal." Associated Press Worldstream, April 23, 2001.

Oliver, Johanna. "The Esquipulas Process: A Central American Paradigm for Resolving Regional Conflict." *Ethnic Studies Report* 17, no. 2 (1999): 149–179.

Organization of the Islamic Conference. "Homepage." http://www.oic-oci.org.

———. "Resolution No. 1/9-P (Is): On the Cause of Palestine and Arab Israeli Conflict." 9th Session of the Islamic Summit Conference, 2000.

———. "Press Release: OIC Attends Inauguration of National Consultation Days in Mauritania." 2005.

Ortega, Daniel, and Miguel Obando y Bravo. "Nicaragua President and Cardinal Discuss Church's Possible Involvement in Peace Process; Amnesty." BBC Summary of World Broadcasts, 1989.

"Pacem in Terris." In *Encyclical of Pope John XXIII on Establishing Universal Peace in Truth, Justice, Charity, and Liberty*, 1963.

Penfold, Peter. "Faith in Resolving Sierra Leone's Bloody Conflict." *The Round Table* 94, no. 382 (2005): 549–557.

Peuraca, Branka. "Can Faith-Based NGOs Advance Interfaith Reconciliation: The Case of Bosnia and Herzegovina." United States Institute of Peace, 2003.

Philpott, Daniel. "Religion, Reconciliation, and Transitional Justice: The State of the Field.": Social Science Research Council, 2007.

———. "Has the Study of Global Politics Found Religion?" *Annual Review of Political Science* 12, (2009): 183–202.

———. "When Faith Meets History: The Influence of Religion on Transitional Justice." In *The Religious in Response to Mass Atrocity: Interdisciplinary Perspectives*, edited by Thomas

Brudholm and Thomas Cushman, 174–212. Cambridge, MA: Cambridge University Press, 2009.
Pope, Stephen J. "The Convergence of Forgiveness and Justice: Lessons from El Salvador." *Theological Studies* 64, (2003): 812–835.
"Resolution on U.S. Support for the International Criminal Court, Adopted by the Commission on Social Action of Reform Judaism." 2002, available at: http://www.amicc.org/docs/CSA_res.pdf.
"Respecting International Law." *America: The National Catholic Weekly*, January 19, 2004.
Reuters. "Guatemala Amnesty Is Passed." *The New York Times*, October 30, 1987.
"Rights Groups Protest Amnesty for Jailed Soldiers." The Associated Press, March 17, 1990.
Rosenblum, Nancy L. "Justice and the Experience of Injustice." In *Breaking the Cycles of Hatred: Memory, Law, and Repair*, edited by Martha Minow, 77–107. Princeton, NJ: Princeton University Press, 2002.
Sampson, Cynthia. "Religion and Peacebuilding." In *Peacemaking in International Conflict: Methods and Techniques*, edited by William Zartman and Lewis Rasmussen. Washington, DC: United States Institute of Peace Press, 1997.
_____. "Local Assessments of Mennonite Peacebuilding." In *From the Ground up: Mennonite Contributions to International Peacebuilding*, edited by Cynthia Sampson and John Paul Lederach, 256–274. Oxford: Oxford University Press, 2000.
Sampson, Cynthia, and John Paul Lederach, eds. *From the Ground up: Mennonite Contributions to International Peacebuilding*. Oxford: Oxford University Press, 2000.
Sanford, Victoria. "The 'Grey Zone' of Justice: NGOs and the Rule of Law in Postwar Guatemala." *Journal of Human Rights* 2, no. 3 (2003): 393–405.
Shenon, Philip. "Timorese Bishop Is Calling for a War Crimes Tribunal." *The New York Times*, September 13, 1999.
Shriver Jr., Donald W. "Forgiveness: A Bridge across Abysses of Revenge." In *Forgiveness and Reconciliation: Religion, Public Policy, and Conflict Transformation*, edited by Raymond G. Helmick, S. J., and Rodney L. Petersen, 151–167. Philadelphia, PA: Templeton Foundation Press, 2001.
_____. "Truth Commissions and Judicial Trials: Complementary or Antagonistic Servants of Public Justice?" *Journal of Law and Religion* 16, no. 1 (2001): 24–25.
Sikkink, Kathryn. "The Role of Consequences, Comparison, and Counterfactuals in Constructivist Ethical Thought." In *Moral Limit and Possibility in World Politics*, edited by Richard Price, 83–111. Cambridge: Cambridge University Press, 2008.
Smock, David R. "Catholic Contributions to International Peace." United States Institute of Peace, No. 69, April 2001.
Smythe, Patrick. *The Heaviest Blow: The Catholic Church and the East Timor Issue*. Munster, Germany: Lit, 2004.
Snyder, Jack, and Leslie Vinjamuri. "Trials and Errors: Principles and Pragmatism in Strategies of International Justice." *International Security* 28, no. 3 (2003–2004): 5–44.
South African Council of Churches. "Homepage." http://www.sacc.org.za.
Sriram, Chandra Lekha, and Suren Pillay, eds. *Peace Versus Justice? The Dilemmas of Transitional Justice in Africa*. Southern Africa: University of KwaZulu-Natal Press, 2010.
Teitel, Ruti. "Transitional Justice Genealogy." *Harvard Human Rights Journal* 16, (2003): 69–94.
Teleonce TV. "President Welcomes Agreement with URNG on Forming a Truth Commission." BBC Summary of World Broadcasts, 1994.
Toft, Monica Duffy, Daniel Philpott, and Timothy Samuel Shah. *God's Century: Resurgent Religion and Global Politics*. New York: W.W. Norton & Company, 2011.
"Top UN Official Addresses NAE." *Insight* (Fall 2007).
"Uganda Rebel Chief 'Still Wanted.'" *BBC News Online* (2006), http://news.bbc.co.uk/2/hi/africa/5150292.stm.
United States Institute of Peace. "Can Faith-Based NGOs Advance Interfaith Reconciliation? The Case of Bosnia and Herzegovina." USIP Special Report No. 103, March 2003.

Villa-Vicencio, Charles. "The Reek of Cruelty and the Quest for Healing: Where Retributive and Restorative Justice Meet." *Journal of Law and Religion* 14, no. 1 (1999–2000): 165–187.

Vinjamuri, Leslie. "Deterrence, Democracy, and the Pursuit of International Justice." *Ethics and International Affairs* 24, no. 2 (2010): 191–211.

Vinjamuri, Leslie, and Jack Snyder. "Advocacy and Scholarship in the Study of Transitional Justice and International War Crimes Tribunals." *Annual Review of Political Science* 7, (2004): 345–362.

CHAPTER 4

Reconciliation as Heterodoxy

Jonathan VanAntwerpen

Tutu and the "Truth Commission Mafia"

Archbishop Emeritus Desmond Tutu sat at the front of the crowded hall, flanked on either side by legal scholars and prominent figures in the field of transitional justice—members of what had once been called the "truth commission mafia."[1] Just as he had before the public hearings of the South African Truth and Reconciliation Commission (TRC)—where as Chairperson of the commission he opened and closed the proceedings with a prayer—Tutu wore his archbishop's vestment, with its long black robe and white clerical collar. There was a large gold crucifix hanging from the chain around his neck.

At one of the first public gatherings of the TRC, held just over a decade earlier in April 1996, in a community hall in East London—and described by one observer as a "theatre of pain and catharsis"—the archbishop had responded to the grief of a widow's testimony by leading those assembled in song. *Senzeni na*.[2] Now it was October 2006, and I was sitting in the Greenberg Lounge at the New York University School of Law, listening to Tutu talk about reparations, reconciliation, and restorative justice. The first volumes of the TRC report had been in circulation for eight years. Many in South Africa had moved on to other preoccupations. "2006 marks the tenth anniversary of the TRC," said Deborah Posel, at a public symposium in Cape Town. "The talk about 'reconciliation' and 'nation-building' that was so common a few years ago now seems rather distant. So, too, does the TRC itself."[3] Yet, as he'd said at the same Cape Town symposium, sponsored by the Institute for Justice and Reconciliation, Tutu remained convinced that South Africans needed "to keep working at reconciliation"—"to listen to one another's stories" and "to heal one another's wounds." The archbishop had also continued to voice his displeasure with the South African government's failure to provide adequate reparations to the victims of human

77

rights violations who had testified in front of the TRC: "I am disappointed with us as a nation." While amnesty had been granted to individual perpetrators who had come before the commission, he asked rhetorically, "What happened to the victims?"[4]

Just a few months later, here was Tutu discussing reparations and reconciliation once again. Yet this time it was a public event in New York City, not Cape Town or East London or Johannesburg, and the occasion was not yet another opportunity to assess the TRC's successes and failures, "10 Years On," but the launch of *The Handbook of Reparations*, a new university press book that the event's promoters described as a "groundbreaking" volume on "repairing the past."[5] In one sense, it was not particularly surprising to learn that Tutu had been given top billing on the New York panel that would launch the new book, a massive volume produced by the International Center for Transitional Justice (ICTJ). Tutu had become one of reconciliation's global prophets, a virtuoso in the world of social and political repair who figured prominently in many contemporary considerations of "coming to terms with the past." Closely associated with the "South African miracle"—South Africa's relatively peaceful transition from apartheid to democracy, symbolized vividly by Nelson Mandela's election and ascendance to the presidency in 1994 and by the subsequent efforts of the TRC—Desmond Tutu was as sought after as ever on the international circuit, even if he was considered controversial by some of its cosmopolitan denizens.

Over the course of the preceding decade, and due in no small part to the international attention lavished upon Tutu and the TRC, a distinctly South African take on "truth and reconciliation" had circulated far and wide. With the international proliferation of truth commissions and a range of other truth-telling modes of response to mass atrocity, the language of reconciliation—if not the reality it sought to bring into being—had gone global, becoming closely intertwined with the field of transitional justice to which the new book was intended to contribute. In the midst of this proliferation there had also been discursive profusion, transformation, struggle, and debate.

While the possibilities associated with the transitional politics of truth and reconciliation were widely touted in the course of these debates, and while the TRC itself was much celebrated, the South African commission and its master narrative of truth and reconciliation were also vigorously and repeatedly critiqued. Reconciliation—closely associated with both amnesty and forgiveness, and explicitly theological in many of its articulations—was tremendously controversial, and in a manner that set it apart from other political keywords. Although the pursuit of reconciliation was frequently figured as closely allied with successful transitions to "democracy," for instance, and although its promotion was said to be crucial if not essential to the building of a sustainable culture of respect for "human rights" and the "rule of law," reconciliation would not enjoy the same ubiquity or acceptance as these global master tropes. The difference here is telling, instructive, and worth pursuing. The emergence of "global human rights culture," it has been claimed, was premised on—or at least facilitated by—a "pragmatic silence on ultimate questions" that helped make the uptake of human rights discourse easier and less controversial.[6] As the philosopher Charles Taylor has remarked, perhaps the culture of human rights "could 'travel' better if it could be separated from some of its underlying justifications."[7] Yet it was precisely reconciliation's connection to and invocation of "ultimate questions" that made its political spectacles so captivating—and so controversial.

As a transnational network dedicated to the work of "transitional justice" began to be consolidated more fully into a recognizable "field"—explicitly named as such by actors claiming both membership and field-specific authority, and with at least some of the characteristics familiar from more established fields—"reconciliation" came to occupy an uncertain and at times somewhat marginal place within it, especially in the context of elite human rights organizations such as the ICTJ. The vast interest in reconciliation—critical and otherwise—did not dissipate. Indeed, the language of reconciliation remained central to the work of many grassroots practitioners of "peacebuilding," and it became increasingly identified with new and more expansive theories of "restorative justice."[8] At the same time, references to reconciliation had become seemingly unavoidable in contexts of transitional justice. Yet embedded within the South African politics of reconciliation, I want to suggest, was a heretical challenge to a normative juridical framework and a form of secular orthodoxy that significantly defined the field—the heterodox promise of nations healed through the political art of forgiveness and the forgoing of full-fledged prosecution.

Thus, within the brief history of the field of transitional justice, South African renderings of reconciliation both loom large and occupy an exceptional and somewhat unstable place. In the pages that follow, I critically examine this placement by considering, first (and all too partially), the history of reconciliation in South Africa and the place of the South African TRC within the recent history of truth commissions, and second, the ambivalent uptake of the language of reconciliation on the part of elite international actors within the field of transitional justice, with a particular view to the ICTJ, founded in the aftermath of the South African TRC and the world's largest nongovernmental organization (NGO) devoted specifically to the theory and practice of transitional justice. In closing, I return to a consideration of Tutu among the "truth commission mafia."

Reconciliation in South Africa

While it has become a ubiquitous element of truth commission discourse, "reconciliation" is a complex, complicated, and frequently slippery term, with many possible significations and multiple historical trajectories. "This much used (but seldom defined) word," claims Jonathan Tepperman in an assessment of South Africa's Truth and Reconciliation Commission, "permeated all of the commission's work."[9] Much used in the South African context—and, in no small part due to the South African experiment, elsewhere throughout the world—the word has (*pace* Tepperman) often been defined. In the context of truth commissions like the South African TRC, "reconciliation" thrives not in the absence of attributed meaning, but in the presence of a multiplicity of at times opposing significations. We might say, therefore, that in this context the word lacks an unchallenged authoritative definition—an importantly different claim than the one Tepperman makes.

To capture something of the diverse uses to which the concept of reconciliation has been put—as well as the specificity of its most central historical significance—consider Michael Hardimon's discussion of Hegel's philosophy of reconciliation. A philosopher, Hardimon is concerned with reconciliation as a basic concept of Hegel's project. In a set of preliminary remarks on that concept, he takes pains to distinguish common understandings of the English word "reconciliation" and the German word Hegel uses, *Versöhnung*. One important difference, Hardimon notes, is that *Versöhnung* "strongly connotes a process of transformation," a process in which "getting along" is the result of a newly transformed relationship. *Versöhnung*, writes Hardimon, "tends to sound churchy," and its etymological roots lie in the word *Sühne*, which means "expiation" and "atonement." "Reconciliation," on the other hand, claims Hardimon, may imply "submission" or "resignation," with suggestions of "surrender" or "acquiescence." A person can, for instance, "become reconciled to a circumstance that is completely contrary to one's wishes." But "if *Versöhnung* is possible," Hardimon writes, "resignation is unnecessary."[10]

We may pick up on Hardimon's discussion of *Versöhnung* and "reconciliation" to suggest that there are at least two quite different ways to think about "reconciliation": first, reconciliation may strongly connote a process of transformation, a process that results in transformed social relations; on the other hand, reconciliation may be figured as a form of resignation, a process that results not in transformed social relations, but in acquiescence to the existing order of things. In the debates about reconciliation that prefigured, attended, and followed the South African TRC, there have in fact been many more attempted figurations of reconciliation's meaning and potential, yet these two divergent sets of significations do suggest how wide the spectrum of possible meanings might be. Indeed, while some have worried that talk of reconciliation signals a call for unjust acquiescence, others have sought to emphasize the transformative potential of "true" or "real" reconciliation. And not a few have worried that certain renderings of reconciliation—and not just those invoking German philosophy—can sound a little too "churchy."

One reason certain renderings of "reconciliation" tend to "sound churchy" is undoubtedly connected to the concept's extensive theological history. A central theme in Paul's *Second Epistle to the Corinthians*, the idea of reconciliation has long had distinctly Christian overtones and implications. It has also been a recurrent topic in modern European theology and philosophy—Karl Barth devoted four large tomes to the subject, and it was one of Hegel's significant preoccupations. While the concept of reconciliation is an old one, however, the conjunction of truth and reconciliation is a discursive innovation. It represents "a new language of social order."[11] Discourses of reconciliation have figured prominently in the historical contexts that gave rise to the first truth and reconciliation commissions. Catholic bishops in Chile called publicly for social reconciliation only one year after a coup that toppled the socialist Salvador Allende and brought General Augusto Pinochet to power, and more than a decade and a half prior to the formation of that nation's Truth and Reconciliation Commission. Likewise, in South Africa, discourses of reconciliation also extend further back than many commentators on the TRC have acknowledged. During the years of struggle against apartheid, activist church leaders and South African theologians regularly debated the meanings and prerequisites of Christian reconciliation. As state repression intensified, and religious leaders were dragged further and further into the anti-apartheid struggle, calls for reconciliation became more controversial. In the years just prior to South Africa's political transition, debates over reconciliation culminated in 1985 in the publication of *The Kairos Document*, a "prophetic" theological intervention in the South African public sphere that critiqued both conservative and liberal invocations of reconciliation. Drawing on and adapting the discursive and theological repertoires made possible by this history, the TRC itself closely associated reconciliation with both forgiveness and *ubuntu* (a central term in Tutu's theological register). In combination with the public and highly mediated spectacles of truth and reconciliation that set the South African TRC apart from those commissions that preceded it, the commission's grand narrative of truth and reconciliation propelled it to greater public prominence, while also making it a subject of intense international scrutiny.

Informed by the history of reconciliation in South Africa, the work of the TRC was also directly shaped by an engagement with and understanding of earlier truth commissions in Latin America. Much more than previous commissions, however, the South African commission would itself quickly become a common reference point within the field, the commission to which all others seemed inevitably to be compared—serving as either an exemplary touchstone to be emulated or an example of the sort of morally compromised truth commission that ought to be rigorously avoided. After the TRC, new commissions proliferated and the international field of transitional justice began to more clearly take shape. In this context, South Africa's commission represented a field-changing moment. It was also significantly controversial, drawing criticisms of its presumption of a causal relationship between "truth" and "reconciliation," and questions about the promotion of reconciliation in the context of both truth commissions and the wider field. As a site for the articulation of an alternative framework for pursuing justice in the midst of political transition, the TRC—along with its theologically inflected discursive frame—was at odds in important respects with the dominant secular, juridical framework that remained hegemonic across "the international community," within the field of transitional justice, and throughout the upper reaches of cosmopolitan human rights culture. When the United Nations issued its 2004 report on transitional justice, while there were relatively vague references throughout the report to the quest for, and promotion of, reconciliation, there was no mention of reconciliation in the section of the report devoted to "facilitating truth telling," which specifically concerned the work of truth commissions.[12] A sign of just how important truth commissions and transitional justice had become, the report was also an example of the tentative and ambivalent approach to the politics of reconciliation on the part of international actors.

The United Nations report wasn't just a sign that truth commissions were being more widely discussed, at the United Nations and elsewhere. There was also a related surge of associations between "truth" and "reconciliation," as more and more observers began referring to the work of "truth and reconciliation commissions" and debating the increasingly prominent rhetorical place of reconciliation in the definition of such commissions. The language of reconciliation had taken a much more prominent place in the lexicon of truth commissions.[13] In multiple ways, South Africa's TRC was the pivotal commission in this historical trajectory. It was a field-shaping "historical event," a remarkable occurrence with "momentous consequences," and a crucial moment in the historical trajectory of the truth commission as an institutional form—not only with respect to the prominence of reconciliation, but also with regard to its innovative use of public hearings.[14] At the same time, the South African commission was also distinctive and even idiosyncratic, including institutional elements that were not widely reproduced elsewhere. The most conspicuous and controversial of these was its individualized truth-for-amnesty provision.[15] Centrally, attention to the TRC also produced a huge pile of commentary and scholarly literature (much of it devoted to the topic of reconciliation), forming an important part of the newly developing field of transitional justice. So much attention was paid to the South African commission, in fact, that the ICTJ regularly found itself burdened with having to remind its partners and constituencies that the TRC was unique—and thus not to be copied thoughtlessly, if at all. A critique—either implicit or explicit—of the TRC's approach to reconciliation, forgiveness, and amnesty often accompanied such reminders.

Proposed as early as 1992, the idea for a truth commission in South Africa became a serious possibility after Nelson Mandela was elected president in April of 1994. Mandela had been a political prisoner for 27 years. Apartheid—its principles and practices of racial separation, discrimination, and oppression implemented in the context of longstanding colonial segregation—had lasted four and a half decades. The proposed truth commission would investigate atrocities and abuses committed during the Apartheid era, in the context of an amnesty agreed to in the course of the nation's negotiated transition. In a post-amble to the 1993 interim constitution, the promise of amnesty had been linked to "acts, omissions and offenses associated with political objectives and committed in the course of the conflicts of the past." This amnesty, wrote the authors of the post-amble, would "advance" reconciliation.[16] Thus, says Erik Doxtader, a scholar of reconciliation closely linked to Cape Town's Institute for Justice and Reconciliation, the post-amble "mandated amnesty in the name of reconciliation." The interim constitution, he writes, "gave its last words to defining reconciliation, announcing its achievement, and calling on citizens to undertake its practice."[17] In the words of the post-amble:

> The pursuit of national unity, the well-being of all South African citizens and peace require reconciliation between the people of South Africa and the reconstruction of society. The adoption of this constitution lays the secure foundation for the people of South Africa to transcend the divisions and strife of the past, which generated gross violations of human rights, the transgression of humanitarian principles in violent conflicts and a legacy of hatred, fear, guilt and revenge.

Hitching amnesty to the language of reconciliation, the post-amble also articulated the "need for understanding but not for vengeance, a need for reparation but not retaliation, a need for ubuntu but not for victimization."[18] Writing about truth and reconciliation, Martha Minow has represented the important concept of *ubuntu* as a matter of "humanness, or an inclusive sense of community valuing everyone," while Doxtader has noted its connection to a "cultural interest in realizing a common humanity," figuring ubuntu as "part of reconciliation's revealing light."[19] Others have represented ubuntu as "an alternative way of being in a hostile world,"[20] and identified it as standing for "an ethic of interdependence, which informs social structures and ethical practices throughout southern Africa."[21] Central to the theology of Desmond Tutu, the chair and leader of the South African TRC, ubuntu came to be closely associated with the commission's discourse of reconciliation, especially as represented by Tutu—so much so that John De Gruchy, a longtime scholar of reconciliation and religion in South Africa, suggested to me that Tutu had come to use the two terms relatively interchangeably. Perhaps even more than reconciliation—though certainly in connection with it—ubuntu has come to stand for the promise of post-apartheid South Africa, especially in global media representations, and this itself is in good part the product of Tutu's transnational prominence and the TRC's global visibility.

According to Tutu, ubuntu "speaks to the very essence of being human," signaling that "we belong to a bundle of life," and that "harmony, friendliness, community are great goods." Ubuntu, wrote Tutu in *No Future without Forgiveness*, says, "My humanity is caught up, is inextricably bound up, in yours," and "a person is a person through other persons." Opposing this notion to "I think therefore I am," Tutu suggests instead that ubuntu says, "I am human because I belong."[22] The opposition to Descartes' well-known philosophical formulation is no accident, and—like the South African brand of reconciliation—ubuntu has frequently been rendered as a distinctively African product, to be contrasted with the ethos of "the West." This is a contrast to which Tutu has regularly returned. As he wrote in "Where Is Now Thy God?":

> Unlike Westerners, Africans have a synthesizing mind set, as opposed to the occidental analytical one. That doesn't mean Africans are better or worse; it just says God is smart. Westerners have analysis. We have synthesis. Westerners have a very strong sense of individualism. We have a strong sense of community. Because Westerners have a strong sense of the value of the individual, they are able to take personal initiatives. It's not so easy, when you are a community-minded person, to go against the stream.... This feel for religious and spiritual realities has made it difficult for atheistic and materialistic ideologies, such as communism, to attract many African adherents.[23]

If ubuntu is thus figured as a central feature of what Tutu once called "the African *Weltanschauung*"—being strategically deployed, in the words of Justin Neuman, as "a rival normative framework to Western ideas about sovereignty, utility, and individual autonomy"—it was also a central and strategic part, along with reconciliation, of the TRC's effort to mobilize these and other "Western" values, and to embed them in South African political culture.[24] As Neuman puts it, ubuntu was "called upon to translate these very norms—and the attendant discourses of human rights and civil society—into African vernaculars."[25]

While the post-amble to South Africa's interim constitution—with its oft-repeated references to reconciliation and ubuntu, and its controversial provision of amnesty—did not, as is often claimed, mandate the formation of the TRC, it did provide the political context for its creation.[26] In this context, the commission would bring together the promise of pardon and the need for understanding, pursuing the project of national reconciliation through truth-telling confessions made in exchange for amnesty. The South African Parliament passed the Promotion of National Unity and Reconciliation Act in 1995, and a 17-member commission, to be led by Archbishop Tutu, was subsequently appointed. Tutu was to become the charismatic leader of the TRC. Bringing a distinctive and influential theological spin to the commission's work, Tutu referred prominently and often to reconciliation, linking it not only to ubuntu but also to forgiveness. "We are a people who know," he said, in response to a statement made in front of the TRC, "that when someone cannot be forgiven there is no future."[27] What has been called Tutu's "ubuntu theology"—with its strong associations with reconciliation and forgiveness—was compelling and widely celebrated, while also controversial and adamantly contested. Along with Nelson Mandela, he became the figure most often taken to represent the truth commission's ways and watchwords. And it was ultimately the archbishop, Antjie Krog would write, who found "language for what is happening." That language, she said, "drags people along with the process" of the TRC.[28]

This language of reconciliation—embodied so powerfully and persuasively by Tutu, but certainly not limited to him—has had a distinctive, contentious, and complicated history in South Africa, a history at once theological and political. Indeed, politics and theology in South Africa have been importantly and at times inextricably intertwined, especially in the years prior to apartheid's demise. Literary critic Susan Gallagher makes this point well, in the course of discussing the significant theological disputes and South African "confessional discourse" of the 1980s:

> Secular observers may find such theological battles esoteric and peripheral. However, because theological paradigms have been repeatedly employed to validate apartheid, and because the political struggles of South Africa are so deeply implicated in religious beliefs and Church politics, anti-apartheid confessional discourse was a much more visible and significant aspect of South African life than similar movements in other countries . . . in South Africa, theological debates about confession have been conspicuous, consequential, and continual, forming a prominent social discourse.[29]

Indeed, the extent to which theological paradigms were "employed to validate apartheid" was significant enough to lead writers of one declaration to refer to a "state theology."[30] A story recounted by Pumla Gobodo-Madikizela puts flesh on this concept of an apartheid state that fell back on theology for its justification. Bibles distributed to soldiers of the South African Defense Force, she writes, included both "the gold star-shaped army insignia embossed on the maroon front cover" and an inscription on the first page, in Afrikaans, from State President P.W. Botha. "Even this tampering with the book that many Christians consider sacred," Gobodo-Madikizela writes, "was not enough to provide the condemnation it deserved from the church: the Afrikaans Church stood by silently and watched apartheid's murderous plan unfold."[31]

If the discourse of the apartheid state was theological, so also was much of the discourse associated with the struggle against apartheid and resistance to the state. In the theologies of struggle and resistance that emerged in direct and explicit response to the South African political context, the language of reconciliation was both central and contested. At the heart of the "church struggle against apartheid," John De Gruchy has written, "was a theology of reconciliation that fundamentally challenged both the politics and theology of racial separation." By de Gruchy's lights, *The Message to the People of South Africa*—published in 1968 by the South African Council of Churches—was, while not the first church statement critical of apartheid, the "most trenchant, unambiguous, and ecumenical to date."[32] The debate that followed the publication of *The Message*, however, was one that took place almost entirely among white South Africans. This fact, combined with the recourse to reconciliation discourse on the part of the "reformist" apartheid state, made many anti-apartheid activists, including proponents of the Black Consciousness movement, suspicious of the rhetoric of reconciliation.

Yet from other positions within the theological field there soon issued new and more radical responses to, and interventions in, the debate over reconciliation, as both subsequent developments within black theology—"the theological reflection of black Christians on the situation in which they live and on their struggle for liberation"—and after it contextual theology, came to ground "a new language of protest."[33] Spearheaded by figures such as Desmond Tutu, Beyers Naudé, Denis Hurley, Allan Boesak, Smangaliso Mkhatshwa, and Frank Chikane, these theological movements evolved in the midst of an increasing "spiral of involvement" in the liberation struggle on the part of South African churches. The result was not only a closer relationship between religious communities and the liberation movement, but also a series of documents, declarations, and other publications that produced and promoted new discourses of liberation, justice, and reconciliation.[34] Products of South African political struggle, these new theologies were influenced intellectually by black theology in the United States, Latin American liberation theology, and European political theology. Like their Latin American counterparts—contextual theology, which according to one scholar replaced black theology and thereby shifted the emphasis from "race" to "class," may be seen as a particular incarnation of liberation theology—South African theologies of liberation have continuously invoked notions of "real reconciliation."[35]

Possibly one of the most important theological statements to be produced in the course of the anti-apartheid struggle—and certainly one of the most controversial—was the 1985 *Kairos Document*, which has been "recognized as the definitive statement of contextual theology in South Africa."[36] The document's multiple authors (there were over 150 individual signatories) critiqued not only the "State Theology" of Apartheid, but also a "Church Theology" that emphasized mediation and liberal reform.[37] As Tristan Borer writes, "For the Kairos theologians, reconciliation through compromise could never be made into an absolute principle that must be applied in all cases of conflict. . . . In contrast to reconciliation, *The Kairos Document* challenged churches to respond with a theology of confrontation and resistance."[38] The "Prophetic Theology" promoted by *The Kairos Document* did not, however, reject the language of reconciliation altogether. Rather, like liberation theologians in Chile and elsewhere, the authors made "true reconciliation" contingent on liberation from unjust and oppressive social structures upheld by a tyrannical regime:

> There can be no doubt that our Christian faith commits us to work for *true* reconciliation and *genuine* peace. But as so many people, including Christians, have pointed out, there can be no true reconciliation and no genuine peace *without justice*. Any form of peace or reconciliation that allows the sin of injustice and oppression to continue is a *false* peace and a *counterfeit* reconciliation. This kind of "reconciliation" has nothing whatsoever to do with the Christian faith.[39]

In seeking to respond to the violent rush of protest, repression, and brutality that characterized South Africa in this period—"in the middle of 1985," writes Doxtader, "the state of emergency in South Africa was both rule and reality"—the authors of *The Kairos Document* figured "Prophetic Theology" as a theology that "would include a reading of the signs of the times."[40] An opening of opportunity, *kairos* has been taken to signify "a time when conditions are right or propitious for the accomplishment of an important task or undertaking."[41] According to Doxtader and Salazar:

> The word *kairos* has in fact two political meanings in ancient Greek. One refers to an opportunity for decisive action arising in the course

of a political debate, and to the ability of one of the contestants to see that there is an opportunity not to be missed in order to resolve an issue. The other is found in the New Testament, to designate that special moment of time when God visits his people to offer them a unique opportunity for repentance and conversion, for change and decisive action. A time of *kairos* indicates a moment when belief is confronted with action, a critical moment (*krisis*, in turn, denotes 'choice').[42]

Doxtader and Salazar go on to figure Tutu's "insistence on reconciliation" as "the recognition of a Christian *kairos*, in politics, and the acknowledgment that a *krisis*, a radical choice (reconciliation, not vengeance), was at hand."[43] As Wendy Brown has emphasized, the practice of *krisis* itself also has "a restorative aim." "Critique as political *krisis*," Brown writes, "promises to restore continuity by repairing or renewing the justice that gives an order the prospect of continuity, that indeed makes it continuous."[44] The link between reconciliation and restoration has in fact been a common one, and it is notable that Tutu and others moved to connect reconciliation with a "restorative" approach to justice. At the same time, there remains some rhetorical distance between reconciliation and restorative justice. As John De Gruchy has written, for example, despite the thematic and theological links to restorative justice—which de Gruchy calls "a form of justice that has to do with healing relationships"—the phrase "does not carry the wealth or the warmth of meaning embedded in the word 'reconciliation.'"[45] Yet *The Kairos Document* was written at a moment of urgency and opportunity when reconciliation's promise of justice restored (let alone the "warmth" of its "healing") could not be immediately fulfilled. And thus the document defined reconciliation, in the words of Erik Doxtader, "as a rhetorical process that could begin a time of transition."[46]

While the publication of *The Kairos Document* was a significant step in the development of contextual theology, earlier South African references to reconciliation had also emphasized its social and material conditions.[47] In an open letter to Prime Minister John Vorster written in May 1976 (a month before the Soweto uprising), Desmond Tutu noted that "a people made desperate by despair, injustice and oppression will use desperate means" and worried about "a point of no return, when events will generate a momentum of their own," and about a "bloody denouement." In this context, Tutu introduced the language and possibility of real reconciliation. "I am deeply committed to real reconciliation with justice for all," he wrote, "and to peaceful change to a more just and open South African society in which the wonderful riches and wealth of our country will be shared more equitably."[48] Thus, Tutu—who would ultimately not sign *The Kairos Document*, objecting to its "attack on the underlying theology of institutional churches"[49]—closely linked reconciliation both with a dream of distributive justice and with the specter of a "bloody denouement," a vision to which he would return upon the submission of the final volume of the TRC's report in March 2003. Reminding President Thabo Mbeki of a proposal to impose a new tax on businesses in order to raise millions of dollars for reparations, Tutu argued that it was in the interest of the business community to make such contributions. "It is not altruistic," he said. "It is in their interest to help narrow the gap between the rich and the poor." "Can you explain," Tutu continued, "how a black person wakes up in a squalid ghetto today, almost 10 years after freedom? Then he goes to work in town, which is still largely white, in palatial homes. And at the end of the day, he goes back home to squalor? I don't know why those people don't just say, 'To hell with peace. To hell with Tutu and the truth commission.'"[50] Without substantial reparations, Tutu implied, real reconciliation—and the peaceful and just society it promised—would not be possible.[51]

The TRC's operation "in the full glare of publicity"—as Tutu put it in his foreword to the TRC Report—was one of the unique features that set the South African commission apart from those that preceded it.[52] As sociologist Tanya Goodman has emphasized, the TRC's representations of reconciliation were a matter of "public ritual." Drawing on the work of Victor Turner, Goodman suggests that in the liminal space occupied by the TRC, public testimonies "were an important part of the ritual bridge building that the TRC undertook." Indeed, such public testimonies were an integral element of both the TRC's everyday practices and its rapid and extensive international celebration, as narratives drawing on the commission's public spectacles of truth and reconciliation—along with the stories of apology and forgiveness that sometimes attended them—circulated widely, both in South Africa and beyond.[53]

The public performances of the TRC, Ebrahim Moosa would write, defied "accepted conceptions of justice, law, order and fairness," and required "faith in the rite of reconciliation" and "belief in the rituals of confession." The TRC, said Moosa, had been a "mysterious" and "grotesque" performative event, a "secular Eucharist."[54] Others recognized the distinctive "liturgy" that developed within the TRC hearings, and called attention to the "spiritual wells" that fed it, while also noting the battles that developed over the "religious trappings" of the commission's public hearings, thus calling into question their supposed secularity.[55] Despite ongoing debates over their overt religiosity, the commission's public hearings soon came to constitute what Deborah Posel has called "the TRC's confessional," the primary site for the commission's "main business of catharsis and expiation."[56] Hearings opened the space for traumatized testimonials and the voicing of "healing truths"—as the commission's fourfold conception of types of truth would have it—and became sites of confession and apology, where requests for forgiveness were sometimes flatly refused, while at other times absolution seemed to be freely offered.[57]

Intersecting importantly with the TRC's mobilization of reconciliation discourse—and further enabling and stimulating its subsequent circulation—the use of public hearings was a major institutional innovation. As Mark Freeman has noted, it was only after the South African TRC that "the idea of a truth commission holding public hearings—especially victim-centered hearings—became the norm." Previous commissions in Argentina, Bolivia, Uruguay, El Salvador, Chile, Chad, and Haiti had not held such hearings. "Everything then changed," says Freeman, "with South Africa's TRC, the first truth commission with a truly international, as opposed to local or regional, impact."[58] While Freeman emphasizes here the TRC's "victim-centered" hearings, just as important to the crafting of its tales of truth and reconciliation were the testimonies and confessions of "perpetrators," for whom commissioners also sometimes served as what Goodman calls "empathic interlocutors."[59] Indeed, both victim and perpetrator hearings were "confessional," Deborah Posel writes, "in the sense that they both created opportunities for the public declaration, acknowledgment, and scrutiny of some sort of inner damage—whether pain, trauma, or guilt—regulated by the listening and questioning role of those experts to whom the confession was made, and with the offer of some sort of transcendence."[60] As Tutu put it, "There is not a single person who has not been traumatized by apartheid—even the perpetrators. We have to pour balm on our tortured souls."[61] In the aftermath of apartheid, says Posel, "*all* were damaged."[62] Thus, in pursuit of truth that would heal the damage, TRC commissioners engaged in practices of active elicitation, and Tutu, in particular, "tutored perpetrators in the art of remorse."[63]

While there were times when Tutu's pedagogy of truth and reconciliation was actively rebuffed, in other cases the discursive and affective results of his tutorials seemed tailor-made for wider circulation. As many critical commentators would note, in order to meet the requirements for the granting of an individual amnesty, perpetrator testimonies before the commission were not required to involve the explicit articulation of regret or remorse. Truth—"full disclosure"—was the standard, not apology or contrition.[64] Yet in the course of the public hearings apologies were encouraged and made, with texts of these being subsequently reproduced in a section on "apologies and acknowledgements" that was part of a chapter on reconciliation included in volume five of the TRC report.

One widely circulated narrative of apology was drawn from commission's consideration of testimony regarding the "Bisho massacre." In the early 1990s, as the collapse of apartheid seemed imminent, political violence was on the rise in South Africa. In September 1992, members of the African National

Congress (ANC) marched through the streets of Bisho, a town in the Eastern Cape, in order to dramatize the ANC's campaign for free political activity. Local Defense Force soldiers fired on the demonstrators, and 28 demonstrators were killed. What happened when the TRC received testimony regarding the killings in Bisho was remarkable, and most would later emphasize that it was also somewhat unique. In a tension-filled hall, packed with local spectators who had been on the ANC's march or who had lost family members killed that day, a white officer, Colonel Schobesberger of the local Defense Force, asked for forgiveness:

> I say we are sorry. I say the burden of the Bisho massacre will be on our shoulders for the rest of our lives. We cannot wish it away. It happened. But please, I ask specifically the victims not to forget, I cannot ask this, but to forgive us, to get the soldiers back into the community, to accept them fully, to try to understand also the pressure they were under then. This is all I can do. I'm sorry, this I can say, I'm sorry.[65]

In response to this plea, another extraordinary thing happened. The people in the audience applauded. Then Tutu, making the link between confession and catharsis, acknowledgement and reconciliation, forgiveness and healing truth, said: "Can we just keep a moment's silence, please, because we are dealing with things that are very, very deep. It isn't easy, as we all know, to ask for forgiveness and it's also not easy to forgive, but we are a people who know that when someone cannot be forgiven there is no future."

In the months that followed, the details of this event quickly became a success story for the TRC, taken to demonstrate that "reconciliation through truth" was a real possibility. Tutu would go on to recount this story in his own book on the TRC process, as would others. In fact, the words of his response that day would come to serve as the title of his book, and in a sense the motto for his approach to the entire TRC process: *No Future without Forgiveness*.

Stories such as this not only indicate the TRC's fundamentally public character—marking a significant shift in the institutional form of the truth commission, and one that set South Africa's TRC apart from the Chilean commission, and others that preceded it. They also clearly demonstrate the explicitly theological vocabulary that substantially shaped the commission's public hearings and report. Tutu, wrote Antjie Krog, "unambiguously mantled the commission in Christian language," even despite the opposition of some commissioners.[66] Along with reconciliation, both *ubuntu* and "restorative justice" were given a prominent place in the TRC report's discussion of the key "concepts and principles underlying the Commission's work."[67]

Over the course of the last decade and a half, this unambiguous mantling of the TRC in Christian language has received a good deal of attention, both in South Africa and well beyond. Not all of it has been positive. In the words of Andre du Toit, "As religious leaders and churches became increasingly involved in the commission's work, the influence of religious style and symbolism supplanted political and human rights concerns."[68] Among international observers, both criticisms of and concerns about the TRC's "theological rhetoric" have also circulated. Political philosopher Dennis Thompson worried that truth commissions adopting such rhetoric might get "bogged down in . . . the therapy of forgiveness."[69] Informed by his own theoretical perspective, Thompson's anxiety was not entirely unfounded. While its formation was the product of a political compromise that brought an end to apartheid, following its launch the South African TRC took on a life of its own, engaging in a theologically motivated quest for forgiveness and healing, and producing in the process not simply the "intangible sacrament" that José Zalaquett had once recommended, but a novel institutional form and a new global discourse of truth and reconciliation.[70]

Reconciliation and Transitional Justice

Founded in New York City, with substantial support from the Ford Foundation, the ICTJ was linked to this new global discourse of truth and reconciliation yet has sought, in various ways, to distance itself from it. The founding of the ICTJ was an important moment in the development of the fledgling field of transitional justice, a "relatively novel field" of both scholarship and expertise, with one foot in the universities and one foot in the world of practical action.[71] Remarkably interdisciplinary and often amorphously defined, the field's porous and disputed boundaries have encompassed the work of both academic researchers and a variety of non-academic actors, while also prominently including those whose own intellectual commitments, concrete life trajectories, personal experiences and organizational efforts effectively blur the distinction between "academics" and "practitioners." Variously recognized actors within the field have included NGO specialists, journalists, policy analysts, political consultants, social movement activists, and academic researchers in a wide range of disciplines, including law, public policy, forensics, political science, economics, psychology, sociology, anthropology, history, philosophy, literature, and the arts. Given this great diversity of actors and efforts, and in light of the wide range of processes and practices associated with "coming to terms with the past," it has been suggested that the term "transitional justice" may not be an adequate discursive marker for the field of action in question.[72] Yet the signifier, along with its attendant discourses and practices—not to mention the support of major philanthropic foundations and the efforts of legions of transnational activists throughout the world—has brought into being a signified, and it has become common to speak of a "field" of transitional justice.[73]

The ICTJ is the world's premier transitional justice organization, and has been explicitly dedicated to field development and expansion. Launched and headquartered in lower Manhattan, the Center later opened offices in Bogotá, Brussels, Cape Town, Dili, Geneva, Jakarta, Kathmandu, Kinshasa, and Monrovia; its staff has worked throughout the Americas, Africa, Asia, Europe, and the Middle East.[74] Local activists dedicated to transitional justice—and to a host of related efforts to confront or overcome a difficult past—are scattered through the world. But the origins of the ICTJ can be traced to South Africa, and its founding was due in no small part to the efforts of its founding president (and former Deputy Chairperson of the South African TRC), Alex Boraine.

Both controversial and acclaimed, the ICTJ styled itself under Boraine's leadership as a different sort of human rights organization, "founded on the concept of a new direction in human rights advocacy: helping societies heal by accounting for and addressing past crimes after a period of repressive rule or armed conflict."[75] In consultation with dozens of legal scholars, human rights activists, and practitioners of transitional justice, all brought together by the Ford Foundation, Boraine put forward a plan for the new organization, along with his former colleague from the South African TRC, Paul van Zyl, an ambitious young lawyer who would eventually become ICTJ's executive vice president, and Priscilla Hayner, a longtime Ford Foundation consultant whose widely cited book on truth commissions was published the year ICTJ opened its doors.[76]

Together, the Center's founders made the rubric of "transitional justice" their overarching framework and broad organizational focus, seeking to "strengthen the field of transitional justice by improving communication among the many scholars, legal professionals, activists, and policymakers engaged in this field," and establishing a series of new research projects, under the leadership of philosopher Pablo de Greiff, who became ICTJ's director of research. Prominently highlighting its ability to provide "comparative information and expertise" and an "overview of lessons learned" to government officials, human rights activists, and others, ICTJ also held training sessions for, consulted with, and provided assistance to, various actors engaged in designing and implementing transitional justice measures.[77] In addition to establishing initiatives aimed at seeking the truth and promoting reconciliation—and in keeping with the central foci of work on "transitional justice"—such measures were taken to include the prosecution of perpetrators of human rights abuses, the provision of reparations to victims of such abuses, the reform of state institutions such as the police and the courts, and the removal of human rights abusers from positions of power. These different approaches to "dealing with a legacy of violence" formed part of what ICTJ dubbed a "Transitional Justice Toolkit," and they were presented not as mutually exclusive options, but rather as component parts of what Boraine referred to as a "holistic strategy" that emphasized "both judicial and nonjudicial mechanisms."[78] Much larger than any other NGO devoted to transitional justice, the ICTJ was soon partnering with dozens of national organizations and consulting with representatives of transitional states throughout the world. Its standing was due in no small part to an expanding international interest in innovative attempts to "come to terms with the past" and to promote national and social healing through the work of truth commissions and other "mechanisms" of the transitional justice.

Based in a metropolitan hub of global human rights activism, the ICTJ very quickly became a relatively powerful and well-funded organization—one indicator of the rising prominence of truth commissions and transitional justice on the international scene. Indeed, the Ford Foundation, writes William Korey of the ICTJ's establishment in 2001, "had moved in an almost revolutionary manner to establish from scratch a human rights NGO."[79] Boraine's stature as a leading South African truth commissioner doubtlessly contributed to the ICTJ's high international profile, and his central role at the ICTJ, where he was positioned to meet regularly with both high-powered visitors to New York and local human rights leaders, put him more squarely on the global stage.

Although the ICTJ was undeniably the leading international organization devoted to the establishment and practice of truth commissions, the organization's representatives increasingly found themselves actively discouraging the premature or "uninformed" establishment of just such commissions, and, despite the impression of some, the ICTJ was not an entirely uncritical proponent of a singular "truth and reconciliation" model.[80] In part because of outside concerns that the organization might not be devoted enough to trials and prosecutions, the founding of ICTJ itself was not uncontroversial, and at an April 2000 meeting convened by the Ford Foundation to discuss the potential organization's mission and parameters, a "rather sharp debate" emerged over the centrality given to truth commissions in a discussion paper produced by Priscilla Hayner, then a consultant for Ford. As Korey reports, Aryeh Neier, the former leader of Human Rights Watch who later became president of the Open Society Institute, challenged the paper's "altogether positive view of truth commissions" and advocated "the need for justice and court decisions for both victims and society as a whole." Justice, Neier and others argued, "could be obtained through legal proceedings in courts, not at disclosures made at the hearings of truth commissions."[81] As Neier had written a few years earlier in a letter to *The New York Review of Books*, while truth commissions had "performed a valuable service in certain Latin American countries"—helping to establish the truth about "disappearances" in countries like Argentina—they would be much less relevant in other contexts. "What is it that a commission could tell us," Neier asked, "about the indiscriminate bombardment of Sarajevo or the radio-incited genocide in Rwanda that would assist in confronting such a past? Only trials of those most responsible would address crimes against humanity committed so brazenly and on so vast a scale." Given that "confronting the abuses of the past" was "a crucial question in many countries," he concluded, it would be "impossible to devise a single approach."[82]

Chairing the Ford Foundation meeting in April 2000, Alex Boraine assured those present that truth commissions would be only a "part of transitional justice." What was needed, as Boraine would go on to emphasize, was a "holistic" approach. Yet as the Ford Foundation and its assembled group of experts discussed how best to respond to the challenges of transitional justice, the question of truth commissions—"always of special interest to the foundation"—stood out. Truth commissions were, Korey reports, "at the very heart" of Priscilla Hayner's preliminary papers for Ford, which had contributed directly to the ICTJ's "founding document."[83]

In fact, while the organization would package and seek to disseminate the contents of the "Transitional Justice Toolkit," the ICTJ's founders were neither recognized masters of all the tools contained in the kit, nor creators of the collective association of those tools with something called "transitional justice," a phrase whose invention and initial proliferation predated the Center's founding by at least several years.[84] Indeed, although the establishment of the ICTJ was "the result of a number of converging streams, starting with the South African TRC," as Alex Boraine would later put it, and although the organization would rapidly expand and diversify its staff, it was clearly the close association of the ICTJ's founders with recent truth commissions—and in particular with the widely discussed South African TRC—that gave the new Center much of its initial cachet (just as those associations contributed to much of the initial debate about the fledgling organization and its mission).[85] The "truth business," wrote one observer, was "booming"—and ICTJ was "the world's first truth commission consulting firm."[86] As a legal scholar and transitional justice expert told me a few years later, the Center in New York had quickly "cornered the market on truth commissions," coming on the scene just as interest in such commissions was on the rise, and positioning itself as an unparalleled source of comparative expertise.

Boraine, van Zyl, and Hayner were already widely seen as important experts on truth commissions, and in that capacity each of them had been traveling the world. With the establishment of ICTJ, they and their colleagues were positioned as global leaders in a swiftly expanding field. During its first year, ICTJ staff members traveled to 15 different countries and informed the efforts of several truth commissions, including direct involvement in the establishment of new commissions in East Timor, Peru, and Sierra Leone.[87] The organization would grow by leaps and bounds in the years that followed. Little more than five years after its founding, ICTJ had offices in several new locations, in addition to its original office in New York, and its staff of more than 100 was working throughout the world.

Early critics worried that ICTJ represented the institutionalization of a "truth commission mafia," a new and controversial organization that might undermine the work of other human rights advocates, "sucking up foundation money" and "likely to stifle other ways of handling state injustice."[88] At least in part as a result of its associations with the South African experience of "truth and reconciliation," the Center was viewed by some in international human rights circles as "soft" on the "duty to prosecute" perpetrators of past abuses.[89] Recognized proponents of the view that standard forms of prosecutorial justice could often be insufficient for grappling with difficult histories of violence, repression, and human rights abuse, ICTJ's leaders were nonetheless at pains to assert their membership in, and solidarity with, the broader human rights community, and thus to disabuse detractors who charged them with seeking to uncritically reproduce the South African "model" in other contexts of transition or to privilege truth commissions over other forms of transitional justice. "We always say that truth commissions and prosecutions should go side by side, and there should never be a hierarchy between them," Paul van Zyl told a reporter from the *New York Times*. "The South African model worked in the South African context, but it's entirely inappropriate in 99 percent of the other contexts in which we work."[90]

If their human rights colleagues in New York and elsewhere were concerned about ICTJ's apparent orientation toward promoting and propelling the work of further commissions like the South African TRC, advocates of reconciliation and restorative justice would note an opposite inclination at the Center—a tendency to focus too heavily on the importance of prosecutions, at the possible expense of supporting broader processes of social and political reconciliation. The theme of reconciliation played an important yet ambiguous and at times contentious role in ICTJ's early days. While the concept of "reconciliation" was at the organizational center of the Institute for Justice and Reconciliation in Cape Town—this one concept, Charles Villa-Vicencio said, best "captures our work"—ICTJ made the aim of "promoting reconciliation" one of the five key elements of its original institutional mission.[91] Yet given the size and diversity of its staff, as well as the organizational and political environment in which it operated, ICTJ experienced persistent difficulties in putting its avowed support of reconciliation into practice, and especially in crafting a coherent organizational strategy regarding how best to promote, advance, or facilitate reconciliation processes.

Alex Boraine was by all accounts deeply committed to the importance of the concept of reconciliation, and indeed devoted substantial attention to the topic in his book on the TRC.[92] Like Villa-Vicencio, Boraine sought to articulate a conception of reconciliation that drew on its long and complicated South African history, while also leaving room for criticism of the overtly religious and Christian character of reconciliation as articulated in the context of the South African TRC, and especially by Archbishop Tutu. Yet not all of his colleagues at ICTJ saw eye-to-eye with Boraine on the question of reconciliation. Continued disagreement made reaching an organizational consensus a significant challenge, and one that ICTJ faced with only limited success during its first few years. Indeed, these initial disputes over reconciliation at the increasingly powerful and influential Center were both representative of and embedded within wider debates regarding truth and reconciliation that were taking place among a diverse and far-flung range of international actors.

As the number and diversity of those engaged in conversations and arguments about "truth" and "reconciliation" continued to expand, so did the number and diversity of commissions seeking some combination of those two social and political goods. "It's amazing," Priscilla Hayner said in late August of 2001, upon her return from a trip to Peru, where she had been advising a new truth and reconciliation commission, "they are cropping up all over the world."[93] Truth commissions, Hayner wrote, in a widely cited book published that same year, were being turned to throughout the world "with great expectation and hope, although often with little appreciation for the complexity of the process and the difficulty of achieving the hoped-for ends."[94] With the advent of new commissions came new challenges, novel approaches, and further innovations. As the institutional form of the truth commission moved from one national location to another, it was transformed in the course of its transnational travel—as were the ideas about "truth and reconciliation" that informed its workings, and in whose name it increasingly operated. There wasn't just one truth commission, but many. At the same time, a recognizable institutional form had clearly taken shape. Built upon "lessons learned" from earlier commissions, discussed and refined in the work of activist scholars and truth commission experts, and conditioned (for better *and* for worse, said the experts) by the lofty aims and outsized rhetoric of the South African TRC, the "truth commission" had come into its own as a transposable tool of political transition. Not infrequently referred to as a "truth and reconciliation commission" (much to the consternation of some truth commission advocates), this ostensibly reproducible traveling institution increasingly took on the goal of "reconciliation" as one of the challenging and difficult to achieve "hoped-for ends" to which Priscilla Hayner had referred. Due in no small part to the prominence of the South African commission—and to widespread fascination with it, subsequent academic attention to it, and desired institutional emulation of it—the conjunction of "truth" and "reconciliation" became an increasingly prevalent, if still contested and controversial, phenomenon.

When Alex Boraine relinquished his position as president of the ICTJ, he was replaced by Juan E. Méndez, a former Washington director of Americas Watch, the nongovernmental human rights organization that later became Human Rights Watch.[95] Under the leadership of Méndez, the staff members of ICTJ persisted in emphasizing that there could be no single blueprint for transitional justice. In particular, they continued to argue that South Africa's unique experiment with truth and reconciliation should not be uncritically replicated elsewhere. "While there is much in the South African Truth and Reconciliation experience to celebrate," said Howard Varney, director of ICTJ's Truth-Seeking Program, in January 2009, "it is unfortunate that the world at large has come to use South Africa as the model or template for all subsequent commissions—or has at least attempted to emulate in one way or another what happened in South Africa."[96] Eduardo González, deputy director of ICTJ's America's program (and later director of its Truth and Memory Program), had earlier voiced a similar sentiment. "The architects of transitional justice policies would pay a more appropriate homage to the South African experience," said González, "by learning both from its strengths and its weaknesses. In particular, the myth that reconciliation will automatically follow from a trade-off of victims' rights needs to be widely debunked."[97]

In its 2006/2007 "annual report magazine," whose cover theme was "Challenging Legacies of Impunity," the ICTJ featured an unsigned "reflection" on "Lessons from South Africa." "In our work," the reflection began, "we have often encountered a yearning for a South African model that could reconcile victims and perpetrators and replace criminal justice. This view is steeped in problematic or self-interested interpretations of South Africa's TRC that compromise reconciliation in the name of political expediency." The feature article highlighted the failure of the South African government to deliver on reparations recommended by the TRC, and criticized the idea of a "back-door" amnesty for perpetrators who had not been granted amnesty by the commission. It went on to criticize those "commissions that claim to model themselves on the South African TRC" while making "thinly disguised efforts to enshrine impunity under a facade of truth-seeking." And it noted the Center's efforts both to challenge the development of plans for "problematic" truth and reconciliation commissions, and "to steer other commissions away from designing their mandates as replicas of the South African model, particularly where TJ [transitional justice] is used as a convenient tradeoff for victims' rights." Itself a telling acknowledgment of South Africa's substantial and controversial influence within the field, the article also recognized in passing the centrality of South Africa's TRC in the ICTJ's own history, closing with an emphasis on the necessity of promoting "best practices" and with a call for efforts to come to terms with the past that would ensure both truth and justice:

> The ICTJ celebrates much of what the South African TRC accomplished—and we trace some of our own institutional origins to it—but we strongly believe that genuine and enduring truth-seeking requires much more than mere imitation. With the enthusiasm for truth commissions unlikely to wane, greater awareness of their real potential is vital. Consequently we are committed to fostering genuine truth-seeking efforts and disseminating basic guidelines and best practices for the implementation of truth commissions. The ICTJ fundamentally believes ... that a crucial lesson from South Africa is that both truth and justice for past crimes are essential to a just and peaceful future.[98]

Crafted in the first-person plural and written in a reflective mood, the closing statement read like a piece of contemporary confessional discourse, a collective statement of strong and fundamental belief celebrating the source of the organization's birth while distancing it from too close an association with problematic dimensions of "the South African legacy." It was, in this sense, a sort of institutional coming-of-age narrative. Yet at the same time the emphasis on challenging impunity was one that had been present from the ICTJ's earliest days.

With the arrival of Méndez, the Center was given a leader who had actively "championed prosecution," a human rights advocate who had been prominently associated with a "prosecutorial approach" (sometimes figured as a distinct alternative to the "restorative approach" favored by the South African TRC).[99] Yet Méndez himself would caution against overdrawn contrasts between reconciliation and prosecution—taking issue with the impression that religious actors mobilizing the language of restorative justice would generally favor the advancement of reconciliation, while international human rights organizations would tend exclusively toward the promotion of prosecutions and "retribution"—since this conjured an "artificial confrontation" between "religious" and "secular" proponents of transitional justice. "Retributive justice," he noted in a memorandum written for a workshop at the Social Science Research Council (SSRC), "is a somewhat loaded term that can be a code for vindictiveness," while "restorative justice is a highly ambiguous term," and one that has in recent usages been appropriated by those promoting alternatives to prosecution. Referring to "the bad faith appropriation" of the language of restorative justice by "those who favor impunity," Méndez challenged those in the SSRC workshop to consider whether the ambiguity of such language might lend itself to this misuse.[100]

Although he was referring in the SSRC Workshop to the language of restorative justice, Méndez would also voice analogous concerns about reconciliation, and indeed his remarks were similar to worries, raised by others, regarding the appropriation of reconciliation discourse. While some focused primarily on critiquing "the saccharin-coated invocations of reconciliation," however, Méndez would take a different stance, especially once he had stepped into his role as the president of the ICTJ.[101] Just as it had at the direction of Alex Boraine, under the leadership of Juan Méndez the ICTJ continued to make reconciliation a positive and central priority of the organization. Thus, when Méndez cautioned against overdrawn contrasts between "reconciliation" and "prosecution," he meant to suggest that the two should be conceived as potentially complementary, even if they had not always been rendered as such in practice.

As Méndez's predecessor, Alex Boraine had persistently defended reconciliation, at times doing so quite vigorously. Yet some of his ICTJ colleagues shared a more critical perspective, if not the precise language in which it was formulated. There had not always been complete consensus among the diverse staff of the ICTJ, and internal dialogues over reconciliation at the Center were marked by significant disagreement over what the concept of "reconciliation" could and should mean in the context of transitional justice. Such disagreements initially inhibited the operationalization of reconciliation as a substantial working principle of the organization, despite its standing as a marker for one of the five original "pillars" of the ICTJ's work. As the internal debates continued, an initial focus on "promoting" reconciliation in ICTJ's mission statement was subsequently shifted to "advancing reconciliation" and then to "facilitating reconciliation processes."[102] But the focus on reconciliation, as one of five "key elements" of the Center's work, remained—despite a continuing lack of internal consensus. While there were internal discussions among senior staff members regarding the possibility of forming a reconciliation program within the organization, nothing major came of these, even given the presence of a number of recognized staff experts on the topic.

At the same time, as the Center's public stance on reconciliation would eventually note, the word "reconciliation" continued "to figure prominently both in the literature and the practice of transitional justice, despite a lack of consensus about what the term means, what activities it encompasses, or what achieving such a condition would require." Through the efforts of Pablo de

Greiff, in particular, in time the ICTJ moved in the direction of a basic organizational consensus, at least in terms of its public representations, coming to endorse a "civic trust model of reconciliation" that focused substantially on the trustworthiness of institutions, a conception of reconciliation that bore strong resemblance to an understanding de Greiff had himself personally articulated and defended in greater detail.[103] As the Center's public statement claimed, this was a conception of reconciliation would neither "lend itself to be offered as a substitute for justice," nor be "likely to lead to an inequitable burdening of victims," nor "rest on the idea that the slate has been wiped clean." It was an understanding of reconciliation that could be "articulated in terms that do not depend entirely on a particular set of religious beliefs," involving an approach that would "not require," although it might lead to, "forgiveness." On this conception, "reconciliation" became the name for "the condition under which citizens can once again trust one another." Put somewhat differently, trustworthy institutions were framed as a "precondition" of reconciliation. "It does not matter how much we talk about restorative justice, reconciliation, apologies, or pardons," the ICTJ statement concluded. "It is necessary to give citizens reasons to trust again. Only then can we properly conceive of reconciliation."[104]

Reconciliation Is a Heresy

In addition to his work on reconciliation—both as a scholar and as a senior staff member at ICTJ—Pablo de Greiff had also taken a significant interest in reparations, directing a large project on the topic in his capacity as the Center's director of research. One result was *The Handbook of Reparations,* the ICTJ volume that Desmond Tutu had come to New York City to help launch in the fall of 2006.[105] The handbook is a big doorstop of a book, weighing in at just over 1000 pages. Published by Oxford University Press, the book consists of contributions from a diverse group of authors. "The field of transitional justice," a note at the front of the book reminds readers, "is varied and covers a range of disciplines, including law, public policy, forensics, economics, history, psychology, and the arts." The volume's final 300 pages are dedicated to a compilation of primary documents and legislation, including excerpts from the reports of truth commissions in Argentina, Chile, El Salvador, Haiti, and South Africa. Those invited to contribute to the handbook included a handful of NGO program officers, two sociologists, a political scientist, an economist, a journalist, a research consultant, a cultural anthropologist, a clinical psychologist, a social psychologist, a psychotherapist, a philosopher, and the former Solicitor General of Argentina, Jaime Malamud-Goti. More than half of the book's 28 contributors were legal scholars, lawyers, or law professors.

Headlining the panel discussion of the handbook at New York University (NYU), Tutu was joined by two of NYU's law professors and two senior staff members of the ICTJ—de Greiff, the book's editor and central organizer, and Paul van Zyl, the South African lawyer and co-founder of ICTJ (who also regularly led courses on "transitional justice" at NYU). Almost predictably, during the Q & A session that followed the opening panel, *no one* asked about the book. All the questioners wanted to talk with Tutu. And, in response to a series of questions, Tutu began to tell stories of the TRC. He told the story of the Cradock Four, of the Guguletu Seven, and of the Bisho Massacre. Maybe this is why an archbishop was asked to chair the commission, he said, rather than "someone entirely legal"—to "remind us that each person has the potential to be a saint." Spoken into a silence that signaled a rapt and expectant audience, in a packed and palatial room at NYU, Tutu's stories—like his very bodily presence (the robe, the collar, the cross, and the legendary and charismatic Christian figure who wore them)—disrupted the secular liturgy of the book launch.[106] There was no big debate over reconciliation, no struggle—as there had been in the course of the TRC's public hearings—over the appropriateness of religious language and symbols in this secular space. "It does not matter," the ICTJ statement on reconciliation would later suggest, "how much we talk about restorative justice, reconciliation, apologies, or pardons." Tutu's words told a different story, and he was allowed his talk of saints, his tales of redemption, and his personal histories of healing truth. Yet the sense that the archbishop was not simply central to this gathering—as he incontestably was—but also, somewhat uncomfortably, an outsider to the institutional practices that had produced the massive tome the event was meant to introduce, was palpable.

As I sat there listening to Tutu elaborate what were by then familiar tales of suffering and hope, my eyes wandering the room in search of local luminaries or gazing at the ceiling high above, something else seemed amiss as well. It wasn't Tutu's admittedly affecting stories of the TRC—at times rendered disturbingly banal by their rampant repetition—that hit me. I was tracking back instead not one decade, but two, not to opening hearings of the TRC, but to the issuance of *The Kairos Document*, with its "prophetic theology," its critique of "*counterfeit* reconciliation," and its call for active participation in the struggle against apartheid. Tutu, I knew, had not signed that document, objecting to its negative characterization of "Church Theology." Yet he had also regularly employed the distinction between "true" and "false" reconciliation—between the "genuine" and the "counterfeit"—and he had long been a widely recognized voice for justice and a symbol of the liberation struggle, and not just among the Christian faithful.[107] A "phalanx of iniquitous laws," Tutu said in his 1984 Nobel Peace Prize Lecture, had propped up "apartheid's ideological racist dream." Until those laws were undone, he said, there would be no justice, and without justice there would be no peace: "We see before us a land bereft of much justice, and therefore without peace and security. Unrest is endemic, and will remain an unchanging feature of the South African scene until apartheid, the root cause of it all, is finally dismantled."[108]

Following Mandela's election, a decade after that lecture was given, Tutu's subsequent leadership of the TRC had made him a more controversial figure in international human rights circles, and in South Africa too—his moral authority muted and muddied by an association with truth commission amnesties laden with the language of forgiveness. Yet as he held sway among the legal scholars in New York, it seemed to me that his position—anchored by an unabashedly theological vocabulary and an emphasis on the ways that restoring justice and repairing the past were intimately bound up with the work of reconciliation and the promise of forgiveness—could still be construed as "prophetic." *The Kairos Document* had explicitly contrasted "prophetic theology" with its "academic" counterpart, and Tutu's own theological position was certainly "no mere academic exercise."[109] Yet that wasn't what set Tutu apart from those around him that day, many of whom had extended their own intellectual engagements well beyond the ivory tower—and in wondering about the potentially "prophetic" qualities of Tutu's current stance, I had in mind not the earlier critiques of the *kairos* theologians, but the sociological analyses of Weber and Bourdieu.[110]

More than 20 years after Tutu's Nobel Peace Prize Lecture and the subsequent signing and circulation of *The Kairos Document*, the struggles within which Tutu was embedded, and the terms in and through which they were carried out, had changed. In the aftermath of the TRC, with the continuing proliferation of truth commissions, an increasing institutionalization of the field of transitional justice, and striking new developments within international law—not to mention his own passage into a different stratosphere within the global elite—Tutu's critical interlocutors and arena of engagement had shifted. Those who actively opposed Tutu here and now, or were at least wary of his consistent recourse to the language of reconciliation, were no longer the defenders of the "iniquitous laws" of apartheid, but rather the promoters of a progressive program of "moral globalization," international law and human rights—fellow members of the "clergy" of world culture.[111] Tutu was in many ways one of them, but he was also dissident and divisive in this context, a critical and heterodox "prophet"—rather than an authority-wielding and orthodoxy-enforcing "priest" of world culture. For many of Tutu's cosmopolitan fellow travelers within the international human rights community, the "duty to prosecute" was a matter of orthodoxy, while assumptions about the dangers of religion were frequently simply tacitly assumed, assimilated as part of a larger framework that was often both unformulated and unchallenged. The "force of secularist spin" was strong.[112] In this milieu, to defend reconciliation—with its intimations of confession and forgiveness, and its associations with amnesty and impunity—was heresy.

And so, despite the international celebration of the TRC, and notwithstanding the vast proliferation of reconciliation discourse, I wondered whether Tutu and other proponents of reconciliation and political forgiveness weren't losing the battle for intellectual hegemony within the field. Piet Meiring had described the struggles over the role of religion in the South African TRC as "the *baruti* [pastors] versus the lawyers."[113] As the battlefield became transnational, were the lawyers—the new high priests of the human rights order—taking over?

Answering such a question, of course, requires more than simply assessing Desmond Tutu's personal trajectory. And, indeed, there has been more to the wider battle over reconciliation and transitional justice—in which I have situated Tutu—than the straightforward language of triumphs and losses would suggest. Likewise, the clash over truth and reconciliation cannot be adequately understood simply as a two-sided power struggle between pastors and lawyers, coded as "religious" and "secular." As the diversity of contributors to *The Handbook of Reparations* indicates, and as those within the field have themselves emphasized, the arena of transitional justice has called forth the participation of a remarkably interdisciplinary bunch.[114] While attempts have been made to sharpen its boundaries and more clearly define its core content, "transitional justice" marks out a diverse and diffuse discursive field, with borders touching on the complementary and competing discourses of "peacebuilding," "restorative justice," "conflict resolution," and justice in the aftermath of "mass atrocity." Indeed, the boundaries of transitional justice are fuzzy and contested at best, and even initially clear conceptions of the field and its limits, articulated among elite actors, have been repeatedly challenged—from within, from without, and along and within the field's borderlands. Border disputes have at times been keyed to disciplinary distinctions, and at times involved contestations over religion and secularity, yet they have also occasionally aligned with other forms of difference and disagreement. Nonetheless, "law" and "theology" are markers for two significant forces within the field, and—as the constellation of contributors to the ICTJ handbook also shows—law had by the time of its publication become a dominant force. Widespread aversion to the South African truth-for-amnesty arrangement can be read in this light.

What came together so powerfully in the South African TRC, however, was the close juxtaposition of both amnesty and forgiveness—or, in the eyes of the commission's many critics, impunity for human rights violations and politically suspect public religion. The language of reconciliation was the discursive linchpin that tied the two together, flying in the face of a hegemonic juridical framework that presumed the moral importance of prosecution and the ethical necessity of a strictly secular politics. The politics of reconciliation challenged, though it did not overturn, these presumptions. What had been a regularly taken-for-granted secularist framework—both within human rights circles and throughout the field of transitional justice, and indeed well beyond—was contested and subsequently more explicitly and persistently articulated, as defenders of transitional justice sought to distinguish themselves from both reconciliation's religious associations and its ostensibly compromised approach to justice, while critics of the field saw reconciliation's place within it as yet another cause for questioning the project of transitional justice itself.

In elite human rights organizations such as the ICTJ, "reconciliation" came to occupy an increasingly contested—and, in a complex way, somewhat marginalized—place. Even at the ICTJ, where reconciliation figured prominently in both the organization's founding and declared mission, the language of reconciliation was only partially assimilated, and proved difficult to institutionalize or fully incorporate. Unlike the cosmopolitan defense of "human rights," the promotion of reconciliation did not come to be seen as "a secular article of faith."[115] Nonetheless, over the course of the past decade and a half or so, there has been both a proliferation and a profusion of "reconciliation" discourse, as the meanings associated with the word have multiplied. New definitions, typologies, and visions of reconciliation have sprouted in the offices of NGOs, at international conferences, in the op-ed columns of prominent newspapers, and within the pages of academic books and journals—not to mention in the programmatic statements of newly emerging truth commissions. Some of these renderings of reconciliation have drawn substantially on the well-established religious affiliations of the word, while others have sought distance from its theological inflections and assumptions, pursuing instead an association with the wildly prolific tropes of "democracy," "human rights," and liberal "tolerance." At the same time, there has been no small amount of promiscuous mixing of reconciliation's various significations—indeed, the South African TRC's own representations of reconciliation had amounted to an only loosely unified amalgamation of meanings and associations—and this gave rise to the production of still further discursive hybrids.

In the midst of this profusion there has also been struggle—not simply between advocates of restorative justice and human rights activists firmly wedded to the widely cited "duty to prosecute" (although such debates have been considerable and significant), but also among the proponents of reconciliation themselves. As reconciliation became a significant topic of study and debate within North America, for example, a series of competing conceptions of reconciliation emerged, some vying for a central place within the growing field and others working its edges. From the perspective of both academic culture and the field of transitional justice, the politics of reconciliation have seemed to be both everywhere and yet stuck at the margins—and some of the most important struggles over reconciliation can be seen as boundary disputes within the field of transitional justice, being caught up in related debates over the meaning, shape, scope, and limits of the field itself.

It was in good part the international prominence of the South African TRC that brought concerns about the specifically "religious"—and, more particularly, Christian—connotations and assumptions of reconciliation discourse to the fore, especially within the growing discussions of transitional justice. It's not that these issues were absent from the debates in South Africa that accompanied the TRC. Such debates—interestingly and importantly—did occur. But as the TRC garnered increasing international attention, debates over its religious particularity proliferated, expanding well beyond South Africa's borders. Critiques of the overt religiosity associated with the South African quest for reconciliation eventually led to various attempts to transform the concept, with the aim of making it more widely, and less controversially, applicable to situations of national transition and the post-transition politics of peace and justice. Both Charles Villa-Vicencio's articulation of a "political" conception of reconciliation and Pablo de Greiff's elaboration of a conception of reconciliation as the condition under which "civic trust" is possible might be interpreted as significant examples of this trend.[116] Among those theories that focused substantially on individuals, more explicitly secular conceptions of reconciliation forwarded its potential associations with liberal "tolerance" as an antidote and preferable alternative to both the political valorization of "forgiveness" and the frequently ambiguous rhetoric of "national healing" (a rhetoric that sometimes mixed Christian discourses of reconciliation with more therapeutic tropes of personal and social repair).

The history of reconciliation's intimate associations with amnesty—and thus, in the eyes of some, with impunity—was a slightly different matter. For transnational activists and human rights lawyers whose activism was rooted especially in the context of Latin America, the aversion to the rhetoric of "reconciliation" was often a strong one—precisely because it was seen as just that, a rhetorical subterfuge intended to hide the grim reality of the state's failure to carry out its "duty to prosecute" perpetrators of human rights violations. The association of reconciliation with the history of impunity in Latin American countries such as Argentina and Chile was thus one important source of critical responses to the South African TRC, where the offer of amnesty was individualized and made demands of those who would apply for it, but resulted nonetheless in amnesty for some of the most notorious agents of the apartheid state. Politically, one activist scholar told me, the conjunction of "truth and reconciliation" in Latin America had sought to satisfy claims emanating from both ends of the political spectrum: "truth" was for "the left," and "reconciliation" for "the right."

Some would attempt to apply a similar logic to the South African situation, a comparison that threatened to miss the different trajectories and significations of reconciliation in that context. But the South African TRC's visions of reconciliation had seemingly made the prospect of political amnesty more palatable, and as a result both the TRC and its prominent conceptions of reconciliation became a lightning rod for debates over amnesty within the human rights movement, and within the "international community" more broadly. Reed Brody's diagnosis of a "South Africa problem" was one indication of this, and his concerns were widely shared by other advocates of the "prosecutorial approach."[117] While Brody would not forward a positive conception of reconciliation, when critics of the idea did approve a specific understanding of reconciliation, it was most often an ostensibly "secular" one—and, indeed, the unease or anger regarding reconciliation's association with amnesty frequently intersected with anxieties about its particularistic Christian vision of political forgiveness and national healing. Thus, efforts to loosen the grip of reconciliation's theological resonances and complicities—and in particular its strong association with forgiveness—sometimes went hand in hand with attempts to sever it from a close association with amnesty, or to critique it on the assumption that such a dissociation was relatively unviable.

Yet opposition to amnesty did not always overlap neatly with concerns about religion's place in the public sphere. While for some the essential problem with reconciliation was its use to justify various state failures to exercise a "duty to prosecute," for others the trouble was located elsewhere—not in reconciliation's associations with impunity, but in its established affiliations with Christian theology. Still others criticized reconciliation's terminological ties to social and political amnesia, bemoaned its insertion as a cheap substitute for wider programs of social justice, or simply decried its discursive ambiguity. With these and other critiques—along with subsequent defenses of reconciliation, involving both re-articulations of its older meanings and revisions of its contemporary possibilities—came new significations of the term, as reconciliation was seen as both a process and a goal, a concrete set of institutional practices and a lofty ideal, a theological master concept and a tool of political transition.

Even with the global celebration of the South African TRC, specifically theological conceptions of reconciliation continued to occupy a relatively uneasy place within an emerging and amorphously defined field of transitional justice. More common than defenses of such theologies—especially within the elite segments of the field—were critical efforts to tame, to contain, and to substantially reconceive reconciliation. Liberal theorists and political scientists looked both to secularize the concept of reconciliation and to render it as a dependent variable subject to social scientific investigation. Proponents of these two approaches (sometimes, but not always, intersecting) attempted to rend asunder what the South African TRC had so controversially joined—"reconciliation" and "forgiveness." Suggesting that forgiveness was not necessary for reconciliation—or, even more forcefully, that forgiveness represented a politically inappropriate and potentially illiberal aim, liberal theorists sought to constitute reconciliation as a scientifically definable end capable of being consistently pursued in a wide variety of transitional contexts. Here the theological language of forgiveness gave way to the liberal discourse of tolerance. If the results of these efforts were uneven, as specifically theological and at times anti-liberal discourses of reconciliation continued to circulate, they nonetheless illuminated powerful political currents and intellectual presuppositions within elite segments of transnational society. In their most familiar, forthrightly theological formulations, theories of reconciliation challenged the secular, broadly liberal orthodoxies that reigned within this sphere. Such theories represented the articulation of a distinctly heterodox position. In the broad shadows cast by the secular presumptions of cosmopolitan culture, the defense of reconciliation was tantamount to heresy.

Notes

1. For the figuring of leaders within the field of transitional justice—including, especially, staff members associated with the International Center for Transitional Justice—as part of the "truth commission mafia," see Lynda Richardson, "Helping Countries, and People, to Heal," *New York Times*, November 23, 2001.
2. For reference to the TRC as a "theatre of pain and catharsis," see Erik Doxtader and Philippe-Joseph Salazar, *Truth and Reconciliation in South Africa: The Fundamental Documents* (Cape Town: Institute for Justice and Reconciliation and David Philip, 2007), xi (citing an article in the *Mail & Guardian*). For many, this was a defining moment for the TRC. The TRC's deputy chairperson, Alex Boraine, recounted this testimony in his insider's account of the commission. He wrote that in the middle of her testimony, Nomonde Calata, the widow of Fort Calata (one of the "Cradock Four" murdered in the Eastern Cape in 1984), "broke down": "The primeval and spontaneous wail from the depths of her soul was carried live on radio and television, not only throughout South Africa but to many other parts of the world. It was that cry from the soul that transformed the hearings from a litany of suffering and pain to an even deeper level. It caught up in a single howl all the darkness and horror of the apartheid years." See Alex Boraine, *A Country Unmasked: Inside South Africa's Truth and Reconciliation Commission* (Oxford: Oxford University Press, 2000), 102. As Antjie Krog would write in her account of the commission, "For me this crying is the beginning of the Truth Commission—the signature tune, the definitive moment, the ultimate sound of what the process is about. She was wearing this vivid orange-red dress and she threw herself backward and that sound . . . that sound . . . it will haunt me for ever and ever." Antjie Krog, *Country of My Skull: Guilt, Sorrow, and the Limits of Forgiveness in the New South Africa*. (Johannesburg: Random House, 1998), 42. Piet Meiring recalled not only the crying and "anguished wails," but Tutu's response, which set the tone for the rest of the day, and in many respects for the rest of the life of

the commission: "Her anguished wails filled the hall. The audience and the Commissioners at the table were shocked into silence. When Tutu, after allowing a few minutes for Mrs. Calata to compose herself, needed to start the session again, he intoned in his own voice the Xhosa hymn *Senzeni na* ('What have we done?'). Everyone, even the journalists and security personnel, joined in the singing. Tears flowed. But the atmosphere was set for the rest of the day. The lesson was properly learnt and at many future meetings, in a particularly difficult situation, the singing of a hymn or prayer saved the day." Piet Meiring, "The Baruti versus the Lawyers: The Role of Religion in the TRC Process" in *Looking Back, Reaching Forward: Reflections on the Truth and Reconciliation Commission of South Africa*, ed. Charles Villa-Vicencio and Wilhelm Verwoerd (Cape Town: University of Cape Town Press, 2000), 126.

3. Charles Villa-Vicencio and Fanie du Toit, *Truth & Reconciliation in South Africa: 10 Years On* (Claremont, South Africa: New Africa Books, 2006), 86.
4. For a transcript of the symposium, convened as part of a conference on the "unfinished business" of the TRC, see Villa-Vicencio and du Toit 2006: 8–15.
5. Pablo de Greiff, ed., *The Handbook of Reparations* (Oxford: Oxford University Press, 2006).
6. Michael Ignatieff, *Human Rights as Politics and Idolatry* (Princeton: Princeton University Press, 2001), 78.
7. Charles Taylor, "Conditions of an Unforced Consensus on Human Rights" in *Dilemmas and Connections: Selected Essays* (Cambridge, MA: Harvard University Press, 2011), 107.
8. The increasing associations between reconciliation and restorative justice in the international arena were due in no small part to the conjunction of reconciliation and restorative justice by leading members of the South African TRC, who had themselves been attentive to work on the concept of restorative justice, as it received increasing attention in the early and mid-1990s. On the history of theories of restorative justice, see Daniel W. Van Ness and Karen Heetderks Strong, *Restoring Justice: An Introduction to Restorative Justice* (Cincinnati: Anderson Publishing Company, 2010), 21–40. For a critical consideration of the relationship between restorative justice and transitional justice, see Jennifer J. Llewellyn, "Restorative Justice in Transitions and Beyond: The Justice Potential of Truth-Telling Mechanisms for Post-Peace Accord Societies" in *Telling the Truths: Truth Telling and Peace Building in Post-Conflict Societies*, ed. Tristan Anne Borer (Notre Dame: University of Notre Dame Press, 2006), 83–114.
9. Jonathan Tepperman, "Truth and Consequences." *Foreign Affairs* 81 (2002): 134.
10. Michael O. Hardimon, *Hegel's Social Philosophy: The Project of Reconciliation* (Cambridge: Cambridge University Press, 1994): 85–87.
11. For "new language of social order," see William Sewell, "Historical Events as Transformations of Structures: Inventing Revolution at the Bastille," *Theory and Society* 25 (1996): 847.
12. Report of the UN Secretary-General, "The Rule of Law and Transitional Justice in Conflict and Post-Conflict Societies," UN doc. S/2004/616 (2004): 17. The report emphasized the importance of accountability through individual prosecutions, truth-telling, vetting and institutional reform, and the delivery of reparations. For an account of these emphases as central to the emergence of the field of transitional justice, see Paige Arthur, "How 'Transitions' Reshaped Human Rights: A Conceptual History of Transitional Justice," *Human Rights Quarterly* 31, no. 2 (May 2009): 321–367.
13. While "commissions of inquiry" had been the most common framework for these commissions when Priscilla Hayner wrote an early article on truth commissions in the mid-1990s, a decade later the field had shifted, and the frame of "truth and reconciliation" had become more much prominent, though there remained variety and complex specificity across different institutions and cases. This is not to say that all of the newer commissions prized reconciliation equally or conceived of it in the same way, and there continued to be great and important institutional diversity in this respect. Yet as a list of truth commissions produced by Amnesty International suggests, something had shifted. For Hayner's early article, see Priscilla B. Hayner, "Fifteen Truth Commissions, 1974–1994: A Comparative Study," *Human Rights Quarterly* 16 (1994): 597–655. For Amnesty International's list of truth commissions, see: http://www.amnesty.org/en/international-justice/issues/truth-commissions. Even at the moment of its initial publication, however, Amnesty's list would not have been universally recognized as definitive and complete. Conceived as a tool of transitional

justice, the "truth commission" is a relatively recent institutional invention, and within the field of transitional justice and beyond there is no small amount of confusion and struggle over its precise definition.

14. For more on this quite specific conception of "historical events," see William Sewell, "Historical Events as Transformations of Structures: Inventing Revolution at the Bastille," *Theory and Society* 25, 1996.
15. Thus, it is not that all of the subsequent truth commissions were suddenly following the lead of the South Africans, mimicking the TRC in every respect, or even being encouraged to do so. Rather, when the possibility of a new commission was identified, South Africa's TRC was frequently the most widely discussed starting point, the commission everyone was talking about.
16. As cited in Priscilla B. Hayner, *Unspeakable Truths: Confronting State Terror and Atrocity: How Truth Commissions around the World Are Challenging the Past and Shaping the Future* (New York: Routledge, 2001), 41.
17. Erik Doxtader, *With Faith in the Works of Words: The Beginnings of Reconciliation in South Africa, 1985–1995* (East Lansing: Michigan State University Press, 2009), 201.
18. As quoted in Erik Doxtader, *With Faith in the Works of Words: The Beginnings of Reconciliation in South Africa, 1985–1995* (East Lansing: Michigan State University Press, 2009), 213.
19. Martha Minow, *Between Vengeance and Forgiveness: Facing History after Genocide and Mass Violence*, (Boston: Beacon Press, 1998), 52. Erik Doxtader, *With Faith in the Works of Words: The Beginnings of Reconciliation in South Africa, 1985–1995* (East Lansing: Michigan State University Press, 2009), 9, 72.
20. Michael Battle, *Reconciliation: The Ubuntu Theology of Desmond Tutu* (Cleveland, OH: Pilgrim Press, 1997), 5.
21. Justin Neuman, "Ubuntu, Reconciliation, and the Buffered Self," The Immanent Frame, Social Science Research Council (2010), http://blogs.ssrc.org/tif/2010/06/07/ubuntu-reconciliation/. Note, however, that Neuman brackets "questions about whether descriptions of ubuntu should be taken as empirical claims about actually existing social norms or are, rather, better seen as utopian longings."
22. Desmond Tutu, *No Future without Forgiveness* (New York: Doubleday, 1999), 31.
23. As cited in Michael Battle, *Reconciliation: The Ubuntu Theology of Desmond Tutu* (Cleveland, OH: Pilgrim Press, 1997), vii.
24. See Desmond Tutu, "Viability" in *Relevant Theology for Africa*, ed. Hans-Jurgen Becken (Durban, South Africa: Lutheran Publishing House, 1973), 38.
25. Justin Neuman, "Ubuntu, Reconciliation, and the Buffered Self," The Immanent Frame, Social Science Research Council (2010), http://blogs.ssrc.org/tif/2010/06/07/ubuntu-reconciliation/.
26. For a more detailed discussion of the post-amble and its centrality in South African discussions of reconciliation, see Erik Doxtader, *With Faith in the Works of Words: The Beginnings of Reconciliation in South Africa, 1985–1995* (East Lansing: Michigan State University Press, 2009).
27. Desmond Tutu, *No Future Without Forgiveness* (New York: Doubleday, 1999), 151.
28. Antjie Krog, *Country of My Skull: Guilt, Sorrow, and the Limits of Forgiveness in the New South Africa* (Johannesburg: Random House, 1998), 201.
29. Susan VanZanten Gallagher, *Truth and Reconciliation: The Confessional Mode in South African Literature* (Portsmouth, NH: Heinemann, 2002), 44. Gallagher's invocation of "confession" is meant to extend not simply to the sorts of confessions made in front of the TRC, but rather to a "confessional mode" that includes, in this context, theological statements and declarations.
30. The Kairos Theologians, *The Kairos Document: A Challenge to the Church*, revised 2nd ed. (Grand Rapids, MI: William B. Eerdmans, 1987).
31. Pumla Gobodo-Madikizela, *A Human Being Died That Night: A South African Story of Forgiveness* (Boston: Houghton Mifflin, 2003), 53. For a detailed consideration of the theology of apartheid and various theological responses to it, see Erik Doxtader, *With Faith in the Works of Words: The Beginnings of Reconciliation in South Africa, 1985–1995* (East Lansing: Michigan State University Press, 2009): 35–84.

32. John De Gruchy, *Reconciliation: Restoring Justice* (Cape Town: David Philip, 2002), 33, 34.
33. Tristan Borer, *Challenging the State: Churches as Political Actors in South Africa, 1980–1994* (Notre Dame, IN: University of Notre Dame Press, 1998), 91.
34. For an extensive discussion of the "spiral of involvement," and of the theological developments that accompanied it, see Tristan Borer, *Challenging the State: Churches as Political Actors in South Africa, 1980–1994* (Notre Dame, IN: University of Notre Dame Press, 1998).
35. Tristan Borer, *Challenging the State: Churches as Political Actors in South Africa, 1980–1994* (Notre Dame, IN: University of Notre Dame Press, 1998), 98–99.
36. Tristan Borer, *Challenging the State: Churches as Political Actors in South Africa, 1980–1994* (Notre Dame, IN: University of Notre Dame Press, 1998), 108.
37. The TRC report would borrow this notion of "state theology" in its consideration of the role of "faith communities as agents of oppression." See *Truth and Reconciliation Commission of South Africa Report*, vol. 4: 69.
38. Tristan Borer, *Challenging the State: Churches as Political Actors in South Africa, 1980–1994* (Notre Dame, IN: University of Notre Dame Press, 1998), 109.
39. For this statement from *The Kairos Document*, see Robert McAfee Brown, ed., *Kairos: Three Prophetic Challenges to the Church* (Grand Rapids, MI: Eerdmans Publishing, 1990), 38. Emphasis in the original. See also: The Kairos Theologians, *The Kairos Document: A Challenge to the Church*, revised 2nd ed. (Grand Rapids, MI: William B. Eerdmans, 1987). A copy of the document's text is also included in Erik Doxtader and Philippe-Joseph Salazar, *Truth and Reconciliation in South Africa: The Fundamental Documents* (Cape Town: Institute for Justice and Reconciliation and David Philip, 2007), 50–56. On *The Kairos Document*, see R. Scott Appleby, *The Ambivalence of the Sacred: Religion, Violence, and Reconciliation* (Lanham, MD: Rowman & Littlefield, 2000), 34–40; Tristan Borer, *Challenging the State: Churches as Political Actors in South Africa, 1980–1994* (Notre Dame, IN: University of Notre Dame Press, 1998), 108–110; Russell Botman, "'Dutch' and Reformed and 'Black' and Reformed in South Africa: A Tale of Two Traditions on the Move to Unity and Responsibility" in *Keeping Faith: Embracing the Tensions in Christian Higher Education*, ed. Ronald A. Wells (Grand Rapids, MI: William B. Eerdmans, 1996), 85–105; Erik Doxtader, "In the Name of Reconciliation: The Faith and Works of Counterpublicity" in *Counterpublics and the State*, ed. Robert Asen and Daniel C. Brouwer (Albany: State University of New York Press, 2001); Erik Doxtader, *With Faith in the Works of Words: The Beginnings of Reconciliation in South Africa, 1985–1995* (East Lansing: Michigan State University Press, 2009); and Susan VanZanten Gallagher, *Truth and Reconciliation: The Confessional Mode in South African Literature* (Portsmouth, NH: Heinemann, 2002).
40. Erik Doxtader, *With Faith in the Works of Words: The Beginnings of Reconciliation in South Africa, 1985–1995* (East Lansing: Michigan State University Press, 2009), 36. Robert McAfee Brown, editor, *Kairos: Three Prophetic Challenges to the Church*. (Grand Rapids, MI: Eerdmans Publishing, 1990), 49.
41. Nicolas Tavuchis, *Mea Culpa: A Sociology of Apology and Reconciliation* (Stanford, CA: Stanford University Press, 1991), 87–88.
42. Erik Doxtader and Philippe-Joseph Salazar, *Truth and Reconciliation in South Africa: The Fundamental Documents* (Cape Town: Institute for Justice and Reconciliation and David Philip, 2007), 99.
43. Erik Doxtader and Philippe-Joseph Salazar, *Truth and Reconciliation in South Africa: The Fundamental Documents* (Cape Town: Institute for Justice and Reconciliation and David Philip, 2007), 100.
44. Wendy Brown, *Edgework: Critical Essays on Knowledge and Politics* (Princeton, NJ: Princeton University Press, 2005), 5, 7.
45. John De Gruchy, *Reconciliation: Restoring Justice* (Cape Town: David Philip, 2002), 2.
46. Erik Doxtader, *With Faith in the Works of Words: The Beginnings of Reconciliation in South Africa, 1985–1995* (East Lansing: Michigan State University Press, 2009), 80.
47. "Reconciliation" does have a longer history in South Africa. I have not attempted to trace that history here. For more detail, see John De Gruchy, *Reconciliation: Restoring Justice* (Cape Town:

David Philip, 2002); and Erik Doxtader, *With Faith in the Works of Words: The Beginnings of Reconciliation in South Africa, 1985–1995* (East Lansing: Michigan State University Press, 2009).
48. Richard H. Bell, *Understanding African Philosophy: A Cross-Cultural Approach to Classical and Contemporary Issues* (New York: Routledge, 2002), 86.
49. Tristan Borer, *Challenging the State: Churches as Political Actors in South Africa, 1980–1994* (Notre Dame, IN: University of Notre Dame Press, 1998), 121.
50. Ginger Thompson, "South African Commission Ends Its Work," *New York Times*, March 22, 2003.
51. Tutu's emphasis on the connection between reconciliation and reparations was written into the final report of the South African TRC, which invoked a conception of "restorative justice" that linked the concepts of reparation and restoration, and he would regularly appeal to the concept of restorative justice when faced with criticisms that the TRC had sacrificed justice in favor of a weak reconciliation and a partial truth. *Truth and Reconciliation Commission of South Africa Report* (Cape Town: Truth and Reconciliation Commission, 1998). At the same time, the report's discussion of truth and reconciliation moved almost seamlessly back and forth between references to "reconciliation" and references to "forgiveness," at times treating the two as if they were inextricably intertwined or even simply interchangeable. Citing a "remarkable magnanimity and generosity of spirit" on the part of those who had "suffered gross violations of their human rights," the commissioners located such generosity not only in the willingness of victims and survivors to "display their pain to the world," but also in a "willingness to forgive" (vol. 1: 116). Indeed, a substantial segment of the report's chapter on "reconciliation"—included in volume 5—involved "remarkable evidence" of this "willingness to forgive" (vol. 5: 371–382). While the TRC report closely associated forgiveness and reconciliation, however, and emphasized the stories of apology and forgiveness that had become a part of the commission's process, the report also warned that forgiveness and reconciliation should not simply be conflated. "It is also crucial not to fall into the error of equating forgiveness with reconciliation," wrote the commissioners. "The road to reconciliation requires more than forgiveness and respectful remembrance" (vol. 1: 117). Indeed, forgiveness itself should not be misunderstood. In response to calls to "close the book on the past"—and perhaps in response to criticisms of its constitution of anti-apartheid activists as "victims"—the commission warned that forgiveness could not be about "forgetting." It was rather a matter of "seeking to forego bitterness, renouncing resentment, moving past old hurt, and becoming a survivor rather than a passive victim" (vol. 1: 116). During a presentation at the University of California, Berkeley, Pamela Reynolds reported that many of the South African youths she interviewed refused to take part in the TRC process, seeing themselves as activists and survivors rather than "victims." From yet another angle, in responding to those who recommended taking up a forgetful rendering of the past, the Commissioners might just as well have been responding to sentiments similar to those voiced by TRC Commissioner Wynand Malan. In his Minority Position (included in volume 5 of the TRC report), Malan attempted to reframe the prerequisites of reconciliation this way: "If we can reframe our history to include both perpetrators and victims as victims of the ultimate perpetrator—namely, the conflict of the past, we will have fully achieved unity and reconciliation and an awareness of the real threat to our future—which is dogmatic or ideological division that polarises the nation instead of promoting genuine political activity" (vol. 5: 443).
52. *Truth and Reconciliation Commission of South Africa Report* (Cape Town: Truth and Reconciliation Commission, 1998), vol. 1: 1.
53. Tanya Goodman, *Staging Solidarity: Truth and Reconciliation in a New South Africa* (Boulder, CO: Paradigm Publishers, 2009), 30–32. A substantial proportion of the TRC's national and international impact, Deborah Posel has written, "derives from one critical element in the commission's range of procedures and performances—namely, its public hearings on gross human rights violations and amnesty. It was these public hearings, televised to millions nationally and internationally, that captured the public imagination and in retrospect, as much as at the time, have become something of a symbolic précis for the TRC as a whole." Deborah Posel, "History as Confession: The Case of the South African Truth and Reconciliation Commission," *Public Culture* 20:1 (2008): 131. For a discussion of the importance of the media in the circulation of such stories,

Reconciliation as Heterodoxy 113

see Tanya Goodman, *Staging Solidarity: Truth and Reconciliation in a New South Africa* (Boulder: Paradigm Publishers, 2009), 73–98. As Teresa Godwin Phelps writes: "The hearings spawned many articles and entire books, thereby creating another level of storytelling: the stories that were told about the process and about the people who observed the process." Teresa Godwin Phelps, *Shattered Voices: Language, Violence, and the Work of Truth Commissions* (Philadelphia: University of Pennsylvania Press, 2004), 108.

54. Ebrahim Moosa, "Truth and Reconciliation as Performance: Spectres of Eucharistic Redemption" in *Looking Back, Reaching Forward: Reflections on the Truth and Reconciliation Commission of South Africa*, ed. Charles Villa-Vicencio and Wilhelm Verwoerd (Cape Town: University of Cape Town Press, 2000), 117.

55. Piet Meiring, "The Baruti versus the Lawyers: The Role of Religion in the TRC Process" in *Looking Back, Reaching Forward: Reflections on the Truth and Reconciliation Commission of South Africa*, ed. Charles Villa-Vicencio and Wilhelm Verwoerd (Cape Town: University of Cape Town Press, 2000), 124–126. Meiring refers to a "friendly debate" between the *baruti* (pastors) and the lawyers on the commission.

56. Deborah Posel, "History as Confession: The Case of the South African Truth and Reconciliation Commission," *Public Culture* 20: 1 (2008): 131. Philip Bonner and Noor Nieftagodien, "The Truth and Reconciliation Commission and the Pursuit of 'Social Truth': The Case of Kathorus" in *Commissioning the Past: Understanding South Africa's Truth and Reconciliation Commission*, ed. Deborah Posel and Graeme Simpson (Johannesburg: Witwatersrand University Press, 2002), 173.

57. The TRC report distinguished between four different notions of truth: factual or forensic truth; personal or narrative truth; social or "dialogue" truth; and healing and restorative truth. See *Truth and Reconciliation Commission of South Africa Report* (Cape Town: Truth and Reconciliation Commission, 1998), vol. 1: 110–114. For discussion of this "rainbow of truths," and an argument that it represents "a very wobbly, poorly constructed conceptual grid," see Deborah Posel, "The TRC Report: What Kind of History? What Kind of Truth?" in *Commissioning the Past: Understanding South Africa's Truth and Reconciliation Commission*, ed. Deborah Posel and Graeme Simpson (Johannesburg: Witwatersrand University Press, 2002), 147–172.

58. Mark Freeman, *Truth Commissions and Procedural Fairness* (Cambridge: Cambridge University Press, 2006), 24.

59. Tanya Goodman, *Staging Solidarity: Truth and Reconciliation in a New South Africa* (Boulder, CO: Paradigm Publishers, 2009), 62.

60. Deborah Posel, "History as Confession: The Case of the South African Truth and Reconciliation Commission," *Public Culture* 20: 1 (2008): 134.

61. Tutu as cited in Giuliana Lund, "'Healing the Nation': Metacolonial Discourses and the State of Emergency from Apartheid to Truth and Reconciliation," *Cultural Critique* 54 (2003): 88–119.

62. Deborah Posel, "History as Confession: The Case of the South African Truth and Reconciliation Commission," *Public Culture* 20 (1), (2008): 135.

63. Leigh A. Payne, *Unsettling Accounts: Neither Truth nor Reconciliation in Confessions of State Violence* (Durham, NC: Duke University Press, 2008), 70.

64. In addition to full disclosure, "The Promotion of National Unity and Reconciliation Act" of 1995 also required that "the act, omission or offence to which the application relates is an act associated with a political objective committed in the course of the conflicts of the past." Erik Doxtader and Philippe-Joseph Salazar, *Truth and Reconciliation in South Africa: The Fundamental Documents* (Cape Town: Institute for Justice and Reconciliation and David Philip, 2007), 19. But it did not require remorse. In a classic sociological account of apology, Erving Goffman once figured apologies as ploys of self-castigation and self-derogation, suggesting that "apologies represent a splitting of the self into a blameworthy part and a part that stands back and sympathizes with the blame giving, and, by implication, is worthy of being brought back into the fold." Erving Goffman, *Relations in Public: Microstudies of the Public Order* (New York: Basic Books, 1971), 113. As Nicolas Tavuchis notes, there is no discussion of sorrow or regret in Goffman's account of apology. "Thus," writes Tavuchis, "it is conceivable that an actor could follow all the steps described by Goffman

without producing a speech act that is socially recognizable as an apology or, its moral reciprocal, forgiveness." Nicolas Tavuchis, *Mea Culpa: A Sociology of Apology and Reconciliation* (Stanford, CA: Stanford University Press, 1991), 138.

65. Colonel Schobesberger's testimony was reproduced in the TRC report's section on "apologies and acknowledgements." *Truth and Reconciliation Commission of South Africa Report* (Cape Town: Truth and Reconciliation Commission, 1998), vol. 5: 382.

66. Antjie Krog, *Country of My Skull: Guilt, Sorrow, and the Limits of Forgiveness in the New South Africa* (Johannesburg: Random House, 1998), 202. See also: Susan VanZanten Gallagher, *Truth and Reconciliation: The Confessional Mode in South African Literature* (Portsmouth, NH: Heinemann, 2002); and Piet Meiring, "The Baruti versus the Lawyers: the Role of Religion in the TRC process" in *Looking Back, Reaching Forward: Reflections on the Truth and Reconciliation Commission of South Africa*, ed. Charles Villa-Vicencio and Wilhelm Verwoerd (Cape Town: University of Cape Town Press, 2000).

67. For the concepts and principles see *Truth and Reconciliation Commission of South Africa Report* (Cape Town: Truth and Reconciliation Commission, 1998), vol. 1, chapter 5. For *ubuntu* and restorative justice, see vol. 1: 125–131.

68. As quoted in Martha Minow, *Between Vengeance and Forgiveness: Facing History after Genocide and Mass Violence* (Boston: Beacon Press, 1998), 55. For an account that emphasizes, alternatively, that "a day at the TRC does contain much religious symbolism and rhetoric," much of which "arises spontaneously from the victims," see Susan VanZanten Gallagher, *Truth and Reconciliation: The Confessional Mode in South African Literature* (Portsmouth, NH: Heinemann, 2002), 119.

69. Henry J. Steiner, ed. *Truth Commissions: A Comparative Assessment.* (Cambridge: World Peace Foundation, 1997), 51.

70. For "intangible sacrament," see Naomi Roht-Arriaza, "The Need for Moral Reconstruction in the Wake of Past Human Rights Violations: An Interview with José Zalaquett" in *Human Rights in Political Transitions: Gettysburg to Bosnia*, ed. Carla Hesse and Robert Post (New York: Zone Books, 1999), 209.

71. For "relatively novel field," see Pablo de Greiff, ed. *The Handbook of Reparations* (Oxford: Oxford University Press, 2006), xi.

72. For example, see Timothy Garton Ash, "The Truth About Dictatorship," *The New York Review of Books*, February 19, 1998. For discussion, Paige Arthur, "How 'Transitions' Reshaped Human Rights: A Conceptual History of Transitional Justice," *Human Rights Quarterly* 31, no. 2 (May 2009): 321–367.

73. At the same time, the field's boundaries have remained ambiguous, its key terms have been contested from within and without, and important critiques and redefinitions of reconciliation have been hatched along and across its borders. In this interstitial space of networked collaboration and discursive struggle, and through the efforts of the prominent theorists and practitioners who have been its worldwide promoters and critics, hybrid discourses of reconciliation have been altered and adapted to suit various political values, institutional purposes, intellectual orientations, and academic perspectives. While elsewhere I have attempted to track some of the post-TRC discourses of reconciliation, here I focus primarily on the tentative handling of reconciliation on the part of ICTJ.

74. "From the President," ICTJ Annual Report 2006–2007: 1.

75. http://www.ictj.org/en/about/mission/.

76. Priscilla B. Hayner, *Unspeakable Truths: Confronting State Terror and Atrocity: How Truth Commissions around the World are Challenging the Past and Shaping the Future* (New York: Routledge, 2001).

77. ICTJ Annual Report 2001–2002: 5.

78. ICTJ Annual Report 2001–2002: 9, 3. See also: "A Holistic Approach to TJ," ICTJ Annual Report, 2006–2007: 4–5; and Alexander L. Boraine, "Transitional Justice: A Holistic Interpretation," *Journal of International Affairs* 60: 1, 2006: 17–27.

79. William Korey, *Taking on the World's Repressive Regimes: The Ford Foundation's International Human Rights Policies and Practices* (New York: Palgrave Macmillan, 2007), 259. Ford's support

of ICTJ built on and extended earlier Foundation support for initiatives engaged in "dealing with the past." For details on Ford's earlier work in this area, see "Memory and Justice: Confronting Past Atrocity and Human Rights Abuse," International Center for Transitional Justice, August 2008.
80. While the ICTJ's work sought to ensure that countries interested in establishing truth commissions and working to implement other mechanisms of transitional justice will not have to "reinvent the wheel," the Center also regularly emphasized that each transitional situation must be seen as unique, and transitional justice mechanisms developed accordingly. Constituting a diverse group that harbored its own potent disagreements, the ICTJ staff had come to represent not simply global moral entrepreneurs of truth and reconciliation at any cost, but rather influential international managers of the complex and often contentious and controversial national and international processes that give rise to truth commissions and other approaches to justice in transition. While some would represent the Center as a group collectively lodged somewhere in between hard-nosed advocates of a universal duty to prosecute and prophets of social reconciliation highlighting the healing power of forgiveness, in reality the ICTJ staff included representatives of both of these two (at times opposing) positions, though the majority tilted toward what Leebaw had earlier called the "prosecutorial approach." Bronwyn Leebaw, *Judging the Past: Truth, Justice, and Reconciliation from Nuremberg to South Africa* (PhD diss., Department of Political Science, University of California, Berkeley, 2002).
81. William Korey, *Taking on the World's Repressive Regimes: The Ford Foundation's International Human Rights Policies and Practices* (New York: Palgrave Macmillan, 2007), 261.
82. Aryeh Neier, "Do Trials Work?" *The New York Review of Books*, October 19, 1995.
83. William Korey, *Taking on the World's Repressive Regimes: The Ford Foundation's International Human Rights Policies and Practices* (New York: Palgrave Macmillan, 2007), 260, 262.
84. Paige Arthur, "How 'Transitions' Reshaped Human Rights: A Conceptual History of Transitional Justice," *Human Rights Quarterly* 31, no. 2 (May 2009): 321–367.
85. For Boraine on the "converging streams," see Alexander Boraine, "A Holistic Approach to TJ," ICTJ Annual Report, 2006–2007: 4–5. "Boraine Takes Lessons of SA Miracle to World" read the headline in the Cape Argus, a newspaper in Alex Boraine's hometown. And, in fact, initial media attention on the ICTJ focused almost exclusively on truth commissions: "Can the Truth Heal a Nation's Wounds?," *Financial Times* (June 16, 2001); Tamar Lewin, "For Nations Traumatized by the Past, New Remedies," *New York Times* (July 29, 2001); Nora Boustany, "Promoting Truth as Antidote In a World of Brutality," *Washington Post* (August 3, 2001); Tim Johnson, "Eager for justice, Peru turns to truth commission," *The Miami Herald* (August 20, 2001); Lynda Richardson, "Helping Countries, and People, to Heal," *New York Times* (November 23, 2001); Tina Rosenberg, "Designer Truth Commissions," *New York Times Magazine* (December 9, 2001).
86. Jonathan Tepperman, "Truth and Consequences," *Foreign Affairs* 81, (2002): 128–145.
87. ICTJ Annual Report, 2001–2002: 7, 11, 18, 21
88. See Lynda Richardson, "Helping Countries, and People, to Heal," *New York Times*, November 23, 2001.
89. On the "duty to prosecute," see Diane F. Orentlicher, "Settling Accounts: The Duty to Prosecute Human Rights Violations of a Prior Regime," *The Yale Law Journal* 100: 8 (1991): 2537–2615.
90. Lynda Richardson, "Helping Countries, and People, to Heal," *New York Times*, November 23, 2001. Nonetheless, the perception that ICTJ was "in part formed with the aim of disseminating the South African experience" has been a durable one. For this particular formulation, see Christine Bell, "Transitional Justice, Interdisciplinarity and the State of the 'Field' or 'Non-Field'" in *International Journal of Transitional Justice* 3: 5–27 (2009), 9.
91. ICTJ Annual Report, 2001–2002.
92. Alex Boraine, *A Country Unmasked: Inside South Africa's Truth and Reconciliation Commission* (Oxford: Oxford University Press, 2000).
93. Tim Johnson, "Eager for Justice, Peru Turns to Truth commission," *The Miami Herald* (August 20, 2001).
94. Priscilla B. Hayner, *Unspeakable Truths: Confronting State Terror and Atrocity: How Truth Commissions around the World are Challenging the Past and Shaping the Future* (New York: Routledge, 2001), 250–251.

95. In March 2010, David Tolbert, a former deputy chief prosecutor of the International Criminal Tribunal for the former Yugoslavia (ICTY), was named ICTJ's new president.
96. "Lessons to Be Learned," *Transitions*, International Center for Transitional Justice, January 2009: 1.
97. ICTJ annual report, 2006/2007: 27.
98. "Lessons from South Africa," ICTJ annual report, 2006/2007: 26–27.
99. Bronwyn Leebaw, *Judging the Past: Truth, Justice, and Reconciliation from Nuremberg to South Africa*, (PhD diss., Department of Political Science, University of California, Berkeley, 2002), 1, 168. Leebaw "charts the evolution of two distinct approaches to transitional justice: the prosecutorial approach, championed by most human rights organizations, and the 'restorative' approach, developed by South African leaders," figuring the 1983 Argentine transition as the "turning point for the human rights movement" that led to the development of the two distinct approaches. "The unprecedented effort to investigate and prosecute human rights violations committed under a prior regime," she writes, "brought together a network of human rights organizations to develop mechanisms to facilitate the prosecution of systematic atrocities. At the same time, the conflicts that derailed Argentina's transitional prosecutions led human rights advocates to debate the meaning of, and relationship between, the values of justice and reconciliation in the context of political transition. Some, such as José Zalaquett, argued that local reconciliation efforts would benefit human rights goals. However, most human rights advocates, including Juan Mendez of Americas Watch, rejected the case for political compromise and began to argue that international human rights law should transcend local struggles" (153–154).
100. Juan Méndez, "Memorandum," Workshop on Religion, Reconciliation and Transitional Justice, Social Science Research Council, May 2, 2008.
101. For "the saccharin-coated invocations of reconciliation," see Richard A. Wilson, *The Politics of Truth and Reconciliation in South Africa: Legitimizing the Post-Apartheid State* (Cambridge: Cambridge University Press, 2001).
102. An initial focus on "promoting" reconciliation in ICTJ's Mission Statement was subsequently shifted to "advancing reconciliation" (ICTJ Annual Report, 2002–2003; ICTJ Annual Report 2003–2004), and then to "facilitating reconciliation processes" (ICTJ Annual Report 2004–2005; ICTJ Annual Report 2006–2007). The other four "key elements" included in ICTJ's Mission Statement (nearly identical in both the 2001–2002 and 2006–2007 Annual Reports) matched the transitional justice measures outlined earlier (while omitting the removal of human rights abusers from positions of power): "prosecuting perpetrators, documenting and acknowledging violations through nonjudicial means such as truth commissions, reforming abusive institutions, providing reparations to victims."
103. Pablo de Greiff, "The Role of Apologies in National Reconciliation Processes: On Making Trustworthy Institutions Trusted" in *The Age of Apology: Facing Up to the Past*, ed. Mark Gibney, Rhoda E. Howard-Hassmann, Jean-Marc Coicaud, and Niklaus Steiner, 120–136 (Philadelphia: University of Pennsylvania Press, 2008), 120–136.
104. See http://www.ictj.org. See also: ICTJ Annual Report 2004–2005.
105. Pablo de Greiff, ed., *The Handbook of Reparations* (Oxford: Oxford University Press, 2006). As with reconciliation, the scholarly literature on reparations is substantial. For a dissection of the "anatomy of reparations politics," see John Torpey, *Making Whole What Has Been Smashed: On Reparations Politics* (Cambridge, MA: Harvard University Press, 2006). On reparations in South Africa, see Erik Doxtader and Charles Villa-Vicencio, eds., *The Repair the Irreparable: Reparation and Reconstruction in South Africa* (Claremont, South Africa: New Africa Books, 2004).
106. For a discussion of "secular liturgies," see James K.A. Smith, "Secular Liturgies and the Prospects for a 'Post-Secular' Sociology of Religion" in *The Post-Secular in Question*, ed. Philip Gorski, David Kyuman Kim, John Torpey, and Jonathan Van Antwerpen (New York: New York University Press, 2012).
107. False reconciliation was also figured as "anaemic" or "cheap." In an earlier address, for example, Tutu had criticized "an attenuated doctrine of reconciliation," which sought to "avoid confrontation at all costs," claiming that reconciliation was "no easy option," nor did it "rule out confrontation." Advocates of an "anaemic reconciliation" did not want to mix religion with politics. But an

examination of the "biblical evidence," Tutu said, required recognizing that "just as there can be no cheap grace so there can be no cheap reconciliation." Desmond Tutu, *Hope and Suffering* (Grand Rapids, MI: William B. Eerdmans, 1984), 38.

108. Erik Doxtader and Philippe-Joseph Salazar, *Truth and Reconciliation in South Africa: The Fundamental Documents* (Cape Town: Institute for Justice and Reconciliation and David Philip, 2007), 46, 48.

109. The Kairos Theologians, *The Kairos Document: A Challenge to the Church*, revised 2nd ed. (Grand Rapids, MI: William B. Eerdmans, 1987), 17.

110. For a critical discussion of Bourdieu's understanding of doxa, orthodoxy, and heterodoxy, to which I am alluding here, see John Guillory, *Cultural Capital: The Problem of Literary Canon Formation* (Chicago: University of Chicago Press, 1995). Bourdieu elaborates the opposition between orthodoxy and heterodoxy (or "heresy") via a reworking of Weber's distinction between "prophets" and "priests." See Pierre Bourdieu, "Legitimation and Structured Interests in Weber's Sociology of Religion" in *Max Weber, Rationality and Modernity*, ed. Sam Whimster and Scott Lash (Boston: Allen and Unwin, 1987), 119–136. To be clear, I invoke these distinctions here—along with the related opposition between "orthodoxy" and "heresy"—to indicate the terms of struggle over power and authority, not in the religious field, but in the wider field of conflict and contestation in which discourses of reconciliation have been mobilized, critiqued, and reconfigured. As Swartz writes, the "fundamental structure of conflict" between "those who defend 'orthodoxy'" and "those who advocate 'heresy'" is, for Bourdieu, "paradigmatic not only in the religious field but in all cultural fields." David Swartz, *Culture and Power: The Sociology of Pierre Bourdieu* (Chicago: University of Chicago Press, 1997), 124. This is figured elsewhere as a distinction between the "creators" and "curators" of culture, or an "opposition between those who reproduce and transmit legitimate bodies of knowledge and those who invent new forms of knowledge;" see Pierre Bourdieu, *Homo Academicus* (Stanford, CA: Stanford University Press, 1988); and Swartz, *Culture and Power*, 226.

111. For "moral globalization," see Michael Ignatieff, *Human Rights as Politics and Idolatry* (Princeton, NJ: Princeton University Press, 2001). For a conception of intellectual elites as the "clergy" of "world culture," see John W. Meyer, "The World Polity and the Authority of the Nation-State" in *Studies of the Modern World-System*, ed. Albert J. Bergesen (New York: Academic Press, 1980), 109–137.

112. I borrow this phrase from Charles Taylor, *A Secular Age* (Cambridge, MA: Harvard University Press, 2007).

113. Piet Meiring, "The Baruti versus the Lawyers: The Role of Religion in the TRC Process" in *Looking Back, Reaching Forward: Reflections on the Truth and Reconciliation Commission of South Africa*, ed. Charles Villa-Vicencio and Wilhelm Verwoerd (Cape Town: University of Cape Town Press, 2000), 124–125.

114. On the field of transitional justice as interdisciplinary, see, for example, Christine Bell, "Transitional Justice, Interdisciplinarity and the State of the 'Field' or 'Non-Field'" in *International Journal of Transitional Justice* 3 (2009): 5–27.

115. For human rights as "a secular article of faith," see Michael Ignatieff, *Human Rights as Politics and Idolatry* (Princeton, NJ: Princeton University Press, 2001), 77.

116. Charles Villa-Vicencio, "Reconciliation as Politics" in *The SA Reconciliation Barometer* 1:1 (Cape Town: Institute for Justice and Reconciliation, 2003); Pablo de Greiff, "The Role of Apologies in National Reconciliation Processes: On Making Trustworthy Institutions Trusted" in *The Age of Apology: Facing Up to the Past*, ed. Mark Gibney, Rhoda E. Howard-Hassmann, Jean-Marc Coicaud, and Niklaus Steiner (Philadelphia: University of Pennsylvania Press, 2008), 120–136.

117. Reed Brody, "Justice: The First Casualty of Truth?" *The Nation*, April 30, 2001.

CHAPTER 5

Accountability

Daniel W. Van Ness

People who commit crimes create rippling circles of injuries. They have broken a law, an act which both violates a norm and challenges the authority of the lawgiver. They have caused multiple kinds of harm for the victims of crime, direct and indirect. They have harmed communities, the spatially-based (or else it should be affinity based) networks that create the relational environment in which they and their victims live. They have harmed themselves and the people close to them. To varying degrees, all these are harmed when someone commits a serious crime. Yet discussions about accountability typically focus on only one of those harms: law-breaking.

Early developments in modern restorative justice practice came in the context of domestic criminal law as a response to the removal of the victim (and even, largely, the offender) from direct participation in State-dominated justice systems. Lawbreaking must be followed by punishment; in serious crimes that usually means imprisonment, if not death. Compensation orders to direct victims may be added, although confinement usually means that they cannot be paid.

So the growth of the procedure by which international bodies hold accountable persons who commit serious human rights abuses or crimes against humanity has been met by some restorative justice proponents with muted celebration.[1] It is important that these offenders be held accountable, but what seems to have become the "gold standard"[2] in addressing these serious international crimes looks very much like domestic criminal courts, with their strengths but also their limitations.

And in fact, accountability for gross human rights violations by States or their agents was historically meted out in domestic courts. Until the past 150 years there was no universally acknowledged international humanitarian law; until the last half century there was no international legal apparatus to enforce such a law. So a great deal of recent attention in the aftermath of genocide and other crimes against humanity has been given to articulating enforceable international norms and creating forums capable of trying those accused of violating those norms.

This chapter will first review the development of domestic and international criminal justice mechanisms and the challenges to those brought by the victim movement and restorative justice. It will then consider two potential justifications for State and international community claims of jurisdiction in determining accountability, victimhood and responsibility, and explain why responsibility is the preferable justification. Finally, it will propose three critical elements of accountability in a restorative framework.

Part One: The Imposition of External Authority in Criminal Justice

We take for granted that the grievances left in the wake of crime should not be left to the victim and offender to settle personally. After all, that could set off cycles of violence and revenge. It was that very threat that led early societies to create mechanisms for resolving such conflicts among members of their communities. But they did not require the parties to accept the judgment of an external third party. By providing participatory forums in which victims could denounce offenders for wrongdoing and demand satisfaction, these societies were able to preserve community peace while giving the parties a role in making decisions. The process and the typical sanctions were designed to restore peace. As Harold Berman observes, this approach was broadly accepted:

> The institution of fixed monetary sanctions payable by the kin of the wrongdoer to the kin of the victim was a prominent feature of the law of all the peoples of Europe prior to the twelfth century, and indeed of every Indo-European people at some stage of its development, including the peoples of India, Israel, Greece, and Rome.[3]

The focus on satisfying the claim of the victim was central to achieving justice until the beginning of the last millennium, when European States began to consolidate and centralize the administration of justice. In England this began shortly after the Norman Conquest. In order to establish preeminence over local governments and ecclesiastical courts, Henry I and his successors decreed the "king's peace" throughout England, meaning that breaches of his peace had to be brought to the king's courts. This jurisdictional claim was based on the legal fiction that the king was harmed when persons in his realm were victimized. Initially the objective of that court proceeding was to hold the offender accountable for repairing the damage that was done to the victim.[4]

The hope was that simply providing the forum would encourage amicable settlement of the claim by the parties. The Leges Henrici Primi "repeatedly emphasized that English law preferred friendly settlement to litigation, *amor* or *amicitia* to *judicium*."[5] But over time the actual victims were replaced by the State as primary complainant against offenders. Kings became legal victims, which is why criminal cases today are titled some version of *State v. Accused*.[6] Reparation to the victim lost favor and was replaced by fines and other sanctions designed to punish offenders and deter future crime.

This surrender by victims to the State of the power to enforce criminal laws was in some ways a useful development. As the modern State grew, it assumed many procedural responsibilities once left to victims and their communities. During the nineteenth and twentieth centuries, professional police, public prosecution, prisons, probation, and parole were established to replace the more informal community-based mechanisms that previously existed. This meant that the State's coercive powers could be used to stop the criminal activity, if possible, and to hold offenders accountable in a proceeding that afforded them procedural protections.

There were practical benefits as well. Private prosecution was burdensome and unpredictable.[7] Victims were required to arrange for the arrest of the offender, interview witnesses and bring them to court, decide what the charge should be, attend the court hearings where indictments were issued, bring witnesses to the grand jury proceeding, make sure witnesses also attended the trial, present the prosecution's case in court, apply for rewards that may come after conviction and disburse them, and oppose (or on occasion support) applications for parole.[8] Victims could hire solicitors to do this for them, but many did not. It is not surprising that many good cases failed because of incompetent prosecution, and unhappiness over this eventually resulted in the creation of public prosecutors.

But State control of domestic criminal justice is now so complete that Nils Christie famously complained that it amounted to a "theft of crime" from victims and offenders.[9] He argued that they have been excluded from meaningful roles in resolving crimes, and certainly from making decisions about sentences that might be imposed on the offender. This "theft" means that the parties and their communities are no longer able to clarify norms in a nuanced and evolving way. Instead, lawyers and judges parse statutes to determine whether the prosecution has proven the defendants guilty of all elements of the crime and if so, how to punish them.

Something similar has happened in creating mechanisms to address violations of crimes against humanity and gross violations of human rights. It is agreed that such crimes should be prosecuted in domestic courts in the countries in which they occur. However, in too many instances this did not happen. During times of transition of power from oppressive to more democratic regimes, governments seek and often receive amnesty for human rights violations that occurred during their time in power. The political will of governments to prosecute members of former governments' ebbs and flows over time. In Argentina, for example, there was an initial effort to try leaders of the military juntas for human rights violations, but threats of military intervention caused the new government to pardon those who had been convicted and to adopt amnesty laws protecting potential defendants. After the Inter-American Court of Human Rights ruled that amnesty laws violated international law, the Argentine Congress repealed them and the Supreme Court invalidated the amnesties that had already been extended, leading to the trial and conviction of several key leaders 25 years after their dictatorship had collapsed.[10]

Traditionally, if a State violated the rights of a citizen of another State, the only hope for redress was through diplomacy or war carried out by the victim's State. With the rise of international law it became possible for States to present legal claims on behalf of their citizens, but it was cumbersome and required the political will of the complaining State. Offending States were reluctant to accept responsibility for crimes committed against individual victims by their agents, even when it involved violations of international human rights or humanitarian law.[11]

The twentieth century was not unique for having mass atrocities, as Minow[12] observes. It was, however, different in that the international community sought to hold perpetrators accountable through prosecutions. Speaking of the tribunals begun in Nuremburg and Tokyo after World War II, and continuing with individual State prosecutions for mass murders and torture, Minow notes:

> These trials have inspired the international movement for human rights and represent in many people's minds the "gold standard" for any public response to mass violence. The use of criminal trials holds out the rule of law as the framework for rendering accountability for unspeakable conduct, for deterring future violations, and for gathering a formal public record so that the attempts to destroy groups of people cannot succeed in destroying their memory.[13]

More recent examples of international criminal prosecutions of serious humanitarian law violations are those conducted at the International Criminal Tribunal for the former Yugoslavia (ICTY) and the International Criminal Tribunal for Rwanda (ICTR). These ad hoc tribunals were created by the United Nations in response to crimes against humanity in both countries. The statutes of both the ICTY and ICTR included provisions for restitution of unlawfully taken property to victims of crime, although neither has issued a single restitution order.[14] Compensation, however, was delegated to national courts or other competent bodies established by national legislation.[15]

More recently the International Criminal Court (ICC) was created as a permanent body to try individuals for violations of crimes under international law. Thanks in large part to the advocacy of a number of NGOs during the negotiations leading to the ICC statute, victims and their families are provided certain opportunities for participation, the right to be informed of progress of the prosecutions, and the possibility of compensation through a special trust fund.[16] However, a formal review of the ICC conducted in 2010 found a significant gap between the statute's aspirations and the actual experience of victims.[17] The ICC, like the tribunals and domestic criminal law, is essentially retributive in purpose and outcome.

CHALLENGES TO DOMESTIC AND INTERNATIONAL CRIMINAL JUSTICE

Two movements arose in the latter part of the twentieth century to protest the State's claim of exclusive jurisdiction in domestic and international criminal matters. Although neither movement sought to exclude the State from involvement in criminal matters, each urged reforms that would allow other voices to join in the determination of accountability in criminal matters. These are the victim rights movement, which seeks to use criminal tribunals as forums in which victims can seek redress, and the restorative justice movement, which seeks opportunities for addressing the relational harms that result from criminalized behavior.

During the last half of the twentieth century, victims of domestic crimes began to protest their exclusion from criminal trials, seeking reforms that would allow them a voice in criminal matters. In many jurisdictions they won procedural concessions allowing them, among other things, information about the status of the prosecution of their cases, access to the courtroom during trials, and the right to address the court before sentencing.[18] They also won the right to request compensation as part of the sentence. However, in increasing numbers of jurisdictions, compensation competes with other financial orders such as fines, fees, and child support, and some of those are given priority over compensation.[19]

However, as Bassiouni observes, too often efforts to recognize the right of victims to compensation appear to have been motivated at least as much to gain victim cooperation with the prosecution of offenders as by recognition that victims deserve this as a matter of justice. Furthermore, social welfare initiatives to provide support and assistance to victims tend to do so because they are in need, not because they are victims.[20] In an article on the UN Basic Principles and Guidelines on the Right to a Remedy and Reparation for Victims of Gross Violations of International Human Rights Law and Serious Violations of International Humanitarian Law (Basic Principles and Guidelines),[21] he proposed adopting as a legal justification for victims' rights to remedies the simple fact of their victimization, which means that those rights would exist independently of the State's decision to prosecute an offender and should shape the criminal procedures that arise when there is prosecution.[22]

This argument becomes important in addressing the rights of victims of gross human rights violations when the perpetrators were States or persons acting as their agents.[23] The first comprehensive process for redress began after World War II with the German government's efforts to compensate Holocaust victims, persons forced to provide slave labor, and those whose human rights were violated in other ways by actions of the previous Nazi government. The total amount paid by Germany and certain private corporations has been over $104 billion (US). Similarly, the US government authorized payments to Japanese interned during WWII, to Native Americans, and to victims of the Tuskegee Syphilis Study and the Rosewood massacre. However, these have been case-specific and the results of special legislation limited to those cases.[24]

A second and related challenge to the State's monopolistic claim to jurisdiction in criminal matters has come from the restorative justice movement. Unlike the international victim rights movement, which seeks new, supra-national tribunals to provide relief, the restorative justice movement argued that formal criminal justice processes had limited potential for building peace. Processes dominated by judges and lawyers, following detailed rules of procedure, determining whether carefully crafted statutes had been violated have their place in addressing law breaking, but they are not well suited to deal with the other harms that victims and communities experience, their relational and material injuries.

In a paper on restorative peacebuilding, McCold, Llewellyn, and Van Ness proposed four principles of restorative justice: it is harm-focused, relational, participatory, and democratic.[25] It is *harm-focused* in that it does not limit itself to broken laws but pays attention to the resulting harms and to the need to repair those harms. A burglary victim needs more than a convicted defendant; she needs assistance in repairing her damaged window and in replacing stolen property. In fact, most criminal laws are intended to prevent just this sort of harm by discouraging proscribed conduct. Restorative justice emphasizes the need to repair that harm when it happens.

Restorative justice is *relational*; it invites us to see the world relationally. Crime does more than cause material or financial harm; it also affects the intersecting network of relationships that create communities, including those between direct victims and offenders, between communities and the victims and offenders that are part of them, and often between groups within the wider community. The burglary that created direct harm to one victim also led her neighbors to install burglar alarms and to restrict their behavior. The response to crime should be one that not only repairs but also strengthens community relationships.

Restorative justice is *participatory*. The parties affected by crime are invited to be part of the solution to that crime. This insight has led to creation of new forums to allow the parties to help determine what happened, how people were harmed, and how to build a better future. In victim-offender conferences or circles, the victim and offender, community and government representatives, and a trained facilitator actually sit down together to design what they feel would be a just response to the crime. Some truth commissions have provided opportunities for similar exchanges.

Finally, restorative justice is *democratic* rather than authoritarian. It reflects the subsidiarity principle that decisions should be taken as closely as possible to and by the parties involved rather than by larger national, regional, or international organizations. This means that the agreement emerging from a victim-offender conference will be tailored to the needs and circumstances of the parties.

Modern restorative justice developed in the context of domestic criminal justice disputes, and is often described in relation to individual or relatively small groups of victims and offenders.[26] But its principles and values can apply as well to national level restorative processes. The important contribution of restorative justice is not its specific processes for bringing victims and offenders together, but the principles and values that underlie restorative thinking. These focus on building an environment in which inclusive, cooperative responses to conflict become viable alternatives to the coercive responses typically used in serious crime. These coercive responses may be imposed through the use of armed force, through judicial proceedings in national or international courts, or through power-based negotiations that rely on the relative weakness of one of the parties seeking to end the conflict. Those measures may be needed if the offender is unwilling to accept responsibility or if other parties refuse to participate in restorative alternatives. But proponents of restorative justice argue that cooperative alternatives should exist and be generally available for those victims and offenders who would prefer that approach.

This is because while coercive responses may indeed end overt conflict, which is good, they do not build peace, which is better. As Braithwaite has said,

> Indeed, the empirical evidence suggests that since World War II power-based elite mediations dominated by major powers have often secured at least temporary peace, though not enduring peace. I have

argued that the peace is usually not enduring because unresolved resentments fester in civil society. This is particularly likely because elite mediation usually involves a mediator who acts for a major power. The greater the power imbalances, the more difficult and intractable the conflict, the greater the temptation to resort to an imposed solution. Indeed, power considerations drive most conflicts, and when power disparity is great, the usual result is unilateral imposition of a solution.[27]

In the latter decades of the twentieth century, a particular restorative mechanism—the truth commission—emerged as an alternative to criminal prosecution for gross violations of human rights in South Africa. There had been previous truth commissions, justified in some instances as the only recourse when offenders have been granted amnesty as part of the transition negotiations or when other pragmatic considerations make that necessary. Such considerations include the impossibility of trying all alleged perpetrators because of financial and professional limitations, the resistance of the military to such trials, and the absence of key perpetrators who have fled the country.

However, after the South African Truth and Reconciliation hearings, some suggest that truth commissions have fundamental advantages over prosecutions in uncovering a reasonably complete understanding of the truth and in laying the ground for reconciliation and peace. As noted, trials have evidentiary limitations that may prevent a full disclosure of what happened and why, they do little to help restore the dignity of victims because they focus on perpetrators, they limit the likelihood of public admission and explanation by perpetrators of what took place, and they seldom offer a forum to victims and survivors that allows them to tell their stories. Although truth commissions also have limited time and resources and even conditional offers of amnesty to secure testimony may limit their public influence, they help underscore the importance of both learning and telling the truth to victims, offenders, and society as a whole.[28]

Part Two: Jurisdictional Justifications for Imposition of External Authority

As noted earlier, the authority of States in criminal matters is well established in domestic law. In the past decades, the UN has acted to create regional tribunals to consider matters of crimes against humanity in the former Yugoslavia and Rwanda, and through treaty in the case of the ICC. However, the arguments for State and international authority are not based simply on positive law or on pragmatics, but also on conceptual grounds. It has been argued that it is just for the State or international authority to take this role for two reasons. One is that the State, and sometimes humanity as a whole, has been victimized by the crimes. The second is that the State, and sometimes humanity as a whole, bears some degree of responsibility for the crimes. Let us consider each of these arguments.

According to restorative theory, offenders are accountable to their victims for the harm they have caused, accountable to do what they can to repair the harm, to make things right.[29] So an initial question—even before "What are the harms?"–is "Who are the victims?" The Basic Principles and Guidelines define victims of gross violations of human rights as "persons who individually or collectively suffered harm, including physical or mental injury, emotional suffering, economic loss or substantial impairment of their fundamental rights," as well as "the immediate family or dependents of the direct victim and persons who have suffered harm in intervening to assist victims in distress or to prevent victimization."[30] So we might speak of *direct* and *secondary* victims, those who have been directly harmed and those who are indirectly harmed because of their close relationship to direct victims such as family members and dependents. People who are injured while assisting victims or preventing victimization are direct victims in their own right.

Restorative justice proponents add a third group: members of the communities of the direct and indirect victims and of the offenders. We might call these communities *tertiary victims*. Communities have much greater prominence in restorative justice thinking than in criminal justice, where they are sometimes considered threats to fairness because of bias or prejudice. The prominence of community in restorative justice is due in part to the importance given to the obligations of relationships (as opposed to obligations imposed by law). Because communities are made up of networks of interconnected relationships, others are harmed when someone commits a crime. They have needs that are independent to those of the direct or indirect victims.[31] Zehr says that criminal justice focuses on the social dimensions of crime in such a way that it "makes community abstract and impersonal."[32] Restorative justice gives it context and personality.

As we saw earlier, a fourth body claiming victimhood is the State; we might call it a *public victim*. Because of the State's power this claim has had significant repercussions. It presents itself as both a direct victim and a representational victim, direct in that its authority has been transgressed by the lawbreaker and representational because it claims to exercise that authority on behalf of society.

Duff speaks of crimes as "public wrongs," explaining that while these are not the wrongs to direct victims, the public is properly concerned about them and their resolution. But the overwhelming reality of the experience of criminal justice to crime victims is that it has far less to do with their needs and interests than it does with securing convictions.[33] It is clear that, although Duff's nuanced arguments are helpful, the State has moved beyond the limitations of appropriate concern for victims to preoccupation with punishing lawbreakers. It has done so by claiming the role of the victim with jurisdictional power: *State v. Defendant*.

Duff is right that the public wrong of a crime is not comparable to the wrong that the direct victim has suffered, but even that leaves open the possibility that in the aggregate the State can claim to be a primary victim. For example, if the "public wrong" for each crime amounted to 0.1 percent of a direct victim's wrong, after 10,000 crimes take place, the State's "victimhood" total would be 10 times that of any single victim. This aggregated victimhood has two characteristics.

First, it is abstract. This is because each specific crime has a negligible effect on the State; the damage it experiences is because of the cumulative effect of many crimes and is consequently generalized. The concern of States has to do with *rates*. Has the crime rate gone up or down? What is the clearance rate of police, the conviction rate of prosecutors, or the incarceration rate of the jurisdiction? Second, the large number of crimes means that States must operate efficiently, which requires applying a degree of uniformity. This leads to generalization, beginning with substantive criminal law and continuing with laws and policies about treatment of victims and offenders in the criminal justice system.

Finally, internationally conducted prosecutions for gross human rights violations in recent decades have marked the rise of another party that asserts authority even over States: the international community. Jurisdiction is invoked not only because of positive law (legislation or treaties) but also on the basis of universal jurisdiction. Ordinarily national courts can try cases only if the alleged crimes happened in their jurisdiction, to or by their nationals, or if treaties grant this authority. However, even without those circumstances, it has been argued that "national courts may nevertheless exercise jurisdiction under international law over crimes of such exceptional gravity that they affect the fundamental interests of the international community as a whole."[34]

The existence of universal jurisdiction not only means that there is a right to prosecute, it

> also means that all States have the duty to prosecute or extradite, that no person charged with that crime can claim the "political offense exception" to extradition, and that States have the duty to assist each other in securing evidence needed to prosecute. But of greater

importance is the fact that no perpetrator can claim the "defense of obedience to superior orders" and that no statute of limitation contained in the laws of any State can apply. Lastly, no one is immune from prosecution for such crimes, even a head of State.[35]

In very recent years there has been the further development of indictments of belligerents for crimes against international law *while the alleged crimes continue to be committed and the conflict rages.* For example, under those conditions arrest warrants were issued for Sudanese president Omar Hassan Ahmad al-Bashir and for the leader of the Lord's Resistance Army in Uganda, Joseph Kony. According to Vinjamuri,[36] this has created four dilemmas. First, it undermines the premise that national legal systems are to be preferred over international for determining accountability. Second, it tends to position those who wish to debate the appropriate timing of international action as seeking to protect offenders from the International Criminal Court. Third, it intensifies the perception of some heads of State that intervention by the international community is biased against them. Fourth, it raises the stakes for justice in that now it not only should determine accountability but it must demonstrably contribute to peace. The first dilemma is of most interest in this discussion of accountability. There now exists a body that seeks to hold even the leaders of States accountable for crimes they have committed or *are in the process of committing.* The claim has been made on the basis of victimhood; the crimes are so serious that the international community—humanity itself—has been harmed.

In conclusion, four kinds of victims might seek accountability from offenders because of the harms they have suffered. Direct, secondary, and tertiary victims have losses that can be described in real and specific terms. States and supra-national bodies, on the other hand, are public victims, sustaining abstract or symbolic damages.

An alternative justification for State or international community jurisdiction is that they bear a degree of responsibility for the crimes. If victims can be identified and classified in terms of the immediacy of the crime, the same can be done with offenders as well. Those with *direct responsibility* are the persons who actually committed the crime. These are the persons who can be charged as defendants in criminal proceedings. They are responsible because of their own actions and intentions.

Another group could be considered *secondarily responsible*. These are persons who stood by as the direct offender acted but did nothing, or who had a special duty to prevent the crime or to protect the victim. These may include people who could be held liable in civil court for negligence that placed the victim in peril. In domestic criminal law these include people whose actions placed the victim in peril. Examples include landlords or property owners who fail to provide adequate security to their tenants or guests when there is a known criminal threat such as gang activity in the immediate vicinity.[37]

A community might bear *social responsibility* for creating conditions that increase the likelihood of crime by, for example, tolerating such social injustices as pervasive discrimination, significantly unequal access to economic opportunities, serious public health problems, and so forth. Social responsibility might also arise when a community is aware of patterns of criminal activity or criminogenic conditions and fails to take action.

But the discussion does not end with determination that there was direct, indirect or social responsibility. Usually the actors are individuals using State power. Can the State be held accountable? Can both be liable? And if so, what form does that liability take?

In a 2007 judgment, the International Court of Justice (ICJ) interpreted the 1948 Convention on the Prevention and Punishment of the Crime of Genocide as it applied to Serbia's support of Bosnian Serb nationalists who carried out a policy of ethnic cleansing in their war of independence from Bosnia. The Court adopted a strict standard for determining the degree of connection needed between the Republic of Serbia and the nationalists to attribute their actions to Serbia: there had to be clear evidence of "effective control" by Serbia over the nationalists as well as specific intent that genocide occur. Mere assistance (even if, without it, the nationalists could not have successfully committed genocide) was not enough. However, it also held that Serbia had failed to prevent genocide because it did not use its influence over the nationalists to stop their actions. In other words, while it did not find Serbia responsible for the commission of genocide, the Court determined that its connection was sufficiently close to justify finding that it had failed to prevent genocide committed by a non-State actor.[38] In the terms used above, the State was not a direct offender, but it bore secondary responsibility for its failure to prevent genocide.

So one basis for holding a State accountable for the actions of non-State actors is that it *exerted effective control* over the non-State actors. A second is that it had a *sufficiently close connection* to the non-State actor to bear secondary responsibility for having failed to prevent them from committing their wrong. It is either directly or secondarily responsible. But some have suggested that it may also have social responsibility for the crimes that occur within it. In domestic law, the question of State responsibility for the acts of an individual has also arisen in arguments for victim compensation. Robert Elias identified a number of theories that might be used to justify victim compensation, several of which stem from the State's responsibility.[39] One is what he called the "strict liability theory," attributed to Jeremy Bentham, which is that the State has a social contract with its citizens to protect them in return for limitations it has placed on individuals' ability to protect themselves. Therefore, when crime occurs this can be considered a failure on the part of the State, providing a basis for compensation from the State. Second, Elias suggests (albeit without citations) that some argue further that the State is responsible for "actually producing or inducing crime in the first place. That is, it is claimed that the State helps produce a social environment that is conducive to crime and it therefore produces crime victims."[40] A third justification is what he called "governmental negligence theory": this would apply when the victimization was caused by the negligence of State employees such as law enforcement officials. A fourth is the "social obligation theory," which draws from the close historical relationship between the victim and society in law enforcement. As the State assumed more control over criminal justice, restitution to the victim was diverted to national treasuries. The argument is that while victims have no *legal* claim for State assistance based on this history, the State nevertheless has a *social* obligation to victims to make amends.

In other words, as the political expression of a community, the State bears social responsibility for all crimes that occur. This suggests that the State may have a social, if not legal, duty to address underlying injustices, which is a significant part of peacebuilding.

It should be noted that a State's negligence and its social obligation are both abstract and generalized. Just as its victimization is not comparable to that of direct victims, neither is its culpability comparable to that of the direct offender. Consequently, whatever amends it owes victims it owes to them as a class, and not as individuals. One way of making amends might be to provide suitable forums for resolving the claims by direct and indirect victims against their direct and indirect offenders.

In restorative theory, responsibility is a preferable justification to victimhood for State or international community action. The notion of accountability obligates offenders to help repair the harm to victims and to restore (or build) harmony. Therefore, Bassiouni argues that the Basic Principles and Guidelines seek three categories of rights for victims: (1) the right to equal access to justice, (2) the right to reparation, and (3) the right to truth.[41] Regarding the first right, access to justice, the relevant principles provide that States should make access to judicial, administrative, and other remedies available to victims; that these should be publicized; that they should be structured so as to minimize inconvenience to victims, protect their privacy, and ensure their safety; that they should receive any assistance needed including legal, diplomatic, and consular initiatives with other States; and that States should develop procedures to allow groups of victims to request and receive reparation.[42]

Regarding the second right, that of reparation, if States indeed bear some degree of responsibility for crime, they must take comparable steps to help victims recover from the harm they have suffered. This includes creation of forums in which immediate, secondary, and tertiary victims are able to pursue remedies from direct and indirect offenders. Some will wish to do so in a judicial process such as criminal or civil courts. But there is sufficient experience with restorative processes to know that other victims want something different: processes in which they can more directly participate. Such forums would incorporate the restorative principles mentioned earlier. They would be harm-focused rather than law-focused, relational rather than impersonal, participatory rather than passive, and democratic rather than authoritarian.

Regarding the third right, that of truth, the Basic Principles and Guidelines provide for creation of an accurate account of what took place. The emphasis is on the duty of the State to verify, commemorate, and provide an accurate report of the violations that happened. This speaks to the need of victims to have answers to questions about what happened, how and why it happened, and what the results were.

The advantage of justifying jurisdiction on the grounds of responsibility rather than victimhood is that there is less likelihood that the State (or the supra-State body) will "steal" the crime from its other owners: victims, offenders, and communities. The outside authority's motive in creating judicial and other remedies is not to vindicate itself, but to make those remedies available in a form and fashion that will be most useful to those who were harmed. An approach based on responsibility as opposed to victimhood will be more humble, more respectful of the interests and values of the direct and indirect victims and offenders, and less likely to insist that justice processes meet its standards alone.

Part Three: Three Elements of Accountability

Restorative justice proponents argue that there are other ways to hold the offender accountable than through traditional criminal justice, ways that have advantages at both the domestic and international levels. This is because criminal justice is offender-oriented and fails to address many needs of victims, communities, and even offenders. It is abstract and fails to deal with actual needs of the parties in their unique contexts.

There are a number of common features among Bassiouni's list of victim rights that are to be observed by the international community and the reforms championed by restorative justice practitioners. Following are three elements common to restorative and victim rights understandings of accountability: reparation, truth-telling, and taking responsibility.

First, let us consider reparation. Harm is a foundational concern in the restorative conception of justice. Crime does more than violate legal norms; in fact, criminal laws were developed to prevent harm to victims from taking place. Therefore, the response to crime must both uphold the law and repair the harm to the extent possible. Walgrave, speaking from a restorative perspective, agrees that harm must be repaired in the aftermath of crime. By this he means "reparation, correcting or remedying a situation that has been degraded."[43] The nature and extent of the harms needing repair may be determined by the parties themselves or by a judge (the former, if possible, is preferred by restorative justice proponents, of course).

When a State is indirectly or socially responsible for gross violations of human rights, certain reparations may be appropriate. Five forms of amends are mentioned in the Basic Principles and Guidelines: restitution, satisfaction, rehabilitation, guarantees of non-repetition, and compensation.

Restitution, defined as the restoration of freedoms, includes a return to normal family life in a home as a full citizen, restoration of employment, and return of property.[44] In other words, it returns the victim to the community without the legal or physical impediments to civic, economic, social, and political life that might have resulted from the human rights abuse.

Satisfaction is related to the idea of vindication and requires actions such as ending human rights violations; searching for the disappeared; declarations restoring the dignity, reputation, and rights of the victim; public apologies; and sanctions against persons liable for violations.[45]

Rehabilitation concerns medical and psychological care as well as legal and social services.[46] These are potentially long-term interventions that may be beyond the capability of individual offenders to offer and which therefore must be provided by society at large.

Guarantees of non-repetition include actions to ensure civilian control of the military; provide that the defendant State will abide by international standards; strengthen the independence of the judiciary; protect lawyers, medical personnel, and human rights advocates; provide human rights training to all sectors of society including military and security forces; promote codes of conduct and ethics; promote monitoring and prevention mechanisms; and make any necessary law reforms.[47]

Some of the particular aspects of reparation outlined in the Basic Principles and Guidelines can be provided by a direct offender either alone or with assistance from the State. For example, *compensation* requires proportional financial reimbursement for physical or mental harm; lost opportunities, including employment, education, and social benefits; material damage and loss of earnings, including loss of earning potential; moral damage; and costs required for legal or expert assistance, medicine and medical services, and psychological and social services.[48]

And what if the wrongdoer does not want to make amends? While not all restorative advocates support coerced compensation, Walgrave argues that this provides an alternative that may be useful when the offender is unwilling to voluntarily assume this responsibility.[49]

Second, accountability requires a willingness to tell the truth about what happened. As Minow writes, "advocates of truth commissions argue that telling and hearing narratives of violence in the name of truth can promote healing for individuals and for society."[50] But where the Basic Principles and Guidelines state that victims and communities have a right to learn the truth, restorative justice argues that it is also a right of the offender. Furthermore, the right extends far beyond merely receiving a truthful account of events; it also invites victims, offenders, and other participants to speak the truth as they understand it.

Court processes seek legal truth, the truth that emerges from a formalized process dominated by lawyers. Evidence is introduced through testimony and exhibits, both constrained by rules of evidence. Furthermore, it is elicited during questioning by attorneys who seek that which supports their side's position in the adversarial judicial process. Restorative justice is more inclusive, and restorative processes (from victim offender dialogue through truth commissions) encourage more active, voluntary conversations that can give the parties a much more robust and nuanced understanding of what took place than is possible in court, where there is little or no opportunity for the parties themselves to elaborate, to ask questions of the others, or to provide background information that while of great interest to them is irrelevant to the narrow legal issues debated in court.

This inclusive and more holistic approach is particularly important in conflict situations where the roles of victims and offenders have changed over time; where today's offender was yesterday's victim, and vice versa; the rebel who kidnaps children and trains them as soldiers was himself kidnapped when he was a child. Clearly the transition from victim to offender took place over time, and it is simplistic to present the individual as entirely one or the other.

The third element of accountability is taking responsibility. Walgrave notes that punishment is typically justified as a method of holding offenders responsible for what they have done. However, it is a limited form of responsibility that requires offenders to passively accept hard treatment in return for their criminal acts.[51] Sanctions are imposed from outside and offenders play little or no affirmative role in accepting and determining the nature of those consequences. Restorative justice values a different kind of responsibility, one that is assumed by offenders who accept the wrongfulness of their behaviors and the duty to help repair the harm that followed that behavior. The voluntary assumption of responsibility is an opportunity for an offender who claims to have changed to demonstrate that to the victims, to the surrounding community, and to those responsible for the justice system.

Passive responsibility focuses on the past; the offender undergoes hard treatment for wrongdoing at an earlier time. Active responsibility has a dual focus; it, too, is retrospective in that it addresses the harm caused in the past, but it also looks toward a future that is better for the victim and the offender. Active responsibility is both retrospective and prospective.[52]

Offenders demonstrate active responsibility when they acknowledge their wrongdoing. This can be done through an admission or an apology, but to be active responsibility it cannot be forced and it must be seen as sincere. Minnow suggests that based on the South African Truth and Reconciliation Commission experience, acknowledgment helped reestablish moral norms, humanized the offenders, and uncovered previously secret information[53]

If the offender will not assume responsibility, then passive responsibility becomes the only alternative. Depending on the form it takes, we might call it restorative punishment.[54] An offender can be required to perform services or pay compensation as a means of repairing the harm caused. Furthermore, the offender can be sentenced to a form of passive responsibility (for example, imprisonment) with the option of moving to a different, more restorative, kind of sanction if the offender (perhaps with the consent of the victim) chooses. What distinguishes "restorative punishment" from retribution is how it affects the people and groups who were harmed by the crime. If it helps restore those who were harmed, then the sanction can be viewed as restorative. If it merely balances the scales of pain, then it is retributive.

Conclusion

State or international involvement in holding offenders accountable for violations of criminal justice or human rights laws requires abstraction and generalization. These may be useful in creating order, but are limited in their ability to build community peace. One does not enter into relationships with groups but with individuals. In fact, a profound realization of victims and offenders during restorative encounters is that each is not the "Other," but "Another."

However, the ability of the State and new international judicial bodies to abstract and generalize, combined with that of the parties to particularize, offers promising opportunities for understanding what is important in responding to violations of the rights of victims. What has prevented this from happening in the past has been the perspective that the State or international community is the victim, which has supplanted the actual immediate, secondary, and tertiary victims. If instead a system of accountability were developed based on the State's or international community's direct, indirect, or social responsibility, its making of amends would include provision of alternative forums for determining responsibility, truth-telling, and reparations.

Notes

1. See, for example, Paul McCold, Jennifer J. Llewellyn, and Daniel W. Van Ness, *An Introduction to Restorative Peacebuilding* (New York: Working Party on Restorative Justice, Alliance of NGOs on Crime Prevention and Criminal Justice, 2007).
2. Martha Minow, "The Hope for Healing: What Can Truth Commissions Do?" in *Truth v. Justice: The Morality of Truth Commissions*, ed. Robert I. Rotberg and Dennis Thompson (Princeton, NJ: Princeton University Press, 2000).
3. Harold J. Berman, *Law and Revolution: The Formation of the Western Legal Tradition*, (Cambridge, MA and London: Harvard University Press, 1983), 55.
4. Daniel W. Van Ness and Karen Heetderks Strong, *Restoring Justice: An Introduction to Restorative Justice*, 4th ed. (Cincinnati, OH: Anderson Publishing, 2010), 9.
5. Berman, *Law and Revolution*, 74.
6. Howard Zehr, *Changing Lenses: A New Focus for Crime and Justice* (Scottsdale, PA: Herald Press, 1990), 107–110; Mark S. Umbreit and Marilyn Peterson Armour, *Restorative Justice Dialogue: An Essential Guide for Research and Practice* (New York: Springer Publishing Company, 2010), 4–5.
7. Van Ness and Strong, *Restoring Justice*, 128–130.
8. Douglas Hay and Francis Snyder, "Using the Criminal Law, 1750–1850: Policing, Private Prosecution, and the State," in *Policing and Prosecution in Britain 1750–1850*, ed. Douglas Hay and Francis Snyder (Oxford: Clarendon Press, 1989), 26.
9. Nils Christie, "Conflict as Property," *British Journal of Criminology* 17 (1977): 8.
10. Jim Cavallaro, "Lessons from the Brutality of Argentina's Dirty War," *Change.org*, April 24, 2010, http://news.change.org/stories/lessons-from-the-brutality-of-argentinas-dirty-war.
11. Ibid., 212.
12. Minow, *The Hope for Healing*, 235–260.
13. Ibid., 235–236.
14. Ilaria Bottigliero, *Redress for Victims of Crimes under International Law* (Leiden and Boston: Martinus Nijhoff Publishers, 2004), 196–200, 202.
15. Ibid., 200–202.
16. Ibid., 213–215.
17. "The Impact of the Rome Statute System on Victims and Affected Communities" was one of four subject areas examined by the review. Annex V(a) contains the final report pertaining to that topic. United Nations, *Review Conference of the Rome Statute of the International Criminal Court; Kampala, 31 May–June 11, 2010; Official Report* (The Hague: International Criminal Court, 2010) 77–101.
18. Van Ness and Strong, *Restoring Justice*, 120–124.
19. In US federal criminal cases, for example, past due child support payments take priority over all other financial obligations, including compensation to the victim of the crime the defendant committed.
20. M. Cherif Bassiouni, "International Recognition of Victims' Rights." *Human Rights Law Review* 6 (2006): 205–206.
21. Basic Principles and Guidelines on the Right to a Remedy and Reparation for Victims of Gross Violations of International Human Rights Law and Serious Violations of International Humanitarian Law. GA Res. 147, March 21, 2006, A/RES/60/147; 13 IHRR 907 (2006). Basic

principles are one of several kinds of criminal justice standards that the United Nations adopts from time to time. They are intended to offer guidance to governments, but do not rise to the level of international law; in fact, they may go beyond the requirements of international law. Because of the process followed in their adoption, however, they are useful to governments and others attempting to discover international norms on a topic.
22. Bassiouni, "International Recognition," 203–279.
23. Ibid., 211–213.
24. Ibid., 219–221. For other examples, including the United Nations Compensation Commission in the aftermath of the Iraq–Kuwait conflict, see Pablo de Greiff, ed., *The Handbook of Reparations* (Oxford: Oxford University Press, 2006).
25. McCold et al., *An Introduction to Restorative Peacebuilding*, 2–3.
26. For example, see Umbreit and Armour's excellent *Restorative Justice Dialogue*, in which the authors propose that four important characteristics of restorative programs are a process of orientation, attention to safety, respectful interaction, and "positive energy." Umbreit and Armour, 101–106.
27. John Braithwaite, *Restorative Justice and Responsive Regulation* (Oxford: Oxford University Press, 2002), 194.
28. However, John Braithwaite and his colleagues at Australian National University's Centre for International Governance and Justice have recently questioned the importance, at least in the relatively short term, of uncovering truth as a means of securing peace. Braithwaite and his team are engaged in a remarkable 20-year project to research each of the major armed conflicts that have occurred since 1990. Through fieldwork interviews with warlords, generals, foreign ministers, peace negotiators, and peacekeeping commanders, the team is collecting detailed information on the conflicts so that they can code 670 variables. This method of data collection produces remarkably detailed information about each armed conflict and the peace and sometimes reconciliation that follows. They have studied seven of eight conflicts in Indonesia that began with the collapse of Suharto's New Order in 1998 and have now ended, resulting in "a remarkable renaissance of peace, unity, tolerance, improved governance and democracy." A pattern they discovered in studying the peace processes in those conflicts has been what they call "non-truth and reconciliation," where "non-truth meant not just forgetting, but lying." John Braithwaite et al., *Anomie and Violence: Non-Truth and Reconciliation in Indonesian Peacebuilding* (Canberra: ANU E Press, 2010), 16 and 42.
29. This raises a number of practical and conceptual questions about whether it is possible to fully repair harm, how to make it feasible for offenders to repair damage that exceeds their means, the sorts of actions that can be considered amends, and so forth. These are discussed elsewhere (Van Ness and Strong, *Restoring Justice*, 83–96).
30. Basic Principles and Guidelines, 8.
31. Zehr, *Changing Lenses*, 184.
32. Ibid.
33. Antony Duff, "Restoration and Retribution," in *Restorative Justice and Criminal Justice: Competing or Reconcilable Paradigms?*, ed. Andrew von Hirsch et al. (Oxford and Portland, OR: Hart Publishing, 2003), 47.
34. Princeton Project on Universal Jurisdiction, *The Princeton Principles on Universal Jurisdiction* (Princeton, NJ: Princeton University, 2001), 23.
35. M. Cherif Bassiouni. "Crimes against Humanity." http://www.crimesofwar.org/thebook/crimes-against-humanity.html.
36. Leslie Vinjamuri, "Deterrence, Democracy, and the Pursuit of International Justice," in *Ethics and International Affairs* 24 (2010): 201–207.
37. James R. Brunet, "Discouragement of Crime through Civil Remedies: An Application of a Reformulated Routine Activities Theory," *Western Criminology Review* 4 (2002): 73–75.
38. Berglind Halldórsdóttir Birkland, "Note: Reining in Non-State Actors: State Responsibility and Attribution in Cases of Genocide," *New York University Law Review* 84 (2010): 1623.
39. Robert Elias, *Victims of the System: Crime Victims and Compensation in American Politics* (New Brunswick, NJ: Transaction, Inc., 1983), 24–26.
40. Ibid., 25.

41. M. Cherif Bassiouni, "International Recognition," 260.
42. Basic Principles and Guidelines, 6.
43. Walgrave, *Restorative Justice*, 27.
44. Basic Principles and Guidelines, 7.
45. Ibid., 8.
46. Ibid.
47. Ibid., 8-9.
48. Ibid., 7-8.
49. Walgrave, *Restorative Justice*, 29.
50. Minow, "Hope for Healing," 241.
51. Walgrave, *Restorative Justice*, 61.
52. Ibid.
53. Minow, "Hope for Healing," 249-251.
54. Christopher D. Marshall, *Beyond Retribution: A New Testament Vision for Justice, Crime, and Punishment* (Grand Rapids, MI: Wm. B. Eerdmans Publishing Co., 2001), 142.

CHAPTER 6

Amnesties in the Pursuit of Reconciliation, Peacebuilding, and Restorative Justice

Louise Mallinder

Introduction

For centuries, amnesty laws were a habitual element of peacebuilding and reconciliation around the world.[1] Amnesties were used to calm insurrections or to mark the ends of wars between states.[2] Ruling elites often portrayed the introduction of these laws as gestures of mercy and benefaction designed to restore relations between the state and the citizenry, or between the peoples of belligerent countries.[3] During the past 30 years, amnesty laws have remained a key component of peace negotiations around the world. For example, a 2007 survey of peace agreements made between 1980 and 2006 found that while "provisions for prosecutions and truth commissions are rare in peace agreements . . . the use of amnesty is comparatively common."[4] However, with the development of the field of transitional justice from the early 1990s, reliance on national amnesty laws to promote peacebuilding and reconciliation has provoked increasing international controversy.[5]

The roots of this controversy lie in the end of the Cold War, which marked the start of a new era in global politics in which legalism and the rule of law became increasingly important in international relations.[6] These changes were manifest in a growing privileging of legal discourse within political transitions,[7] and a rapid expansion of international criminal law and institutions, including the creation of the ad hoc tribunals, the hybrid courts, and the International Criminal Court (ICC).[8] These developments had multiple and contrasting impacts on amnesty laws. For example, whereas previously, transitions from conflict and repression were usually achieved through pragmatic bargains brokered between political elites often entailing de facto impunity, the expansion of international criminal law caused these elites to demand and enact a growing number of amnesty laws to shield themselves from prosecution.[9]

Concurrent to the growing legalism creating incentives for the enactment of new amnesty laws, the emergence of international legal obligations for states to investigate, prosecute, and punish serious human rights violations resulted in international attitudes toward amnesty laws shifting. During this period, as is documented in United Nations' reports, perceptions of amnesties as tools for the "safeguard and promotion of human rights and fundamental freedoms"[10] were replaced with increasing condemnation of amnesty laws as forms of impunity.[11] The anti-impunity critiques, as articulated for example in the 2005 United Nations' *Updated Set of Principles to Combat Impunity* understand impunity as "the impossibility, de jure or de facto, of bringing the perpetrators of violations to account—whether in criminal, civil, administrative or disciplinary proceedings." The principles continue that both judicial and nonjudicial proceedings should lead to perpetrators of serious crimes under international law "being accused, arrested, tried and, if found guilty, sentenced to appropriate penalties, and to making reparations to their victims."[12] Under this approach, holding perpetrators to account is viewed as synonymous with criminal trials, and a state's failure to investigate violations and to ensure that "those suspected of criminal responsibility are prosecuted, tried and duly punished" by, for example, enacting amnesty laws, is perceived as resulting in impunity, even when the amnesty is "intended to establish conditions conducive to a peace agreement or to foster national reconciliation."[13]

The desire to prosecute and punish serious human rights violations is of course understandable; however, this anti-impunity approach has some limitations. For example, it is narrowly focused on primarily Western, legalistic, and formal understandings of justice, accountability, and the rule of law.[14] As this chapter will explore, this overlooks the role that informal or traditional accountability mechanisms can play in combating impunity and delivering more holistic forms of justice.[15] In many parts of the world, informal justice processes[16] are used to respond to both ordinary crime and mass violence. Indeed, the United Nations Development Program estimates that "informal justice systems usually resolve between 80 and 90 percent of disputes" in many countries.[17] Although the mandates, composition, processes, and outcomes of these mechanisms can vary considerably between communities, they are often permeated by common elements of restorative justice, which are outlined below. As the field of transitional justice has developed, informal approaches to justice have attracted increasing attention as a way of redressing past crimes,[18] and some transitional justice institutions have explicitly embraced restorative justice principles, even while implementing amnesties.[19] However, as will be explored below, supporters of legalistic approaches to combating impunity often view restorative approaches as compromised forms of justice to be pursued where "full" justice in the form of trials is not possible. This chapter will argue, however, that such narrow approaches to justice fail to acknowledge the full extent to which restorative justice can contribute to peacebuilding and reconciliation.

A second critique of amnesty-as-impunity arguments is that they overlook the considerable diversity that exists among amnesty laws today in terms of the crimes they cover, their implementation processes, and their diverse relationships to transitional accountability mechanisms, including trials, truth commissions, and vetting programs.[20] In particular, although amnesty laws bar criminal proceedings against certain categories of crimes or offenders, no amnesty laws to date have prohibited offenders participating in restorative justice processes; indeed, some require it. As this chapter will explore, understanding how amnesties can coexist with or even be integrated into restorative justice mechanisms can cast light on how victims, offenders, communities, and wider societies can engage with amnesty laws in ways that seek to deliver truth, accountability, reparations, and the articulation of non-violent social norms.

This chapter will begin by exploring how the concepts of peacebuilding, reconciliation, and transitional justice have evolved since the 1990s. This analysis will focus in particular on how perceptions of amnesty laws as promoting (or inhibiting) the goals espoused by these concepts have shifted over the past two decades, and conversely how amnesties themselves have adapted to take these goals into account. This chapter will then analyze interpretations of restorative justice within the transitional justice literature. Drawing on restorative justice theory and the experiences of amnesty processes in Timor-Leste, South Africa, and Uganda, this chapter will tentatively propose elements that should be considered when designing a "restorative amnesty." This analysis will include addressing how amnesty laws can facilitate inclusive restorative processes, promote truth recovery, enforce restorative outcomes, and provide reparations. However, due to the context-dependent nature of restorative justice, these proposals should not be viewed as a template to which all amnesties should conform, but rather as themes to be considered when tailoring bespoke amnesty laws for local contexts.

Restoring Relationships: Exploring the Nexus Between Peacebuilding, Reconciliation, and Transitional Justice

Although they share a concern in identifying how war-torn societies can achieve lasting peace, over recent decades, multidisciplinary scholars working on peacebuilding, transitional justice, and reconciliation have employed distinct conceptualizations, normative positions, and research questions. For example, the growth of transitional justice was strongly influenced by international human rights law and international legal scholars and jurists.[21] This meant that transitional justice programs were often highly legalistic and focused on promoting universal standards of rights protection. This contrasted with peacebuilding or conflict resolution strategies that sought to develop bespoke political solutions to tackle the problems faced by war-torn states, or with reconciliation programs that for well-intentioned or nefarious reasons often emphasized the importance of forgiving and forgetting in rebuilding post-conflict states. Amnesty laws to prevent the enforcement of legal penalties for human rights abuses were often at the epicenter of clashes between these different concepts, although as this section will explore, in recent years, there has been considerable convergence on the status of amnesties within each concept.

Reconciliation is an ancient notion that has its roots in the religious scriptures of Judaism, Christianity, and Islam, and the cultural traditions of indigenous communities in many parts of the world.[22] Historically, it was often associated with the restoration of personal relationships between individuals, or within communities. Where reconciliation did feature in legal or political discourse, it was often interpreted narrowly to mean simply an end to violence. As a result, it was primarily used to justify policies to promote national unity through a public forgetting of past crimes. Indeed, reconciliation has long been invoked as both the objective and justification for enacting amnesty laws and was even frequently proclaimed in the titles of amnesty legislation.[23] This narrow understanding of reconciliation as closing a door on the past clearly contrasts to wider-ranging transitional justice objectives such as delivering truth, accountability, and reparations. As a result, during the early development of the field of transitional justice, "transitional justice institutions were ... seen as a threat to national reconciliation" as according to their critics they were "charged with 'opening old wounds,' generating political instability and interfering with forward-looking political change."[24]

From the mid-1990s, theoretical and empirical inquiries into conflict began to emphasize the role that unequal relations can play in the onset of conflict, the ways in which rupturing relationships within and between communities can be a central objective of combatant factions, and ways in which fractured relationships can undermine the durability of peace and reconciliation programs.[25] These insights contributed to the emergence of what Philpott describes as a new "ethic of political reconciliation," which situated reconciliation as both a process and outcome that is central to transitional justice.[26] Philpott defines this ethic as a concept of justice that involves the will to restore victims, perpetrators, citizens, and the governments of states who have been involved in political injustices to a condition of right relationship within a political order or between political orders—a condition characterized by human rights, democracy, the rule of law, and respect for international law, by widespread recognition of the legitimacy of these values, and by accompanying virtues.[27]

This definition illustrates how under the newly evolving ethic of political reconciliation, national reconciliation policies moved from being primarily negative measures, whereby states refrained from delving into their violent pasts, to processes in which states committed themselves to more positive obligations to investigate political injustices, to repair the harms that they created, and to work toward a more just society. Thus, the recognition of the causes, nature, and long-term impacts of conflict shifted scholars and practitioners toward understandings of reconciliation as the longer-term restoration of relationships. In this way, the concept of reconciliation has deepened and come to share an emphasis on rebuilding relationships with restorative understandings of justice. However, within both concepts, "restoring" social relationships does not imply restoring the status quo ante, but rather establishing conditions whereby each individual's "rights to equal dignity, respect and concern" are respected in society.[28] The evolution within the concept of reconciliation has meant that rather than being in tension with transitional justice, sustainable reconciliation has become a central objective of many transitional justice institutions, most notably, the South African Truth and Reconciliation Commission,[29] as well as a key element of peacebuilding programs.

For several decades, peacebuilding scholars, influenced by the work of Johan Galtung, have distinguished between "positive peace" and "negative peace."[30] In this distinction, negative peace is defined as the "absence of violence, absence of war," whereas positive peace is a much richer concept entailing "the integration of human society."[31] In his later writings, Galtung expanded this definition of positive peace to denote the absence not just of physical violence, but also of structural and cultural violence.[32] This distinction between negative and positive peace echoes the evolution in the concept of reconciliation and has become a central element of peacebuilding theory. It can be used to differentiate between short-term efforts to bring stability and security to postconflict states, and longer-term projects that seek to address the root causes of violence and restore societal relationships that have been fractured by conflict.

Despite its decades-old academic existence, the term peacebuilding only entered into widespread policy usage with the UN secretary-general's 1992 *Agenda for Peace* report.[33] This report defined peacebuilding as the process of "rebuilding the institutions and infrastructures of nations torn apart by civil war and strife."[34] It argued that such intervention into war-torn states was necessary to "preserve peace once it is attained" and to "prevent the recurrence of violence among nations and peoples."[35] In addition, the report provided for wide-ranging intervention including

> Disarming the previously warring parties and the restoration of order, the custody and possible destruction of weapons, repatriating refugees, advisory and training support for security personnel, monitoring elections, advancing efforts to protect human rights, reforming or strengthening governmental institutions and promoting formal and informal processes of political participation.[36]

Interestingly, these measures are all forward-looking and, despite the acknowledgment of the need to "preserve peace," none provide for more sustained engagement to promote reconciliation between previously antagonistic communities. As such, the initial UN peacebuilding definitions focused primarily on delivering negative peace. In line with this approach, during the early 1990s, unconditional amnesty laws were widely used, in some cases with UN endorsement, to facilitate peace negotiations or the surrender of combatant factions.

The failure of many peace agreements to deliver lasting peace resulted in peacebuilding programs placing greater emphasis on longer-term projects to ensure sustainable peace. These developments mirrored the greater emphasis placed on the rebuilding of relationships within the concepts of reconciliation and transitional justice. The UN began to broaden its approach to include sustainable peace and reconciliation with the publication of the 2000 "Brahimi" report. This report defined peacebuilding as "activities undertaken on the far side of conflict to reassemble the foundations of peace and provide the tools for building on those foundations something that is *more than just the absence of war*" (emphasis added).[37] To construct this more positive form of peace, the report identified the following non-exhaustive list of measures that could be undertaken:

> reintegrating former combatants into civilian society, strengthening the rule of law (for example, through training and restructuring of local police, and judicial and penal reform); improving respect for human rights through the monitoring, education and investigation of past and existing abuses; providing technical assistance for democratic development (including electoral assistance and support for free media); and promoting conflict resolution and reconciliation techniques.[38]

This list illustrates that reconciliation and the reintegration of former combatants had become central elements of peacebuilding strategies, together with rule of law projects and transitional justice mechanisms to investigate past crimes. Drawing on these developments, Borer argues that the shared objective of reconciliation provides a key point of intersection between peacebuilding and transitional justice.[39] However, with regard to amnesty laws, it is interesting to note that the Brahimi report calls for past abuses to be investigated, although not prosecuted. This is surprising given that from 1999, the UN had adopted guidance for its mediators that prohibited them from endorsing amnesties for serious human rights violations.[40] The emphasis on post-conflict justice was incorporated more fully into the UN's approach to peacebuilding with the UN secretary-general's 2004 report on *Transitional Justice and the Rule of Law*. In this report, the secretary-general proclaimed that "justice, peace and democracy are not mutually exclusive objectives, but rather mutually reinforcing imperatives."[41] The UN secretary-general further proclaimed the importance of inclusive participation in peacebuilding strategies by stating that "ultimately, no rule of law reform, justice reconstruction, or transitional justice initiative imposed from the outside can hope to be successful or sustainable."[42] Instead, he argued that reconciliation programs should be "based upon meaningful public participation involving national legal professionals, Government, women, minorities, affected groups and civil society."[43]

This section has demonstrated how over the past two decades the concepts of reconciliation, peacebuilding, and transitional justice have gradually converged to recognize the importance of rebuilding relationships at all levels within transitional states. The coalescence between these concepts has meant that the emphasis on investigating, prosecuting, and punishing past human rights violations within legalistic approaches to transitional justice has caused the use of amnesty laws to deliver peace and reconciliation to become controversial. Although unconditional amnesty laws for serious human rights violations continue to be enacted, new amnesties now explicitly exclude such crimes more often, and scholars and practitioners have become more skeptical of the capacity of amnesties for serious offenses to deliver sustainable peace. Instead, amnesty laws, if adopted, are increasingly being designed not as an end point, but rather as one component in wider, longer-term peacebuilding programs. In addition, as will be explored below, some of these amnesty processes seek to promote reconciliation by soliciting the participation of all stakeholders in society, including the perpetrators of violence. Such explicit engagement with and attempt to hold responsible those who commit crimes or who are involved in other forms of socially or personally destructive behavior is of course a key tenet of restorative justice.

Restorative Theories of Transitional Justice

Around the world, restorative justice has been practiced in diverse forms by many communities since ancient times. However, the label of restorative justice has been applied to a variety of settings with the result that restorative justice "is often used as a catchall phrase to refer to any alternative practice that does not look like mainstream justice practices."[44] Due to the array of mechanisms that have been described as restorative, no widely accepted definition of the concept has yet developed and there is no clear consensus on restorative justice principles, either in relation to ordinary crime or mass violence.[45]

Although restorative principles are contested, several elements of restorative justice appear to be broadly accepted in the literature. First, in contrast to criminal justice approaches that focus on crime and punishment, restorative justice primarily views crime as "a violation of people and relationships."[46] As a result, rather than privileging the illegality of the action, restorative approaches emphasize the "harms" caused by the offenders' actions, both to individual victims and the wider community.[47] Second, the notion that restorative justice processes should aim primarily to repair the harm rather than punish the perpetrators appears largely uncontested.[48] Indeed, restorative theories argue that causing harm creates "responsibilities" for offenders to right their wrongs.[49] Third, the focus on encouraging offenders to fulfill their responsibilities in repairing such damage emanates not just from the urge to "restore" victims but also from an acceptance that the aim of restorative justice should also be to reintegrate the offenders rather than "alienate and isolate" them from society.[50] Breaking cycles of recidivism is, from a restorative perspective, not just in the interests of individual offenders, but also has obvious benefits for the community and society to which they return. In this way, the outcomes of restorative justice processes are "forward looking" as they seek to address the "implication of a wrong in the future," rather than punishing the offender "for what she did in the past."[51] Finally, throughout the process of identifying the harms and the necessary remedies, restorative justice processes are generally geared toward encouraging the involvement of all stakeholders, including the direct victims, the offenders, the families of the victims and offenders, and their wider communities.[52] This inclusive approach recognizes that all these persons, including the offenders themselves, can suffer harm as a result of the offenders' actions. It therefore encourages a version of justice wherein the participants are encouraged to work collaboratively to develop remedies that are acceptable to all parties. This more inclusive approach contributes to the identification of harms and remedies that are not commonly discussed in formal justice processes, encourages healing and responsibility among all the participants, and envisages a sufficiently broad understanding of harm to include structural injustices that affect people and communities beyond the immediate participants.[53]

The theory of restorative justice has primarily been applied in indigenous justice processes or domestic criminal justice procedures in liberal, democratic states.[54] To a lesser extent, restorative justice has also been invoked in transitional states in the work of truth commissions,[55] local justice mechanisms,[56] and indeed with regards to the rights of victims before the International Criminal Court.[57] In addition, as explored above, restorative goals of rebuilding relationships today form part of the objectives of peacebuilding programs around the world. However, the application of restorative justice to past crimes in transitional contexts remains comparatively undertheorized by scholars and advocates.[58] Where theorizations of transitional justice as restorative justice have been attempted, they generally fall into one of the following camps: (1) restorative justice as compromised justice or (2) restorative justice as exceptional justice. However, as this chapter argues, restorative justice can be theorized as a full theory of justice.

Restorative Justice as Compromised Justice

In recent critiques of transitional justice, scholars have argued that transitional knowledge and practice have become dominated by legalism.[59] As noted above, this has resulted in a privileging of Western forms of prosecution and punishment as the appropriate means to hold perpetrators accountable for serious human rights violations. However, it is increasingly becoming evident that in most transitional contexts, prosecuting all perpetrators is impossible. For example, in his 2004 report on *Transitional Justice and the Rule of Law*, the UN secretary-general argued that "[i]n the end, in post-conflict countries, the vast majority of perpetrators of serious violations of human rights and international humanitarian law will never be tried, whether internationally or domestically."[60] The difficulties in prosecuting offenders can result from a number of factors, including the limitations posed by compromised and under-resourced legal and penal infrastructures, large numbers of offenders and victims, the time that may have elapsed since the crimes occurred, the reluctance of some victims and witnesses to come forward, the difficulties in obtaining evidence, the ongoing military or political strength of some perpetrators or their supporters, and the existence of legal obstacles, such as amnesty laws. Where these difficulties exist, restorative justice is sometimes advocated as "partial" justice, where "full" justice is not possible. Llewellyn argues that "implicit in this approach is the view that restoration is just one of the goals served by retributive justice of prosecution and punishment," rather than being a full theory of justice itself.[61]

Under this approach, where full justice in the form of trials and punishment cannot be implemented for some or all offenders, restorative justice can offer a partial, second-best form of justice that will identify perpetrators, acknowledge victims' suffering, and provide reparations, and which can be pursued through other transitional justice mechanisms such as truth commissions or local justice processes. In this way, alternative transitional justice mechanisms operating according to restorative justice principles can be used to address the "impunity gap" created by the limitations of formal criminal proceedings, either in conjunction with limited trials or as a substitute for prosecutions.

As amnesty laws are generally viewed as obstacles to full justice, the theorization of restorative justice as "compromised" justice has contrasting implications for amnesty laws. First, for many advocates of legalistic approaches to transitional justice, the obligations to prosecute and punish serious human rights violations imply that restorative justice should only accompany rather than replace formal prosecutions. This approach suggests that amnesty laws should be omitted from restorative processes so that crimes dealt with by these processes can also be prosecuted and punished by the courts once conditions are more favorable (for example, following reforms of the criminal justice and judicial systems, or the stabilization of the democratic transition). Although trials become increasingly difficult as time elapses, advocates of this approach can point to examples such as the recent reopening of human rights trials in Argentina and Chile decades after the crimes occurred as evidence that the passage of time does not always block trials.[62] However, the South American experiences of annulling or narrowing preexisting amnesty laws have not been replicated in other parts of the world. Furthermore, the experience of Bosnia-Herzegovina, where serious human rights violations were excluded from amnesty legislation, shows that, 16 years after the conflict ended, even with substantial international involvement in creating the international tribunal, supporting initiatives to build the capacity of the domestic criminal justice system, and the establishing of a hybrid court, only a small fraction of the total number of perpetrators have been prosecuted. From this it can be speculated that in the majority of transitional states, which do not enjoy such high levels of international involvement, but which today often face pressure to exclude serious crimes from amnesty legislation, pursuing prosecutions for these crimes will face even more difficulties and delays.

This points to the second implication of viewing restorative justice as "partial" justice. Where it is accepted that "full" justice for most offenders is and will remain impossible, restorative justice approaches then become not a temporary stopgap until trials can be conducted, but rather a replacement for trials. As amnesties do not bar participation in restorative justice approaches, accepting that trials will not be conducted means that the arguments against amnesty laws as an impediment to prosecutions would no longer be persuasive. Instead, amnesty laws could be used to remove obstacles to offender participation in the restorative justice processes, where without the amnesty offenders would be reluctant to incriminate themselves through participation. In this way, amnesty laws can be used to promote rather than inhibit "partial" justice, where "full" justice is not possible.

Restorative Justice as Exceptional Justice

The second rationale often proposed for using restorative approaches in transitional contexts advocates that they are better suited to the exceptional conditions of political transitions than pursuing accountability through criminal prosecutions. This rationale draws on criminological analyses of the causes of mass violence to argue that focusing on pursuing individual criminal responsibility results in only some individuals being labeled as "evildoers," while concealing the responsibility of broader sections of society who benefited from or supported the violence.[63] In addition, Drumbl argues that trials of individual offenders "conveniently or unwittingly swaddle the myriad structural factors that permitted that evildoer to perpetrate evil on such a large-scale to the point that those factors become masked."[64] Lundy reasons that concealing these factors is risky, as the focus on legal remedies for physical violations against direct victims, "tends to leave the injustices that caused the conflict untouched."[65] This omission arguably leaves open the possibility of renewed conflict in the future.[66] In addition to the risks posed by the limited criminal accountability, the punitive nature of formal criminal proceedings may encourage offenders to lie or conceal their crimes rather than inculpating themselves. This denial will further prevent the nature and causes of the conflict being revealed, and it will undermine acknowledgment for victims.[67] Other critiques of trials for mass atrocity argue that formal court proceedings often marginalize victims, rather than providing them with a forum "to tell their stories and receive redress."[68]

Proponents of restorative justice in political transitions argue that inclusive restorative processes in which harms are revealed and appropriate remedies are developed are better suited to addressing the communal dimensions of mass violence in ways that are supportive to victims, can reintegrate offenders, and can restore damaged communal relationships. From such a vantage point, amnesty laws that remove obstacles to offender participation in restorative processes can facilitate a broader understanding of justice, not simply impunity. In other words, under this approach, amnesties to encourage offenders to participate in restorative processes and reveal their crimes are not viewed as compromised justice, but rather as "alternative forms of accountability, through flexible processes of conversation and negotiation."[69] For example, according to Bell and O'Rourke, restorative processes that offer amnesty in exchange for truth arguably "deliver a differently textured accountability by moving beyond overly proceduralized forms of adversarial justice as adjudications of individual guilt toward a more complex account of individual, communal and institutional accountability."[70]

This theorization offers a more positive role for restorative justice in political transitions than theorizations of restorative justice as compromised or partial justice. However, it too has been critiqued by some restorative justice proponents as portraying restorative justice only as an *exceptional* measure to be implemented during the exceptional political conditions that exist in transitions from mass atrocity.[71] This position implies that once a community or state has transitioned toward peace and democracy, ordinary criminal justice procedures will be possible and preferable. However, as the next section will explore, this position can be criticized as failing to recognize that restorative justice offers a full theory of justice.

Restorative Justice as Full Justice

In the restorative justice literature, the relationship between restorative justice and retributive justice has long been disputed. Gavrielides succinctly summed up these debates as arguments between commentators who assert that restorative justice "is a complete, consistent and independent justice paradigm that has the power to stand alone, and which should replace the current one," and those who argue, conversely, that restorative justice "can exist only if supported by other paradigms namely the present justice system."[72] In transitional settings, restorative processes commonly exist in mixed systems consisting of trials, restorative justice in the form of truth commissions or local justice, and other mechanisms, including amnesty. The relationship of the restorative justice mechanisms to prosecutions can be separate, such as in Uganda, where the local justice ceremonies have been operating independently of the courts to reintegrate returning combatants.[73] Alternatively, restorative processes can choose to work with the courts by providing relevant information to prosecutors. For example, in 2003, the South African Truth and Reconciliation Commission (TRC) presented the National Director of Public Prosecutions with a list of over 300 names of persons it recommended for prosecution.[74] However, such mixed approaches may face many of the obstacles and limitations noted above of conducting trials for human rights violations in transitions.

In contrast, some theorists argue that restorative justice has the potential to offer a complete framework to address mass atrocity. This approach has been cogently reasoned by Llewellyn, who argues that restoration is not simply one of the goals of justice (along with retribution, deterrence, incapacitation, rehabilitation, and expression of social norms), "nor is it a theory about a *kind* or *type* of justice appropriate only in certain circumstances. Restorative justice is, rather, a comprehensive theory about the meaning of justice." (emphasis in original)[75] Under this approach, harms or crimes are viewed as creating inequalities in the relationships between victims and offenders. Consequently, justice is viewed as a process that seeks to respond to wrongdoing through the restoration of relationships between the "the victim(s), wrongdoer and the respective communities" so that "each party enjoys equal dignity, respect and concern."[76] As noted above, the restorative goal of rebuilding relationships can be interpreted as a central tenet of both reconciliation and peacebuilding.

In contrast to restorative processes, where prosecution and punishment seek to isolate the offender, although they may "prevent further harm to relationships where there is a continuing risk of harm—that is where the perpetrator is not willing or able to restore the relationships," but they will do little to restore ruptured relationships.[77] As a result, Llewellyn argues if justice is understood as the restoration of relationships, prosecution and punishment "are only able to serve the interests of justice in part."[78] In contrast, amnesty laws that aim to deliver peace may also contribute to delivering restorative justice and reconciliation, where they are designed to encourage offenders to take responsibility for their actions and engage with accountability through participation in restorative justice processes. In this way, by encouraging offender participation, amnesty laws can potentially contribute to creating the conditions for the restoration of relationships. I would argue that for amnesties to be understood as an expression of restorative justice they must be designed according to restorative justice principles. The ways in which this might be achieved are explored in the following sections.

Designing Amnesties on Restorative Principles

As noted above, amnesty laws are generally considered to be a denial of justice.[79] This portrayal is accurate for amnesties that are granted unconditionally to human rights abusers, in the absence of alternative accountability mechanisms, in order to shield the abusers from investigations or punishment for their crimes. However, amnesty laws have diverse objectives and take many forms, with the result that amnesty processes often coexist with restorative justice processes, and some even have restorative goals. For example, following state repression, transitional governments have often enacted amnesty laws for political prisoners, in which the amnesty itself is a form of restoration to individuals who were victimized by the state.

In addition, in the wake of armed conflicts, amnesties may be unobjectionable from a restorative justice perspective according to leading restorative justice scholar, John Braithwaite. However, he stipulates that for this to be the case amnesties must "contribute to the ending of war" and all the stakeholders must be given "a voice in the amnesty negotiations."[80] The objective of ending the war is a common feature in peace agreement amnesties, many of which are negotiated by representatives of the leading factions. To a lesser extent there are also examples of amnesty negotiations that have listened to voices from other constituencies, such as victims' groups or civil society negotiations, or amnesty processes that were subject to national plebiscites. These criteria indicate the role of amnesty in delivering negative peace. However, Braithwaite adds a further criterion that links post-conflict amnesties more directly to the restorative objective of rebuilding relationships by stating that within restorative amnesty processes all amnesty beneficiaries must be "willing to show public remorse for their crimes and to commit to service to the new nation and its people to repair some of the harm they have done."[81] In the midst of peace negotiations where the conflict may still be ongoing, the political and military elites are likely to be unwilling to bind themselves and their supporters to obligations to admit guilt and acknowledge their actions as criminal offenses. In such circumstances, the political context in which the amnesty negotiations are occurring could shape how pressures to achieve "negative peace" are balanced against the need to create the conditions for sustainable peacebuilding, reconciliation, and restorative justice. However, even where the amnesty is initially agreed upon as a pragmatic political bargain, the experience of the South African amnesty process indicates that these balances may not be static and restorative justice principles can be incorporated into amnesties that originate as the product of political compromises.

The transitional amnesty process in South Africa began life as the product of an elite pact agreed to in the final stages of the transitional negotiations, but its ultimate shape was determined in the legislation to establish the TRC, which was promulgated by the democratically elected transitional government following public consultations. The enacted law created the Amnesty Committee of the TRC, which was empowered to grant amnesty for civil and criminal liability to individual offenders who fully disclosed their political offenses,[82] with offenders who did not apply for amnesty or did not comply with the conditions remaining liable for prosecution. The conditional and individualized nature of this process introduced elements of accountability, reconciliation, and restorative justice into the process that was originally the product of political compromise. This was recognized by the TRC in its final report, when responding to criticism of the amnesty as a denial of justice, the TRC argued that amnesty could be viewed as a form of justice if justice is conceived, not as retribution, but as restoration.[83] Although the extent to which the South African amnesty process was conducted according to restorative principles has rightly been critiqued by several authors,[84] the framing of the amnesty within the restorative framework transformed a contentious transitional compromise into a process that delivered greater truth and accountability.

Drawing on the example of the South African amnesty process, together with amnesties in Timor-Leste and Uganda, this section will explore how amnesty laws can be designed to promote restorative justice.[85] This analysis will be structured around the contribution that amnesty laws can make to delivering key restorative justice elements identified from the literature, namely: inclusive stakeholder participation, truth recovery, enforcement, and repairing harm.[86] The elements identified here represent ideal types and as yet no amnesty has fully addressed *all* of these criteria within a single process. Indeed, and as noted above, the ability or desirability of transitional states to do so will depend on the specific political context and the nature of the harms to be addressed. Instead, this section seeks to review the experience of existing amnesties to illustrate the role and potential of amnesties to move from impunity to more victim-centered approaches within restorative justice, reconciliation, and peacebuilding frameworks.

Inclusive Stakeholder Participation

As noted above, restorative justice has been described as "relational," as it offers a "vision of justice that is concerned primarily with addressing the harm that wrongdoing causes to relationships."[87] As a result, restorative processes seek to include all persons who might have been harmed or affected by crimes, such as the victims, the offenders, the families of the victims and offenders, and their wider communities. In addressing damaged relationships, restorative justice focuses on the restoration of social relationships, rather than personal or intimate ones.[88] These social relationships relate to the interactions between individuals that arise from sharing "the same physical or political space."[89]

In contexts of communal violence, as noted above, negative social relationships have contributed to and been generated by violence. As a result, inclusive stakeholder participation in designing and implementing restorative peacebuilding and reconciliation strategies is central to building positive social relationships. In this section, the ways in which amnesties contribute to restoring relationships will be analyzed through considering how they encourage community participation, facilitate victim-offender encounters, and reintegrate offenders.

Inclusive community participation should form a component of all stages of the amnesty process. First, affected persons should be given a voice when designing amnesty processes. This participation can be instigated by grassroots movements that mobilize to lobby political elites to enact amnesty laws. For example, in Uganda, the Amnesty Act of 2000 was enacted following a prolonged campaign by religious, cultural, and political leaders from the region worst affected by the conflict between the Ugandan government and the Lord's Resistance Army.[90] Alternatively, governments can consult with local communities during the process of drafting the legislation. For example, in Timor-Leste, following complaints from local leaders that grassroots dynamics were being overlooked by international actors and political elites, the National Council for Timorese Resistance (the UN's local governing partner) created a Steering Committee comprising government officials, non-governmental organizations, and international experts to consult on national reconciliation strategies.[91] This committee conducted consultations with "different political and human rights groups from the village to regional level" over six months, which contributed to the design of the Community Reconciliation Process (CRP).[92]

Second, following the initial consultations and enactment of amnesty legislation, inclusive participation should continue during the law's implementation. For example, the Ugandan Amnesty Act of 2000 mandates the Amnesty Commission to coordinate a program of public sensitization to the amnesty law, to consider and promote appropriate reconciliation mechanisms in the conflict-affected areas, and to promote dialogue and reconciliation within the spirit of this Act.[93] In fulfilling this mandate, the Amnesty Commission has sought to engage not just in dissemination but also in dialogue with affected communities. For example, Moses Draku, the commission's Principal Public Relations Officer, states that the commission approaches the traditional cultural leaders to say "We would like you to help us know how to bring peace in your own area, because your people are going to obey and respect what you tell them. If we come through you, we are likely to get peace in this area."[94] This cooperation has also entailed the commission working with family and community members to promote social reintegration through "traditional reconciliation mechanisms, religious meetings and community-welcoming gatherings."[95] In Uganda, participation in these traditional reconciliation processes is not a condition of amnesty process, but linking these participative community processes to the amnesty process offers a way of using the amnesty to facilitate reconciliation.

Third, where hearings are held to determine whether individual applications for amnesty should be approved or whether amnestied persons should be able to reintegrate into the community, all stakeholders should be able to participate in the hearings to discuss the ways in which the offenders' actions have caused harms, to present evidence or question offenders, and to contribute to devising appropriate outcomes. This participation can include identifying harms that are not commonly discussed in formal justice processes, such as structural injustices. In addition, as noted above, these discussions can acknowledge the harms the offenders to caused victims and the wider community but also how the offenders harmed themselves by their actions. For example, in Timor-Leste individuals who were suspected of minor crimes, such as theft, minor assault, or arson,[96] could participate in a CRP facilitated by the truth commission.[97] The CRP drew on a traditional form of justice known as *lisan*, so that offenders who wished to benefit from the amnesty had to take part in this justice process.[98] During the CRP, community members could listen to the statements of the victims and offenders but could also ask questions or add relevant information to the discussion. In addition, local community leaders often formed part of the panels that adjudicated these hearings.[99] Local communities could also contribute to the decisions on the appropriate form of reparations to be made and, as discussed below, this could include offenders undertaking community service.

In addition to creating a forum for inclusive participation, restorative amnesty processes can facilitate victim-offender encounters. Llewellyn argues that "these encounters are fundamental to restorative justice processes as they provide the opportunity for dialogue about the nature of the harms experienced by the parties and how to address them."[100] By creating a space for dialogue between victims and offenders, these encounters can potentially highlight how victim and offender identities are often politically complex and overlapping.[101] For example, as Mani highlights, "categories such as 'victim' or 'perpetrator' are fluid in situations of dynamic conflict and can change over time. Victims can and do become aggressors and often have done so in the past, just as former perpetrators may become victimized."[102] For victims, such encounters can be important for obtaining truth about events and being able to question offenders, which can be an empowering experience. Furthermore, exposing these complex identities during restorative justice processes can encourage participants to recognize one another's humanity.[103]

Among the case study amnesty processes, victim-offender encounters could occur in several ways. For example, in South Africa there was some scope for the presence and participation of victims in the Amnesty Committee hearings. Victims' rights in these hearings included the right to be notified of the hearings, to provide evidence to be taken into consideration, to give formal testimony, to question amnesty applicants, either personally or through legal representatives,[104] and to make impact statements, either orally or in writing. These statements could include "their feelings or intuition about the facts, how the events being related had affected them and their families, what their and their families' current needs were, requests for explanations of what had happened and sometimes statements of forgiveness."[105] Finally, in addition to the Amnesty Committee's formal hearings, in exceptional cases following a victim request, the hearings were accompanied by "behind the scenes interpersonal dialogues" between victims and perpetrators, facilitated by TRC staff.[106] Overall, the South African amnesty process offered victims more extensive participation rights than had featured in previous amnesties around the world. This represents a significant innovation and contributes to the restorative nature of the process, even though in practice the extent to which individual victims exercised their rights was constrained by the legalistic focus of the Amnesty Committee and its limited investigative and financial resources.[107]

Victims and offender encounters are also often part of local justice initiatives. For example, in Timor-Leste the CRP created a space where victims could respond to statements made by the offenders by "detailing the impact of the crimes committed against them or members of their families." In addition, they could question the perpetrator to clarify his or her precise role and responsibility.[108] Also, although victims could not veto the grant of immunity, they could be involved in determining the nature of the reparation that the perpetrator should make.[109]

As victim participation in the South African and Timorese amnesty processes was voluntary, the case studies indicate some victims will wish to use the restorative amnesty process as a forum to participate in dialogue with the offenders and to have their voices heard in the amnesty hearings. Such participation can provide a sense of acknowledgment and empowerment for individual victims. Personal participation in restorative amnesty processes can also contribute to the reintegration of offenders into the community.

Finally, as noted above, in contrast to retributive criminal justice, which seeks to isolate offenders through penal sanctions, restorative justice aims to reintegrate offenders.[110] The importance of offender reintegration following conflict has been emphasized by Villa-Vicencio, who argued that "for the kind of sustainable peace to be achieved that makes the restoration of victims possible, it is crucial for perpetrators to be incorporated into the emerging new society."[111] Amnesty laws can play an important role in reintegrating offenders by simply preventing the use of "isolating punishment mechanisms."[112] Additionally, amnesties frequently contain measures to facilitate reintegration.[113] For example, the Ugandan Amnesty Commission is tasked with monitoring the demobilization, reintegration, and resettlement of reporters.[114]

This reintegration can require both preparing communities for the return of offenders and supporting offenders who are reintegrating into society. Often offenders need considerable assistance in reintegrating as they may have physical or psychological problems, including drug or alcohol dependencies, as a result of their experiences. They may also require educational or vocational training to help them find employment.[115] Providing these services to offenders can create tensions within communities, particularly where those they harmed are also in need of government support. As a result, this reintegration must be managed within a process of communal participation.

In addition to providing financial or medical support, amnesty processes can provide a forum for cultural or religious forms of offender reintegration. For example, by performing local reintegration or justice processes, amnesty beneficiaries can show their desire to change and to respect the norms of society.[116] For example, in Uganda, although traditional justice processes are not formally part of the amnesty process, offenders have participated in traditional forms of justice in order to seek reacceptance from their community. In addition, these rituals may be of spiritual value to former combatants, as many in Uganda express fear of *cen* (haunting by the spirits of the dead),which the traditional cleansing rituals are believed to remedy.[117]

Truth Recovery, Answerability, and Incentivized Testimony

Amnesty laws have historically been described as "acts of oblivion" that seek to "forget" past crimes. Transitional societies' need to forget their violent pasts is an idea with a long lineage.[118] Today, some memory scholars continue to suggest that forgetting can play an important role in reconciliation and healing within transitional states, particularly where cultural traditions do not support "verbally recounting memories of violence."[119] In contrast, scholars and activists in the fields of restorative justice and transitional justice widely emphasize the importance of truth recovery in preventing a repetition of crimes and contributing to the healing of victims and society. Furthermore, in recent years, legal scholars and jurists have highlighted the emerging right to truth of victims and societies in the wake of mass atrocity.[120]

In addition to potential benefits for victims and societies, where truth recovery processes are empowered to hear testimony from offenders and can offer incentives such as amnesty to encourage them to recount their crimes, the process of testifying can potentially benefit the offenders. For example, Parmentier et al. have contended that transitional justice mechanisms designed according to restorative justice principles "should provide the conditions necessary to . . . allow perpetrators and survivors to tell their own story and allow them to gain back the control over their position and their role in the conflict, and later also their place in the community."[121] This suggests that testifying may contribute to offenders' reintegration into the community, and where their testimony is permitted to address the wider context in which their acts were committed, rather than just the facts of the case; it may contribute to greater social understanding of the causes of the violence.

Furthermore, although the transitional justice literature frequently equates accountability with criminal prosecutions, in other disciplines the term is understood more broadly to encompass *answerability* and *enforcement*. Whereas the legalistic focus in transitional justice emphasizes the need for enforcement and punishment in accountability processes, studies in fields such as public administration or criminology place greater emphasis on the importance of answerability within any understanding of accountability. Roche has described answerability as the requirement for offenders to literally "account for" their actions.[122] According to Schedler, this may require offenders to outline the facts of what took place and to explain or justify their decisions and actions. Their version of events may then be scrutinized, judged, and recorded.[123] Encouraging offenders to answer in this way for their crimes can be a feature of criminal proceedings, particularly where plea agreements are available. However, in general, the punitive nature of trials may cause offenders to lie, obfuscate, or conceal the full extent of their crimes. Indeed, the deficiencies of trials as truth recovery processes have been succinctly summed up by Cohen, who stated "[o]nly cultural dummies would think of reading a legal verdict as a historical record of the event, let alone its context and why it happened."[124] In contrast, although amnesties impede some criminal enforcement mechanisms, recent amnesty laws in several jurisdictions have been designed to promote the answerability component of accountability through granting amnesty as an incentive for offenders to offer testimony, or at least through removing obstacles to such testimony.

The most high-profile example of exchanging amnesty for truth occurred before the South African TRC. Under this process, the requirement that perpetrators fully disclose their criminal acts was a crucial element of the amnesty process. The Constitutional Court emphasized the amnesty's importance for truth recovery in the *AZAPO* case, which stated that without the amnesty, "there is nothing to encourage such persons to make the disclosures and to reveal the truth which persons in the positions of the applicants so desperately desire."[125] In practice, the procedures of the TRC's Amnesty Committee in receiving and processing offender testimony have been criticized for taking a narrow, legalistic, and somewhat inconsistent approach toward the information the offenders were required to disclose,[126] while the unwillingness of large numbers of offenders to apply or to disclose certain crimes created gaps in the information revealed. However, despite these difficulties with the mandate, resources, and proceedings of the Amnesty Committee, it is widely argued that the process obtained more truth than would have been possible without the offer of amnesty. It resulted in the revealing of gross human rights violations, in the resolution of disappearances, in the exposing of incidents in which individuals "had been suspected of involvement in acts against their own people" as acts of terror by the state, and in the exoneration of individuals who had been wrongly accused. In its final report, the TRC argued that even if trials had been pursued, they "would probably have contributed far less than did the amnesty process towards revealing the truth about what had happened to many victims and their loved ones."[127] The TRC further argued that by providing a space to listen "carefully to the complex motives and perspectives of all" those involved in the "divisions of the past," the amnesty process contributed to social or "dialogue" truth.[128] The TRC argued that this discourse was important, as "it was through this process that the essential norms of social relations between people were reflected. It was, furthermore, through dialogue and respect that a means of promoting transparency, democracy and participation in society was suggested as a basis for affirming human dignity and integrity."[129]

Although the South African model of empowering a truth commission to grant amnesty for serious human rights violations in exchange for testimony has not been exactly replicated in other contexts, it has nonetheless shaped the design of other transitional justice processes. For example, in Timor-Leste individuals who were suspected of minor crimes[130] could participate in the CRP facilitated by the truth commission.[131] This process was initiated by written statements from offenders in which they detailed the relevant acts, admitted their guilt, and asked to participate in the CRP.[132] These statements were reviewed by the prosecutorial authorities and if the offender was deemed not to have committed serious crimes, then the CRP could be held.[133] At the hearing, the offender would then read this statement to the mediators, victims, and community members who were present.[134] According to Zifcak, following this reading, the offender "might make any further oral statement that he or she wished by way of elaboration, explanation or apology."[135] These statements could then be followed by questions from the mediators, victims, or community members. Although, according to Pigou, this process was not "strictly a truth seeking exercise,"[136] the CRP resulted in statements from over 1,500 offenders, which considerably exceeded expectations.[137]

In addition to the importance of offender testimony for truth recovery and creating a forum in which offenders can answer for the crimes, as will be explored below, the obligation of offenders to testify and admit guilt for their criminal actions has been viewed as also addressing some of the enforcement elements of accountability.[138]

Enforcement and the Role of Punishment

As discussed above, accountability entails both *answerability* and *enforcement*. Enforcement comprises the notion of a judgment being passed on the offenders' behavior by an accountability forum, such as a court, truth commission, or traditional justice process. Although for serious human rights violations, legalistic approaches to transitional justice argue for the need for offenders to be punished following adverse judgments, the role of punishment is more contested in the literature on accountability. For example, Bovens argues that it is the *possibility* of punishment—not its actual imposition—that marks the difference between the "non-committal provision of information and being held to account."[139] Similarly, among restorative justice scholars and advocates there is considerable debate on the extent to which restorative justice processes can and should be punitive.[140] This debate ranges from views that restorative processes should primarily be constructive and seek to reintegrate the offender, rather than punish them, to understandings that restorative justice can be viewed as punishment as it creates responsibilities for offenders.[141]

In transitional settings, restorative justice processes have been used in combination with selective prosecutions and punishment for high-level offenders or for persons who did not comply with amnesty processes. However, the notion of punishment with restorative justice can entail a range of alternative measures, not simply conviction and sentencing. These alternatives include requiring offenders to demonstrate remorse for their crimes and imposing penalties for recidivism or non-compliance. In addition, as will be explored below, offenders could be required to contribute to repairing the harm that they caused. The flexibility of the restorative justice approach to punishment offers the opportunity for an amnesty law that precludes penal sanctions to be reconciled with a legitimate justice process in which the needs of the victims are acknowledged.

Where amnesties are conditioned on truth-telling, offenders are required to acknowledge their guilt. As noted above, answering for their actions can represent a form of accountability. For example, the South African TRC contended in its report: "[i]f one accepts . . . that punishment is not a necessary prerequisite for the acknowledgement of accountability, it is possible to see that qualified amnesty does contain certain of the essential elements required by justice. Thus, individual perpetrators were identified and, where possible, the circumstances that gave rise to the gross violations of human rights they had committed were explained."[142] However, recounting their crimes may not automatically result in offenders experiencing shame or demonstrating remorse for their actions through apologies or reparative measures. Instead, perpetrators of political offenses who feel their actions were morally justified may seek to "use restorative mediation to 'explain' why they took recourse in violence."[143] In such circumstances, John Brewer contends that seeking to impose shame or guilt may risk "perpetuating the conflict."[144] In addition, requirements that offenders apologize for their actions might dissuade offenders from participating and where they do apologize, the mandatory obligation to do so could devalue genuine expressions of remorse by causing the apologies to appear self-serving and insincere.[145] Forced apologies may also be particularly unwelcome among victims, where they are perceived as creating pressure on victims to reciprocate by forgiving those who harmed them.

Although requiring offenders to demonstrate feelings of shame and remorse could prove risky for any restorative amnesty process, this does not mean that shame has no role in such processes. For example, some offenders may decide to participate in public amnesty hearings due to preexisting feelings of shame,[146] while others may come to experience shame through being confronted by the pain their actions have caused for victims, their own family, the community, and perhaps even the wider society.[147] Where such feelings of shame occur, this can be interpreted as an indication of the offenders' acceptance of responsibility. In his analysis of whether the South African amnesty process was a mechanism for accountability, Ron Slye found that "[t]here is no doubt that the South African amnesty holds applicants to account for their actions."[148] In particular, he argued that "[a]mnesty does not come cheap" for the perpetrators as they face considerable public, personal, and professional repercussions, and that "[p]ublic shame, personal alienation and familial rejection should not be dismissed as insignificant."[149] In addition, although apologies were not required by the Amnesty Committee, encounters with their victims did motivate some offenders to apologize for their actions.[150]

Offenders also apologized for their actions during the Community Reconciliation Process in Timor-Leste. Here, also, apologies were not mandatory for all offenders, but rather the legislation establishing the CRP stipulated that apologies or other acts of contrition were possible requirements to demand of offenders in the reconciliation agreements reached during the CRP.[151] In its final report, the Commission for Reception, Truth and Reconciliation stated that "[t]he number of cases in which the deponent [amnesty beneficiary] was required only to make a public apology was far higher than had been expected,"[152] and in many villages it was the only form of reconciliation that communities asked offenders to perform. The commission then speculated that the requests for apologies, rather than other possible outcomes such as community service or contributing to reparations, may be due to "the close-knit nature of East Timorese communities."[153] However, the truth commission report noted that where apologies did not appear to be sincere, they failed to satisfy the victims and the community members. In contrast, where apologies are viewed as genuine they can open the way for forgiveness among participants in restorative processes. According to Philpott, "forgiveness is a practice of reconciliation and a tool of peacebuilding," and by creating a forum in which it can occur, restorative justice can support these processes.[154]

The issue of punishment can also arise in individualized amnesty processes, where offenders are granted immunity from civil or criminal liability in exchange for pledging in oral or written statements not to re-offend.[155] These conditions can help to assuage public concerns about the ongoing threat posed by the offenders or about the possibility of the amnesty creating or reinforcing cultures of impunity.[156] In some countries, individuals who have promised to obey these conditions can face stiff penalties for recidivism. For example, a 2002 amendment to the Ugandan Amnesty Act of 2000 provided that if, after receiving an amnesty certificate, a person commits crimes of war or armed rebellion, they cannot then be granted amnesty for that act and will be liable for prosecution for it, although not for the acts that were previously amnestied.[157] More restrictive still was the 1991 Lebanese amnesty, which stated that those committing crimes covered by the amnesty, after the date of its promulgation, would be liable for prosecution for their original offenses together with any new offenses.[158]

An alternative way of ensuring offender compliance with an amnesty process is to withhold the amnesty until offenders have fulfilled their obligations under any agreements reached in restorative hearings. For example, in Timor-Leste, offenders only benefited from immunity for the acts they had disclosed in the hearing once they had "fully complied with all obligations" arising from their Community Reconciliation Agreement.[159] Depending on the nature of the restorative outcome, such measures would help to fulfill the victims' rights to reparations. Furthermore, as the threat of punishment remains for noncompliance, the possibility of non-recidivism penalties could work as enforcement mechanisms.

Repairing Harm

Again, as discussed previously, the focus of restorative justice is not whether laws have been broken but rather on identifying the harms that resulted from the offenders' actions and considering how these harms might be repaired.[160] According to restorative justice theory and practice, these harms should be interpreted broadly to include those endured by the victims, their community, the wrongdoers and their surrounding relationships, and the wider community.[161] This inclusive approach contrasts with criminal law, which views the state as the principal party harmed by the crime.[162] Furthermore, restorative approaches understand harm more broadly than simply physical, emotional, or material harms experienced by the victims of physical violence, but it also recognizes other forms of harm, including those resulting from structural injustice.[163]

Once harms have been identified through inclusive dialogue involving all stakeholders, restorative justice mandates that these harms should be repaired. The appropriate reparations measures should also be agreed in inclusive processes involving victims, offenders, and their communities. Such reparations measures can help to "appease the anger and indignation that victims and the public may feel towards" offenders, thereby assisting with their reintegration.[164] Encouraging offenders to contribute to reparations, Llewellyn argues, "is crucial for the reintegration of the perpetrator, and, ultimately for the restoration of relationships."[165] According to international human rights law and transitional justice, reparations can be made in various material and symbolic forms, including restitution, compensation, rehabilitation, and guarantees of non-repetition.[166] Given the centrality of reparations to restorative justice theory, for amnesty processes to comply with restorative principles, the issue of reparations is crucial,[167] and as demonstrated by some of our case study jurisdictions, reparations can be included directly in the amnesty process.

In South Africa, where amnesty was granted for political offenses, including gross violations of human rights, the Amnesty Committee was empowered to forward the names of any victims identified to the TRC's Reparation and Rehabilitation Committee. Similarly, even where amnesty was denied, if the committee was of the opinion that a gross violation of human rights had occurred, it could forward the name of the victim to the reparations committee.[168] Despite these provisions, the reparations issue was very contentious in South Africa, particularly since grants of amnesty shielded offenders from civil as well as criminal liability. This controversy arose for several reasons, the most important of which for restorative justice theory is that in the South African amnesty process, other than the requirement to disclose their crimes, offenders were not involved in the process of redressing harm.[169] This meant that offenders "were not required to make reparations, nor was there any formal mechanism through which they could voluntarily participate in making reparation to their victims and to the community."[170] Llewellyn argues that this omission is problematic both for victims who see the offenders benefiting from the amnesty without making any practical effort to repair the harm, and for offenders, who may be stigmatized by the amnesty processes without the possibility of making amends for their actions.[171] This omission was even criticized by the TRC, which, arguing against its own legislatively mandated procedures, stated that "the fact that people are given their freedom without taking responsibility for some form of restitution remains a major problem with the amnesty process."[172]

In contrast, requirements that offenders or their communities pay reparations are often part of local justice initiatives. For example, in Timor-Leste, the participants in the CRP can agree that offenders must pay compensation to their victims. Where the perpetrator fails to pay, Amy Senier notes, the "responsibility falls to his family."[173] Similar approaches are part of the local justice initiatives used in Uganda to reintegrate returning combatants.[174] However, as noted above, in many post-conflict situations reintegrating offenders often have limited financial resources or vocational skills, and therefore may not be in a position to contribute financially to compensation programs. Furthermore, offenders may not be able to rely on their family or community to provide reparations, as they too may have been impoverished by the conflict.

Where they are unable to make financial reparations, offenders can demonstrate their remorse and make reparations through contributing to community service projects. These projects can provide symbolic reparations to victims while also making a practical contribution to improving their living standards. The approach taken to community service can vary from projects designed by victims, offenders, and their communities in mediation hearings to more centralized approaches. For example, the CRP in East Timor provided for the reconciliation agreements to require amnesty beneficiaries to perform community service. According to the Timorese truth commission, this "usually consisted of a task performed once a week over a set period that was usually no longer than three months. Examples of required tasks included: the repair of public buildings, tree planting, the erection of a village flagpole, and cleaning of church grounds or other facilities."[175] In some cases, the community joined the offender in carrying out the agreed task. Furthermore, in Uganda, the Amnesty Commission has begun to provide reintegration funds to groups of former combatants to fund development projects to be carried out together with the local community. Where offenders are encouraged to repair the harms they have caused through material or symbolic reparations, it can provide a manifestation of the offenders' remorse, improve conditions for those harmed by the offenders' actions, and facilitate the offenders' reintegration into society.

Conclusion

In the past two decades, theories of restorative justice and reconciliation have attracted increasing attention from scholars and activists who are interested in peacebuilding and transitional justice. For some commentators, restorative justice offers a justification for granting amnesties for past crimes in order to obtain other social goals such as peace and truth recovery. For others, including the contributors to this edited collection, restorative justice can be understood as a theory of justice that is better suited to addressing the communal dimensions of mass violence than trials that seek to individualize criminal responsibility and alienate offenders. In accordance with the latter approach, rather than being a denial of justice, amnesty laws can complement restorative justice principles by encouraging offenders to participate in restorative processes in exchange for immunity from prosecution.

This chapter has sought to explore the extent to which amnesties can complement the principles and goals of restorative justice, peacebuilding, and reconciliation. Drawing on restorative justice theory and the experiences of amnesty processes in Timor-Leste, South Africa, and Uganda, this chapter explored how amnesty laws can be designed to facilitate inclusive stakeholder participation, promote truth-telling, enforce restorative outcomes, and provide reparations. It demonstrated that amnesties could potentially fulfill all these goals and thereby contribute to the restoration of relationships within transitional states. However, as yet, no amnesty process has contained all of these restorative elements. Furthermore, tensions may exist between different elements of a restorative amnesty. For example, if incentivizing perpetrator testimony is prioritized in order to gain access to information such as the location of the remains of disappeared persons, then encouraging offenders to come forward may require providing anonymity or allowing them to provide testimony behind closed doors. While such measures could potentially lead to greater truth recovery, they could reduce the extent to which the amnesty inspires communal discourse. In addition, it seems likely that the more conditions are placed on the grant of amnesty the less desirable it may appear to some offenders. However, experiences in several transitional states indicate that the voluntary testimony of even relatively small numbers of perpetrators can make significant contributions to the level of truth revealed and to public perceptions of the past.

Amnesty laws are a constant feature of peacebuilding and reconciliation endeavors in many parts of the world, and despite the growth of international criminal law in recent decades, amnesties are likely to continue to play a role in transitions from war to peace. This role will vary from country to country depending on the balance of power in the transition, the nature of the criminality, and societies' perceptions of justice. In all contexts, however, designing amnesty laws in accordance with restorative principles can offer a way to move from impunity for conflict-related crimes toward more inclusive and holistic approaches that seek to repair the multiplicity of harms suffered by diverse stakeholders and to help societies move toward more just forms of governance.

Notes

1. The author would like to thank Jennifer Llewellyn, Daniel Philpott, Kieran McEvoy, Leslie Vinjamuri, and Aaron Boesenecker for their thoughts and comments on the earlier drafts of this chapter. She would also like to thank the participants at the authors' workshop, University of Notre Dame, September 17, 2010, and participants at the *Reconciliation, Peacebuilding, and Restorative Justice* conference, New York, November 10, 2011, for their feedback on this chapter.
2. For a historical overview of the use of amnesties, see Fania Domb, "Treatment of War Crimes in Peace Settlements—Prosecution or Amnesty?" in *War Crimes in International Law*, ed. Yoram Dinstein and Mala Tabory (Hague: Martinus Nijhoff Publishers, 1996), 305; Robert Parker, "Fighting the Siren's Song: The Problem of Amnesty in Historical and Contemporary Perspective" *Acta Juridica Hungaria* 42, no. 1–2 (2001): 69–89.
3. For an analysis of the motivations for introducing amnesty laws see Louise Mallinder, *Amnesty, Human Rights and Political Transitions: Bridging the Peace and Justice Divide (Studies in International Law)* (Oxford: Hart Publishing, 2008), 39–70.
4. Leslie Vinjamuri and Aaron Boesenecker, *Accountability and Peace Agreements: Mapping Trends from 1980 to 2006* (Geneva: Centre for Humanitarian Dialogue, 2007), 5.
5. See, e.g., Diane F. Orentlicher, "Rule-of-Law Tools for Post-Conflict States: Amnesties," Office of the United Nations High Commissioner for Human Rights (Geneva) HR/PUB/09/1.
6. Cesare P.R. Romano, "The Proliferation of International Judicial Bodies: The Pieces of the Puzzle," *New York University Journal of International Law and Politics* 31 (1998): 709–751.
7. Kieran McEvoy, "Beyond Legalism: Towards a Thicker Understanding of Transitional Justice," *Journal of Law and Society* 34, no. 4 (2008): 411–440.
8. See, e.g., Kai Ambos and Otto Triffterer, eds., *Commentary on the Rome Statute of the International Criminal Court: Observers' Notes, Article by Article* (Baden-Baden: Aufl edn Nomos Verlagsgesellschaft, 1999), 1295; Laura A. Dickinson, "The Promise of Hybrid Courts," *American Journal of International Law* 97, no. 2 (2003): 295; Roy S. K. Lee, ed., *The International Criminal Court: The Making of the Rome Statute—Issues, Negotiations, Results* (Hague: Kluwer Law International, 1999), 657; Cesare Romano, André Nollkaemper, and Jann K. Kleffner, eds., *Internationalized Criminal Courts and Tribunals: Sierra Leone, East Timor, Kosovo, and Cambodia* (Oxford: International Courts and Tribunals Series, Oxford University Press, 2004), 491; William A. Schabas, *The UN International Criminal Tribunals: The Former Yugoslavia, Rwanda and Sierra Leone* (Cambridge: Cambridge University Press, 2006); William A. Schabas, *An Introduction to the International Criminal Court*, 3rd ed. (Cambridge: Cambridge University Press, 2007).
9. Louise Mallinder, "Amnesties' Challenge to the Global Accountability Norm? Interpreting Regional and International Trends in Amnesty Enactment." In *Amnesty in the Age of Human Rights Accountability: Comparative and International Perspectives*, ed. Leigh A. Payne and Francesca Lessa (Cambridge: Cambridge University Press, 2012).
10. UN Sub-Commission on Prevention of Discrimination and Protection of Minorities, Resolution 1983/34 The administration of justice and the human rights of detainees. UN Doc E/CN.4/Sub.2/RES/1983/34 (September 6, 1983).
11. These criticisms are most evident in the reports of human rights organizations; see, e.g., Amnesty International, "'We Cry for Justice': Impunity Persists 10 years on in Timor-Leste," AI Index ASA 57/001/2009; Sara Darehshori, "Selling Justice Short: Why Accountability Matters for Peace," Human Rights Watch. New York: July 2009.
12. UNCHR, *Updated Set of Principles for the Protection and Promotion of Human Rights through Action to Combat Impunity*. Commission on Human Rights, 2005.
13. Ibid. Principles 1 and 24.
14. See, e.g., Payam Akhavan, "Are International Criminal Tribunals a Disincentive to Peace? Reconciling Judicial Romanticism with Political Realism" *Human Rights Quarterly* 31 (3) (2009): 624.

15. For an analysis of the concept of accountability within transitional justice, see Louise Mallinder and Kieran McEvoy, "Rethinking Amnesties: Atrocity, Accountability and Impunity in Post-Conflict Societies," *Contemporary Social Science: The Journal of the Academy of Social Science* 6, no.1 (2011): 107–128.
16. Within the scholarly literature, a range of terminology is used to describe these processes, including traditional justice, local justice, informal justice, customary justice, indigenous justice, and restorative justice. Each of these terms has its strengths and limitations but it is beyond the scope of the chapter to analyze these debates. Instead, "informal justice" has been selected as the most appropriate here to contrast these processes with formal prosecutions, although the author acknowledge this term is not unproblematic.
17. Ewa Wojkowska, *Doing Justice: How Informal Justice Systems Can Contribute* (UNDP, 2006), 5.
18. E.g., in his August 2004 report on *The Rule of Law and Transitional Justice in Conflict and Post-Conflict Societies*, the UN secretary-general proclaimed that "due regard must be given to indigenous and informal traditions for administering justice or settling disputes, to help them to continue their often vital role and to do so in conformity with both international standards and local tradition." See UNSC, *Report of the Secretary-General: The Rule of Law and Transitional Justice in Conflict and Post-Conflict States*, UN Doc S/2004/616 (August 23, 2004), para. 36.
19. E.g., in its final report, the South African Truth and Reconciliation Commission expressly characterized its work as a form of restorative justice. See Truth and Reconciliation Commission of South Africa Report, vol. 1, ch. 5, para. 82 ("TRC Report"). See also e.g., Erin K. Baines, "The Haunting of Alice: Local Approaches to Justice and Reconciliation in Northern Uganda" *International Journal of Transitional Justice* 1, no. 1 (2007): 97; Patrick Burgess, "A New Approach to Restorative Justice: East Timor's Community Reconciliation Process" in *Transitional Justice in the Twenty-First Century: Beyond Truth Versus Justice*, ed. Naomi Roht-Arriaza (Cambridge University Press, Cambridge 2006), 176; Sinclair Dinnen, Anita Jowitt, and Tess Newton Cain, *A Kind of Mending: Restorative Justice in the Pacific Islands* (Canberra: Pandanus Books, 2003); Carola Eyber and Alastair Ager, "Conselho: Psychological Healing in Displaced Communities in Angola," *Lancet* 306 (2002): 871; Paulo Granjo, "The Homecomer: Postwar Cleansing Rituals in Mozambique" *Armed Forces & Society* 33, no. 3 (2007): 382; Alcinda Honwana, "Children of War: Understanding War and War Cleansing in Mozambique and Angola" in *Civilians in War*, ed. Simon Chesterman (Boulder, CO: Lynne Rienner Publishers, 2001), 1137; Pat Howley, *Breaking Spears and Mending Hearts: Peacemakers and Restorative Justice in Bougainville* (London: Zed Books, 2002), 222; Victor Igreja, Gamba Spirits and the Homines Aperti: Socio-Cultural Approaches to Deal with the Legacies of the Civil War in Gorongosa, Mozambique (paper presented at the Building a Future on Peace and Justice conference, Nuremberg, 25–June 27, 2007) available at http://www.peace-justice-conference.info/download/WS10-Igreja%20report.pdf; Justice and Reconciliation Project, "The Cooling of Hearts: Community Truth-Telling in Acholi-Land," Liu Institute for Global Issues and Gulu District NGO Forum (Vancouver, July 2007); Coel Kirkby, "Rwanda's Gacaca Courts: A Preliminary Critique" *Journal of African Law* 50, no. 2 (2006): 94; Andre Le Sage, "Stateless Justice in Somalia: Formal and Informal Rule of Law Initiatives," Centre for Humanitarian Dialogue (Geneva, July 2005) 1; Kieran McEvoy and Anna Eriksson, "Restorative Justice in Transition: Ownership, Leadership and 'Bottom Up' Human Rights" in *Handbook of Restorative Justice*, ed. Dennis Sullivan and Larry Tifft (Routledge, Abingdon: Routledge International Handbooks, 2006), 321; Agnes Nindorera, "*Ubushingantahe* as a Base for Political Transformation in Burundi," http://www.ksg.harvard.edu/wappp/research/working/bc_nindorera.pdf; Josiah Osamba, "Peace Building and Transformation from Below: Indigenous Approaches to Conflict Resolution and Reconciliation among the Pastoral Societies in the Borderlands of Eastern Africa" *African Journal on Conflict Resolution* 2, no. 1 (2001): 71; A. S. J. Park, "Community-Based Restorative Transitional Justice in Sierra Leone" *Contemporary Justice Review* 13, no. 1 (2010): 95; Jessica Raper. "The *Gacaca* Experiment: Rwanda's Restorative Dispute Resolution Response to the 1994 Genocide" *Pepperdine Dispute Resolution Law Journal* 5, no. 1 (2005): 1; Thomas Harlacher and others, *Traditional Ways of Coping in Acholi* (Kampala, Uganda:

Caritas Kampala, 2006), 160; Lars Waldorf, "Rwanda's Failing Experiment in Restorative Justice," in *Handbook of Restorative Justice: A Global Perspective*, ed. Dennis Sullivan and Larry Tifft (Routledge, London: Routledge International Handbooks, 2006), 422; Spencer Zifcak, "Restorative justice in Timor-Leste: The Truth and Reconciliation Commission," *Development Bulletin* 68 (2005): 51.

20. Louise Mallinder, "Can Amnesties and International Justice Be Reconciled" *International Journal of Transitional Justice* 1, no. 2 (2007): 208–230. Louise Mallinder, "Beyond the Courts? The Complex Relationship of Trials and Amnesty," in *International Criminal Law*, ed. William A. Schabas (Cheltenham: Edward Elgar Publishing Ltd., 2011); Mallinder, *Amnesty, Human Rights and Political Transitions*, 165–195.

21. See, e.g., Paige Arthur, "How 'Transitions' Reshaped Human Rights: A Conceptual History of Transitional Justice," *Human Rights Quarterly* 31, no. 2 (2009): 321–367.

22. Daniel Philpott, *Just and Unjust Peace: An Ethic of Political Reconciliation* (Oxford: Oxford University Press, 2012).

23. See. e.g., Ley de Amnistía para el Logro de la Reconciliación Nacional, Decreto N° 805, Diario Oficial N° 199, October 28, 1987 (El Salvador); Ley de amnistía general y reconciliación nacional, n° 81, La Gaceta, March 23, 1990, No. 53, p. 429–430 (Nicaragua).

24. Bronwyn Leebaw, "The Irreconcilable Goals of Transitional Justice," *Human Rights Quarterly* 30 (2008): 95–96.

25. See, e.g., Mary Kaldor, *New and Old Wars: Organized Violence in a Global Era*, 2nd ed. (Cambridge: Polity Press, 2006); Dinka Corkalo and others, "Neighbors Again? Intercommunity Relations after Ethnic Cleansing" in *My Neighbor, My Enemy: Justice and Community in the Aftermath of Mass Atrocity*, ed. Eric Stover and Harvey M. Weinstein (Cambridge: Cambridge University Press, 2004), 143.

26. Philpott, *Just and Unjust Peace*.

27. Ibid.

28. Jennifer J. Llewellyn, "Restorative Justice in Transitions and Beyond: The Justice Potential of Truth Telling Mechanisms for Post-Peace Accord Societies," in *Telling the Truths: Truth Telling and Peace Building in Post-Conflict Societies*, ed. Tristan Anne Borer (Notre Dame, IN: University of Notre Dame Press, 2006), 91–92.

29. Article 3(1) of the Promotion of National Unity and Reconciliation Act 1995 provided that "The objectives of the Commission shall be to promote national unity and reconciliation in a spirit of understanding which transcends the conflicts and divisions of the past."

30. Johan Galtung, "Editorial," *Journal of Peace Research* 1 (1964): 1. Johan Galtung, *Peace by Peaceful Means: Peace and Conflict, Development and Civilization* (Oslo: International Peace Research Institute, 1996).

31. Galtung, 'Editorial'., 2.

32. Johan Galtung, "Violence, Peace and Peace Research" *Journal of Peace Research* 6 (1969): 167; Johan Galtung, "Cultural Violence" *Journal of Peace Research* 27 (1990): 291.

33. UN Secretary-General, *Agenda for Peace: Preventive Diplomacy, Peacemaking and Peace-keeping* (1992) UN Doc A/47/277.

34. Ibid., para. 15.

35. Ibid., para. 21.

36. Ibid., para. 55.

37. Lakhdar Brahimi, *Report of the Panel on United Nations Peace Operations*, UN Doc S/2000/809 (2000), para. 13.

38. Ibid., para. 13.

39. Tristan Anne Borer, "Truth Telling as a Peace Building Activity" in *Telling the Truths: Truth Telling and Peace Building in Post-Conflict Societies*, ed. Tristan Anne Borer (Notre Dame, IND: University of Notre Dame Press, 2006), 28.

40. William A. Schabas, "Amnesty, the Sierra Leone Truth and Reconciliation Commission and the Special Court for Sierra Leone," *U.C. Davis Journal of International Law & Policy* 11 (2004): 148–149.

41. UNSC, *Report of the Secretary-General: The Rule of Law and Transitional Justice in Conflict and Post-Conflict States*, UN Doc S/2004/616 (August 23, 2004).
42. Ibid., para. 17.
43. Ibid., para. 17.
44. Llewellyn, "Restorative Justice in Transitions and Beyond," 91.
45. An omission which, as noted elsewhere in this collection, this project has set out to address.
46. Howard Zehr, "Doing Justice, Healing Trauma: The Role of Restorative Justice in Peacebuilding," *South Asian Journal of Peacebuilding* 1, no. 1 (2008).
47. Miriam J. Aukerman, "Extraordinary Evil, Ordinary Crime: A Framework for Understanding Transitional Justice," *Harvard Human Rights Journal* 15 (2002), 39–97. 78.
48. Stephan Parmentier, Kris Vanspauwen, and Elmar Weitekamp, "Dealing with the Legacy of Mass Violence: Changing Lenses to Restorative Justice," in *Supranational Criminology: Towards a Criminology of International Crimes*, ed. Smeulers Alette and Haveman Roelof (Antwerp: Intersentia, 2008), 335–356, 344.
49. Zehr, "Doing Justice, Healing Trauma."
50. Parmentier, Vanspauwen, and Weitekamp, "Dealing with the Legacy of Mass Violence," 344.
51. Llewellyn, "Restorative Justice in Transitions and Beyond," 96.
52. Ibid., 91.
53. See, e.g., Rama Mani. "Rebuilding an Inclusive Political Community after War," *Security Dialogue* 36, no. 4 (2005): 511.
54. Paul McCold, Jennifer Llewellyn, and Daniel W. Van Ness, *An Introduction to Restorative Peacebuilding* (Working Party on Restorative Justice, 2007), 1. Available at www.restorativejustice.org/10fulltext/mccoldp/at_download/filey.
55. See, e.g., Jennifer J. Llewellyn, "Truth Commissions and Restorative Justiee" in *Handbook Of Restorative Justice*, ed. Gerry Johnstone and Daniel W. Van Ness (Cullompton, UK: Willan Publishing, 2007), 351; Jennifer J. Llewellyn, "Restorative Justice in Transitions and Beyond: The Justice Potential of Truth Telling Mechanisms for Post-Peace Accord Societies" in *Telling the Truths: Truth Telling and Peace Building in Post-Conflict Societies*, ed. Tristan Anne Borer (Notre Dame, IN: University of Notre Dame Press, 2006), 83; Jennifer J. Llewellyn, "Justice for South Africa: Restorative Justice and the South African Truth and Reconciliation Commission" in *Moral Issues in Global Perspective: Moral and Political Theory*, 2nd ed. (Peterborough ON: Broadview Press, 2006). Louise Mallinder, "Can Amnesties and International Justice Be Reconciled?" *International Journal of Transitional Justice* 1, no. 2 (2007): 208.
56. See, e.g., Luc Huyse and Mark Salter, eds, *Traditional Justice and Reconciliation after Violent Conflict: Learning from African Experiences* (Stockholm: International IDEA, 2008); Patrick Burgess, "A New Approach to Restorative Justice: East Timor's Community Reconciliation Process" in *Transitional Justice in the Twenty-First Century: Beyond Truth Versus Justice*, ed. Naomi Roht-Arriaza (Cambridge: Cambridge University Press, 2006), 176; Kieran McEvoy and Anna Eriksson, "Restorative Justice in Transition: Ownership, Leadership and 'Bottom Up' Human Rights" in *Handbook of Restorative Justice*, ed. Dennis Sullivan and Larry Tifft (Routledge, Abingdon: Routledge International Handbooks, 2006), 321.
57. See, e.g., Janine Natalya Clark. "The Three Rs: Retributive Justice, Restorative Justice, and Reconciliation," *Contemporary Justice Review* 11, no. 4 (2008): 331; Tim Allen, "The International Criminal Court and the Invention of Traditional Justice in Northern Uganda" *Politique Africaine* 107 (2007): 147; Nancy Amoury Combs, *Guilty Pleas in International Criminal Law: Constructing a Restorative Justice Approach* (Stanford, CA: Stanford University Press, 2007); D. Radosavljevic, "Restorative Justice under the ICC Penalty Regime" *Law & Practice of International Courts & Tribunals* 7, no. 2 (2008): 235; Mark Findlay and Ralph J. Henham, *Transforming International Criminal Justice: Retributive and Restorative Justice in the Trial Process* (Cullompton, UK: Willan Publishing, 2005), 413.
58. Llewellyn, "Truth Commissions and Restorative Justice," 352.
59. See e.g., Patricia Lundy and Mark McGovern. "Whose Justice? Rethinking Transitional Justice from the Bottom Up" *Journal of Law and Society* 35, no. 2 (2008): 265; Kieran McEvoy, "Beyond

Legalism: Towards a Thicker Understanding of Transitional Justice" *Journal of Law and Society* 34, no. 4 (2008): 411.
60. UNSC, *Report of the Secretary-General on the Rule of Law and Transitional Justice in Conflict and Post-Conflict Societies* (2004), para. 46.
61. Llewellyn, "Restorative Justice in Transitions and Beyond," 87.
62. See, e.g., Cath Collins, *Post-transitional Justice: Human Rights Trials in Chile and El Salvador* (Philadelphia: Pennsylvania State University Press, 2010); M. K. O'Donnell. "New Dirty War Judgments in Argentina: National Courts and Domestic Prosecutions of International Human Rights Violations" *Northwestern University Law Review* 84 (2009): 333; Pablo F. and Pellegrini Parenti Lisandro, "Argentina" in *Justicia de Transición: Informes de América Latina, Alemania, Italia y España*, ed. Kai Ambos, Ezequiel Malarino, and Gisela Elsner (Berlin: Konrad-Adenauer-Stiftung, 2009), 133; Terence Roehrig, "Executive Leadership and the Continuing Quest for Justice in Argentina" *Human Rights Quarterly* 31 (2009): 721.
63. Mark A. Drumbl, "Collective Violence and Individual Punishment: The Criminality of Mass Atrocity," *Northwestern University Law Review* 99, no. 2 (2005): 538–539.
64. Ibid., 538–539.
65. Lundy and McGovern, "Whose Justice?," 274.
66. Drumbl, "Collective Violence and Individual Punishment," 538–539; Paul Gready, "Reconceptualising Transitional Justice: Embedded and Distanced Justice," *Conflict, Security and Development* 5, no. 1 (2005), 3–21, 18–19.
67. Stanley Cohen, "Unspeakable Memories and Commensurable Law," in *Legal Institutions and Collective Memories*, ed. Susanne Karstedt (Oxford: Hart Publishing, 2009), 27–38.
68. McCold, Llewellyn, and Van Ness, *An Introduction to Restorative Peacebuilding*, 5.
69. Christine Bell and Catherine O'Rourke, "Does Feminism Need a Theory of Transitional Justice? An Introductory Essay," *International Journal of Transitional Justice* 1, no. 1 (2007): 40.
70. Ibid., 40.
71. See e.g., Llewellyn, "Restorative Justice in Transitions and Beyond."
72. Theo Gavrielides, "Restorative Justice—the Perplexing Concept: Conceptual Faultlines and Power Battles within the Restorative Justice Movement," *Criminology and Criminal Justice* 8, no. 2 (2008): 170.
73. The Agreement and Annexure on Accountability and Reconciliation that resulted from the now-defunct Juba peace process had planned that local justice ceremonies would become part of more holistic strategies to address the crimes committed during the conflict between the Ugandan government and the Lord's Resistance Army.
74. Ken Oh and Theresa Edlmann, "Reconciliatory Justice: Amnesties, Indemnities and Prosecutions in South Africa's Transition," in *After the Transition: Justice, the Judiciary and Respect for the Law in South Africa—A Collection of Papers from a Project on Justice and Transition*, ed. Center for the Study of Violence and Reconciliation (Johannesburg: CSVR, 2007), 13.
75. Llewellyn, "Restorative Justice in Transitions and Beyond," 91.
76. Jennifer Llewellyn, "Justice to the Extent Possible: The Relationship between the International Criminal Court and Domestic Truth Commissions," in *La Voie Vers La Cour Pénale Internationale: Tous Les Chemins Mènent à Rome*, ed. Hélène Dumont and Anne-Marie Boisvert (Montreal: Journees Maximilien-Caron, 2003), 334.
77. Llewellyn, "Justice to the Extent Possible," 334.
78. Ibid., 334.
79. Amy Gutmann and Dennis Thompson, "The Moral Foundations of Truth Commissions," in *Truth v. Justice: The Morality of Truth Commissions*, ed. Robert I. Rotberg and Dennis Thompson (Princeton, NJ: Princeton University Press, 2000), 32.
80. John Braithwaite, *Restorative Justice and Responsive Regulation* (Oxford: Oxford University Press, 2002) 203.
81. Ibid., 203.
82. Promotion of National Unity and Reconciliation Act 1995, sec. 20(1).

83. Truth and Reconciliation Commission of South Africa Report, vol. 1, ch. 5, para. 82 ("TRC Report").
84. See e.g., Graeme Simpson and Paul Van Zyl, "South Africa's Truth and Reconciliation Commission," *Temps Modernes* 585 (1995): 394; Hugo Van der Merwe and Audrey R. Chapman, "Did the TRC Deliver?" in *Truth and Reconciliation in South Africa: Did the TRC Deliver?* ed. Audrey R. Chapman and Hugo Van der Merwe (Philadelphia: Pennsylvania Studies in Human Rights, University of Pennsylvania Press, 2008), 241.
85. It should of course be noted that amnesty provisions can work in different ways, and are not always designed to promote restorative justice.
86. These broad categories will be explored here only in relation to amnesty laws. For more detailed analysis of the relationship of each category to restorative justice, see relevant chapters in this book.
87. McCold, Llewellyn, and Van Ness, *An Introduction to Restorative Peacebuilding*, 2.
88. Llewellyn, "Restorative Justice in Transitions and Beyond," 91–92.
89. Ibid., 91–92.
90. Gilbert M. Khadiagala, *The Role of the Acholi Religious Leaders Peace Initiative (ARLPI) in Peace Building in Northern Uganda* (USAID, 2001).
91. Amy Senier, "Traditional Justice as Transitional Justice: A Comparative Case Study of Rwanda and East Timor," *Praxis: Fletcher Journal of Human Security* XXIII (2008): 67–88, 76.
92. Ibid., 76.
93. Amnesty Act 2000 (Uganda) sec. 9.
94. Moses Draku, Principal Public Relations Officer, Amnesty Commission, cited in Joanna R. Quinn, "Tradition: Traditional Cultural Institutions on Customary Practices in Uganda," Paper presented at International Studies Association conference, New York (2009).
95. Ibid.
96. Individuals responsible for serious crimes such as murder, rape, and torture were intended to face prosecution before special panels of the District Court of Dili.
97. Regulation No. 2001/10 on the Establishment of a Commission for Reception, Truth and Reconciliation in East Timor (2001) (Timor-Leste) sec. 1.
98. Senier, "Traditional Justice as Transitional Justice," 78.
99. Ibid.
100. Llewellyn, "Restorative Justice in Transitions and Beyond," 99.
101. John D. Brewer, *Peace Processes: A Sociological Approach* (Cambridge: Polity, 2010), 164–165.
102. Mani, "Rebuilding an Inclusive Political Community after War," 522.
103. Parmentier, Vanspauwen, and Weitekamp, "Dealing with the Legacy of Mass Violence," 353.
104. Antje du Bois-Pedain, *Transitional Amnesty in South Africa* (Cambridge: Cambridge University Press, 2007), 223–224.
105. Ilan Lax, "Amnesty, Reparation and the Object of Reconciliation in the Context of South Africa's Truth and Reconciliation Commission," in *To Repair the Irreparable: Reparation and Reconstruction in South Africa*, ed. Erik Doxtader and Charles Villa-Vicencio (Claremont, South Africa: David Philip Publishers, 2004), 236–237.
106. Audrey R. Chapman and Hugo Van der Merwe, eds., *Truth and Reconciliation in South Africa: Did the TRC Deliver?* (Philadelphia: University of Pennsylvania Press, 2007), 11.
107. Lax, "Amnesty, Reparation and the Object of Reconciliation in the Context of South Africa's Truth and Reconciliation Commission," 227; Jeremy Sarkin, "An Evaluation of the South African Amnesty Process," in *Truth and Reconciliation in South Africa: Did the TRC Deliver?*, ed. Audrey R. Chapman and Hugo Van der Merwe (Philadelphia: University of Pennsylvania Press, 2008), 93–115.
108. Zifcak, "Restorative Justice in Timor-Leste," 53.
109. Ibid., 53.
110. Ibid., 95.
111. Charles Villa-Vicencio, "Transitional Justice, Restoration, and Prosecution," in *Handbook of Restorative Justice: A Global Perspective*, ed. Dennis Sullivan and Larry Tifft (London: Routledge, 2006), 395.

112. Llewellyn, "Restorative Justice in Transitions and Beyond," 98.
113. Mallinder, *Amnesty, Human Rights and Political Transitions*, 387–390.
114. Amnesty Act 2000 (Uganda) s 9.
115. John Braithwaite, "Restorative Justice: Assessing Optimistic and Pessimistic Accounts," *Crime and Justice* 25 (1999): 69.
116. M. Cherif Bassiouni, "Searching for Peace and Achieving Justice: The Need for Accountability," *Law and Contemporary Problems* 59, no. 4 (1996): 21.
117. Julian Hopwood et al., *With or without Peace: Disarmament, Demobilisation and Reintegration in Northern Uganda* (Justice and Reconciliation Project, 2008), 5.
118. Barbara A. Misztal, *Theories of Social Remembering* (Oxford: Open University Press, 2003), 146.
119. Rosalind Shaw, "Rethinking Truth and Reconciliation Commissions: Lessons from Sierra Leone" (Special Report 130, United States Institute of Peace, 2005), 7. See also John Braithwaite et al., *Anomie and Violence: Non-Truth and Reconciliation in Indonesian Peacebuilding* (Canberra: Australian National University Press, 2010).
120. The right to truth is not explicitly contained in any international human rights treaty but it is increasingly viewed as part of emerging customary international law and its existence has been highlighted in the decisions of international human rights treaty monitoring bodies. The nature of this right was described in UNCHR, "Updated Set of Principles for the Protection and Promotion of Human Rights through Action to Combat Impunity," Commission on Human Rights (February 8, 2005) E/CN.4/2005/102/Add.1 1.
121. Parmentier, Vanspauwen, and Weitekamp, "Dealing with the Legacy of Mass Violence," 347.
122. Declan Roche, *Accountability in Restorative Justice* (Oxford: Oxford University Press, 2004), 44.
123. Andreas Schedler, "Conceptualizing Accountability," in *The Self-Restraining State: Power and Accountability in New Democracies*, ed. Andreas Schedler, Larry Diamond, and Marc F. Plattner (Boulder, CO: Lynne Rienner Publishers, Inc., 1999), 14–15.
124. Cohen, "Unspeakable Memories and Commensurable Law," 27.
125. *Azanian Peoples Organisation (AZAPO) and Others v. the President of the Republic of South Africa and Others* 1996 (4) SA 671 (CC), para. 17.
126. Graeme Simpson, "'Tell no Lies, Claim no Easy Victories': A Brief Evaluation of South Africa's Truth and Reconciliation Commission," in *Commissioning the Past: Understanding South Africa's Truth and Reconciliation Commission*, ed. Deborah Posel and Graeme Simpson (Johannesburg: Witwatersrand University Press, 2002), 220–251; Sarkin, "An Evaluation of the South African Amnesty Process"; Chapman and Van der Merwe, *Truth and Reconciliation in South Africa: Did the TRC Deliver?*, 26.
127. TRC Report, vol. 1, ch. 5, para. 66.
128. Ibid., para. 41.
129. Ibid., para. 42.
130. Individuals responsible for serious crimes such as murder, rape, and torture were intended to face prosecution before special panels of the District Court of Dili.
131. Regulation No. 2001/10 on the Establishment of a Commission for Reception, Truth and Reconciliation in East Timor (2001) (Timor-Leste) sec. 1.
132. Senier, "Traditional Justice as Transitional Justice," 77–78.
133. Ibid., 77–78.
134. Zifcak, "Restorative Justice in Timor-Leste," 52–53.
135. Ibid., 52–53.
136. Piers Pigou, *The Community Reconciliation Process of the Commission for Reception, Truth and Reconciliation* (UNDP Timor-Leste, 2004), 96.
137. Ibid., 6.
138. Elizabeth Kiss, "Moral Ambition within and Beyond Political Constraints: Reflections on Restorative Justice," in *Truth v. Justice: The Morality of Truth Commissions*, ed. Robert I. Rotberg and Dennis Thompson (Princeton, NJ: Princeton University Press, 2000), 77.
139. Mark Bovens, "Analysing and Assessing Accountability: A Conceptual Framework," *European Law Journal* 13, no. 4 (2007): 451.

140. Gavrielides, "Restorative Justice—the Perplexing Concept," 174.
141. Ibid., 174.
142. TRC Report, vol. 1, ch. 5, para. 61.
143. Brewer, *Peace Processes*, 124.
144. Ibid., 124.
145. Kent Greenawalt, "Amnesty's Justice," in *Truth v. Justice: The Morality of Truth Commissions*, ed. Robert I. Rotberg and Dennis Thompson (Princeton, NJ: Princeton University Press, 2000), 199. With reference to the guilty plea process in the Rwandan *gacaca* system, see Lars Waldorf, "Rwanda's Failing Experiment in Restorative Justice," in *Handbook of Restorative Justice: A Global Perspective*, ed. Dennis Sullivan and Larry Tifft (London: Routledge, 2006), 428.
146. Conversely, feelings of shame may dissuade some offenders from participating, particularly where their friends and family members are unaware of their crimes.
147. Mark A. Drumbl, "Restorative Justice and Collective Responsibility: Lessons for and from the Rwandan Genocide," *Contemporary Justice Review* 5, no. 1 (2002), 5–22. 11. For a comprehensive analysis of the role of shame in restorative justice processes, see John Braithwaite, *Crime, Shame, and Reintegration* (Cambridge: Cambridge University Press, 1999).
148. Ronald C. Slye, "Amnesty, Truth and Reconciliation: Reflections on the South African Amnesty Process," in *Truth v. Justice: The Morality of Truth Commissions*, ed. Robert I. Rotberg and Dennis Thompson (Princeton, NJ: Princeton University Press, 2000), 170–188. 178.
149. George Bizos, "Why Prosecutions Are Necessary," in *The Provocations of Amnesty: Memory, Justice, and Impunity*, ed. Erik Doxtader and Charles Villa-Vicencio (Claremont, South Africa: David Philip Publishers, 2003), 5–9. 6–7.
150. Kiss, "Moral Ambition within and Beyond Political Constraints," 82. See also Pumla Gobodo-Madikizela, "Empathetic Repair After Mass Trauma: When Vengeance is Arrested," *European Journal of Social Theory* 11, no. 3 (August 1, 2008), 331–350.
151. UNTAET, Regulation No. 2001/10 on the Establishment of a Commission for Reception, Truth and Reconciliation in East Timor, 2001 (E. Timor) sec. 27.7.
152. Commission for Reception, Truth and Reconciliation in East Timor (CAVR), *Chega! The CAVR Report* (Dili, 2006) ch. 9, 33.
153. Ibid., 33.
154. Philpott, *Just and Unjust Peace*.
155. Ibid., 163.
156. The Northern Ireland (Sentences) Act 1998 (UK).
157. Amnesty (Amendment) Act 2002.
158. Loi d'amnistie générale No 84/91 (1991) art 2 (Lebanon).
159. Regulation No. 2001/10 on the Establishment of a Commission for Reception, Truth and Reconciliation in East Timor, sec. 32 (2001) (Timor-Leste).
160. McCold, Llewellyn, and Van Ness, *An Introduction to Restorative Peacebuilding*, 2.
161. Llewellyn, "Restorative Justice in Transitions and Beyond," 93.
162. Ibid., 93.
163. Ibid., 94.
164. Susan Sharpe, "The Idea of Reparation," in *Handbook of Restorative Justice*, ed. Gerry Johnstone and Daniel W. Van Ness (Cullompton, UK: Willan Publishing, 2007), 31.
165. Ibid., 100.
166. UNCHR, *Updated Set of Principles for the Protection and Promotion of Human Rights through Action to Combat Impunity*, 1–19.
167. Jennifer Llewellyn and Robert Howse, "Institutions for Restorative Justice: The South African Truth and Reconciliation Commission," *University of Toronto Law Journal* 49 (1999): 355–388.
168. Lax, "Amnesty, Reparation and the Object of Reconciliation in the Context of South Africa's Truth and Reconciliation Commission," 233.
169. Other criticisms highlighted that although offenders could benefit from amnesty immediately after a positive amnesty decision by the Amnesty Committee, victims had to wait years for the TRC to recommend reparations, and then for the government to make compensation payments.

Furthermore, the payments that were eventually made fell below the amounts recommended by the TRC and were considerably less than the amounts that could have been awarded following a successful civil claim.
170. Llewellyn, "Restorative Justice in Transitions and Beyond," 100.
171. Llewellyn and Howse, "Institutions for Restorative Justice," 388.
172. TRC Report, vol. 1, ch. 5, para. 100.
173. Senier, "Traditional Justice as Transitional Justice," 70. In addition, Sharpe argues that where the state is responsible for serious human rights violations, the state should also make reparations "for crimes committed by state agents, or to contribute to reparations programs where offenders are unable to make a sufficient financial contribution." See Sharpe, "The Idea of Reparation," 31.
174. Baines, "The Haunting of Alice"; Erin Baines, *Roco Wat I Acoli—Restoring Relations in Acholi-Land: Traditional Approaches to Reintegration and Justice* (Vancouver: Liu Institute for Global Issues, 2005).
175. Commission for Reception, Truth and Reconciliation, *Chega! The CAVR Report*, ch. 9, para. 112.

CHAPTER 7

The Role of Forgiveness in Reconciliation and Restorative Justice: A Christian Theological Perspective

Stephen J. Pope

Relational anthropology provides a framework for appreciating how peacebuilding can be promoted by forgiveness, reconciliation, and restorative justice. Some contemporary conceptions of transitional justice, however, make it difficult to see their relevance to post-conflict contexts. First, peacebuilders in post-conflict societies often understand peace too thinly as the mere cessation of armed conflict rather than as an ongoing, long-term process of reintegration. Second, justice is often equated with judicial retribution rather than being seen, more broadly, as right relations within community. Third, peacebuilders often work with predominantly secular assumptions that lead them to ignore the potential contribution of religious communities to social reintegration. Contemporary peacebuilding efforts often overdraw competition between justice and peace, truth and reconciliation, and accountability and forgiveness. Restorative justice grounded in a more relational anthropology can provide a useful corrective to these dichotomizing tendencies.

This chapter focuses on ways in which forgiveness might contribute to the emerging relationally based theory of peacemaking. It is divided into six sections that examine, in order: the meaning of forgiveness, the relation of forgiveness to reconciliation, the relation of forgiveness to restorative justice, the meaning of forgiveness in theological perspective, the church's promotion of forgiveness, and the role of forgiveness in the public life of post-conflict societies. This chapter argues that an ethic of forgiveness can support the political and social goals of reconciliation and restorative justice.

The Meaning of Forgiveness

In recent years, social scientists and ethicists have produced an extensive body of writings on the meaning of forgiveness.[1] Forgiveness, like any morally significant term, has been subject to many interpretations and so cannot be reduced to one simple, clear, and distinct formula. Forgiveness is often described in terms of acts and processes that move victims from negative to positive attitudes toward their perpetrators. Psychologist Michael McCullough defines forgiveness as "a private process of getting over your ill will and negative emotions, and replacing these 'negatives' with 'positives' such as wishing the offender well or hoping for a new and improved relationship."[2] It is not clear why McCullough describes this process as "private," since forgiveness has profound implications for the quality of life within and between communities. He focuses on "motivational and emotional changes" in the person who learns to forgive, so perhaps by a "private" he means a "personal" process that involves choices over which agents have some control, freedom, and rights. Forgiveness, in McCullough's view, is not antithetical to justice. People can be forgiving, he writes, "without also having to be doormats."[3] His research has led him to appreciate the potentially close relationship between forgiveness and reconciliation, which he defines as "the restoration of a fractured relationship that happens because the victim has forgiven the offender and because the offender has mended his or her evil ways."[4] He proposes an interpersonal model of reconciliation wherein the victim forgives a repentant offender and freely chooses to resume their friendship.

McCullough's work on the relation between forgiveness, reconciliation, and restorative justice introduces the themes of this chapter. He speaks explicitly of reconciliation as a restoration of friendship on the basis of a new commitment to justice by the offending party and of forgiveness as a voluntary commitment by the harmed party to accept the offender despite the latter's offensive conduct. His research focuses on human adaptations of a common tendency in many groups of living species (which he calls the "forgiveness instinct") to resolve conflicts by means of conciliatory behaviors.[5] While his view of reconciliation is especially apt as a description of the healing of interpersonal relationships, we have to keep in mind that the restoration of interpersonal friendship is not the goal of political reconciliation. Yet both the capacity for forgiveness, particularly the tendency not to exact revenge, and the desire for reconciliation are relevant to inter-group relations, even on a large-scale. Developing a culture of peace, McCullough argues, depends on elaborating on favorable, pro-social evolved capacities and reducing the pull of unfavorable, anti-social evolved capacities. Our natural social capacities for forgiveness and reconciliation must be enlisted in the attempt to counteract our evolved proclivity toward in-group favoritism. Cooperation within and between groups is often more useful than competition and enmity.[6]

Many commentators hold that forgiveness involves a shift in the victim's attitudes and/or emotions. This shift can be described by way of negation: as ceasing to hate, no longer wanting to exact revenge, letting go of anger, renouncing grudges, abandoning resentment, transcending bitterness, and the like. We can distinguish the victim's duty to treat the offender with justice from the victim's willingness to forgive. The latter is a free gift done out of generosity, not something to which an offender has a right.

McCullough's account of forgiveness can be complemented by that suggested by the medieval Roman Catholic theologian, Thomas Aquinas. Forgiveness, according to Aquinas, is rooted in an agent's choice to love an offender despite his or her unjust act toward the self or others.[7] The term "love" here refers neither to warm feelings nor erotic attraction, but rather to "willing the good" to the offender. To love the neighbor is to will what is good for the neighbor, even if the neighbor does not perceive it as such. This can include willing a just punishment for the sake of the offender as well as for the community. Forgiveness is contextually specific and so might involve remission of punishment for an offender in one context and punishment for a particular offender in another context.

Forgiveness, thus, generally involves renouncing destructive internal dispositions like hatred for the offender or thirsting for revenge. The persistence of resistant negative emotional tendencies challenges the agent to continue to choose to will the good to the offender. It does not, however, exclude acknowledgment of the offender's guilt—far from it, since an agent cannot forgive a person whom he does not believe needs forgiveness.

We can note several further qualifications regarding the meaning of forgiveness, particularly as based on the religious perspective rooted in the theology of Thomas Aquinas and then developed in Roman Catholic social teachings. First, the act of forgiveness is, at its best, an expression of an agent's compassion for a person who acted unjustly. True forgiveness, in other words, flows from an agent's mercy and not from a manipulative desire to have power over the offender.

Second, the more severe and repeated the unjustified harm, of course, the more difficult the process of forgiveness. Forgiveness in cases of significant harm is typically not accomplished in one decisive act, but rather approached gradually over the course of many decisions and acts. This implies that forgiveness runs a spectrum from partial to complete, or from weak to strong.

Third, forgiveness is more readily elicited by repentant than unrepentant offenders. It can be either unilateral, flowing one-way from the victim to the unrepentant offender, or bilateral, from the victim to a repentant offender.

Some agents choose to resume goodwill for a transgressor even in the absence of the offender's acknowledgement of wrongdoing. The granting of forgiveness to a contrite offender is bilateral when both parties take an active role in the process that leads to forgiveness.

Fourth, forgiveness can in some cases affect healing in the forgiver, the recipient of forgiveness, and even in third parties. Forgiveness can bring a degree of liberation from bitterness, burning resentment, and other negative emotions in victims. This notion resonates with psychologist Robert Enright's description of forgiveness as a "path to freedom."[8] The acceptance of forgiveness, moreover, can help perpetrators move to a new level of self-understanding and provoke a positive change in moral character.

A number of ethicists from a variety of backgrounds maintain that since forgiveness involves the exercise of moral agency, groups can neither forgive nor be forgiven. Christian theologian Anthony Bash, for example, argues that since groups "do not have a moral 'self,'" we cannot properly speak of groups "forgiving" or "being forgiven."[9] This challenge can be met, however, if we use the term "forgiveness" in an *analogous* sense to refer to ways in which groups or some of their members learn to renounce hatred for another group, cease clinging to threatening or otherwise negative stereotypes about the other, commit themselves, in institutional and cultural ways, to overcome a habitual resentment toward historic oppressors, and work to dismantle structural barriers to good relationships.

Consider the civil rights movement in the United States, particularly under the leadership of Martin Luther King, Jr. King was committed not only to changing unjust laws that supported segregation, unequal education, and racial oppression, but also to improving the attitudes of whites toward blacks and vice versa. King's integrationist vision generated both prophetic denunciation of racism and segregation but also affirmed that "white America ... could be redeemed" in a society in which whites and blacks could be reconciled.[10] King's dual message of accountability and forgiveness, it should be noted, was directed not only to individuals but also to entire communities. Concerned about the force of oppression coming from communities marked by structural evil as well as personal sin, King called for a collective commitment to justice and love. As he explained in a famous sermon given in 1957, "Time is cluttered with the wreckage of communities which surrendered to hatred and violence. For the salvation of our nation and the salvation of mankind, we must follow another way.... While abhorring segregation, we shall love the segregationist. This is the only way to create the beloved community."[11]

The injustice that comes from powerful groups can amount to more than the aggregate sum of the unjust choices made by all their individual members. King's comment suggests that groups as well as individuals can be forgiven for the evil they have done and can be forgiving of the evil done to them. He suggests that "redemptive good will" (resonating with Aquinas's love of enemies) can grow within a community in a way that is roughly analogous to the way it can increase with a particular moral agent's conscience. If so, we can speak of groups forgiving and being forgiven, albeit, it is important to note, in an *analogous* sense. We can also see cases in which institutional leaders issue apologies on behalf of their communities, as seen in a range of cases from Pope John Paul II's apologies for Christian sins of racism and anti-Semitism[12] to President Mauricio Funes's apology for the brutalities of the Salvadoran military in that country's civil war.[13]

Forgiveness and Reconciliation

We can now turn to the question of how forgiveness is related to reconciliation. Reconciliation can be described as the restoration of relationships that have been damaged by some kind of wrongdoing. The giving and receiving of forgiveness among friends ordinarily leads to reconciliation. McCullough believes that, "reconciliation, at least in humans, seems to be the point of forgiveness."[14] Under some circumstances of course, e.g., in the case of a battered wife or a profoundly betrayed friend, a victim who is willing to forgive an offender may legitimately decide not to seek reconciliation. In some particular circumstances, individuals must go their own way. Yet such a course of action is a regrettable necessity, not a moral ideal. The decision to forgive naturally leads to reconciliation unless exceptional circumstances make it impossible for a given relationship to be resumed. In the extreme realm of mass atrocities, of course, undertaking a commitment to forgive can itself be a major moral accomplishment. In the wake of "horrendous evils,"[15] reconciliation between victims and offenders (most of whom tend to show little repentance) is a rarity and certainly not the norm. In cases such as these, it is important that survivors not be burdened with moral guilt for their inability to reconcile with perpetrators. Sometimes refusing to reconcile can be a condition of security, self-respect, and even mental health.

Some advocates of transitional justice regard forgiveness and reconciliation as morally preferable to the pursuit of criminal justice. Forgiveness and reconciliation have often been regarded as alternatives to justice and accountability. Those who identify forgiveness with forgetfulness insist that we can only make progress in reconciliation by focusing on the future rather than the past. After the twelve-year civil war in El Salvador, for example, the then president of the republic, Alfredo Cristiani, repudiated the UN Truth Commission report on the grounds that its content would not contribute to national reconciliation.

He urged Salvadorans to forgive and forget the past rather than open up old wounds. "What must be done now," he said in a national address, "is to see what has to be done to erase, eliminate, and forget everything in the past."[16]

An alternative view, however, regards authentic forgiveness as facilitated by disclosure of the truth about prior wrongdoing. Christian as well as secular ethicists have argued that acknowledgment of truth is essential to long-term, large-scale efforts at peacebuilding. They regard justice as essential for the vindication of the dignity of victims. The "basic form" that vindication takes, theologian Nigel Biggar holds, is that of "recognizing the injury as such, and thereby acknowledging the dignity of the direct victim."[17] It also rests on worry about the psychological tendency, as David Tombs puts it, that "the more victims try to forget and leave their terrible experience in the past, the more they tend to reproduce it in the present in the form of emotional illness."[18] The Jesuit rector of the University of Central America, José María Tojeira, S.J., was thus willing to express his community's forgiveness for those who masterminded the massacre of six Jesuits, their housekeeper, and her daughter at the Jesuit campus on November 1989, but he still insists on public accountability for the intellectual authors of the crime and vindication for the victims.[19]

Relational theory argues for the proper place of both forgiveness and acknowledgment. It also advocates that a more central role be given to large-scale reconciliation as complementary to the promotion of justice. South African theologian John De Gruchy offers a helpful distinction between "political reconciliation," a process of moving beyond collective forms of enmity, and "social reconciliation,"[20] the overcoming of alienation between and within communities at local levels. The latter, for example, includes intra-communal processes that bring together factions within divided neighborhoods, schools, or political groups.[21]

Political reconciliation runs along a spectrum from weak to strong. A weak version is found when former enemies have begun to establish a basic working ability to exist together as citizens without resorting to violence as a means of settling disputes. It is established with cease-fires, peace negotiations, and peace treaties. In El Salvador, for example, weak political reconciliation was produced by a negotiated peace following a prolonged, brutal, and deadlocked civil war.[22] In Chile, a stronger degree of political reconciliation was attained after General Augusto Pinochet narrowly lost a plebiscite. President Patricio Alywin issued a public apology and several truth commissions documented the Pinochet regime's extreme abuse of human rights.[23] Even weak political reconciliation is a moral achievement when contrasted with the lethal violence it replaces. Yet it is typically unstable, marked by social polarization, and contains the seeds of future violence.

Some degree of forgiveness must accompany collective reconciliation, if only as a renunciation of violent retaliation and a commitment to recognize the rights of the opponents qua citizens. Strong forgiveness does not necessarily precede collective reconciliation, but some form of willing the good to the other is implied in any resumption of civil cooperation after violent conflict. South African theologian Charles Villa-Vicencio in fact maintains that political reconciliation does not necessarily involve forgiveness. In his terminology, political reconciliation pursues a much more modest agenda than widespread social healing. It involves "a minimum level of political harmony and cooperation between former enemies as a basis for pursuing holistic justice, which includes accountability, human rights, economic development, and the rule of law."[24]

Villa-Vicencio is right to be reserved about the tendency of some advocates of transitional justice to focus primarily on the pursuit of high-profile prosecutions while ignoring the more important need for political reconciliation. He properly wants to avoid aiming at an excessively lofty social goal of reconciliation in ways that devalue basic political reconciliation. His reference point is the South African commitment to the priority of political justice over criminal justice for the sake of promoting sustainable peace. By "peace" he means "a sustainable positive peace" that involves not only the end of organized violence but also a strengthening of the "capacity of societies to deal with conflict nonviolently and to be willing to build healthy structures and institutions to deal with the underlying causes of conflict."[25] Peace thus begins with political reconciliation but is further advanced with growth in social reconciliation, the restoration of relationships and communities.

Critics of course have faulted South Africa's Truth and Reconciliation Commission (TRC) with confusing interpersonal and religious forms of reconciliation with the political goal of "national unity and reconciliation."[26] Some individuals who testified before the TRC forgave their offenders and even reconciled with them, yet critics ask whether this exercise actually has anything to do with the collective goal. This controversy becomes especially acute when amnesty is said to be a necessary condition of national reconciliation. Those who prioritize justice argue that truth commissions should, out of respect for individual autonomy, allow individual survivors to decide about how they want to respond to their perpetrators.[27] No commission, they insist, should presume to urge forgiveness upon victims or push them to reconcile with their former tormentors.

Yet one can respond to this position in a variety of ways. First, while a truth commission cannot require offenders to extend forgiveness to their oppressors, it can establish conditions that in some cases facilitate forgiveness for individuals (either offenders or victims) who are open to it. In communicating a sense of collective guilt on behalf of the state, it can vindicate victims and encourage particular perpetrators to admit their guilt. Moreover, truth commissions can focus on a variety of forms of reconciliation with the intent of aiding long-term peace. The TRC, for example, has often been said to represent the beginning, not the achievement, of reconciliation in that country. Large-scale collective projects can encourage, not require, reconciliation for the sake of the common good, as long as reconciliation efforts accord with respect for the victims and the promotion of the common good.

Chilean human rights attorney José Zalaquett describes collective reconciliation as, "a process of reconstructing the moral order [in a way] that is more healthy than punishment."[28] Political reconciliation is promoted by the full recognition of the equal rights of all citizens in legal and political spheres. What political scientists Amy Gutmann and Dennis Thompson call "democratic reciprocity"[29] involves a set of social, economic, and political conditions "that enable adults to engage with each other as civic equals."[30] If political reconciliation moves forward by a shared commitment to democratic governance, protection of human rights, and respectful dialogue between citizens who have equal standing before the law, social reconciliation works in civil society to promote civic friendship, social trust, social cohesion, and solidarity. Social reconciliation at its best involves a union of previously estranged people and communities, a "shared comprehensive vision, mutual healing and restoration, or mutual forgiveness."[31] It is promoted in what De Gruchy describes as "a process in which there is a mutual attempt to heal and overcome enmities, build trust and relationships, and develop a shared commitment to the common good."[32] Social reconciliation is promoted by a commitment to social justice that addresses long-term structural conditions that lead to unrest, social tension, and violence.

Reconstructing a moral order involves the whole community, perpetrators and bystanders as well as survivors and their loved ones. De Gruchy, Villa-Vicencio, and Zalaquett all agree that this restored moral order must institutionalize justice to prevent future relapse into injustice and violence. The growth of institutional justice over time generates conditions that make more likely the growth of social forgiveness and social reconciliation.

Forgiveness and Restorative Justice

Moral skeptics generally worry about how these broad reconciliatory ideals can be used to evade or diminish the enforcement of justice.[33] They insist that justice is a more basic moral standard than reconciliation and should not be sacrificed for the sake of other goals, no matter how noble. The rights of victims, for example, in cases of torture or forced disappearance, cannot be ignored for the sake of future beneficial consequences for society as a whole. Social and political reconciliation are morally wrong, it is argued, if they involve compromising any aspect of what is due in justice to either victims or their perpetrators.

This moral warning must be taken seriously, but should not be allowed to reduce the meaning of justice to effective criminal prosecution. Justice should not be identified with retribution nor reconciliation with forgetfulness. As Jennifer Llewellyn and Daniel Philpott argue in the introduction of this volume, some of the multiple meanings of the term "justice" are compatible with reconciliation.

The TRC was not the only enterprise seeking the goal of restorative justice. Restorative justice has also been used in programs of conflict mediation and negotiation in a variety of community-level settings around the world, especially in victim-offender programs directed at young people.[34] Instead of rendering a proportionate amount of pain to the violator as a way of rectifying an imbalance, restorative justice strives to restore the relationship between offender and victim and to restore both to right relations with the wider community. The TRC promoted these goals by allowing victims to tell their stories in public fora. The practice of having perpetrators present for victims' testimony encouraged the former to come to a greater realization of the harm they had done and to accept responsibility and express contrition for their wrongdoing. It also underscored the need for the state to make reparations.

Restorative justice attempts to address the harm done to victims, the wider community, and perpetrators themselves. It is best attained when offenders take responsibility for their conduct and seek to repair the damage they have inflicted on others. On the interpersonal level, restorative justice thrives when perpetrators explicitly acknowledge their guilt and ask for forgiveness, and when victims choose to forgive them. On the social and political level, restorative justice operates in a less explicit, more symbolic ways to incorporate forgiveness. Public rituals, memorials, and the like encourage and express the value of group forgiveness and reconciliation.[35]

The dialogic nature of restorative justice allows it to take advantage of traditional mores and community wisdom about forms of reconciliation appropriate to particular historical contexts. The inclusion of these local practices enhances their probability of success. Restorative justice has also been valued for its ability to incorporate local practices and grassroots methods of social recovery, reintegration, and reconciliation. One well-known example is Desmond Tutu's creative fusion of Christian forgiveness with the African notion of *ubuntu*.[36]

Social reconciliation is promoted when the state and civil society take measures to correct the injustice done to victims as much as possible. This includes, as Chilean psychologist Elizabeth Lira argues, the provision of mental health resources, educational opportunities, compensation for harm done, and social recognition of the dignity of the victims.[37] These goods cannot be simply delivered by the state to passive recipients but must rather involve the input, choices, and actions of survivors. This goal implies the development of survivor agency.

Reparative measures must be multi-faceted, extensive, and long-lasting. Lira argues that society as a whole, and not only victims' groups or NGOs, must take responsibility for the promotion of justice. The state, acting as the embodiment of the people as a whole, has a duty to take responsibility for what happened to the victims. Political reconciliation begins with social coexistence based on the protection of the human rights of everyone, but restorative justice strives to strengthen the moral agency of victims and their communities. Increased moral agency can help to provide survivors degrees of personal freedom that make it possible for them to offer forgiveness to their offenders and to the communities who support them. Deep harm cannot be negated by singular decisions to forgive. Like reconciliation, true and lasting forgiveness is not the first response to transgression but rather the end of a long process.

A Christian Perspective on Forgiveness, Reconciliation, and Restorative Justice

The notions of forgiveness and reconciliation have been used in public discourse for some time. In the West, they are rooted in Jewish, Christian, and Islamic religious traditions. The definition of forgiveness offered above—the resumption of good will to an offender—is an ethical extrapolation from the work of Catholic theologian Thomas Aquinas and subsequent Catholic social teachings. It is important to note that the Catholic church has struggled to implement its teachings within its own institutions. The clerical sexual abuse crisis underscores the importance of promoting the various forms of justice within the church as well as the world.

There is a strong theoretical and practical resonance between Christian theological accounts of forgiveness and recent work in restorative justice and reconciliation. To illuminate some of these resonances, we now focus more explicitly on a theological interpretation of forgiveness, reconciliation, and restorative justice. The core of Christian faith lies in the Trinitarian religious affirmation of God as "Father," "Son," and "Spirit."[38] Popular Christian piety often mistakenly either identifies God with Jesus or treats the three "persons" of the Trinity as if they were three separate gods. It frequently identifies punishment and justice with the Father, love and mercy with the Son, and holiness and special spiritual gifts with the Spirit. This view divides God against God, or at least regards each person as related to creation in a temporal sequence: first, the Father creates, then the Son offers salvation, and then the Holy Spirit inspires the church. Jesus offers love now but if we refuse we deserve God's retributive justice in the final judgment. In contrast, Christian belief in the unity of God, the Son's involvement in creation, and the Spirit as an integral basis of Christian life provides an important theological ground supporting our responsibility to seek harmony with one another and to work for forgiveness and reconciliation.[39]

Trinitarian theology in particular offers a profoundly social notion of the human person as made in the "image of God." God is an eternal community of love who freely chooses to share the divine goodness with creatures. God's goodness is reflected within creation to the extent that creatures live in right relationship to God and to one another; it is violated when an individual turns from right relationship out of a misdirected quest for his or her own private good.

Popular Christian piety often views sin as involving particular acts that transgress moral rules or violate certain taboos. A theologically more helpful account regards sin as a core alienation from God, rooted in a self-absorbed refusal fully and rightly to trust in God. "All sin, all mis-relationship with God," theologian Nicholas Lash writes, "is a matter of setting our minds and hearts, our hopes and fears, on something other than the mystery of God; in other words, it is a matter of idolatry."[40] Religious mistrust can generate wider social estrangement as well as interpersonal wrongdoing. The paradigmatic murder of Abel by Cain in chapter 4 of Genesis offers a vivid depiction of how alienation from God leads us to human destructiveness. Sin, as Lash puts it, denies "solidarity with each other and with all the world, and seeks alchemically to transmute 'communion' into ownership, gift into private property."[41]

If the effect of sin is alienation, then grace, God's free and forgiving self-communication to humanity, restores our relationship with God, and with one another and all of the creation (Col. 1:18–23). If God is reconciling, then the person restored to God wants to reconcile with others when possible. Whereas sin damages relationships, reconciliation heals them; whereas sin separates and excludes "them" from us, reconciliation establishes an inclusive "us" in which all are welcome; whereas sin brings a sense of isolation, reconciliation brings a sense of belonging and communion.

The most fundamental form of reconciliation is made possible by the redemptive work of Christ, who, Christians affirm, gave his life so that we could be reconciled to God (Rom 5:6–11; 2 Cor 5:18–20). Theological reconciliation is initiated and sustained by God but its effect can only be realized to the extent that we freely and fully cooperate with divine love. Reconciliation is based on forgiveness and healing that lead us to be "new creatures" (2 Cor 5:17) marked by self-giving friendship with God and one another. The Christian affirmation of eternal life as a "communion of saints" suggests that this healing produces comprehensive restoration of right relationships. The "sacraments of baptism, Eucharist, and penance demonstrate the theological significance of forgiveness, reconciliation, and restorative justice". (see Gal 5:5).

This overarching theological framework profoundly shapes Christian interpretations of forgiveness, reconciliation, and restorative justice. First, Jesus taught forgiveness as a central expression of God's love for us. Christ lived and died for the "forgiveness of sins" out of a love for humanity without reserve, conditions, or limits. Jesus extended love to enemies as well as friends, the unrepentant as well as the repentant, outsiders as well as insiders. The Lord's Prayer petitions, "forgive us our trespasses as we forgive those who trespass against us" (Mt 6:12). Those who have been forgiven are inclined to forgive one another, and also the Christian community is constantly repaired by practices of forgiveness (see Mt 18:15–20). The offer of forgiveness ought to be directed to every offender, but perpetrators can only appropriate it when they respond with repentance, conversion of heart and mind, and a commitment to reparations.

Second, forgiveness by its very nature moves to reconciliation. Christ comes to the world for the sake of reconciliation, and as the "body of Christ" (Rom 12:108; I Cor 12:12–31) in the world, the church must be a community of reconciliation. Jesus thus teaches in the Gospel of Matthew that worship should only be conducted after estranged members have been reunited—"if you bring your gift to the altar, and there recall that your brother had anything against you, leave your gift there at the altar, go first and be reconciled with your brother, and then come and offer your gift" (Mt 5:23–24). The annunciation of this ethical ideal, of course, should not be confused with the imperfect and halting practice of actual Christians in their daily lives.

Whereas the human experience of reconciliation is usually initiated by the guilty party's apology, divine reconciliation begins with God's gracious offer of forgiveness (akin to the father's love in the parable of the Prodigal Son, Luke 15:11–32). As theologian Robert Schreiter explains, the divinely initiated process moves from reconciliation to forgiveness to repentance.[42] The experience of the resurrection for the disciples was first of all one of forgiveness. As Schreiter observes, "[t]hey experienced Jesus' forgiveness even before they could ask for it."[43] The heart of the church, the people of God, lies in its mission to reconcile the estranged and to live for its vision of heaven as an eternal community of reconciled friends.

Because sin affects the common good and not only individuals, we have a distinct need to address the unjust harm perpetrated by social structures and not just the conversion of individual hearts and minds. Commenting on sins against other Christians, for example, Pope John Paul II wrote that, "Not only personal sins must be forgotten and left behind, but also social sins, which is to say the sinful 'structures' themselves have continued and can still contribute to division and to the reinforcing of division."[44] Reconciliation is thus intrinsically connected to justice, right relationship, as well as mercy, rightly ordered care for the needy.[45]

Third, restorative justice complements forgiveness and reconciliation. Restorative justice receives its distinctive theological basis in the standard of "right relationship" that is central to both the covenant of the Hebrew Bible and to Jesus's central announcement of the in-breaking of the "Kingdom of God." Popular Christian piety sometimes confines forgiveness to private relationship and assigns justice to the public world. Yet if we understand biblical justice to concern what John R. Donohue, S.J., calls "fidelity to the demands of a relationship,"[46] then this dichotomy is not legitimate. Justice that renders punishment in a manner that is constructive and reparative can also be an expression of mercy. As Christopher Marshall puts it, "if justice is understood in more relational and restorative terms—making things right and repairing relationships—then justice is actually consummated in forgiveness and reconciliation."[47]

Assumptions about Biblical ethics as exclusively punitive ignore the richness and variety of the tradition's views of justice.[48] Christian piety often assumes a strict division between the just God of the Hebrew Bible and the loving God of the New Testament. This theological dualism both ignores the many texts in the Hebrew Bible that speak in effusive terms of God's love (for example, God's loving kindness, *hesed*, in Hosea 2:19, Micah 6:8, Psalms 103) and overlooks the many judgment texts of the New Testament (e.g., the parable of the last judgment in Mt 25:31–46 or the vengeance of God in 2 Thess 1:8–9). It also mistakenly identifies justice in the Hebrew Bible with condemnation, punishment, and destruction. The latter certainly play important roles in some Biblical texts, but as Marshall has shown, they are best understood as negative aspects of the more over-arching divine commitment to maintaining and protecting the covenant. God acts in order to protect the covenanted people from both external threats (e.g., Pharoah) and internal threats (e.g., false prophets, corrupt kings, and popular idolatry). Marshall describes God's wrath as "double-sided": "It is positive insofar as it is directed at evil and oppression that hinders God's purposes of deliverance for the covenant people;

it is negative in that God's people, both corporately and individually, suffer under punishment for their own sinfulness and injustice."[49]

Biblical judgment is aimed at sin because it is destructive of human beings. In general, Marshall argues, when "wrongdoing occurred, Israel's law was more concerned with the restoration of *shalom* than the punishment of the offender."[50] Jesus's teaching about the Kingdom of God responds to sin in the same way. The Kingdom arrives when God intervenes to "put things right on earth," becomes present to human beings on a new level of intimacy, and creates a messianic community bound to live in a way that is worthy of the new age.[51]

If justice is to be in right relation to God, even punishment must be seen as a means of repairing what has been damaged rather than as either an end in itself or an expression of the purely vindictive anger of an emotionally overwrought deity. Reestablishing right relations within community can only be brought about through overcoming fractures based on injustice. This theme is taken up in the early church's vision of eschatological hope for the renewal of the world (2 Cor 5:11–20).

The Gospel of Luke describes Jesus as scandalizing locals by visiting the house of a well-known and wealthy "sinner," the chief tax collector Zacchaeus. Zacchaeus responds to Jesus's unexpected attention by proclaiming, "Behold, half of my possessions, Lord, I shall give to the poor, and if I have extorted anything from anyone I shall repay it four times over" (Lk 19:8). Zacchaeus's words indicate both a religious conversion to the "Lord" (about whom he was merely curious prior to this encounter) and a moral conversion to caring for the needy and for those whom he had previously exploited through tax collection. As collaborators with Romans, Jewish tax collectors were considered traitors as well as economic predators. Jesus's action inspired Zacchaeus to a change of heart, to reform his life, and to repair the damage he did to his victims. The story culminates in Jesus's announcement of Zacchaeus's reinstatement to the community: "Today salvation has come to this house because this man too is a descendent of Abraham. For the Son of Man has come to seek and to save what was lost" (19:9–10).[52]

This emblematic story does not employ the concepts "forgiveness" or "reconciliation" but both are implied in its invocation of "salvation." Salvation came not only to Zacchaeus but also to his entire "household." It is not about "going" to heaven, but living in an entirely new set of relationships. Forgiveness is thus not a matter of one's soul being "wiped clean" but about seeing oneself in a new way and living accordingly. Zacchaeus' transformation is not only interior but also flows into his material and social existence. He begins to act with a new awareness of how possessions can serve human needs and ought not be treated as ends in themselves. If sin is marked by an attempt to "transmute 'communion' into ownership," Lash reminds us, then holiness, "takes the form of dispossession, letting go, surrendering the title-deeds we forged."[53] Jesus's care inspired Zacchaeus's responsive proclamation of his own "dispossession" for the sake of his community, and particularly its most vulnerable and abused members, and Zacchaeus's change led Jesus joyfully to declare his restoration to the community.

Catholic sacramental theology regards forgiveness as based on three conditions: contrition, confession, and intention to make satisfaction.[54] Pope John Paul II employed these features of sacramental forgiveness to analogous contexts of social transformation following collective wrongdoing. Perpetrators of large-scale social injustice must face their crimes with honest contrition, admission of guilt, moral amendment, and reparations. As he explained in his Message for the World Day of Peace of January 1, 1997, "forgiveness, far from precluding the search for truth, actually requires it. The evil which has been done must be acknowledged and as far as possible corrected . . . [because an] essential requirement for forgiveness and reconciliation is justice."[55] The establishment of truth commissions around the world has been a "first step" toward reconciliation.

Justice in this theological perspective is clearly not reducible to punishment, let alone the exaction of revenge. It requires that evil be corrected (as far as possible) by recognizing the truth of what happened to victims and by taking serious steps to repair the damage done by collective evils. Christian forgiveness here, as in the case of Zacchaeus, is offered to all offenders, but comes with serious implications for concrete actions. A restorative approach to justice acknowledges the importance of establishing the rule of law, but it cannot end there.

Social reconciliation and forgiveness are promoted more deeply through the "healing of memories" that is facilitated by honest disclosure of harm rather than by either denial or amnesia. After the civil war in El Salvador, Archbishop Arturo Rivera y Damas pointed out that, "So many wounds cannot be cured by overlooking them. On the contrary, I believe these sores must be uncovered no matter how noxious they are. Then they can be carefully cleansed so that they heal properly and do not become infected again."[56] The healing process may be advanced when perpetrators acknowledge their own guilt and victims are able to express their own anguish.

This is not to say that conditional amnesty ought to be ruled out in all circumstances.[57] After reminding his listeners of the importance of making decisions prudently in ways that do not make reconciliation "even more difficult," John Paul II held that willingness to "grant an amnesty to those who have publicly admitted crimes . . . can be regarded favorably as an effort to promote good relations between groups previously opposed to one another."[58] The pope was willing to accept the moral legitimacy of conditional amnesties as long as they are structured in a way that respects the needs of victims. Indeed, he taught that justice is an "essential requisite for forgiveness and reconciliation."[59] Thus rather than offering forgiveness or reconciliation in place of justice, John Paul II saw them as mutually complementary.

The Church as Agent For Forgiveness, Reconciliation, and Restorative Justice

The church is uniquely positioned by its core beliefs, universal scope, concern for the common good, and integrated structure of dioceses, social agencies, schools and parishes to promote forgiveness, reconciliation, and restorative justice. This complex network of relationships puts the church in position to provide a context for rebuilding relationships and even to promote positive relationships when none had previously existed.

The church has in fact successfully engaged in "top down" diplomacy, but has also understood that the commitment to peace and reconciliation must be pursued in "bottom up" directions as well—through the impact of networks of relationships in small-scale groups, local parishes, particular religious communities, primary and secondary schools, and local initiatives that provide opportunities for direct face-to-face dialogue.[60]

The church's support for reconciliation and justice at the regional and national levels includes not only public promotion of truth and reconciliation commissions, but also, more generally, defense of human rights through pastoral letters, litigation, public policy advocacy, funding and administering social services to the needy, and willingness to provide space within which competitors can engage in discussion, deliberation, and negotiations. The church has at times also been involved in mediation in places as disparate as Colombia, Burundi, and the Philippines. None of this of course gainsays the occasions on which the church has failed to act as mediator and peacemaker. In any case, the church is often positioned to encourage the formation of the public conscience, exercised by ordinary citizens as well as politicians, and to support public moral criteria of forgiveness, reconciliation, and restorative justice as the bases of true and lasting peace. As will be noted below, this Catholic ethical perspective can contribute to public moral discourse in pluralistic societies because it appeals to what promotes human dignity and the common good.

The church pursues reconciliation at local levels. The ministry of reconciliation is communicated through the sacraments of baptism, reconciliation, and the Eucharist, and through pastoral counseling and retreats. The church can lead communities formed in schools, parishes, colleges, and seminaries to embrace a spirituality that supports and flows from fundamental ethical principles of neighbor-love, mercy, forgiveness, accountability, rebuilding trust, etc. Local churches engage in grassroots community-building by fostering parishes and schools as communities of forgiveness and reconciliation, accompanying victims, and creating spaces of solidarity, safety, memory, and hope where survivors can come together for mutual support and be empowered to act as leaven in society. This is displayed, for example, in base ecclesial communities in El Salvador, Chile, and elsewhere in Latin America.[61] The local church can be a model to society to the extent that the church itself is, and is seen to be, a community in support of forgiveness, reconciliation, and restorative justice. When the church supports the oppressed and seeks to empower victims, it is more likely that they will have the ability to forgive those who have abused them.

Like other communities, the church faces significant obstacles to the promotion of forgiveness, reconciliation, and restorative justice. Socio-political divisions are reflected in divisions within the church that are reinforced by alternative historical memories. Authoritarian Christians in Chile, Argentina, and El Salvador, for example, continue to justify the repression on purportedly Christian grounds. Lack of clarity about what must be done can present an obstacle to efforts for reconciliation. As noted above, theological resistance comes from those who maintain an excessively otherworldly spirituality or a purely individualistic understanding of the Christian message. The legitimate fear of over-politicizing Christian faith can lead to the other extreme of passivity, indifference, or quietism. Some religious leaders worry that prophetic speech exacerbates divisions within the church. All of the societies discussed here have church members who were complicit with or even directly active in the previous regime's repression. The question is not whether there is division within the church, but how it should be dealt with—either ignored and suppressed or faced with honesty and ethical resolve. The church's own ethic favors the latter.

Forgiveness in Public Life

After having discussed the relevance of forgiveness for the life and thought of the church, we will now turn to the public relevance of forgiveness for peacemaking within pluralistic societies. While forgiveness is often assumed by both religious and non-religious people to pertain only to interpersonal relationships, there are reasons for thinking that the collective offering and granting of forgiveness can play a role in large-scale reconciliation and restorative justice efforts within pluralistic societies.

One objection to the effort to construct a public ethic holds that forgiveness is a religious concept that cannot be detached from its particular context and used more broadly. This claim is made not only by secular critics of religion but also by religious thinkers. Marshall, for example, argues that, "Christian values and principles cannot be separated from the larger narrative framework of the Christian story without loss to either and without substantially altering their meaning." According to him, "it is the biblical narrative of God's creative love and redemptive justice made known in the life of Israel and in the person of Christ and the experience of his followers, rather than in a set of timeless moral axioms, that represents the real Christian contribution to collective ethical discourse."[62] This criticism of "middle axioms" is a bit anachronistic, since it refers to an approach to Christian social ethics prominent in the 1960s and 1970s; few people today endorse "timeless moral axioms" or would even be able to explain with much clarity what this phrase even means. The important question today is whether the biblical narratives themselves, and the moral standards they communicate, can elicit moral insights in those who do not profess religious belief. In a Catholic perspective, biblical narratives bear public (and not just distinctively religious) significance today because they speak to general human needs, goods, and aspirations that make sense to people from ordinary human experience from many different cultural backgrounds. We can see, for example, the value of family, community, compassion, human dignity, and right relationship. In traditional Catholic language, these and related goods form the basis of the "natural law" that emerges in human experience and that gives us indications of what constitutes the conditions for living well, both personally and communally.

This "natural law" approach to public morality runs contrary to a certain tendency in both religious and secular circles to expect an all-or-nothing approach to religious ethics. According to this perspective, a religious narrative is either affirmed as true and taken as the definitive guide to human existence, or judged as completely false and therefore dangerous to public life. Yet we need to do better than this simplistic dichotomy. It is of course true that forgiveness, reconciliation, and restorative justice have certain meanings and religious resonances for Christians (and people of other faiths) that they do not have for other people. Yet it is not the case that Christians cannot talk about the meaning of these ideals in ways that are intelligible to people from other religious traditions or none at all. There is a deeply human dimension to many strains of biblical literature that can be helpful for public conversations about the meaning of forgiveness and reconciliation. The relevant task is to discuss how we understand the meaning of these ideals and moral standards and to explore how their use might play a constructive role in public life.

Marshall is of course right to say that the Christian story is not reducible to a moral code. The biblical story, he writes, "reveals the *character* of God demonstrated in word, deed, and relationship; it mediates *participation* in the life of God; and it has the power to shape *moral* character in conformity to God, both individually and communally."[63] Yet Christian narratives also communicate moral insights about forgiveness, reconciliation, and restorative justice that can be broadly helpful, even if different perspectives vary in the inferences and interpretations they draw from these texts.[64] It is important, then, to distinguish the nourishment of the Christian moral life within communities of faith from our responsibility as citizens to participate in public life. While they are distinct, there is some overlap between the virtues cultivated in Christian character and those taught in the formation of good citizens. Public moral discourse must at times be subjected to criticism, but opposing it to religious ethics as a matter of general principle is both unnecessary and counterproductive. As the opening discussion of this chapter indicated, a great deal of literature has been produced in the last decade from non-theological researchers like psychologist Michael McCullough who appreciate the wide moral significance of forgiveness, reconciliation, and restorative justice for peacemaking today.

The public conversation surrounding the work of the TRC in South Africa was significantly informed by these ideals and, despite the commission's weaknesses, still continues to be regarded by a consensus of scholars as the most successful experiment of its kind. Villa-Vicencio judges that while the TRC hearings did not accomplish all that their advocates had hoped, they did play an important role in what should be a long process of healing: "The nation was confronted with a body of testimony that few could ever ignore or simply dismiss as untrue. This helped South Africans begin to challenge the systemic denial that characterizes so many situations of violence, abuse, crimes against humanity, and genocide in other parts of the world."[65] This is in itself a major accomplishment. The conversation is unfinished, but it was at least a strong beginning to what should be a lengthy national conversation.[66] Unfortunately, societies like El Salvador that have been deprived of such reconciliatory processes are left without such a "strong beginning."

Conclusion

This chapter has attempted to argue that an ethic of forgiveness can play a central role in wide-scale efforts to promote social reconciliation and restorative justice. It explored the meaning of forgiveness as a commitment to will the good to the offender. It argued that while this commitment typically takes place in an interpersonal context, it can also be sought, analogously, in communal contexts. This chapter also maintained that forgiveness often gives rise to various forms of reconciliation. Political reconciliation involves the construction of equal rights within political community and social reconciliation seeks broader and deeper forms of reintegration within civil society. It also argued that restorative justice can play an integral role in promoting social reconciliation. Distinctively Christian approaches to forgiveness carry important implications for the communal structures and life of the church but they can also play a significant role in the broader moral conversation that takes place within the public life of pluralistic societies.

Notes

1. Important social scientific literature includes Everett L. Worthington Jr., ed., *Handbook of Forgiveness* (New York: Routledge, 2005); Worthington Jr., ed., *Forgiving and Reconciling: Bridges to Wholeness and Hope* (Downers Grove, IL: InterVarsity Press, 2003); P.E. Diseger, *Political Forgiveness* (Ithaca, NY: Cornell University Press, 2001); Richard D. Enright, *Exploring Forgiveness* (Madison, WI: University of Wisconsin Press, 1998); Michael McCullough, *Beyond Revenge: The Evolution of the Forgiveness Instinct* (Somerset, NJ: Jossey-Bass, 2008). For an ethical exploration of forgiveness as public goal, see Donald W. Shriver, *A Ethic for Enemies: Forgiveness in Politics* (New York: Oxford University Press, 1995); Raymond G. Helmick, S. J., and Rodney L. Petersen, eds., *Forgiveness and Reconciliation: Religion, Public Policy, and Conflict Transformation* (Philadelphia: Templeton Foundation Press, 1998).
2. McCullough, *Beyond Revenge*, 114.
3. Ibid., 116.
4. Ibid., 115.
5. Ibid., 147 ff.
6. Ibid., ch. 9.
7. Thomas Aquinas, *Summa Theologiae*, II-II, 23–26. See also, H. J. M. Schoot, *Tibi Soli Peccavi: Thomas Aquinas on Sin and Forgiveness* (Utrecht, The Netherlands: Peeters, 1998) and Jules Toner, *Love and Friendship* (Milwaukee, WI: Marquette University Press, 2003).
8. Robert D. Enright, *Forgiveness Is a Choice*, ch. 1. (Washington, DC: APA, 2001). See Nancy Nyquist Potter, ed., *Trauma, Truth and Reconciliation: Healing Damaged Relationships* (New York: Oxford, 2006) and Donald Shriver, *An Ethic for Enemies* (New York: Oxford, 1998).
9. Anthony Bash. *Forgiveness and Christian Ethics* (New York: Cambridge University Press, 2007), 115.
10. James H. Cone, *Martin and Malcolm and America: A Dream or Nightmare?* (Maryknoll, NY: Orbis, 1999), 69.
11. Martin Luther King Jr. *Strength to Love.* (Cleveland: Collins, 1963), 54.
12. "Pope Says Sorry for Sins of Church," *The Guardian*, March 13, 2000, at http://www.guardian.co.uk/world/2000/mar/13/catholicism.religion, accessed May 17, 2000.
13. "El Salvador's Funes Apologises for Civil War Abuses," *Reuters*, January 10, 2010, at http://www.reuters.com/article/2010/01/16/us-elsalvador-idUSTRE60F26M20100116, accessed May 17, 2011.
14. McCullough, 116.
15. This phrase is used by Marilyn McCord Adams, *Horrendous Evils and the Goodness of God* (Ithaca, NY: Cornell, 2000).

16. Presidential Address to the Nation (March 18, 1993), cited in Margaret Popkin, *Peace without Justice: Obstacles to Building the Rule of Law in El Salvador* (University Park: Pennsylvania State University Press, 2000), 150. The current president has rejected this denial. See Emilio San Pedro, "El Salvador President Mauricio Funes in Abuse Apology," BBC, January 17, 2010, at http://news.bbc.co.uk/2/hi/americas/8463929.stm, accessed January 18, 2010.
17. Nigel Biggar, "Making Peace or Doing Justice: Must We Choose?," in *Burying the Past: Making Peace and Doing Justice after Civil Conflict*, ed. Nigel Biggar (Washington, DC: Georgetown University Press, 2003), 3–24 at 8.
18. David Tombs, "Unspeakable Violence: The UN Truth Commissions in El Salvador and Guatemala," in *Reconciliation, Nations and Churches in Latin America*. ed. Ian S. Maclean (London: Ashgate, 2006), 57–84 at 77.
19. Stephen J. Pope, "The Convergence of Forgiveness and Justice: Lessons from El Salvador," *Theological Studies* 64 (2003): 812–835.
20. John De Gruchy, *Reconciliation Restoring Justice*. (Minneapolis: Fortress, 2002), 26. Emphasis added.
21. Ibid., 27.
22. On the civil war in El Salvador, see Tommie Sue Montgomery, *Revolution in El Salvador: From Civil Strife to Civil Peace* (Boulder, CO: Westview Press, 1992) and Aldo Lauria-Santiago and Leigh Binford, eds., *Landscapes of Struggle: Politics, Society, and Community in El Salvador* (Pittsburgh: University of Pittsburgh Press, 2004).
23. Pamela Constable and Arturo Valenzuela, *A Nation of Enemies: Chile under Pinochet* (New York: Norton, 1991).
24. Charles Villa-Vicencio, *Walk with Us and Listen: Political Reconciliation in Africa*, (Washington, DC: Georgetown University Press, 2009), 2.
25. Ibid., 3.
26. Wilmot James and Linda van de Vijver, eds., *After the TRC: Reflections on Truth and Reconciliation in South Africa* (Athens: Ohio University Press, 2000).
27. Richard A. Wilson, *The Politics of Truth and Reconciliation in South Africa: Legitimizing the Post-Apartheid State* (New York: Cambridge, 2001), 119 f.
28. José Zalaquett in Alex Boraine, Janet Levy, and Ronell Scheffer, eds., *Dealing with the Past: Truth and Reconciliation in South Africa* (Cape Town, S.A.: IDASA, 1994), 11.
29. In Robert I. Rotberg and Dennis Thompson, eds., *Truth v. Justice: The Morality of Truth Commissions* (Princeton, NJ: Princeton University Press, 2000), 35 f.
30. Ibid., 36.
31. David A. Crocker, "Truth Commissions, Transitional Justice, and Civil Society," in Rotberg and Thompson, ed., *Truth v. Justice*, 99–121, at 108. Crocker's argument here is ambiguous in that it moves from allowing truth commissions to encourage deep reconciliation to opposing any effort to impose a legal requirement to forgive. The latter concern is a red herring, since no one proposes forgiveness as a legal obligation. Gutmann, Thompson, and Crocker are skeptics of forgiveness and criticize Tutu for promoting it.
32. De Gruchy, *Reconciliation*, 15.
33. See Wilson, *The Politics of Truth*, ch. 1.
34. Gordon Bazemore and Lode Walgrave, *Restorative Juvenile Justice: Repairing the Harm of Youth Crime* (Monsey, NY: Criminal Justice Press, 1999).
35. Villa-Vicencio, *Walk with Us and Listen*, ch. 6.
36. Desmond Tutu, *No Future without Forgiveness* (New York: Random House, 1999), 103 et passim; also Villa-Vicencio, *Walk with Us and Listen*, ch. 5.
37. Elizabeth Lira, "The Reparations Policy for Human Rights Violations in Chile," in *The Handbook of Reparations*, 55–101, ed. Pablo de Greiff. (New York: Oxford University Press, 2006). See also David Becker, Elizabeth Lira, Maria Isabel Castillo, Elena Gomez, and Juana Kovalskys, "Therapy with Victims of Political Repression in Chile: The Challenge of Social Reparation," *Journal of Social Issues* 46.3 (1990): 133–149.

38. Karl Rahner, "Trinity, Divine" in *Encyclopedia of Theology: The Concise Sacramentum Mundi, 1755–1764*, ed. Karl Rahner (New York: Crossroad, 1982).
39. These claims are contested within the Christian tradition. For some of the important issues, see Christopher D. Marshall, Beyond Retribution: A New Testament Vision For Justice, Crime, and Punishment (Grand Rapids: Eerdmans, 2001).
40. Nicholas Lash, *Believing Three Ways in One God: A Reading of the Apostles' Creed* (Notre Dame, IN: University of Notre Dame Press, 1993), 100.
41. Ibid., 103.
42. Robert J. Schreiter, C.PP.S., *The Ministry of Reconciliation: Spirituality and Strategies* (Maryknoll, NY: Orbis, 2005), 64.
43. Ibid.
44. *Ut Unum Sint*, no. 34. Available at http://www.vatican.va/holy_father/john_paul_ii/encyclicals/documents/hf_jp-ii_enc_25,051,995_ut-unum-sint_en.html, accessed January 4, 1010.
45. The prophet Zechariah communicated this oracle: "Execute true justice; deal loyally and compassionately with one another. Do not defraud the widow, the orphan, the stranger, and the poor; and do not plot evil against one another" (7:9–10). Commenting on this passage, Jon Levenson argues, "It would be a mistake to see in these words a call to justice tempered by compassion, or to a compassion that goes beyond justice.... Rather, justice here is constituted by compassion, by special solicitude for the powerless and disadvantaged, a determination that they not be victimized." Jon D. Levenson, *Creation and the Persistence of Evil: The Jewish Drama of Divine Omnipotence* (Princeton, NJ: Princeton University Press, 1994), 104.
46. John R. Donohue, S.J., "Biblical Perspectives on Justice," in *The Faith That Does Justice*, ed. John C. Haughey, S.J. (Mahwah, NJ: Paulist, 1977), 69; see also Donohue, "The Bible and Catholic Social Teaching," in *Modern Catholic Social Teaching*, ed. Kenneth R. Himes (Washington, DC: Georgetown, 2004), 9–40.
47. Marshall, 26.
48. Moshe Weinfield, *Social Justice in Ancient Israel and in the Ancient Near East* (Minneapolis: Fortress, 1995).
49. Ibid., 170.
50. Ibid., 4.
51. Ibid., 70–71.
52. Robert C. Tannehill, *Luke* (Nashville: Abingdon, 1996), 275–279.
53. Lash, ibid., 103.
54. See *Catechism of the Catholic Church* (Washington, D.C.: USCCB Publishing, 1995), para. 1450–1460.
55. "Message of His Holiness Pope John Paul II for the Celebration of the XXX World Day of Peace: Offer Forgiveness and Receive Peace," January 1, 1997, no. 5, at http://www.vatican.va/holy_father/john_paul_ii/messages/peace/documents/hf_jp-ii_mes_08121996_xxx-world-day-for-peace_en.html, accessed December 27, 2013.
56. Cited in Jon Sobrino, "Theological Reflections on the Report of the Truth Commission," in *Impunity: An Ethical Perspective: Six Case Studies from Latin America*, ed. Charles Harper (Geneva: World Council of Churches, 1996) 118. See also Jon Sobrino, "Latin America: Place of Sin and Place of Forgiveness," in *Forgiveness*, ed. Casiano Floristán, Christian Duquoc, and Marcus Lefébure (Edinburgh: T & T Cark, 1986), 45–56.
57. Jennifer Llewellyn, "Just Amnesty and Private International Law," in *Torture as Tort: Comparative Perspectives on the Development of Transnational Human Rights Litigation*, ed. C. Scott (Oxford: Hart Publishing, 2001), 567–600.
58. Message for World Day of Peace of 1997, para. 5, available at http://www.vatican.va/holy_father/john_paul_ii/messages/peace/documents/hf_jp-ii_mes_08,121,996_xxx-world-day-for-peace_en.html, accessed January 4, 2011.
59. Ibid.
60. Robert Schreiter, Scott Appleby, and Gerald Powers, eds., *Peacebuilding: Catholic Theology, Ethics, and Praxis* (Maryknoll, NY: Orbis, 2010).

61. Andrew Dawson, "The Origin and Character of the Base Ecclesial Community: A Brazilian Perspective," in *Cambridge Companion to Liberation Theology*, 2nd ed., ed. Christopher Rowland (New York: Cambridge University Press, 2007), 139–158.
62. Marshall, ibid., 30.
63. Marshall, 30. Emphasis in original.
64. See John Paul II, "No Peace without Justice, No Justice without Forgiveness," World Day of Peace Message, 2002, http://www.vatican.va/holy_father/john_paul_ii/messages/peace/documents/hf_jp-ii_mes_20,011,211_xxxv-world-day-for-peace_en.html.
65. See Villa-Vicencio, *Walk with Us and Listen*, 95.
66. Ibid., 111.

CHAPTER 8

Pursuing Inclusive Reparations

LIVING BETWEEN PROMISE AND NON-DELIVERY

Charles Villa-Vicencio

We are told in hard-selling ads that what we see is what we get—with the assurance that there are no prejudices, hidden agendas, or fine print to worry about. Not so in politics. In most countries around the globe, what is promised on political platforms, even in law and constitutions, is rarely delivered. This is especially the case in countries that reach a negotiated political settlement after a period of large-scale human rights violations and violent conflict. It is clearly the case in South Africa, where the Constitution reflects a liberal understanding of human rights and the Truth and Reconciliation Commission (TRC) recommends the payment of reparations to victims of past atrocities. This raises the important question concerning what it means to live between promise and non-delivery in a democratic society.

In what follows I argue that realistic debate in pursuit of human rights and reparations requires a good set of multifocal lenses that enable us to respond to the immediate, middle, and distant needs of those denied these rights, and of the victims seeking redress. I am indebted to Howard Zehr for his formative text, *Changing Lenses*,[1] which has inspired a generation of scholars and students to wrestle with the key categories of restorative justice. Changing his metaphor from "camera" to "spectacles"—I seek to capture the fact that we all see life through our own spectacles, ground as they are by our location in life. I shall not repeat or endeavor to improve on what Zehr and others say about restorative justice. I shall also refrain from engaging the many important dimensions of transitional justice and reparations, discussed in this volume and elsewhere. Pablo de Grieff's *Handbook of Reparations* and Daniel Philpott's *Just and Unjust Peace: An Ethic for Political Reconciliation* provide insightful overviews of the reparations debate and are implicit to my discussion.[2]

I am also indebted to Ernesto Verdeja's critical theory on reparative forms of justice, in which he projects two ideal-type axes, resulting in the creation of four conceptual dimensions of reparations as a basis for defining the scope of a coherent, general theory of reparations. One axis refers to acknowledgment, which can be either symbolic or material. The other axis concerns recipients, who can be collective or individual. This enables him to speak of four interrelated dimensions of a comprehensive understanding of reparations: collective symbolic and individual symbolic reparations, as well as collective material and individual material reparations.[3]

De Grieff's overview of reparation models is prefaced by the important reminder that any viable program of reparations is required to heed the contextual features, the necessary trade-offs, and the different measures required to redress a particular situation of gross violations of human rights.[4] Philpott, in turn, identifies six normative practices to bridge the gap between abstract debate and the particular. These are building socially just institutions, acknowledgment, reparations, apology, punishment, and forgiveness. The notion of restoration suggested in the schemata offered by both de Grieff and Philpott presuppose the pursuit of a reconciled society that is shaped by justice, mercy, and peace.

This, I argue in what follows, requires the creation of a post-conflict society in which former enemies and adversaries learn to live together at a level of cordiality, human respect, and civic trust that enables them to manage and transcend the fundamental causes of the conflict they are seeking to overcome. It is here that I draw on Verdeja's "critical theory of reparative justice," together with the concerns of others whose work I acknowledge in the argument below, in an attempt to promote restoration and peacebuilding on the basis of relational identity theories. Verdeja seeks to transcend liberal theory of reparations that bases repair and compensation in what is essentially a Lockean conception of rights that suggests that those who "hath received damage has besides the right of punishment . . . a particular right to receive reparation."[5] Central to Verdeja's argument is the need "to secure victims' sense of dignity and moral worth in ways that are compatible with social justice and equality."[6] His concern is the promotion of ontological transformation among all parties (perpetrators, bystanders, victims) to ensure that "animosity and bitterness are rejected in favour of broad-based public repentance and forgiveness." Verdeja's fear is that the simple payment of damages is insufficient to correct the structural and ideological imbalances of society.

The surveys of reparations offered by De Grieff and Philpott recognize the need for transitional justice and restorative justice interventions, ranging from appropriate prosecutions to truth-telling, the acknowledgment of victims' suffering, and apologies, all in order to promote the level of victim dignity that

Verdeja projects. The essays in this volume by Daniel W. Van Ness on accountability through restorative justice, John Braithwaite on traditional justice, and Louise Mallinder on restorative amnesties are particularly pertinent in this regard.

Against this background I seek to engage in the restorative justice and reparations debate from a meta-ethical perspective. In so doing I seek to goad individuals and communities who are *not* victims or survivors of a particular political catastrophe to consider the underlying perspectives that influence their response to the overall needs of those who are victims. In South Africa non-victims include most whites, recognizing that they overwhelmingly rejected the Home for All campaign of a few years back that merely asked that they *acknowledge* the privileges they enjoyed under apartheid. Some among the new black elite are, in turn, becoming separated from those who have failed to extract themselves from the economic and social ravages of apartheid. As a result there are those who defend their newfound wealth, as do many whites, as a right to enjoy rather than something to ponder.

The questions I raise regarding the responsibility of "non-victims" in post-conflict societies are considered in relation to the ambitious challenge in the mandate of the South African TRC, which is to "restore the human dignity" of victims. My focus is a practical or political one, rather than a theoretic or academic one. I do not address the important procedural and legal questions concerning the delivery of reparations in different truth commissions and compensation bodies. The wisdom, or otherwise, of the alien tort law cases in the US Court of Appeals in New York concerning US-based multi-national companies that did business in apartheid South Africa is addressed only in passing. The Holocaust reparation claims against Swiss banks and other reparation-related endeavors are only present by implication.

I seek rather to consider what is involved in a realistic understanding of reparations at a generic level that is driven by a dialogical or reciprocal sense of being. It involves a perception of ourselves and others—whether rich or poor, oppressors or victims—through the lens of how others see us and we see them.

I do so by addressing four interrelated aspects of the reparation debate.

1. The way we view others.
2. The need to take a second look at ourselves.
3. What it means to live between promise and non-delivery regarding basic human rights and the payment of reparations.
4. The importance of reparations within the context of development theory.

In closing, I argue that the promotion of a holistic understanding of reparations aimed at restoring the human dignity of victims is a slow and contested process. It is one that tests the patience of victims who struggle to know how far they can take their demands without causing the settlement to collapse. The endeavor to respond to the demands of victims, in turn, causes both the former oppressors and those who assume power to face the question regarding how much political and economic influence each can afford to concede in the continuing struggle for power.

Others

A serious attempt to *restore the human dignity* of victims necessarily influences the way in which we view those who suffer the wounds of the past—whether they be supporters of our own cause, adversaries, former enemies, alienated people, or strangers. In all cases it requires us, inter alia, to deal with difference, which is arguably among the biggest challenges facing the world in the twenty-first century.

Important in this regard is the need to recognize that the encounter between different groups, each of which produces its own victims, varies from one context to another. The Hutu-Tutsi conflict in Rwanda is different from the wars involving child soldiers elsewhere in Africa, the standoff between blacks and whites in South Africa is different from the division between the descendents of slaves and indentured laborers and the ruling classes in Mauritius, the suffering of comfort women in Japan is different from the suffering of young girls in Sudan, and the unresolved trauma of the disappeared in Argentina is different from the theft of children in Afghanistan and Haiti.

These differences require us to focus and refocus our lenses anew in each particular situation to see and realistically understand the political forces at play as a safeguard against repeating the near- and long-sighted errors of judgment that the best-intentioned do-gooders and proponents of international aid sometimes impose on a situation. There is an urgent need to recognize that for human rights to prosper in any situation, offenders and victims are required to co-exist and to strive to reach a modest level of reconciliation. Obvious as this may be, many international agencies and governments seeking the immediate implementation of international human rights law in conflict situations run the danger of undermining local initiatives aimed at facilitating cooperation between adversaries. This lies at the heart of many failed development and peacebuilding initiatives in post-conflict situations around the world. The standoff between the United Nations' Security Council and the African Union regarding Darfur is but one example. Although the African Union endorsed the Rome Statute (which established the International Criminal Court (ICC) in 1998) at its June 2010 ICC Review Conference in Kampala, Uganda, when the African Union met at its own summit a little more than a month later, it reiterated the need to find a settlement to the Darfur conflict that excludes the arrest of Sudanese President al-Bashir, whom the ICC has indicted for war crimes.

Whether in Sudan or elsewhere, the chances of political enemies finding an equitable settlement to conflict is questioned by those favoring an international retributive intervention. The likelihood of finding a "quick fix" in these situations is minimal, which raises questions concerning the trendy developments that draw on a spectrum of thinking, ranging from a pre-colonial African notion of *ubuntu* to post-modernist ideas of seeing and engaging the stranger in a manner that allows for peace. Captured in the proverb, *umuntu ngumuntu ngabantu*, *ubuntu* translates to mean that a person is a person through other people. This philosophy, which is built on a restorative principle of drawing offenders back into a community for healing and rehabilitation, is often exploited by white South Africans who argue it is time to forget the evils of apartheid by creating a new South Africa within which yesterday's racists can find a home. There is, at the same time, a residual dimension of *ubuntu* at the heart of the South African Constitution, which enables restorative justice to find its rightful place in the post-apartheid nation-building process.[7]

As *ubuntu* is at the pre-colonial end of the chronological spectrum of dealing with the past, so post-modernist thought, popularized by the adoption of the appealing and marketable phrases of Emmanuel Lévinas, Michel Foucault, and others, is at the present end. Emmanuel Lévinas' well-known dictum that tells us if we look one another in the eye with integrity and meaning, we will not be able to look away again, is an obvious example of the popular appropriation of aspects pertaining to post-modernism.[8] His *Otherwise Than Being: Asking for Patience*,[9] in turn, reminds us just how difficult it is to do so. In a similar vein, Michel Foucault argues that we come to recognize the humanity of the other through authentic, free, fearless, and truthful speech, embedded in such "moral, ethical and spiritual conditions" that render human respect and honesty possible. The difficulty of truth-seeking, he emphasizes, is directly linked to the "problem of the truth-teller" and his or her place in the inevitable power relations involved in political debate.[10] In so doing, Foucault guards against the trap of romanticizing or sentimentalizing the other, as the views and opinions of others are not necessarily in all respects correct. Fearless speech brings the dominant views of the prevailing order and the alternative view of others into dialogue.

All options for reparations must be fearlessly debated by those not only directly involved in the giving and receiving of reparations (government and victim representatives), but also in participatory public debate, where the promise for reparations must be continually addressed, discussed, and evaluated in relation to changing realities in society. There is no blueprint for reparations—no one size fits all. Each society must decide on what best meets its particular needs in an open, unrestricted debate. Dialogue between stakeholders decidedly should include those who have borne the brunt of inequality and abuse. Realistically, it also needs to incorporate those who are required to pay for reparations, which encompasses the benefactors of the old order and those who hold the purse strings of the new. Successful negotiations concerning restorations that reach beyond a one-off acknowledgment grant or penalty require what Harold Saunders defines as "a cumulative, multilevel and open-ended process of continuous interaction over time, engaging significant clusters of citizens in and out of government and the relationships necessary to solve public problems."[11]

Such a level of respect for the views and humanity of others, in both cooperation and confrontation, constitutes a departure from normative Western patterns of engagement with the other, shaped as they are by an impulse to conquer, colonize, master, and proselytize. In such engagements "good natives" are customarily absorbed into the culture of those who judge themselves to have reached a superior level of human worth, while the recalcitrant are effectively put to the sword. Conquerors executed both options with a kind of arrogance that claims superiority and looks anxiously upon human differences. The threat of the "barbarians" is always there. Borders are sealed, townships are built on the other side of the railway line, and informal settlements are developed at a safe distance from the city.

So deeply entrenched is the sanctity of our own values and the fear of different value systems that it is invariably only when we are confronted with a collapse of our society that we dare to explore and seek to understand the needs, values, and demands of others whom we have come to view as the enemies of peace, moral decency, and the common good. Roelf Meyer, the chief negotiator in the 1990s for the former South African government, contends that politics, not least in times of conflict, is driven by self-interest, with little thought being given to the interests and needs of others. He argues:

> It is usually only when the implications of the conflict of interests stare us in the face and we realise that neither side can impose their interests on the other that we begin to recognise the need to accommodate one another. When you look into the abyss you realise just how much you and your enemy need one another. You begin to realise you need to talk . . . This realisation is one of the most important lessons I take away with me from the negotiations between the former government and the ANC in the 1994 settlement. After years of alienation and the fear of an escalating civil war staring us in the

face, we began to see the necessity of accommodating one another. It was once we began to realise that we both needed to honour our commitments to one another that a measure of trust began to develop between us.[12]

Cyril Ramaphosa, the chief African National Congress (ANC) negotiator and Meyer's counterpart, concurs. He affirms that "a failure to find trust had destroyed thousands of people in tens of decades of fighting.... It was clear that a political settlement simply had to be found and a way of building trust became essential.... We needed to recognise the human needs of one another.... We had no alternative."[13] At the heart of democratic debate is the question of how to normalize dialogue within a context of trust and friendship that allows for honest and fearless speech without having to pay the price of abyss politics.

In South Africa and elsewhere, the demand for reparations has been trivialized for the simple reason that non-victims—those who have either benefited from the old order or those who have inherited a share of it—have not experienced the kind of pressure required for them to take the demands of victims as seriously as their humanity requires.

For reparations to be critically recognized they must be driven by the kind of political vigor that enables those in power to recognize that it is in their interest to respond to and recognize the human needs of victims. They must be forced to see the humanity of the oppressed and marginalized who threaten their security. The balance in this regard needs to be finely tuned. Get the balance wrong and the coalition of old wealth and the nouveau riche, with a dependent working class in tow, will defend the status quo against the threat of change. Without sufficient pressure though, the elite will prevail.

The question is how to enable victims, offenders, and bystanders to recognize the human needs of others before the standoff between enemies and adversaries plunges a nation into chaos. The answer has something to do with creating space for fearless speech and the need for proportionality of political power, backed up with the necessary checks and balances of fair politics. Above all, it has to do with the creation of a culture that recognizes that those who constitute the other are not necessarily the vile aggressors worthy of ridicule and silencing, if not death. They are often no more than members of the human family struggling for identity, acceptance, and the opportunity to survive and prosper. The limitations of South African society aside (and these are numerous), many who were estranged from one another by apartheid and some who saw themselves as enemies are beginning to recognize each others' shared humanity, at least in the sense of "live and let live"—largely as a result of political necessity, but sometimes because of an emerging sense of civic trust and friendship.

Restoring the human dignity of others ultimately requires that reparations, in addition to all else, inject a transformative dimension into society at a social, psychological, and spiritual level, as well as at an economic or material level. In brief, there is a need to integrate material and other forms of human and economic development, along with a self-determined growth path in a realistic and sequential manner if the human dignity of victims is to be realized. Democracy requires development, with the novelty of electing public representatives soon wearing off if voters do not have access to basic resources. Development, on the other hand, requires democracy. Despots can build houses. This does not, however, promote human dignity or self-fulfillment. The affirmation of human dignity requires that victims participate in their own development as an essential part of affirming their human worth and dignity.

Ourselves

At the heart of *ubuntu* thought as introduced above is the belief that one's human potential can only be achieved in interaction with others. It suggests that where we are out of harmony with others it is not only harmful to the well-being of the community, but also diminishes us as individuals. In brief, to the extent that there is enmity between me and another I am a lesser human being and so is the person alienated from me.

Again, the link between the principles of pre-colonial *ubuntu* and of post-modernism warrants inviting someone (other than myself) to investigate this "family resemblance" further. The common ground exists in Jean-Francois Lyotard's commentary on Hannah Arendt's observation "that a man, who is nothing but a man, has lost the very qualities which make it possible for others to treat him as a fellow man."[14] Building on Arendt's thought, Lyotard argues that a person who lives in isolation from others, failing to develop relations with others, undermines his or her *own* humanity. "To banish the stranger," writes Lyotard, "is to banish the community and thereby to banish yourself from the community."

To take this a step further, where we narrow the scope of who we are to our immediate associates—those who are effectively an extension of ourselves, those who share our ideas, our culture, our prejudices, and our social class—we open the way to constricted forms of classism, tribalism, and nationalism. A human being, Lyotard contends, "does not precede but results from interlocution."[15] Italian feminist Adriana Cavarero develops her literary theory in a similar vein by speaking of self through what she calls the "narratable self."[16] Her thesis is that humans cannot help but speak. They are compelled to speak, although often inadequately. There is perhaps always more to say in all human speech, resulting in people being drawn into deeper conversation with others and with themselves. They become fuller and more complete beings through telling stories and engaging the stories of others.

This broadening of self through interlocution and in community with the other does not, as is sometimes feared, undermine our capacity to engage in the intimacy of personal relations with those that share our culture, identity, and outlook on life. We can indeed only relate to the whole through the immediate. Marshal McLuhan's sense of the "global village" does not require us to neglect "our village" and the "warmth of our home." Starry-eyed notions of "world citizenship" carry the danger of replacing belonging in a particular community or nation with a sense of anonymity in a crowd. The different level of interlocution with those in and adjacent to our immediate environment is a given. It is an inescapable reality and, for many, a cherished sense of attachment. We relate to those whom we know, whose interests we share, and whose language we speak, more easily than we do to those more distant from us. There are also dangers involved though, as demonstrated by the extremists in the abortion debate, those favoring traditional forms of circumcision in Africa, racial extremists and others who lock themselves into situations of group-think in order to not face the questions posed by those whose experiences and thinking are different from their own. This raises the question: To what extent can the desire to belong and take comfort among one's own ultimately be detrimental to oneself and one's own?

The marvels of interlocution through modern vehicles of communication are such that we as individual people, communities, and nations are able to grow into appreciating the values, challenges, and needs of ourselves and others. In so doing, our values, sensitivities, and perceived needs, and those of our village and nation, are broadened, enriched and challenged. It is only through this invariably slow and sequential development of self, recognizing what has shaped my successes and contributed to my failures and those of my family, my community, and my nation, that we are able to begin to understand and respond to the challenges and needs of others. Without embracing Bronisław Malinowski's refusal to allow that there are no superior or inferior cultures, we would do well to ponder the importance of his pioneering ethnographic work, which tells us that "to judge something, you have to be there."[17] Unless we allow others to influence and shape us—our feelings, attitudes, and understanding of ourselves—the possibility of our being involved in the restoration of the human dignity of others is rendered inadequate.

The emergence of who we see and understand ourselves to be in relation to others is at the heart of forging reparations that reach beyond, without excluding, the need for reparations in the form of acknowledgment grants. An appropriate relationship between ourselves and others involves not only a realization that we are our brothers' and sisters' keepers, but that we need others to realize our own identity and fulfillment. It is this understanding of the other that underpins an African sense of communalism, as a corrective to notions of liberal individualism that have the capacity to degenerate into a fight between competitors for a limited offering. Only within a sense of shared belonging can a viable relationship emerge between haves and have-nots, between victims and perpetrators, and between winners and losers as a foundation for sustainable forms of restorative justice and transformative reparations.

To allow restoration and reparations to be no more than a one-off intervention is to reduce our endeavors to no more than a one-off holiday before returning to the exploitative world where the playground bully goes home with the prize. A one-off intervention sometimes does no more good than enabling us to convince ourselves that we have done our duty, which results in being able to get back to business with a good conscience.

Reparations within the restorative justice model require that we recognize the importance of a material acknowledgment of the suffering of others through a form of compensation. It also requires that those responsible for the predicament of victims agree to mend their ways through a change in their behavior in pursuit of a new way of doing business amidst the harsh realities of life. Above all, it involves the need to transform the structures and institutions that determine business and related forms of behavior.

The alien tort law cases in the US Court of Appeals in New York concerning the demand for reparations from US-based companies that did business in apartheid South Africa ought to recognize this need. In order to meet the calls of restorative justice and transformative reparations, the Court must give serious consideration to what restorative measures are required to transform the way in which multinationals do future business in developing countries and elsewhere. It is simply not enough to pay off victims for the abuse they suffered. The limited and delayed reparations paid by the South African government to individuals found to be victims of gross violations of human rights by the South African TRC pose similar questions. Despite the belated and reduced nature of the grants paid by the South African government to victims, the eventual acknowledgment of their suffering through the payment of reparations was important to their morale. In addition, it obliged the public to recognize the wrongdoing of a state that most whites in South Africa either tacitly or openly supported. Nevertheless, it is unclear whether these grants contributed in a significant way to institutional change in South Africa. The transformation that has happened in South Africa has rather come as a result of political reform and communal development that are only circuitously related to the payment of individual reparations. Some in government and elsewhere indeed argue that it is only through infrastructural change, job creation, and social development that the well-being of victims can be advanced. The rejoinder to this line of thought is, of course, that reparation is something more than development. For reparations to be seen as such, they need necessarily to involve more than government simply doing what it is required to do at the level of welfare relief and social development.

The symbolic acknowledgment of their suffering is an expectation that victims bring to the national process and is something that the government can only dismiss at the cost of its own integrity. The question is how and by what criteria such reparation packages can best be developed to allow both short-term and long-term restoration of inner psychological and emotional needs, as well as longer-term material development.

Between Promise and Delivery

How does all this play out in a negotiated settlement? It obviously depends on the nature of the settlement, although the South Africa paradigm, which is widely celebrated as an example for other countries undergoing political change, provides a rich example of what is involved in a resolution that requires compromises by all participating parties.

South Africa was spared a revolution, in the sense of one side being vanquished by the other. Political power was transferred to the ANC, as a representative of the oppressed masses of the country, while economic power remained largely in the hands of whites. The new government, in turn, committed itself to a macro-economic program of reconstruction and development that has since been tinkered with and modified without radically deviating from being an investor- and business-friendly initiative. The outcome is that the government found it increasingly difficult to deliver on the impressive aspirational clauses in the Constitution that favor social and economic rights for all South Africans. It has also chosen to be restrained in offering reparations for apartheid's victims. The outcome is a nation living between promise and delivery.

It would be naïve to suggest that no victims of past abuse have a desire to see perpetrators brought to justice and punished. It is, on the other hand, clear that many victims are prepared to settle for something other than retribution. They are willing to explore the kind of alternative appeasements suggested by proponents of restorative justice as a viable way of bringing a measure of closure to their suffering, keeping alive the promise of something new and hoping things will change—without destroying all that is in pursuit of that goal.

The ruling of the South African Constitutional Court in response to the application brought by the Azanian Peoples' Organisation (AZAPO) and other victims of apartheid concerning the validity of the Promotion of National Unity and Reconciliation Act is instructive in this regard.[18] The court upheld both the criminal and civil clauses of the Act, presenting reparations as a quid pro quo for victims and survivors, who, in turn, were required to surrender their right to prosecution. It further ruled that parliament was justified in adopting a wide concept of reparations, to be seen in relation to other programs of reconstruction and development. The separate judgment of Justice John Didcott is particularly important in this regard. It stated that any notion of reparations at the time needed to be indecisive for the simple reason that the government was not in a position to either assess the cost of reparations or to state whether it was possible to compensate all victims of apartheid.[19] Often overlooked in the reparations debate, Didcott's words are as telling today as they were in 1996.

The tardy response by the South African government to paying reparations was not primarily driven by budget restraints. Rather, the delay was due to political priorities, with some in government arguing it had to do with development choices. The Achilles heel of proposals on reparations in most developing nations is, however, often a financial one. It is this that makes the establishment of the ICC's Trust Fund for Victims (TFV) such an important development, with consideration being given through this Fund to a range of restorative services, including vocational training, counseling, reconciliation workshops, and reconstructive surgery. The TFV website indicates that there are an estimated 42,300 direct beneficiaries and an additional 182,000 families and community members who are recipients of funding.[20] Spokespersons for the TFV, at the same time, indicate that funding in Uganda and the Democratic Republic of the Congo resulting from decisions made within the Pre-Trial Chamber on the Court alone cost an estimated 1.8 million Euros. There are also restrictions imposed on the Fund by the mandate of the ICC and the separate mandate of the TFV.[21] Reparation funding is further a victim of bureaucratic distinctions made by UN agencies and elsewhere between reparations and development, with officials responsible for development funding seeking to ensure that development funds are used for self-sufficiency projects and economic growth rather than victim dependency. There is also reluctance on the part of governments to embrace the concept of reparation due to the sense of guilt and responsibility associated with it.

The reparations debate is complex. Victims need immediate relief, while the long-term overcoming of deprivation requires sustainable development and institutional reform to make this possible. The question is what happens in the interim between promise and non-delivery? The simple answer is revolution versus the perpetuation, if not the intensification, of the gap between the haves and the have-nots. The more complex response is to inquire whether a society in transition can find a *via media* between both options, by avoiding the destruction of the past in the hope that it produces something new, while refusing to accept the perpetuation of former exclusion. To this end black South Africans have (for the present) placed their trust in the liberation politics of the ruling party. Indications are, however, that they are becoming increasingly skeptical as to whether the government can meet their basic needs. Torn between the politics of liberation and a hunger for jobs, the poor vote to keep the present government in power, while their frustration manifests in protests, strikes, anger, and violence, as well as threats and attempts to form new and realigned political movements.

The demands of South African blacks, while at times self-destructive and costly to those who are asked to support strikes and radical political action in the streets, point to what has been called a "maturing democracy." At best, the deep fissures in the ruling alliance and the ANC itself give expression to the beginning of a deep conversation concerning the nature of post-apartheid society that is likely to live in the interregnum between the old and the new, between promise and non-delivery, for the foreseeable future. This requires a level of fearless and honest speech and a level of truth-telling that few political parties are ready to engage. It is seen in the debate concerning the meaning of blackness between black South Africans who have benefited materially and politically from the 1994 political transition, and those who failed to escape the structural oppression of the past. Above all, it involves deep reflection on the essence of non-racism, gender equality, and what it means to be South African in a diverse and economically unequal society.

Njabulo Ndebele suggests that "perhaps citizenship right now is about responding to the imperative to be more questioning and more rigorous: Something South Africans may have been disinclined to do since 1994."[22] This has resulted in a conflict of words, if not always dialogue, that gives expression to the anguish that many black South Africans face concerning the unfulfilled grand promises of the 1994 political settlement.

Living within the contradictions of contemporary existence in South Africa, marred by the entrenched wealth of the few and the structural poverty of the many, South Africa is experiencing a level of restlessness not seen since 1994. Ndebele argues that this sense of restlessness, together with interrogation of prevailing policies and practices, is a requirement for a democracy to be in a "constant source of renewal." This means that if democracy and reconciliation are to mean anything in South Africa, the nation is obliged to protect the public space within which emboldened and fearless critical debate is happening. It is here that the meaning of post-apartheid peace, the contours of a negotiated settlement, and indeed the reparations must be renegotiated if the

South African settlement is to be more than illusionary peace within which the poor continue to experience the cold winds of exclusion.

Reparations and Development

I suggest that advocates of restorative justice, practitioners of transitional justice, and others concerned with repairing the irreparable in their respective societies ought to wrap their minds around two practical questions. The first asks how to challenge and change the practices of governments and businesses in deeply unequal societies, within which disparity is unlikely to be overcome in the immediate to medium-term future. The second question is how to enable those who hold political and economic power to recognize and accept the need to affirm and promote the human dignity of those who are unlikely to break out of poverty in their lifetime. These are questions that reach to the heart of what constitutes a liberal democracy within a situation of gross material inequality in transitional societies.

This requires poverty relief and economic change to be accentuated in the appropriation of development as understood by Amartya Sen and Martha Nussbaum and others.[23] Their formative contribution to development theory is unprecedented. What should be resisted is a tendency among some who seek to use a distorted reading of their theory to "explain" if not justify the reason why western capitalism has succeeded where Third World economies have failed. These Afro-pessimists fail to address the exploitative trade policies embedded in earlier forms of colonialism and current trade policy by the world's dominant economies that contribute to the undermining of the freedom that a holistic understanding of development emphasizes. Development involves more than charitable aid. It involves all that is contained in the richness of Sen and Nussbaum's theories of development. It requires, however, a critique of global economics and trade policy and their impact on poor nations.

The need to redress the prevailing under-development in the world is a direct consequence of the underlying principle developed in this paper, which emphasizes the need to build a new sense of *human inclusivity*. Julius Nyerere's observation in the heady days of 1961 continues to be valid still today: "Capitalism went wrong when it divorced wealth from the true purpose of life . . . [which] is to satisfy very simple needs: the need for food, the need for shelter, the need for education and so on. There is enough wealth in every state for every individual to satisfy these basic needs."[24] Suffice it to say, there is enough wealth *in the world* to satisfy these needs. A simple hierarchy of needs in Third World countries shows that unless what Nyerere calls the "very simple needs" of human existence are addressed, higher human needs cannot be met.

The prevailing policies of First World countries and those of many developing countries suggest that the ruling classes in these countries are unlikely to welcome such realities. These are questions that require what Ernesto Verdeja calls the "reconceptualising of the we," in society.[25] They force leaders and citizens to rethink the nature of citizenship in a society that aspires to some form of social democracy. Such democracy requires a balance between the good life (of rights and privileges) in relation to a shared or communal life (with those whose life is not in all respects a "good" one). This is a balance that few modern societies have managed to achieve.

In tentative conclusion: Shortly before his death in 2001, I interviewed Govan Mbeki, father of President Thabo Mbeki and a veteran ANC and South African Communist Party leader who spent 24 years in a cell adjacent to that of Nelson Mandela on Robben Island. I asked him what it would take to repair the damage of apartheid. His answer was decisive: "having and belonging." He noted, "For political renewal to happen, the economy needs to be restructured in such a way that the poor and socially excluded [the victims of apartheid] begin to share in the benefits of the nation's wealth." "People," he insisted, "all people, both black and white . . . need to feel they are part of the new nation. Those who do not feel welcome or at home in it will not work for the common good. They can also cause considerable trouble."[26]

There are no quick fixes and few morally satisfying solutions to historic conflicts in the world. There is no holy grail through which to restore the human dignity of victims of gross violations of human rights. In addition to all that we can do in pursuit of creating a modestly decent society, it takes a significant amount of what Bernard Williams calls "moral luck" to heal and restore a nation.[27]

This luck can perhaps only emerge when victims, survivors, perpetrators, benefactors of the former regime, and aspirant benefactors of the emerging new order are allowed and prepared to muddle along in deciding what to concede and what to demand in resolving a dispute. In desperate settlements this involves more than a case of "who blinks first." It means a choice between life and death. The help of the international community is important but the solution requires local ownership. In the words of Kofi Annan, the former UN secretary-general: "Peace programmes that emerge from national consultations are . . . more likely than those imposed from outside to secure sustainable justice for the future that is in accordance with international standards, domestic legal traditions and national aspirations."[28] These solutions take time, in situations where the poor have the right to be impatient. In the words of Lévinas: "One has to be patient oneself, without asking patience of others" in encountering the other and in building a nation with which to do so.[29]

Notes

1. Howard Zehr, *Changing Lenses* (Scottsdale, PA: Herald Press, 1995).
2. Pablo de Grieff, ed., *Handbook of Reparations* (Oxford: Oxford University Press, 2006); Dan Philpott, *Just and Unjust Peace: An Ethic of Political Reconciliation* (Oxford: Oxford University Press, 2012).
3. Ernesto Verdeja, "A Critical Theory of Reparative Justice," *Constellation* 15 (June 2008), no. 2, 208–222.
4. de Grieff, *Handbook of Reparations*, 467.
5. John Locke, "The Second Treatise," in *Two Treatises of Government*, ed. Peter Laslett (Cambridge: Cambridge University Press, 1988).
6. Verdeja, "A Critical Theory of Reparative Justice," 212.
7. Mark Saunders, *Ambiguities of Witnesses: Law and Literature in the Time of a Truth and Reconciliation Commission* (Stanford, CA: Stanford University Press, 2007); Charles Villa-Vicencio, *Walk with Us and Listen: Political Reconciliation in Africa* (Washington, DC: Georgetown University Press, 2009).
8. Emmanuel Lévinas, *Ethics and Infinity Ethics and Infinity* (Pittsburgh: Duquesne University Press, 1985), 89.
9. My knowledge of this book comes via an article by John Muckelbauer and Erik Doxtader, "Reading Otherwise Than Being: Asking After Patience" *JAC* 29, no. 3 (2010), 493–509.
10. Michel Foucault, *Fearless Speech*, ed. David Pearson (Los Angeles: Semiotext (e)/MIT, 2001), 169.
11. Harold H. Saunders, *Politics Is about Relationship: A Blueprint for the Citizens' Century* (New York: Palgrave Macmillan, 2005), 7.
12. Interview, 2007, Pretoria.
13. Geoffrey R. Heald, "Learning Amongst Enemies: A Phenomenological Study of the South African Constitutional Negotiations from 1985–1998" (PhD diss., University of the Witwatersrand, 2006).
14. Hannah Arendt, *The Origins of Totalitarianism* (New York: Harcourt Brace Jovanovich, 1951), 300.
15. Jean-Francois Lyotard, "The Other's Rights," in *On Human Rights: The Oxford Amnesty Lectures*, ed. Stephen Shute and Susan Hurley (New York: Basic Books, 1993), 136.
16. Adriana Cavarero, *Relating Narratives, Storytelling and Selfhood* (New York: Routledge, 2000).
17. Ryszard Kapuściński, *The Other* (London: Verso, 2008).
18. AZAPO and Others vs. The President of the RSA and Others, 1996 (8) BCLR 1015 (CC).
19. Section 2, 32 (4) of the Interim Constitution allows that no section of the Constitution, including the postscript on amnesty, should be regarded as having less validity than any other part of the Constitution. Of the nine judges, J. Didcott provided a separate concurring judgment, suggesting there is no way for the court to assess the cost involved or whether it is impossible to compensate all victims of apartheid. Arguing that the Act allows for "some *quid pro quo* for the loss" suffered as a result of gross human rights violations, he concedes that nothing "more definite, detailed and efficacious could feasibly have been promised at this stage." His substantial argument is, however, that Section 33 (2) of the Interim Constitution allows for amnesty for vicarious liability.
20. Trust fund for victims in International Criminal Court [database online]. Available from www.trustfundforvictims.org/; Rome statute of the international criminal court. Available from http://untreaty.un.org/cod/icc/statute/romefra.htm.
21. Heikelina V. Stuart, "The ICC Trust Fund for Victims: Beyond the Realm of the ICC," Radio Netherlands Worldwide [database online]2009. Available from http://static.rnw.nl/migratie/www.rnw.nl/internationaljustice/specials/commentary/090204-ICC-TFV-redirected.
22. See Amartya Sen, *Development as Freedom* (New York, NY: Alfred A Knopf, 1999); and Martha Nussbaum, *Women and Human Development: The Capabilities Approach* (Cambridge, UK: Cambridge University Press, 2001
23. Njabulo Ndebele, "Suspect Reconciliation!" Background paper, Eighth Nelson Mandela Annual Lecture by Ariel Dorfman, 2010.
24. Thabo Mbeki, "The Imperative of Our Time," *The Thinker* 52 (May 2013): 13.
25. Verdeja, "A Critical Theory of Reparative Justice," 218.

26. Charles Villa-Vicencio, *Walk with Us and Listen: Political Reconciliation in Africa* (Washington, DC: Georgetown University Press: 2009), 95–96; Interview with Mbeki, 2000, Cape Town.
27. Bernard Williams, *Moral Luck: Philosophical Papers, 1973–1980* (Cambridge: Cambridge University Press, 1981).
28. Diane Orentlicher, *Independent Study on Best Practices, Including Recommendations, to Assist States in Strengthening Their Domestic Capacity to Combat All Aspects of Impunity.* United Nations, E/CN.4/2004/88. 2004.
29. Muckelbauer and Doxtader, "Reading Otherwise Than Being."

CHAPTER 9

Traditional Justice

John Braithwaite

Respect for Specificity in Justice Traditions

In chapter 2 of this volume, Jennifer Llewellyn and Daniel Philpott argue that we live in an age of peacebuilding, though hardly an age of peace.[1] Part of the character of that age of peacebuilding is the search for a concept of justice that might inform a just peace, positive peace that can be distinguished from negative peace as no more than absence of war.[2] Restorative justice is advanced in this volume as a candidate for such a concept of justice. Reconciliation is advanced as a partner concept, so together restorative justice and reconciliation can provide a framework for peacebuilding. Louise Mallinder, for example, explores how reconciliation and restorative justice might be advanced through restorative amnesties. Other chapters tweak these partner concepts together and apart at other points of peacebuilding policy. Jonathan VanAntwerpen's chapter reveals something of the way an institution like the International Center for Transitional Justice became a battleground for contestation between reconciliation/restorative justice and justice as putting war criminals in prisons, as well as a space for combining these concepts and packaging the combination as holistic.

The problem in focus for this chapter is that all these contested concepts have mainly been crafted in the West. Restorative justice and penitentiary-style prisons for housing criminals long-term (as opposed to police lock-ups or castle dungeons) are transitional justice institutions that have conceptual and practice origins in the Northeast of North America. In that sense, the International Center for Transitional Justice in New York is in the right place to be a battleground for competing conceptions of how reconciliation and punishment might or might not cohere. I have my own, somewhat different, views on how to integrate restorative justice and punitive justice within a responsive regulation policy framework[3] and according to civic republican values of freedom as non-domination.[4] The objective of this chapter is not to defend that alternative, but to explore the problem faced by all the alternative peacebuilding paradigms at the UN, because their influences are so Western. Still, respect and learning from specificity in justice traditions, it must be said, does not require one to step back from republican advocacy of freedom as non-domination, of separations of powers. Republican thought must value a niche for non-state justice in a separation of powers, and freedom as non-domination requires meaningful space for traditional forms of contestation. While no case is made for why freedom as non-domination, separations of powers, women's rights, restorative justice, and reconciliation are worthy discourses for the local traditions of all societies to engage, we can say that these are candidates for two-way global dialogue because they lean on principles discussed by Llewellyn and Philpott, like equality of relationship, respect, and dignity, which are of concern in all national conversations about justice.

First, this chapter explores its topic of traditional justice by urging respect for specificity in non-state justice traditions. It also urges respect for reconciliation and restorative justice as encompassing traditions of thought and practice that can both enrich and be enriched by non-state justice in developing societies. But reconciliation and restorative justice can only be combined in a spirit of humility. It is possible to embark on a journey of learning how to work with reconciliation and restorative justice in a way that is better informed by the wisdom of traditional justice. This journey is opened up with a consideration of ways that traditional justice agreements can invoke superior compliance mechanisms than court orders. Then we contemplate how reconciliation might be conceived sufficiently broadly as to encompass *gotong royong* (what Clifford Geertz[5] describes as an Indonesian philosophy of "joint bearing of burdens"). The implication of this analysis is that the West may have an impoverished conception of reconciliation because it does not extend to *gotong royong*. Finally, we consider what restorative justice and reconciliation can learn from the use of humor in traditional justice.

I am not especially fond of the term traditional justice. It is the term chosen by International IDEA (Institute for Democracy and Electoral Assistance) for their influential volume by Huyse and Salter, *Traditional Justice and Reconciliation after Conflict: Learning from African Experiences*.[6] Like Huyse and Salter, I will argue that alternatives for conducting comparative research—customary justice (which I take to be a synonym of traditional justice), indigenous justice, informal justice—have equal or greater problems.

One important conclusion of this chapter is that if one is promoting the utility of restorative justice principles and practices for peacebuilding in a particular place and finds that a traditional justice practice considerably realizes restorative justice ideals, it is normally best to work with or through that traditional practice. And when one does that, it is best to call that justice work by its traditional name rather than import the Western term restorative justice to describe the practice. So if villagers in Rwanda describe what they are doing as *gacaca*, a researcher discussing non-state justice in Rwanda should use that term to describe that practice. Doing so is not only more precise and grounded, it is also more respectful of local ownership of justice traditions. This does not help the comparativist, who is not likely to find it very helpful to describe one society's justice system as more *gacaca*-like than another's. In this chapter, Sally Engle Merry's[7] work is used to locate a path for synthesis of a global discourse like restorative justice or reconciliation and local traditional discourses. As in Merry's work, this chapter uses questions of gender and rights to explore some of the dilemmas of reconciliation, restorative justice, and peacebuilding.

State and Non-State Justice

In the twenty-first century, all nations have a state justice system. The idea of having one has utterly globalized in the past six centuries. All but a handful are based on one European system of formal law or another, or some hybrid of different European systems (such as Louisiana's or Quebec's French-English hybrids). The major exceptions are around seven states with Islamic law systems.[8] The most analytically useful distinction is perhaps between state justice processes and non-state ones; though one must not allow it to blind us to the way state and non-state systems influence, capture, and constitute one another.[9] One problem with such a conception is that in the kind of organizational society in which we live, so many of the most important non-state justice processes are rather non-traditional creations of private corporations. So, if we work in the private sector, we will have more encounters with the company's justice system than with the state system. That will not usually be described as a contact with the corporate justice system, but with the corporate compliance group, the occupational health and safety office, the comptroller, the general-counsel, the anti-discrimination officer, the auditor. The quality of the justice might not be all that great! There will usually be some sort of appeal processes available, however, if we believe we have been unjustly demoted or disciplined, and there will be a body of rules and precedents we can appeal to. Even those of us who are university professors have more encounters during our lives with just and unjust university sanctioning systems than with state ones. So even in the Western societies with the best resourced state justice systems, most people feel the pinch of a non-state justice system more often during their life. This is even more true of the societies that have been experiencing armed conflict within their borders during the twenty-first century, all of them non-Western, all of them with much more weakly resourced state justice systems than in the west.

It is nevertheless helpful to think about the non-traditional non-state justice of late modern corporations. When conservative politicians in a country like Australia say that our legal system should not recognize Aboriginal or Torres Strait Islander law because they believe in "one law for all Australians," the best way for legal pluralists to respond is to say that is not true. If we work in a university and engage in serious plagiarism, we will be subjected to a university justice process that will probably decide to end our job, indeed our entire career. But if we are an ordinary citizen and engage in plagiarism that is not a breach of copyright, no one is able to drag us before any justice system for that. If we are a professional rugby league player and say publicly that the referee was terribly unfair, we might be dragged before a body called the "National Rugby League Judiciary" and fined for "bringing the game into disrepute." A sports fan who shouts the same thing from the grandstand is viewed by national law as exercising freedom of speech and is beyond legal sanction. So my first conclusion is that in no country is there "one justice system for all" and in no country is the state system the most important vehicle for delivering justice (or injustice) to most of us.

Justice research focuses disproportionately on state systems. In a state like Timor-Leste, where I have been doing fieldwork since 2006, large private organizations are thin on the ground, but the survey evidence is overwhelming that most citizens take most of their grievances about injustice to a traditional justice system, and more than 80 percent of people prefer that to recourse to the state's courts.[10] A problem with calling that Timorese justice with people literally sitting "on the mat" with village "traditional" or "customary" or "indigenous" justice is that it might be infused with Christian traditions of prayer, hymn-singing, and Christian concepts of forgiveness that, for the most part, only arrived in the southeast corner of the globe in recent centuries. This is even truer with traditional reconciliation following the conflicts in Bougainville and the Solomon Islands, where the infusion of Christianity into traditional justice is both stronger and more historically recent.[11]

A lot of traditional justice is not very traditional. It constantly adapts. Its practitioners often sought out hybridity with Christianity to bolster legitimacy for their justice practices, just as Christianity sought out hybridity with the animism of traditional justice in the South Pacific to bolster its legitimacy. Most creation of culture through communities is highly creolized, and this seems particularly true of the creation of traditional justice.[12]

Indigenous justice has an additional set of problems as a comparative framework. It is a concept well-attuned to the justice discourses of white settler societies—Australia, Canada, New Zealand, the United States—as a way of referring to the justice practices of indigenous minorities. But indigenous justice is not part of the discourse of how the British refer to the traditional justice of Scottish clans. Miranda Forsyth argues that the term indigenous justice is not attractive in a nation like Vanuatu where the state legal system is fully operated by indigenous professionals yet is distinguished from what locals prefer to describe with the *Pidjin* word *kastom*. For this reason, she prefers the analytic frame of distinguishing state and non-state justice systems.[13]

Informal justice has the different limitation that some non-state or traditional justice systems are quite formal. For example, Huyse and Salter[14] conclude that Rwandan *gacaca* and some other African traditional justice practices have formal attributes. A limitation of local justice is that non-state systems such as religious justice systems can be non-local, even transnational.[15]

So for many comparative analytic purposes, it is useful to distinguish state and non-state justice and then consider how restorative is state justice in that society and how restorative are its various non-state justice systems. Harry Blagg[16] and others legitimately worry that such a method can involve a kind of "orientalism,"[17] where indigenous custom is appropriated to a Western project like restorative justice, putting indigenous ideas into foreign contexts where it is detached from the cultural moorings that give the indigenous project point and purpose. While that is a risk, it is another kind of risk to write books on restorative justice that only learn from Western justice practices. Disrespect resides in finding it perfectly natural that non-Western peoples should come to the West to undertake courses in Western state law, yet failing to see the value in Westerners travelling east and south to learn from the wisdom of non-Western non-state justice and then incorporating that wisdom in their restorative justice writing.

It can be crudely simplifying and Westernizing to think of a traditional form of dispute resolution in a village society as restorative justice. It can be equally misleading to think of the practice as any kind of justice, including indigenous justice. Justice is a Western concept too. Much of what we describe as traditional or indigenous justice is actually thought of by the people who practice it with concepts that could never be translated as justice, concepts such as making things right, restoring balance, establishing harmony through and with the ancestors. Justice is like rights in that sense. There may be no concept of justice or rights in the traditions of a particular people. That is not to say that there are not ways of thinking about what Westerners call justice for women that might resonate with and enrich Western discourses on these matters. Nor is it to deny that these societies, and especially women within them, might not draw benefits from being part of a global conversation about justice or rights for women, and from being part of a global feminist politics that can deliver them some resources to do things their women value.

Others in this volume, like myself in the past,[18] have dedicated many pages to arguing why restorative justice is a meaningful and powerful concept, and other pages on how it should be conceptualized. I will not rejoin those debates and conclusions here, but rather take them as my starting point. I take restorative justice to be a banner around which a global social movement politics valued by the contributors to this volume has rallied. I see it as a social movement originating in the West, but a social movement about a form of practice whose richest instantiations are in developing countries, and especially those that have had long histories of armed conflict. The social movement actually originated at the center of Western power in North-eastern North America, the early hot spots being in a semi-circle running from Ontario to Minnesota to Pennsylvania. In the 1980s in Australia, my own research group was studying exit conferences following regulatory inspections in places like nursing homes and coal mines and in the early 1990s we were studying what the New Zealanders had dubbed family group conferences for youth crime. Neither we nor the New Zealanders started calling this conferencing innovation restorative justice until some time between 1991 and 1993. In Australia, we did that quite consciously because we believed there was power in ideas that connected into the circuitry of northern knowledges, and we decided to be obeisant to the fact that the design of global circuitry was mostly defined in the North Atlantic. We were conceptually obeisant but not ideationally humble. We thought extant North Atlantic practices of victim-offender mediation were inferior to conferencing and we had a variety of theoretical positions on why we believed that.

By the same lights, these days I think many of the restorative practices I see in village societies have virtues that are lacking in Western restorative justice conferencing. Some will be discussed in this chapter. For the same reason that it was good to encourage New Zealanders to do so, I think it is good to encourage the master practitioners of those village methods for seeking justice to engage with the social movement for restorative justice. It is good for village practitioners to acquire that comparative lens on why their practice is so unique and valuable, and yes, to pick up some useful ideas from other places, and it is good for Western restorative justice to be likewise engaged with southern voices.

Vernacularization

One of the most important contributions to the law and development literature addressing these issues is Sally Engle Merry's *Human Rights and Gender Violence*.[19] It is a study of how local actors creatively adopt human rights ideas, find a way of channeling them through indigenous discourses, of justice or balance, to reshape social relationships. Merry's vision is for the foreign researcher as a multisite ethnographer of the comparative project of understanding the diffusion of human rights approaches to gender violence. At various points of space-time across the globe, the researcher engages with only fragments of a larger local system that is neither coherent nor fully graspable. One of Merry's case studies is the reaction of the international human rights and feminist communities to the Fijian reconciliation tradition of *bulubulu*. The concern at the Convention on the Elimination of All Forms of Discrimination against Women (CEDAW) hearings at the UN has been that *bulubulu*—enacted as a person apologizes for wrongdoing, offers a whale tooth and a gift and asks for forgiveness—has been widely used for rape. After Fiji's 1987 coup, the indigenous coup leaders declared the use of *bulubulu* for rape legal, and *bulubulu* rape cases increased. It is a significant case for restorative justice because as Fijian society changed, the custom became in some senses more restorative: it "changed from a practice that focuses on preventing vengeance between clans to one that supports a victim and holds the offender accountable."[20] The Western human rights and feminist resistance fueled ethnic nationalist defiance, even from Fijian feminists, and the use of *bulubulu* for rape increased rather than decreased. The upshot was that discourses of restorative justice, human rights, and feminism were all discredited.

Merry's book also describes a number of much more positive encounters between local tradition and global discourses of women's rights. In these more optimistic cases what happened was that rights discourse was translated into local vernacular ("vernacularized"). The key actors in these accomplishments were local intermediaries who had a "double consciousness" that combined logics of global human rights and local ways of thinking about grievances. "They move between them, translating local problems into human rights terms and human rights concepts into approaches to local problems."[21] Just as human rights discourse and local justice vernaculars about resolving specific grievances can and should be natural allies most of the time, so restorative justice discourse and traditional justice vernaculars should be allies in most contexts. The authority of human rights as a global movement is enhanced in such encounters and the capacity of traditional justice to prevent local injustice can also be enhanced when it successfully appeals to rights discourse. For example, in village justice conversations, rights might be used to assert that "unwanted sex" is actually rape and to mobilize resources from international donors to support consciousness-raising about the right to freedom from rape and other forms of exploitation of women.

We can learn from this work that effective restorative justice advocates might seek a "double consciousness" of indigenous ways of thinking about justice and of the global movement for evidence-based restorative justice. As Merry learned with rights discourse, we should not be so naïve as to think that Western trainers can convince locals with restorative justice discourse. What we can do is train local trainers in ways that allow them to acquire a helpful double consciousness. Restorative justice discourse will not be helpful post-conflict unless it is vernacularized into the language of local traditions, and unless it shows respect to those traditions. Of course there will be conflicts between effective and just restorative practice and traditional justice, just as there are endless conflicts between traditional justice and state justice and between restorative justice and traditional justice. These conflicts can be approached conversationally rather than coercively. The key mediators of the conflicts must not be foreign ideologues of restorative justice who threaten to withdraw funding, but locals with a double restorative-traditional sensibility. A formidable degree of field experience in many post-conflict contexts like Bougainville[22] now reveals that trainers with the double sensibility, like Chief John Tompot,[23] can resolve conflicts between restorative justice principles and tradition with profound wisdom.

The final sections of this chapter argue that one reason things so often work out this way is that justice is immanently holistic. Different conceptions of justice are different in major ways, but also have shared features and foundations that are forged in recurrently common human experience of injustice and oppression. Rape is a good example of such recurrence across all societies that is experienced by its survivors as oppression. Not only can locals with dual traditional-restorative sensibilities mediate in ways that enhance the legitimacy of both restorative and traditional justice, they can also be facilitators of each learning valuable lessons from the other. And the conversation can foster creolized adaptation by both sets of justice practices. Such creolization throughout human history has been a driver of justice innovations worth evaluating. Llewellyn and Philpott[24] go further to argue that justice and reconciliation are immanently holistic. So one might take the analysis of this chapter further, that locals with shared traditional, reconciliatory, and justice sensibilities might mediate fertile new hybrids.

Conversely, it is destructive of both the virtues of traditional justice and the virtues of global restorative justice to seek to resolve the real conflicts that arise between them by coercive Western imposition. This parallels Merry's lesson of the *bulubulu* contest between traditional justice and the global regime on the rights of women as a conflict that reduced the legitimacy and efficacy of both.

A final lesson of Merry's work is her empirical finding that global discourses (of rights) were translated "down" more than grassroots perspectives were translated "up." Restorative justice advocates need to contemplate the structural drivers of stronger downward than upward translation and seek to compensate for a lopsided appropriation of meaning by special efforts to listen to the voices of the periphery and to honor them in restorative justice writing and training. C. Wright Mills's sociological imagination is about converting personal troubles into public issues.[25] To accomplish global public consciousness about how to do a better job of peacebuilding, we must learn how to connect a personal story of transcending violence in the periphery to larger principles of human rights, of restorative justice. We can become effective in our global politics of peacebuilding when we translate local stories of reconciliation into global discourses with social movement momentum. Restorative justice is slowly acquiring that momentum.

Learning from Traditional Peacemaking

This section seeks to make the foregoing abstractions concrete by illustrating three ways in which restorative justice might learn from traditional peacemaking. The first is about increasing the probability that what is agreed in restorative justice processes will actually be delivered. The second is about the Indonesian philosophy of *gotong royong* or joint bearing of burdens. The third is about the role that humor can play in clearing a path to healing.

THE SPIRIT OF COMPLIANCE

The evaluation literature on restorative justice suggests that its strongest effect is that the agreement in a restorative circle is more likely to elicit compliance than the order of a court, even though the latter is backed by the law of contempt and the restorative circle is not.[26] We think this is because loved ones have a superior capability of holding offenders to their undertakings to do work for victims, attend a drug rehabilitation program, and the like, than are the police.[27]

In light of this, I was intrigued to learn from my fieldwork with Hilary Charlesworth and Aderito Soares in Timor-Leste between 2006 and 2009 that one reason most Timorese preferred traditional justice on the mat even in towns, but especially in villages, for cases of gang violence connected to political and ethnic conflict, was that undertakings to desist from future gang violence were much less likely to be complied with after court cases. Worse than that, the belief was widespread among Timorese that if a court punished someone after a complaint to the state justice system, the court case would run a serious risk of triggering a revenge attack by the defendant's group. Conversely, when those involved in traditional justice literally sat down on the mat that village elders spread out for this ritual purpose, there was a belief that breaking the agreement would lead to dire things happening to the individual who broke the reconciliation agreement. This was because the agreement on the mat had a spiritual significance that undertakings to a court did not. In my 2013 fieldwork in the Pakhtun areas of northwest Pakistan with Ali Gohar, all the differences between state and non-state justice discussed in this paragraph were present. So much so that children were advised to stay away from the entrance to the prison after 4:00 p.m., which is the time when prisoners were released after serving their sentence, lest the children were to get caught in crossfire.

We have found similar beliefs about traditional post-conflict reconciliation in Bougainville and across many other parts of Melanesia,[28] in the Moluccas, and across many parts of Indonesia.[29] In Bougainville peace processes, once spears and arrows had been ritually broken and a stone buried to indicate the permanence of the peace, anyone who broke that peace would be at risk of dying from sorcery that would naturally flow from that breach. In Sulawesi, Indonesia, we discovered something similar, though it was the head of a ritually slaughtered buffalo that was buried rather than a large stone.

Returning to the Timor-Leste case, in circumstances where there was fear that the punishment of a court would fuel revenge attacks, it was viewed as important for the elders to lead a reconciliation process on the mat that might result in compensation (in buffalo, other livestock, or goods) not only for the original violence but also for the punishment resulting from state justice. There would be apology for harsh things said and done in the past, including in the courtroom. Likewise in northwest Pakistan.

In Merry's terms, vernacularizing justice through moving it to the mat not only connects peacemaking to restorative justice principles that make more local sense than Western restorative-justice-speak, it also connects peacemaking to the commitment to comply with conference outcomes in a way that makes sense in Timorese terms. In some contexts in Melanesia and further across to the Moluccas, rituals of Christian prayer are hooked into belief systems regarding the spiritual unbreakability of peace agreements. The priest's prayers, informants said, might mention descent into hell for spoilers of the peace. This is Christian vernacularizing of beliefs with more animist origins.

The point is that neither transplants of Western state justice, nor Western restorative justice, nor Western-style diplomacy in these contexts are likely to deliver the commitments to a peace distinctively available from traditional peacemaking. Second, skillful translation of one form of peacemaking or justice into the vernacular of another by mediators with dual sensibility across these discourses can render one form of justice less vulnerable to being ravaged by the other when it is seen as an affront to the other form of justice.

One form is less likely to be ravaged by another form of justice process when vernacularizers of justice search for holistic justice in a spirit of deep respect of one justice tradition for another. One font of respect for state justice from village elders who translate Timorese justice wisely on the mat is a recognition that some actors are too powerful, too determined to fight, or too well-armed for village elders to be able to manage them on the mat. Wise elders in these contexts call in the police or military to handle the matter. Obversely, wise police tend to defer a lot to village elders when they wish to handle a matter on the mat, yet stand ready to step in (calling in military backup where needed) in cases where this is what village elders request.

A difference between New Zealand and Australian practices of restorative justice conferencing is that in New Zealand it is common for conferences to open and close with a Christian prayer, especially when participants include Maori or Pacific Islanders, while in Australia this almost never happens. This is because Australian thinking is that the church should be kept out of a state domain like criminal justice. An implication of the analysis in this section is that we might consider seeing the Australian approach as doctrinaire, at least so long as non-believers say, without feeling pressured, that they are fine with believers saying a prayer. Before committing too strongly to the value of spirits in compliance with restorative justice agreements, however, it is worth considering the mixed reviews of the role of *magamba* spirits as (male only) dead ex-combatants who returned following the civil war in Mozambique to reject punitive justice and demand a form of restorative justice (according to the account of Ingreja and Dias-Lambranca).[30] As those believed to have suffered most, dead warriors demand post-war healing of war-related wounds. Bad things are said to happen to those who eschew the injunction to embrace reconciliation. Unfortunately, however, *magamba* do not empower the living through dialogue. Their messages are only transmitted through the bodies of designated individuals who can then abuse their special line to the dead warriors to make demands that advance their personal political projects. We might therefore be agnostic, seeing the spirits of all religions as resulting in mixed bag of effects.

GOTONG ROYONG

In the Indonesian research for the *Peacebuilding Compared* project, we found non-truth and reconciliation much more common than truth and reconciliation.[31] This contrasts with the greater prominence of "truth" as an objective of various modalities of traditional African reconciliation.[32] High integrity truth-seeking was rarely present in Indonesian peacebuilding, refuting

Braithwaite's starting model of peacebuilding.[33] Indeed, this starting model, grounded in the empirical literature on truth and reconciliation in South Africa,[34] has actually not been validated in any of our first 12 conflicts of *Peacebuilding Compared*.

Nevertheless, we concluded that Indonesian non-truth and reconciliation has supported peace, though we cling to the suspicion that truth, justice, and reconciliation might have made that peace more resilient. Like Susanne Karstedt,[35] we have learned that it is important to focus on the *longue durée* of reconciliation that may overcome the non-truth of short-term reconciliation. Karstedt discovered in post–World War II Germany that the creation of a space for "moving on" was initially based on a non-truth that just those in Hitler's inner circle who were convicted at Nuremberg were culpable.[36] That distorted truth, however, laid a foundation for subsequent testimony that gave voice to victims of the Holocaust. Victim testimony from the 1960s ultimately became a basis for an acknowledgment of the full, terrible truth. Deeper reconciliation between the German people and their former enemies and victims then occurred.

Remarkable accomplishments of the reintegration of combatants from organizations such as *Laskar Jihad*, in which religious leaders showed great leadership for peace, was a feature of Indonesian peacebuilding. So was reconciliation through sharing power combined with the sharing of work (*gotong royong*) for reconstruction. *Gotong royong* is a core tenet of Indonesian philosophy that means mutual aid or "joint bearing of burdens."[37] *Gotong royong* is a widespread modality of healing. The Indonesian military, whose actions in fueling the conflict in Poso, and whose inaction in preventing it, caused so much resentment on both sides, participated widely in *gotong royong* by rebuilding Poso houses that had been lost to victims on both sides.[38] One reason why reconciliation has been less studied in Indonesia than elsewhere is perhaps that little of it has been done by national elites or even provincial elites. The politics of reconciliation that mattered happened from the bottom up as a micro-politics massively dispersed among thousands of leaders of villages, clans, churches, mosques, and subdistricts.

Reconciliation is a word that can mean many things. We can see the point of view of some restorative justice scholars who think it is a concept with too little precision.[39] Changing hearts, changing minds, restoring relationships, forgiveness, apology, helping one another through *gotong royong*, former enemies shaking hands and agreeing to put the past behind them—these are all very different things. We do, however—perhaps unproductively, perhaps not—lump them together in a discussion of types of reconciliation.

On the other hand, as Duane Ruth-Heffelbower pointed out in a sermon he gave in Indonesia in 2000, reconciliation is a word that travels surprisingly well across languages and religions,[40] while allowing different peoples to impute somewhat different meanings to it as it travels. Ruth-Heffelbower in that sermon argued that the teaching of Paul was that different groups and individuals should each find their own different paths to reconciliation so these differences will constitute resilience of reconciliation:

> In his second letter to the church at Corinth the Apostle Paul was trying to explain his goals, and describe goals Christians should have ... [T]he goal Paul set was simple: be reconciled to God—*punyalah rekonsiliasi dengan Allah*, and help others to be reconciled as well.... Reconciliation is a big word. What do we really mean by "the message of reconciliation?" That's *rekonsiliasi* in Bahasa Indonesia, and means the same thing. The word "conciliation" means the process of bringing two people or things together, to help them fit together. To reconcile means to fit together again two people or things that have come apart. It is similar to *mencocokkan*, but *mencocokkan* has the feeling of forcing things to fit together, while reconciliation has the feeling of inviting things to fit together.[41]

It may be that United Nations discourse is more attracted to reconciliation than to restorative justice precisely because it is even more open-textured than restorative justice, allowing different traditions to connect to the concept with their own meanings. Much of the reconciliation work in Indonesia during the past decade was indigenous, pre-Islamic, and not especially "Indonesian"; it was to a degree *pela-gandong* in Maluku,[42] *hibua lamo* in Halmahera,[43] *maroso* in Poso,[44] and *peusijuek* in Aceh,[45] among other local reconciliation traditions that were even more variegated among Dayaks and Papuans.[46] Yet there were two definite patterns to post-conflict reconciliation in Indonesia: non-truth and reconciliation and *gotong royong*. We consider each in turn. At first, we found the low level of political commitment to high-integrity truth-seeking at all levels of politics and in most civil society networks disturbing, especially when non-truth meant not just forgetting, but lying. The most common kind of lie was widespread blaming of "outside provocateurs" for atrocities that were committed mostly by locals against locals.

So how was reconciliation without truth accomplished in most of these cases? Thousands of meetings across these conflict areas in the early 2000s were called reconciliation meetings. Some included only a dozen or so leaders; quite a number had hundreds of participants, some had more than 1000. The most common number was approximately 30 people who were key players from two neighboring villages or the Christians and Muslims from the same village, who had been at war with each other not long before. Other meetings were called interfaith dialogues, others *adat* rituals bearing various customary names for reconciliation meetings among the ethnic groups of that locality.

Sorrow, even remorse, for all the suffering was commonly expressed at these meetings. Tears flowed and there were often deeply sincere hugs of forgiveness. No one ever, in any of the reports we received of these meetings, admitted to specific atrocities that they or their group perpetrated against the other. Most of the agenda was dominated by practical concerns of rebuilding and reintegration. Sometimes the ethnic group that ended with control of the village would invite back only a small number of trusted families of the ethnic other as a first step toward rebuilding trust. A common gesture of practical reconciliation was for a Christian community to start rebuilding a mosque they had burned down or a Muslim community to start rebuilding a church they had razed. The cleansed group might be invited back to the village to see this for themselves as a sign of the sincerity of the desire for reconciliation and to give advice on how to do the rebuilding. They might then do some work together on the project.

When the cleansed group returned, their former enemies would often organize a moving welcome ceremony for them. Former enemies who, before the conflict, had also been friends and neighbors, would shower them with gifts of food and other necessities in a steady stream of visits to their home. The point of this summary narrative is not to say this always happened. There were also unpleasant exchanges, bitterness, and people who were shunned. The point is to give a sense of how reconciliation without truth worked when it did work, which was quite often. When a mosque substantially built by Christian hands was opened, the Christian community would be invited and Christian prayers would sometimes be said inside the mosque. We also found rituals of everyday life to be important to reconciliation. Christians attending the funeral of a respected Muslim leader and embracing Muslims soon after the conflict were sites of reconciliation. So were Christians being invited to the celebration of Mohammed's birthday, Muslims to Christmas celebrations, to *halal bi halal* (a forgiveness ritual among neighbors that occurred at the end of the fasting month of Ramadan),[47] and so on. In our interviews, we were told of simple acts of kindness that were important for building reconciliation from the bottom up: an *ulama* who picked up an old Christian man in his car and dropped him at the market, the loan of a Muslim-owned lawnmower to cut the grass of the Christian church. There were a great variety of locally creative and meaningful ways that people reconciled without ever speaking the truth to one another about who was responsible for crimes.

If non-truth is the first pattern of Indonesian reconciliation we have identified, *gotong royong* manifests the second. This has already become apparent in many of the examples above. Healing happens through sharing in community work projects, in building that mosque or school together. Indonesians are good at having fun when they work together; they bond through work more than Westerners do partly because the division of labor in village society is less differentiated, but also because sharing communal work and community welfare burdens is overlaid with cultural meanings of *gotong royong*. Backbreaking work that must be done to rebuild might be seen as a burden on reconciliation in the West, infused with resentment as people struggle to do it. In Indonesia, it is much more a resource for reconciliation. Valerie Braithwaite thinks power sharing is a way to transcend disengagement and dismissive defiance more broadly.[48] Perhaps *gotong royong* offers prospects of a different form of reengagement through doing, through sharing in work rather than sharing in power. For some village folk who have limited interest in sharing even local political power, there can be a kind of empowerment through work, in deciding where and how the mosque will be rebuilt. This can be confidence-building and ultimately commitment-building by other (rural Indonesian) means, especially when the military also joins in the *gotong royong*, as it has done from Aceh and Poso to Papua. Power sharing and work sharing together enable a dual assault on post-conflict disengagement and disruption of the peace.

To make this more concrete, village forums sometimes envision what their village would look like in 20 years if they choose to use the planning resources they are empowered to spend, by, for example, building a bridge at a particular spot. That is what they then decide to spend local infrastructure money on when the government provides it. Then, together, in a spirit of *gotong royong*, with some outside engineering help, they build it. Deciding together and doing together can weave a stronger fabric of peace.

The intertwining of sharing power and sharing rebuilding work through *gotong royong* that we take to be a lesson of reconciliation in Indonesia can also be important as a means of restoring dignity. All our Indonesian cases pulsate with assaults on people's dignity as drivers of conflict. We give dignity back to people who feel a loss of it when we agree to share power with them and when we pitch in to work with them on projects that they are empowered to shape and that they care about more than we do.

We can learn something about the politics of indignity and the reconciliatory politics of dignity from telling this recent history of Indonesia. We have learned from Shadd Maruna's work that "redemption scripts" that help Liverpool criminal offenders "make good" often involve, particularly at first, much less than full acknowledgment of responsibility.[49] Serious offenders say to themselves, "that was not the real me," "that was me recovering from abuse by my father," "that was the alcohol speaking, not me," and the like. Clarity of commitment to a non-violent me can nevertheless be a starting point for desistance from violence. It seems possible to link criminological lessons from Maruna's work to peacebuilding lessons from Indonesian *gotong royong*. Consider a man who fails to fully own personal responsibility for his crime in any way that could be accepted by a victim. There have been examples in Canberra of such offenders agreeing to supervised work for the victim that in the best circumstances became work with a victim (say when the wheelchair-bound victim needs more carer support than the state will provide). This illustrates the possibility that Western reintegration practice might learn from Indonesian *gotong royong*.

In Bougainville, initial post-conflict reconciliation encounters rarely involved individuals admitting specific murders or rapes. A more common scenario involved a company of the Bougainville Revolutionary Army admitting to rape and pillage of a village and asking forgiveness. If forgiveness were proffered in return, and if over time, the admission did not lead to payback, then individuals one by one might find the courage to confess, apologize, and offer compensation to mothers that symbolizes the blood of a son killed or a daughter raped. So while Bougainville is a truth and reconciliation case with increasingly widespread acceptance of individual responsibility for war crimes, and Indonesia a case of mostly non-truth and reconciliation, in Bougainville individual responsibility tended to come much later than collective responsibility. In a similar way, we might hope *gotong royong* can become in time a foundation for full responsibility for war crimes. No reconciliation destination is ever reached in a journey with just one stop.

JUSTICE HUMOR

I often contemplate what might be the critical differences between really great restorative circle facilitators like my Australian colleague Terry O'Connell and rather ordinary ones like myself. One answer I come up with is that part of the greatness of the style of an O'Connell is his use of humor, skillfully attuned to local norms. In the New South Wales country center of Wagga Wagga, I saw O'Connell many times put people at ease in the midst of awful conflicts with deft use of passing humor. It was humor that fitted the milieu of country New South Wales, relaxed in its timing, often poking fun at authority. It seems to me that you have to be confident in your place within the cultural milieu of a particular people to be able to use humor without offense in such tense situations.

I have been surprised and interested to learn how much humor there is in Asia and the Pacific in reconciliation processes concerning terrible wartime atrocities. The documentary, *Passabe*, focuses on a Community Reconciliation

Process that was part of the East Timor Commission for Reception, Truth and Reconciliation.[50] The men from Passabe village had attacked nearby villages, burning them down, killing 74 independence supporters on orders from militia leaders backed by the Indonesian military. All but one of the Passabe perpetrators arrived for the reconciliation to tell the same story. One by one each gave their testimony saying yes, they had arrived for the attack on the village, but they personally "did nothing," were at the rear, by the time *they* arrived everything was already burning, waited in the vehicle. This was not greeted with anger so much as contagious laughter from the crowd of victims attending the reconciliation. There were interjections like: "You saw nothing?" Reply: "Nothing!" Then more laughter. This spirit of the meeting changed when finally one man started his testimony by confessing his shame for the fact that he had clubbed a man to death on orders of the militia leader and had beaten others. He was full of remorse and offered help and compensation to the families of his victims. His testimony was not greeted by laughter but by applause, embrace, tears, and gestures of respect, forgiveness, and compassion for the man who had been courageous enough to take responsibility for his crimes.[51]

It is not that humor never occurs in Western courts. Yet it is the case that the institutional ambience of the Western criminal trial is about solemnity. In contrast, much traditional justice oscillates between comedy and tragedy, as in the story of Passabe above. When I was an anthropology student living in a village in Bougainville in 1969, there was gossip that our chief, who in the matrilineal tradition had gone to live on the land of his wife in a nearby hamlet, had been treating his wife badly. The villagers were reluctant to share such shocking gossip with me, but I got the message that part of it was that the wife had been pushed to have a baby she did not want. Then one day a traditional justice process to put this right occurred. Suddenly, all the women from the wife's village arrived and took whatever property they wanted from our village—from fishing poles to bush knives. I was worried about them taking my camera; my best defense was to use it taking photos of their joyous shopping spree in our village. The justice process really was a lot of fun for them, and for us too, even though we were madly rushing around trying to hide things. One very old man puffing on a pipe joined the marauding women, and much to my chagrin, took the only chair in the village. I used to enjoy a break away from sitting on the ground to read in that chair. Our people shouted out, "Old man, you are not allowed to take things. Only the women are allowed." He chuckled behind his pipe, then took it out to retort, "If you are worried about losing things, you should get your chief to behave properly." The good humor of the occasion made the old man's point rather forcefully to us without stirring anger between the two villages.

The Poso Conflict Resolution Group and the Institute for the Development of Legal and Human Rights Studies were local NGOs that led reconciliation efforts with funding from Mercy Corps following the Christian-Muslim fighting and the founding of a terrorist training camp in Poso, where the 2002 Bali bombers trained. The Institute conducted reconciliation dialogues in a Christian village, then a Muslim village, then with a meeting of the two villages, with an average of 30 people attending more than 300 meetings. Their meetings did not involve apologies and rituals of forgiveness; rather, they focused on practical issues of refugee return. The hope was that forgiveness might follow in time. Facilitators said humor that might seem morbid or inappropriate to outsiders often worked in dealing with tension. For example, one man laughingly said, pointing to a friend with whom he had a minor disagreement in the meeting: "When we have the conflict again, you are my target." Another said, smiling: "Are we attending this meeting as the victims or the actors?"

Just as I could never be confident in the country town milieu of Wagga Wagga to use the humor Terry O'Connell deployed, it is even more unimaginable that I could utter the kind of apparently humorous remarks that were passed in those Poso meetings. Humor is a quirky thing culturally. Even TV sitcoms do not travel particularly well between the US and UK, two predominantly Anglo-Saxon societies that have much heritage in common. If it is a good hypothesis that humor has important value in helping people cope with confronting severe violence, and if the solemnity of state justice rules humor out too often in comparison with traditional restorative justice, then we may only be able to seize this advantage by having only locals facilitating local reconciliations. This takes us back to the conclusion that the practice of flying in Western experts for reconciliation processes may be less valuable than training local trainers, keeping cultural dopes away from the direct conduct of reconciliations beyond their home culture.

Justice as Immanently Holistic

Erik Luna has argued that holism is fundamental to the philosophy of restorative justice.[52] He contends that in the give and take of dialogue in restorative justice processes, competing justice theories are allowed space to contribute to decision-making. Often there will be practical agreement on an outcome from this dialogue, though the philosophical motivation for the agreement will be very different for different participants in the conversation. One reason this happens is that in practical reasoning based on contextualized conversation it is hard for listeners not to become concerned about the worries of others in the conversation. Hence, they seek to craft integrated solutions that redundantly cover all the worries on the table.

Justice is to a degree immanently holistic, though not totally holistic; otherwise there would be no point in distinguishing procedural justice from the justice of outcomes. Procedural justice has been conceived in the literature as having a number of facets—including consistency, correctability, decision accuracy, impartiality, ethicality, and process control—yet these facets tend to be moderately highly intercorrelated.[53] Second we find that procedural and distributive justice tend to be positively correlated and that both are positively correlated with restorative justice. Hence, one of the arguments of restorative justice theorists has been that restorative justice, compared to existing justice practices, contributes to procedural justice, perceived fairness of outcomes (distributive justice), and indeed social justice.[54] Howard Zehr argues that this holism in the conception of justice is to be found in the biblical notion of justice as *shalom*.[55] The intuition about the immanent holism of the *shalom* way of thinking about justice is that a restorative justice process that seeks to empower stakeholders to repair the harm of an injustice will produce outcomes that are more distributively satisfying to stakeholders than a process that seeks to deliver equal punishments to equal wrongs. Heather Strang's writing suggests one reason is that a narrower just-deserts or proportionality objective allows less leeway for a wider contract zone in which a win-win outcome can be crafted—hence restorative justice outcomes are produced that are more generally conceived as fair.[56] The greater control of process in the hands of stakeholders as opposed to justice professionals might also explain why restorative justice is perceived as more procedurally fair. We can also intuit why justice may be immanently holistic by going in the opposite direction in ways suggested by the writings of John Rawls and indeed most other writers on justice.[57] An unjust procedure will be more open to domination by the person with the most power rather than the person with the best case, and so will lead both to less fair outcomes and to social injustice by virtue of domination of the powerful.

The fact that justice is not fully holistic—that procedural, restorative, and distributive justice often conflict—means that there is value in studying the tensions between different versions of justice. Restorative justice innovation takes a different tack, however. It says that because there appears to be an immanent holism of justice as *shalom*, which our editors would add includes justice as reconciliation, why not search for institutional ideas that maximize the synergy of holistic justice? Then it theorizes restorative justice and reconciliation as those institutional ideas. Religion, we argue in this chapter, is one institution that when mobilized with respect for the other, including non-believers, can promote holistic justice synthesis.

Holistic Justice, Peace, and the Good Society

A theme I have long pursued in my research and politics is that the struggle for restorative justice is part of a wider social movement politics for justice (that is holistic). This chapter advances that agenda by showing through the work of Merry[58] the considerable space for shared struggle between the global social movement for restorative justice, the global human rights movement, and feminism. In the discussion of Merry in the pages above, there was no consideration of procedural rights such as the prohibition of detention without trial. But this is obviously another arena of shared struggle between rights advocates and restorative justice advocates, who are joined in the belief that procedural justice is part of what makes holistic justice just. And therefore restorative justice advocates are often active in supporting the work of groups like Human Rights Watch and Amnesty, but more importantly of local human rights NGOs in conflict zones.

The theoretical contention here is that societies that are more holistically just are likely to have less crime and less armed conflict. Broken down, societies that have more social justice, more procedural justice, and more restorative justice are likely to be societies with less crime and less war. I started working on this research program by arguing in an evidence-based manner that societies with greater inequality of wealth and power and greater gender inequality are likely to have higher levels of both common crime and white-collar crime.[59] On armed conflict, it is Paul Collier who has made the most powerful case that one of the most effective things we could do to reduce warfare in today's world is lift "the bottom billion," the poorest billion people in the world, out of extreme poverty.[60] Collier reaches this conclusion in an evidence-based way by showing that extreme poverty of nations, controlling for other variables, consistently and strongly predicts warfare in the historical conditions of the past half century. My research group has leaned heavily on Tom Tyler's[61] work on the theme that procedural justice might reduce lawbreaking, and on the holistic connections between procedural justice and restorative justice.[62] We have made limited progress in exploring the empirical connection between treating people with procedural fairness and armed conflict; but this connection has already begun to emerge, particularly as ethnic or religious groups take to arms when they feel they have been denied a fair hearing of their grievances from institutions they see as dominated by another group.[63] In *Restorative Justice and Responsive Regulation* I first sought to advance the hypothesis that restorative justice has potential to contribute to both the reduction of crime and the reduction of war.[64]

This holistic justice agenda is of course massively macro-sociological, and therefore the contributions of our research community have been limited.

Yet the agenda seems a worthy one with which new generations of scholars can persist in an evidence-based fashion. Part of the tiny contribution of this chapter is in helping us to see that while we might be interested in a bold macro-sociological agenda, we will find a need to put aside macro terms like "justice" and "rights" when we connect the macro vision to micro struggles for non-violence. The contribution is so little because it is so derivative of the work of Sally Engle Merry.[65] Macro theories are useless unless they are micro-macro. Merry's contribution is in showing vernacularization as a macro-micro-macro path. For restorative justice advocates it implies, "Do not conduct struggle for justice in conflict-ridden developing countries in the language of restorative justice." It means finding ways to support feminists with dual commitments to holistic justice and traditional justice that can be fluently transacted in the language, even leaning on the humor, of traditional cultural forms.

Conclusion

In this spirit, let us reinforce our conclusion, within the methodology that generates it, with a final ethnographic fragment. It starts with a glimpse of the war-making potential of fundamentalist actors who shun Merry's double consciousness, and then the peacemaking potential of culturally adept locals who embrace it. Conditions of warfare bring to the fore fundamentalist interpreters of tradition of the first type. During the conflict in Poso,[66] myopic Islamists interpreted the longstanding Christian-Muslim cultural tradition of dancing the *dero* (traditionally symbolizing harmony with young people holding hands dancing in a circle) as a morally corrupt Christian tradition that allowed inappropriate touching between adolescent boys and girls. Traditionally, it was actually a ritual of harmony embraced by Poso Muslims and Christians alike that probably pre-dated the arrival of Islam and Christianity in Poso. These *ulamas* also associated the *dero* with the evil of alcohol, which sometimes was consumed by young people of all faiths at these events. *Ulamas* banned the *dero* during the armed conflict between Christians and Muslims in Poso. Part of the process of reconciliation negotiation was that more moderate *ulamas* became willing to interpret the *dero* not within a Christian frame, nor a corrupted "boy-meets-girl" frame, but within a framework of traditional inter-group harmony and reconciliation. As we found in Maluku and North Maluku with *pela-gandong* and *hibua lamo*,[67] in Poso traditions like the *dero* and *maroso* that had been waning pre-conflict and during the height of the conflict have been reinvigorated and reinvented as more syncretically Muslim-Christian "brotherhood" (and sisterhood) traditions.

Simply because tradition is the tool of the war-maker, we must not fail to see it as a central vehicle for vernacularizing peace. As in the discussion of the role of the *magamba* spirits in Mozambique, however, elements of oppression and of liberation can be vernacularized simultaneously within the one ritual. We must therefore be diagnostic in our dual sensibilities about when each arises; we must be deft in our engagement to strengthen freedom and weaken domination.[68] There are growing numbers of examples of such engagement transforming traditional justice institutions that were once utterly male-dominated—one is *bashingantahe* justice of "men of integrity" in Burundi, including 33 percent women in all local management committees,[69] another is *gacaca* courts in Rwanda—into institutions where female participation is substantial and increasing. Sometimes critiques of traditional justice as dominated by male elites enable regulation that renders it much more representative of disadvantaged strata of the population than the courts. We saw this with the 1993 amendments to the Indian Constitution that required *Panchayats* (village governance institutions in all states, village courts in some) with at least one-third of the officers women and with seats reserved for Scheduled Castes in proportion to the representation of each lower Caste in that area.[70] Thence a new platform is created for questioning why the courts cannot manage comparable proportions of women and judges from lower castes. Restorative justice and reconciliation, even while being relational forms of justice, can in such ways contribute to the creation of a "vibrant 'agonistic' public sphere of contestation where different hegemonic political projects can be confronted."[71]

Notes

1. Jennifer Llewellyn and Daniel Philpott, "Restorative Justice and Reconciliation: Twin Frameworks for Peacebuilding," this volume.
2. The concepts of negative and positive peace originated in the work of John Galtung; John Galtung "Violence, Peace and Peace Research," *Journal of Peace Research* 6, no. 3 (1969): 167–191.
3. John Braithwaite, *Restorative Justice and Responsive Regulation* (Sydney; New York: Federation Press and Oxford University Press, 2002).
4. Philip Pettit, *Republicanism* (Oxford: Clarendon Press, 1997); John Braithwaite and Philip Pettit, *Not Just Deserts: A Republican Theory of Criminal Justice* (Oxford: Oxford University Press, 1990).
5. Clifford Geertz, *Local Knowledge: Further Essays in Interpretive Anthropology* (New York: Basic Books, 1983).
6. Luc Huyse and Mark Salter, *Traditional Justice and Reconciliation after Conflict: Learning from African Experiences* (Stockholm: International IDEA, 2008).
7. Sally Engle Merry, *Human Rights and Gender Violence: Translating International Law into Local Justice* (Chicago: University of Chicago Press, 2006).
8. Philip R. Wood, *Maps of World Financial Law* (London: Allen and Overy, 1997).
9. Miranda Forsyth, *A Bird that Flies with Two Wings: Kastom and State Justice Systems in Vanuatu* (Canberra, ACT: ANU E Press, 2009).

10. Asia Foundation, *Law and Justice in East Timor: A Survey of Citizen Awareness and Attitudes Regarding Law and Justice in East Timor* (Dili, East Timor: Asia Foundation, 2004); UNDP, *Justice for All? An Assessment of Access to Justice in Five Provinces of Indonesia* (Jakarta: UNDP, 2007), 2.
11. John Braithwaite, Hilary Charlesworth, Peter Reddy, and Leah Dunn, *Reconciliation and Architectures of Commitment: Sequencing Peace in Bougainville* (Canberra, ACT: ANU E Press 2010); John Braithwaite, Sinclair Dinnen, Matthew Allen, Valerie Braithwaite, and Hilary Charlesworth, *Pillars and Shadows: Statebuilding as Peacebuilding in Solomon Islands* (Canberra, ACT: ANU E Press, 2010).
12. Jean Comaroff and John Comaroff, "Occult Economics and the Violence of Abstraction: Notes from the South African Postcolony," *American Ethnologist* 26 (1999): 279–303.
13. Forsyth, *Bird that Flies*.
14. Huyse and Salter, *Traditional Justice and Reconciliation*.
15. I am indebted to Miranda Forsyth for this point.
16. Harry Blagg, "A Just Measure of Shame? Aboriginal Youth and Conferencing Australia," *British Journal of Criminology* 37 (1997): 481–501.
17. Edward W. Said, *Orientalism: Western Conceptions of the Orient* (Harmondsworth, UK: Penguin, 1995).
18. Braithwaite, *Restorative Justice*.
19. Merry, *Human Rights and Gender Violence*.
20. Merry, *Human Rights and Gender Violence*, 122.
21. Ibid., 229.
22. Patrick Howley, *Breaking Spears and Mending Hearts* (London; Sydney: Zed Books and The Federation Press, 2002).
23. Prison Fellowship International "Prison Fellowship International Award Peace Foundation Melanesia," (2007) accessed August 11, 2010 http://www.thefreelibrary.com/Prison+Fellowship+International+award%3A+Peace+Foundation+Melanesia...-a0180102731.
24. Llewellyn and Philpott, "Restorative Justice and Reconciliation."
25. C. Wright Mills, *The Sociological Imagination* (New York: Oxford University Press, 1960).
26. Jeff Latimer, Craig Dowden, and Danielle Muise, *The Effectiveness of Restorative Justice Practices: A Meta-Analysis* (Ottawa, Canada: Department of Justice, 2001).
27. Braithwaite, *Restorative Justice*, 51–69.
28. Braithwaite et al., *Reconciliation and Architectures*.
29. John Braithwaite, Valerie Braithwaite, Michael Cookson, and Leah Dunn, *Anomie and Violence: Non-Truth and Reconciliation in Indonesian Peacebuilding* (Canberra, ACT: ANU E Press, 2010).
30. Victor Ingreja and Beatrice Dias-Lambranca, "Restorative Justice and the Role of Magamba Spirits in Post-Civil War Gorongosa, Central Mozambique," in *Traditional Justice and Reconciliation after Conflict: Learning from African Experiences*, ed. Luc Huyse and Mark Salter (Stockholm: International IDEA, 2008).
31. Braithwaite et al., *Anomie and Violence*.
32. Huyse and Salter, *Traditional Justice*.
33. John Braithwaite, "Between Proportionality and Impunity: Confrontation-Truth-Prevention," *Criminology* 43, no. 2 (2005): 283–306. (For this starting model see Figure 1, p. 290).
34. Particularly grounded in James Gibson's survey and other empirical work: James Gibson, *Overcoming Apartheid: Can Truth Reconcile a Divided Nation?* (New York: Russell Sage Foundation, 2004).
35. Susanne Karstedt, "The Nuremberg Tribunal and German Society: International Justice and Local Judgment in Post-Conflict Reconstruction" (paper presented at the Asia Pacific Centre for Military Law Conference, The Australian National University, Canberra, 2005) 4.
36. Ibid.; Susanne Karstedt, "From Absence to Presence, from Silence to Voice: Victims in Transitional Justice since the Nuremberg Trials," *International Review of Victimology* 17 (2010): 1–8.
37. Geertz, *Local Knowledge*.
38. Braithwaite et al., *Anomie and Violence*, ch. 4.

39. Stephen Parmentier and Elmar Weitekamp, eds., *Crime and Human Rights* (Amsterdam; Oxford: Elsevier Publishers 2007) 109–144.
40. "The ultimate goal of traditional justice systems among the Kpaa Mende (and indeed among most African communities) is reconciliation." (Joe A.D. Alie, "Reconciliation and Traditional Justice: Tradition-Based Practices of the Kpaa Mende in Sierra Leone," in *Traditional Justice and Reconciliation after Conflict: Learning from African Experiences*, ed. Luc Huyse and Mark Salter (Stockholm: International IDEA, 2008)).
41. "No Stumbling Blocks to Reconciliation," http://peace.fresno.edu/docs/2Cor5_20-6_10.pdf, Sermon at Yogyakarta International Congregation, Indonesia (March 5, 2000).
42. Braithwaite et al., *Anomie and Violence* ch. 3.
43. *Hibua lamo* is a cultural tradition in North Maluku of binding Christian and Muslim villages together in pacts of peace and mutual help that is similar to *pela-gandong* in Maluku. It is seen as a pluralist custom pre-dating the arrival of Islam and Christianity that involves "equality among the differences" (Gorua interview). It was believed that when Islam arrived, *hibua lamo* meetings were held to agree that "this religion will be welcomed, but some will accept it and others will not. But we will still all be brothers together in spite of this." It was widely believed that in the decades leading up to the conflict the bonds of *hibua lamo* had weakened across North Maluku. At the early post-conflict reconciliation meetings, the mayor told the story of a famous historical figure of the district. He was a wealthy man with a big home and, in the spirit of *hibua lamo*, he allowed his home to be used for both Sunday Christian services and Friday Muslim prayers. In the *hibua lamo* ritual itself, one side gives sri fruit and the other panang fruit placed on swords and exchanged to indicate they are friends. Sugar cane juice (representing sweet, happy things) combined with traditional cooking oil (representing sincerity, peace, kindness, and justice) is then poured over swords, shields, arrows, and other weapons. Then there is an agreement called *koboto*, a sacred declaration to maintain peace. Anyone who tries to destroy it will never succeed in life and will live in misery. Part of the agreement in Tobelo, where hundreds had been slaughtered, was to hand over weapons to the military. The fact that some who failed to do so later found themselves in trouble with the military for this was interpreted as evidence that the sacred power of the declaration worked.
44. Braithwaite et al., *Anomie and Violence*, ch. 4.
45. Local officials encouraged former GAM (Free Aceh Movement) fighters to participate in traditional reconciliation rituals—*peusijuek* ceremonies. Ross Clarke, Galuh Wandita, and Samsidar, *Considering Victims: The Aceh Peace Process from a Transitional Justice Perspective* (New York: International Center for Transitional Justice 2008, 14) reported that *peusijueks* (welcome-home ceremonies) for amnestied GAM prisoners returning to their villages were attended mostly by AMM (Aceh Monitoring Mission peacekeepers), military, and police representatives, and went off smoothly. One AMM officer had attended one *peusijuek* ritual attended by 112 GAM fighters and another in which 25 GAM families stood with 25 non-GAM families who were victims of the war, many at the hands of GAM. The World Bank found that almost all villages had experienced some form of *peusijuek* or *kenduri* ceremony and 77 percent of active GAM members surveyed reported that they had experienced welcome ceremonies in their village—sometimes family *peusijuek*, sometimes village *peusijuek*. Often every member of the village attended these rituals (World Bank, *GAM Reintegration Needs Assessment: Enhancing Peace through Community-Level Development Programming* (Jakarta: The World Bank, 2006), 25). *Peusijuek* usually involves pouring sacred water, yellow rice, or powder on those blessed after reconciliation of a dispute, returning from the *hajj*, and other important events. Separate processes before a *peusijuek* would normally work through the resolution of the dispute. For example, *suloh* is a more complicated process involving many people in reconciliation by negotiation and testimony, related to the Arabic (and Jewish) restorative justice practice of *sulha*. The *peusijuek*, in contrast, symbolizes only the fact that the parties are at peace. It can also be a cooling down that prepares parties in conflict to subsequently sit down to talk. So these watering ceremonies are "social practices, not discursive practices. It's actions. Not in the mind, it's in the practice" (Personal communication, Mustafa Arahman, State Institute of Islamic Studies, Banda Aceh.) Watering "cools people down," watering them as if they were plants. Widows and other conflict victims were often also blessed

in these rituals. Ex-combatants also widely experienced religious welcomes of reconciliation and forgiveness, as in sermons by imams in mosques and village halls. *Peusikuek* is probably a pre-Islamic tradition that has some elements widely interpreted as suggestive of the earlier Buddhist/Hindu influence on Aceh. Sometimes people who have been in conflict shake hands in the presence of a traditional leader who has worked on reconciliation between them, and selected prayers for peace and selected verses of the Koran for peace may be recited. Some of these were between GAM leaders and leaders of militias opposed to them, who made commitments to each other in the mosque and hugged in front of the mosque afterwards, with important figures on both sides adding gravitas to the occasion—for example, a minister from Jakarta and the Governor of Aceh.

46. Braithwaite et al., *Anomie and Violence*, ch. 2 and 5.
47. Christians go to Muslim homes at the ritual of *halal bi halal* to ask for forgiveness for any (non-specified) thing they had done to treat their Muslim neighbor badly in the past. It is common to read in the Jakarta press how *halal bi halal*—this ritual of mutual asking for forgiveness that is unique to Indonesia—has lost all meaning. People ask forgiveness ritualistically, with no depth of feeling, from people whom they do not feel need to forgive them for anything. After the terrible inter-village wars of the turn of the millennium, however, the ritual acquired a new depth of meaning. People would hug each other for long periods, weeping, after forgiveness was offered. Both parties would know of the acts of arson or violence for which forgiveness was very much needed, but these specific acts would not be vocalized in the context of the *halal bi halal* ritual.
48. Valerie Braithwaite, *Defiance in Taxation and Governance: Resisting and Dismissing Authority in a Democracy* (Cheltenham, UK: Edward Elgar, 2009).
49. Shadd Maruna, *Making Good: How Ex-Convicts Reform and Rebuild their Lives* (Washington DC: American Psychological Association, 2001).
50. James Leong and Lynn Lee, *Passabe*, DVD (Singapore: Lianain Films, 2004).
51. Under pressure from the victim community, this confessor who paid the compensation and asked for forgiveness was not prosecuted for the murder or the assaults he confessed. This was absolutely in breach of the legal framework for the Community Reconciliation Process of the East Timor Commission for Reception, Truth and Reconciliation, which precluded community reconciliation for murder.
52. Erik Luna, "Punishment Theory, Holism, and the Procedural Conception of Restorative Justice," *Utah Law Review* 1 (2003): 205–260.
53. G. S. Leventhal, "What Should Be done with Equity Theory?" in *Social Exchange: Advances in Theory and Research*, ed. Kenneth J. Gergen, Martin S. Greenberg, and Richard H. Willis (New York: Plenum Press, 1980), 27–55; Allan E. Lind and Tom R. Tyler, *The Social Psychology of Procedural Justice* (New York: Plenum Press, 1988).
54. Braithwaite, *Restorative Justice*, 54–130.
55. Howard Zehr, *Changing Lenses: A New Focus for Criminal Justice* (Scottsdale, PA: Herald Press, 1995).
56. Heather Strang, *Repair or Revenge: Victims and Restorative Justice* (Oxford: Oxford University Press, 2002).
57. John Rawls, *A Theory of Justice* (Cambridge, MA: Belknap Press of Harvard University Press, 1971).
58. Merry, *Human Rights and Gender Violence*.
59. John Braithwaite, *Inequality, Crime and Public Policy* (London: Routledge, 1979); John Braithwaite, "Poverty, Power, White-Collar Crime and the Paradoxes of Criminological Theory," *Australian and New Zealand Journal of Criminology* 24 (1991), 40–50.
60. Paul Collier, *The Bottom Billion: Why the Poorest Countries are Failing and What Can Be Done about It* (Oxford: Oxford University Press, 2007).
61. Tom Tyler, *Why People Obey the Law* (New Haven, CT: Yale University Press, 1990); Tom Tyler and Steven Blader, *Cooperation in Groups: Procedural Justice, Social Identity, and Behavioural Engagement* (Philadelphia, PA: Psychology Press, 2000); Tom Tyler and Yuen J. Huo, *Trust and the Rule of Law: A Law-Abidingness Model of Social Control* (New York: Russell Sage, 2001).
62. Braithwaite, *Restorative Justice*, 98–99.
63. See Braithwaite et al., *Anomie and Violence*; Braithwaite et al., *Pillars and Shadows*.

64. Braithwaite, *Restorative Justice*.
65. Merry, *Human Rights*.
66. Braithwaite et al., *Anomie and Violence*, ch. 4.
67. Ibid., ch. 3.
68. As required when our perspective is a civic republican one (Pettit, *Republicanism*; Braithwaite and Pettit, *Not Just Deserts*).
69. Assumpta Naniwe-Kaburahe, "The Institution of Bashingantahe in Burundi," in *Traditional Justice and Reconciliation after Conflict: Learning from African Experiences*, ed. Luc Huyse and M. Salter (Stockholm: International IDEA, 2008).
70. *Indian Constitution* Part IX (the Panchayats) art. 243(d).
71. Chantal Mouffe, *The Return of the Political* (London; New York: Verson, 2005), 3.

CHAPTER 10

Doing Justice Differently: From Revolution to Transformation in Restorative Justice and Political Reconciliation

Jason A. Springs

Copernicus looked upon a night sky wholly different from the one that Claudius Ptolemy had charted. In fact, with the advent of Copernicus's helio-centric worldview, Ptolemy's perfectly spherical, geo-centric cosmos—and the countless epicycles that held it in place—was overturned. Of course, actual conversion to the Copernican world view required more than a century of dispute, controversy, disbelief, and, at times, inquisition. In time, however, the earth-centered worldview that had held sway since long before Aristotle would melt into air. More importantly, Copernicus's revolutionary innovations laid the groundwork for successive breakthroughs and revolutions in comprehending the cosmos, and the advance of science generally—from Galileo to Newton to Kepler, to Einstein and beyond.

The Copernican revolution in astronomy proved equally influential as a model for the revolutionary transition—the "paradigm shift"— in the development of Western thought more broadly.[1] The eighteenth- to nineteenth-century philosopher Immanuel Kant described his own accounts of the nature and basis of ethics and politics as marking revolutions of a kind comparable to that of Copernicus. On Kant's account, prior to his own revolutionary intervention, human moral action and freedom had depended upon authorities like divine command, natural law, the deliverances of religious tradition, or the conditional urgings of inclination, desire, or sentiment. Kant repositioned the rational will of individual agents as the center-point—the only unconditional source of value and freedom—in the realms of ethics and politics.[2]

Though far from the lone predecessor for what the present volume refers to as the "liberal peace," Kant clearly stands among its most influential originators. The revolution he helped set in motion laid indispensible groundwork for the social institutions, political conceptions, and legal implements that have come to structure many Western societies. Many of these have become deeply sedimented in Western common sense understandings and moral intuitions. They have come to inform the emergent international institutions and conceptions of justice and peace as well. As Kant had it, a peaceable society emerges in the pursuit of what he called "the kingdom of ends"—the ideal outcome of autonomous individuals existing together in political community, each like a self-determining, sovereign state that binds his or her actions by principles that take the form of universalize-able law.[3]

With the "kingdom of ends" as his model, Kant envisioned an international league of sovereign states, each freely binding itself to deal lawfully with the others, and holding the others accountable to categorical dictates of justice.[4] Yet, even with Kant's philosophical groundwork in place, it was not until the wake of the Second World War that what have come to be termed the "juridical revolution" and "enforcement revolution" in international law and human rights would begin to materialize and take hold.[5] In effect, these revolutions marked the realization of a Copernicus-like paradigm shift to the prevailing normative and interpretive framework for justice and peace in the international community—the "liberal peace."

The chapters in this volume participate in a vision that contrasts powerfully to Kant's Copernican revolution of the eighteenth and nineteenth centuries, and the world that revolution did so much to bring into being in the twentieth and twenty-first. In fact, it is tempting to describe what unfolds in these pages as the makings of yet another "paradigm shift"—a shift that overturns the prevailing conception of "justice" (as that virtue according to which each receives his or her due), "peace" (achieving conditions in which explicit violence or deadly conflict are absent), and the deep sociological presuppositions that hold those conceptions in place. What is at stake in these essays is not merely an effort to amend or supplement these prevailing conceptions. And yet, too much would be lost in identifying what unfolds in these pages as a new paradigm purely and simply—another revolution in justice and peace—or so I will argue in these concluding reflections.

The chapters here give voice to, theoretically enrich, and innovatively press forward a vision that, on one hand, diverges from the so-called liberal peace. At the same time, this vision engages the liberal peace in order to incorporate, reorient, and carry forward its most indispensable insights. In concluding this volume synthetically and constructively I draw the preceding chapters into conversation. My aim is to refine and illuminate precisely how they converge upon a *transformational* vision, and thereby move beyond the prevailing accounts of reconciliation and restorative justice as revolutionary challenges to—would-be paradigm shifts beyond—the liberal peace.

Perhaps the most instructive attempt to position the emergence of restorative justice as a paradigm shift is to be found in the book largely responsible for the consolidation of the restorative justice movement in North America, Howard Zehr's *Changing Lenses*.[6] In this path-marking text, Zehr mapped the emergence of "state-centered" justice as itself a revolutionary transition out of medieval European contexts and into the early modern period. He argued for the viability—perhaps the necessity—of thinking in terms of a new revolution beyond a state-centered, retributive orientation to a restorative justice frame. If an actual shift had yet to materialize at the time of his writing, articulating the vision and ideals of such a shift was a pivotal early step. Prescribing a paradigm shift in justice from state-centered to restorative is the central leit-motif of *Changing Lenses*. And, in fact, that motif resurfaced as a point of contention in much of the ensuing restorative justice literature.

For all its gravitas and explanatory effectiveness, Zehr's use of the "paradigm shift" motif brought its own difficulties in train. One of the most pronounced of these is the oppositional character to which the notion of rival paradigms lends itself. Over-emphasizing the revolutionary character of the break between contrasting models and the displacement of an earlier by a later scheme implies that the people embedded in the different schemes, in effect, dwell within distinctive worldviews that play out at odds with one another.[7] Just such an opposition between state-centered retributive justice versus restorative justice haunted the first edition of *Changing Lenses*.

Read by some as a program of replacement, Zehr found himself needing to defend against criticisms of "utopian daydreaming." Several pressing questions ensued. How best to conceive the relation of a restorative framework to the prevailing retributive model in a way that was accurate in principle, and yet also realizable in practice? Should restorative justice forward itself as an *alternative* to the actually existing realities of retributive, state-centered justice? Should it present itself as a humanizing *complement* to those realities by which a hybrid model might be fashioned? Was it more realistically conceived as a corrective and pragmatic *supplement* within a basically retributive justice system, but a system in which certain retributive impulses had run amok?[8]

Zehr opted for a model of compromise between the realities of a retributive justice system that might, as much as possible, be rendered more restorative. To overturn or abandon the pivotal gains of modern state-centered justice (the rule of law, due process, human rights, "orderly development of law"[9]) would surely be a mistake. In fact, by the third edition of *Changing Lenses*, Zehr had come to describe his vision for restorative justice as targeting "a realistic goal." What Zehr described as "real world justice" positioned retribution and restoration as opposite poles on a single continuum. A further set of questions followed. If the hybrid model that Zehr proposed was sufficient to overcome the temptation of idealism to which the oppositional framing of paradigms was prone, could it remain true to the genuinely transformational elements of the restorative orientation? This question continues to press in upon the restorative justice movement. It highlights a point at which the present volume makes pivotal steps past the theoretical options on offer so far.

Philpott and Llewelyn take the above lessons from the restorative justice literature to heart. Their framing of the volume indicates that there can be no un-revised comparison between scientific "paradigm shifts" and the reorientation of justice and peace upon which restorative and reconciliation models converge. The conceptualization they articulate, and which encompasses the contributions to the volume, steps past the perils of incommensurable rivalry between state-centered justice and restorative justice, on one hand, and straightforwardly supplemental, complementary, or hybrid models, on the other. Their framing of this volume aims not simply to replace without remainder the indispensable accomplishments of the liberal peace. Nor does it position retribution and restoration at either ends of a continuum, proposing a truce in the interests of piecemeal collaboration. The framing here aims, rather, to integrate holistically the most pivotal—indeed essential—insights of each, and yet to do so in a way that revalues and repositions them by a more basic vision of justice.

It is in answering the above challenges that Llewelyn and Philpott give us perhaps the most enunciated contribution of the integrationist model they propose—a robust, theoretically rich, and orientational account of *relational personhood* from which the holistic model of justice emerges. This includes insights from the "encumbered self" of the liberal-communitarian debates among political theorists of the 1990s—a self whose deepest beliefs, commitments, relationships, memories, and history are constitutive of the perspon, and not simply optional or dispensable (like clothes he or she can put on and take off as need or desire dictate).[10] And yet, the conception on offer here retains the viability of individual identity, holding it in tandem with the relational constitution of individual selves. There is no question of whether individuals are in relationship with others. The operative questions are, rather, whether those relationships will be destructive or just, what the means are by which to diminish the former and cultivate the latter. As a result, one finds in this framing no trace of resentment toward human rights discourse (as was sometimes the case among communitarian advocates of the idea that selves are constituted by their social roles). One finds, rather, rapprochement between the indispensible idea of human beings as rights-bearing agents, and the relational formation and constitution of those agents.[11]

Of course, a conception of self that is intrinsically relational is not unique to the present volume, nor even with the practices of reconciliation and restorative justice. Various of the chapters here gesture toward the pivotal role that such an account of personhood drawn from indigenous African traditions played in the South African Truth and Reconciliation Commission.[12] Villa-Vicencio makes much of the fact that a relational conception of personhood resonates with so-called postmodern thinkers such as Jean Francois Lyotard and Emmanuel Levinas. Llewelyn points out that later twentieth-century feminist theorists have perhaps most effectively theorized relational personhood for purposes that range from critique and resistance to forms of domination infused in social structures and practices, to innovation and self-creation.[13] But even these thinkers did not invent the model from scratch. Its nature and basis, as well as its ethical and political implications, reach back to the likes of Aristotle, Hegel, Ludwig Feuerbach, Martin Buber, Karl Barth, and John Dewey. Relational conceptions of personhood emerge from well beyond the philosophical canons of Europe and North America. They find articulation in numerous indigenous traditions and worldviews. Relational conceptions of personhood have been read as forming a powerful counter-current that runs throughout the European Enlightenment, contrasting with Kant's Copernican revolution. These conceptions emerge from, at times, radically different religious, philosophical, and cultural traditions, stretching into the twentieth century as resources that aided in some of the most important gains on behalf of justice and peace.[14] Yet, in so far as the work of the present volume is to do more than contribute an (albeit, much needed) theoretical "tilt" to the manifestation of a genuinely integrative era of restorative justice and reconciliation, then there remains to identify and cultivate these broader points of contact, to capitalize on the breadth of ethical and political resources they afford, to incorporate the ways they have been theoretically refined over years of critique. There remains, furthermore, to broaden the scope of investigation in order to draw in, and learn from, relational conceptions of personhood available cross-culturally.

The further tack of inquiry I am suggesting might appear to prod an already theoretically inclined set of chapters into even deeper and more expansive theoretical background. Is it necessary? Is it advisable? Surely, after all, Karl Marx was correct that the perennial risk—perhaps the folly—of theoretical depth and persistence is that it occupies one with merely interpreting the world, whereas the point is to effect some actual change in it. And yet, as the previous chapters clarify, conversations about reconciliation and restorative justice— still fledgling in many ways—remain richly practice-directed, and as of yet, under-theorized. The advantage in this occurs in the fact that efforts at theoretical reflection upon reconciliation derive from, and are grounded in, several decades of on-the-ground lived experiences and efforts at implementation.

Theoretical efforts serve to historically contextualize, to illuminate fine-grained challenges and problematical interstices through empirical mapping and comparison. They are indispensible for evaluating, correcting, refining, enriching—where necessary, justifying, defending, and bolstering—reconciliatory and restorative understandings, practices, and institutions. These tasks enable practitioners and theorists alike to better understand past efforts and aid future implementations. They draw into focus a perennial obligation for any vision of justice and peace that would be thoroughly integrationist and holistic. Such a standing obligation comes in cultivating a praxis orientation—a practical sensibility that integrates the lessons and realities of on-the-ground practice with the full breadth and historical depth of theoretical analysis of practice, and persistently so over time. To grant praxis an orientational position is to recognize that the dialectical process of practical implementation, its theoretical enrichment through critical reflection, and then further implementation in light of that enrichment, is never finished.

The present volume contributes a crucial and needed theoretical angle to the reconciliation and restorative justice discourses. The volume itself attests to the fact that much remains to be done to deepen further the theoretical connections illuminated here. After all, revolutionary developments effected by the likes of Copernicus and Kant unfold amid the concrete realities of social history. They force into the light of day antinomies, oppositions, and countless anomalies for which the prevailing framework cannot fully account. They inspire disputations, intellectual and procedural controversies that worked themselves out only over time, often in fits and starts, and never without the prospect of marginalization or the possibility of failure. So much more so for the holistic and integrationist account of restorative justice and concomitant framing of social and political transformation on offer here; one that aims, in effect, to reorient a replacement account of paradigm shifts.

One of the most pressing theoretical dimensions of immediate consequence to the prospects for reconciliation and restorative justice is the contest of secularization. VanAntwerpen's chapter offers meticulous exposition of the ways in which the South African Truth and Reconciliation Commission (TRC), in particular, emerged as an exemplary instance—a "field orienting" case—of truth and reconciliation processes in the wake of mass violence. By re-narrating this exemplar's theoretical significance and institutional impact upon truth and reconciliation discourse, he illuminates how this process of exemplification at the level of international elites and institutions opened new vistas to be admired and explored. And yet, he also demonstrates how these developments became assimilated into the international consensus, routinized, and, in some of their features, anathematized.

Most pointedly, the South African TRC's theological resonances inspired broadly reaching allergic reactions at the level of international organizations, in particular, human rights organizations such as the International Center for Transitional Justice. VanAntwerpen's account of how this happened casts into relief the sometimes tacit, but nonetheless prevailing, "normative juridical framework" interwoven with the presumption of a dichotomous opposition between religion-specific practices and commitments, and those that are "secular." Within a "secular" framing, the theological and religious elements of the South African TRC come to be categorized as anomalous. They show up as context-specific particularities that can (and perhaps must) be filtered or bracketed out, or at least rendered tangential, in so far as the TRC is to exert exemplary influence across different contexts. This is especially true amid an international milieu already circumscribed by the common denominator of human rights norms and increasingly by a frame of international law oriented by a retributive model of criminal justice.

VanAntwerpen re-narrates these developments in a way that affords glimpses of how the received dichotomous opposition between secular and religion-specific meanings and commitments exerted itself in various institutional configurations at the international level. Particularly controversial is the notion that societies suffering in the wake of mass atrocity might be "healed through the political art of forgiveness and the forgoing of full-fledged prosecution." Charges of "heresy" erupt in so far as these notions (i.e. forgiveness) become interwoven (to the ears of some, synonymous) with amnesty—allegedly surrendering accountability in ways that fuels impunity, and mocks true justice. The conceptual vortex created by the prevailing "spin of the secular" means that the religious resonances of the word "forgiveness," and its presumed interwoven-ness with "reconciliation," "restoration," and "amnesty," come tainted with controversy.

For the purposes of theoretically contextualizing and further enriching the holistic-integrationist approach unfolding in the present volume, the orthodoxy of secularism that VanAntwerpen so thickly describes remains to be positioned amid the groundswell of criticisms of secularist presuppositions (as well as constructive applications of those critical insights). This literature has emerged across multiple fields of inquiry relevant to the international consensus.[15] These developments present a potentially fruitful, if not pressing, avenue for conversation among the ideas unfolding in this volume's pages. And, in fact, when positioned within the proper conversational framing, the present volume makes its own—if at moments, subtle—contributions to this broader literature.

VanAntwerpen's contribution initiates this conversational thread in raising the instructive comparison that the UN's *Universal Declaration of Human Rights* (UDHR) emerged in controversy no less deeply dichotomized between religious identities and secular presuppositions. Do human rights need God? Do they require some ultimate basis to be conceived as universally binding and effective?[16] As a Cold War document born in the wake of the atrocities of the Nazi holocaust, the parties to the formulation of the UDHR had no choice but to settle for a "pragmatic silence" about the ultimate nature and basis of the rights.[17] Is the same necessary for the practices of political reconciliation? Would "comprehensive doctrines"—claims about what truth and reconciliation require that may be either specific to, or derive explicit support from, particular religious, moral, philosophical, and/or cultural traditions—need to be bracketed, or translated into terms that can be embraced as common to everyone? If such translation was deemed necessary at the level of international actors and institutions, could the terms of translation ever be sufficiently robust for particular tradition-situated actors and societies? Would those terms be weighty enough in meaning and substance to sustain and perpetuate transitions to the cultivation of peace, healing, and restoring and reconciling relationships among peoples that had undergone the horrors of ethnic cleansing, mass murder, and apartheid?

If the pragmatic silence on the nature of human rights was sufficient for what Michael Ignatieff has called the "juridical" and "enforcement revolutions" that emerged in the wake of World War II,[18] surely that sufficiency was accommodated—if not necessitated—by the legal and procedural nature of the institutions and principles that they served. The chapters in this volume gesture toward accruing agreement that far too much is at stake in pursuing reconciliation in the wake of mass atrocity to rely upon a "pragmatic silence." The pursuit of reconciliation and restorative justice in such contexts is fleshy and embodied. It is interwoven with the suffering of peoples living through particular circumstances and histories. It is caught up in the healing of wounds, the reclamation and restoration of human dignity, and the transition to societies oriented by the integration of justice and peace. These are aims far too weighty to be achieved by bracketing out the kind of ultimate resources and commitments often bound up with the cultural, religious, and moral identities of the people living through these circumstances and processes. In short, political reconciliation and restorative justice require more than concepts, values, and processes that restrict themselves (either pragmatically or in principle) to facilitating political utility, procedural expedience, and disinterested objectivity in seeing that each receives his or her due.

One attempt to circumvent a "pragmatic silence" on these questions has been to take what some philosophers and theologians call a hermeneutical-phenomenological approach toward ultimate claims, commitments, and the tradition-specific comprehensive doctrines in which they find articulation. Such an approach aims to grapple with the challenges of the (at times, conflicting) diversity of traditions and identities with the claim that any appeal to universal ultimacy must first set its sights upon particular claims of those traditions. This line of thinking states that the deeper one moves into the particularities of different traditions of meaning (whether moral, cultural, philosophical, theological, or some mixture of these), the more weighty in relevance and trans-contextual—the more universal—become the themes, motifs, and significances of the descriptions one finds there. On this line of thinking, the vast array of religious, philosophical, and secular moral traditions share complementary ends in so far as they attempt to describe reality in its ultimate significance (e.g., the ontological basis of human dignity, the depth-existential dimensions of the human condition, the Good, the Real). Therefore, one must press beyond the particularities of philosophical, theological, cultural, and ethical traditions—and what may appear prima facie to be conflicting truth claims and commitments—to the ontological concerns, presuppositions, and aims that they share. Some argue that, for purposes of promoting reconciliation in pluralist societies, it is imperative to plumb the ontological concerns of tradition-specific manifestations. Otherwise, the political realities with which reconciliation and restorative justice concern themselves will float indeterminately adrift upon the waves of history and political utility.[19]

Yet another approach has been to take particular religious, moral, philosophical, and cultural traditions in their full particularity—including the often mutually exclusive truth claims, commitments, and the stories in which they originate—and then engage in the work of finding points at which they agree, parallel, and can become conversant with one another. This approach seeks to avoid reducing the particular truth claims and thick commitments of religious and moral traditions to more basic, common-denominator terms for a number of reasons. At the level of argument, such positions claim that to translate them into allegedly more basic claims is to translate them into something they are not. It is to ascribe alien terms of meaning to them.[20]

The two approaches in question highlight a pressing antinomy that is present in attempts to grapple with the "spin of the secular."[21] And it is at this point that the chapters in the present volume contribute positively to reconceptualizing the prevalent dichotomous opposition between "the religious" and "the secular." Together, they enrich the multiple ways that tradition-specific commitments, identities, and resources from across the spectrum (moral, religious, secular, cultural, political traditions) might contribute to, and are needed for, the flourishing of arts of political reconciliation and restorative justice. Villa-Vicencio, for example, draws upon an appeal to the ontological repositioning that intentional, public truth-telling in the service of reconciliation ought to include. Here we glimpse the way that an appeal to ontological depth might anchor even the seemingly thinnest features of reconciliation.

Villa-Vicencio presents a meta-ethical case as to why the integrative account of justice on offer in this volume is able to encompass within its framework even the thinnest elements of reconciliation and restorative justice. A holistic and integrative account of restorative justice promotes a vision far more robust than merely tending to immediate material needs or acknowledging the basic status of other's humanity. He makes a case for what these "thin" features of reconciliation—when moored to ontologically freighted conceptions of personhood—entail in terms of reparations. Such a contribution is pivotal in that it side-steps the temptation to simply contrast conceptions of "live and let live" tolerance, or thin recognition of some other as fellow-citizen—conceptions typically taken as hallmarks of "the liberal peace"—as that which political reconciliation overturns in order to move revolutionarily beyond. In a society that has been ravaged by violence and human rights violations—where the most basic forms of relational recognition were denied to some group, where the members of that group could appear only as to be despised and dominated, if acknowledged at all—the capacity to look each other in the eye, to exist side by side in the absence of explicit violence, to speak to one another frankly and without fear cannot be relegated to the status of tell-tale indicators of "the liberal peace." They become, rather, repositioned and revalued as necessary (if, in themselves, insufficient) elements of the capacious conception of *relational justice* at the heart of a holistic, comprehensive account of reconciliation in the wake of mass atrocity.

The transformational move in Villa-Vicencio's account comes in anchoring his treatment of reparations to—as the title of the chapter portends—a "way of being," yet without claiming to be doing onto-theology. Rather than bracket his ethical claims from questions of ethical ultimacy, this move anchors the thin forms of tolerance, mutual recognition, and reciprocal speech in more basic ontological significance. Such an account subsumes into itself (rather than supersedes) the liberal account of rights and responsibilities (Villa-Vicencio references John Locke's account as an example). So anchoring these elements implies that even the thinnest features of recognition, respect, and reparation must be reconceived and appropriated for the purposes of societal transformation. Viewed through an ontological lens, victims' dignity and moral worth requires transformation among all the parties to the conflict. On such an account it is insufficient to speak of reconciliation in terms of compensation for damages. Instead, reparations entail broader forms of transformation. In Villa-Vicencio's South African context, this means reconfiguration of the business and government sectors of the society toward a more distributively just orientation—toward, in effect, a preferential option for the poor. Based on his own work and experience in South Africa, Villa-Vicencio confesses that such reconfigurations take long periods of time. They require luck. At the same time, the victims have the need, indeed the right, to be impatient.

Pope's contribution offers both challenge and complement to Villa-Vicencio's chapter. For, if Villa-Vicencio tells us *why* a holistic account of justice can and should encompass within its framework "thin" recognition, tolerance, and the basic reparative meeting of immediate needs in the wake of violence, Pope demonstrates *how* it is possible to think in this way. Perhaps the most distinctive contribution of Pope's chapter is its demonstration that a tradition-specific account of forgiveness—indeed in the case he treats, a robustly and irreducibly Christian theological account—can collaborate in, support, and even enrich, reconciliation as a political art unfolding at the level of civic practice and institutions. If we generalize this point, we find that the claims of particular traditions—not only theological, as in Pope's example, but also moral, cultural, and philosophical—need not first be reduced to general ontological or meta-ethical claims in attempt to shear them of their "sectarian" features, so as to increase the likelihood of their broad reception, perceived plausibility, or basic utility in religiously, morally, and culturally plural contexts. What is required, rather, is fine-grained, intentional, reflexive, conversational engagement that respects crucial differences by acknowledging, first, that such differences are real, and not simply fungible—not reducible to an allegedly more basic, common level of reality. At the same time, such engagements must facilitate illuminating and cultivating the parallel points of agreement for purposes of allowing suffering to speak and promoting the possibility of healing—and transformation—by facilitating reconciled and restored relationships. Such conversational intimacy may seem like much to ask. Yet, it is precisely such conversational intimacy of which the South African TRC offers an example.

Pope's chapter illustrates, further, what it looks like to find points of ad hoc agreement and overlap between different religious, philosophical, cultural, and moral-tradition-specific truth claims and perspectives. In the instance he considers, Pope describes how the most orientational and axiomatic Christian commitments about the nature of God's triune life entail a relational anthropology that is able to move outward from its own theologically distinct, central claims, to identify and develop points of contact and overlap with claims deriving from other particularistic points of origin. On this view, a participant motivated by Christian commitments (or others motivated by comprehensive outlooks that are philosophical, humanistic, or emerge from some other religious tradition) need not necessarily remain silent about the pivotal role that forgiveness might play in political reconciliation from such a perspective (for either pragmatic or principled reasons). In fact, as circumstances afford, they *ought* not remain silent. This is because commitment-specific contributions might actually deepen, enrich, support, and facilitate recovery, restoration, reconciliation, healing of wounds, and the cultivation of just peace. The key transformational move here is to develop capacities to engage in deeply plural contexts with a flexible, collaborative pragmatism for specific purposes of reconciliation and restorative justice, yet without either merging or bracketing the integrity of tradition-specific claims.

VanAntwerpen's contribution at once historicizes the emergence of the "transitional justice orthodoxy," and complicates that orthodoxy by illuminating some of its deepest—and perhaps most un-interrogated—presuppositions, and providing a thick description of the counter-currents and developments that the prevailing orthodoxy occludes. Villa-Vicencio and Pope converse provocatively and instructively from meta-ethical and theological angles, respectively. Such a vector is crucial for its potential to intervene in the broader discussions surrounding the "secularist orthodoxy," and to do so from the grounded histories and practices of truth and reconciliation, and restorative justice. Yet, in itself, the conversation I have sketched above is insufficient. It is here that the contributions by Boesnecker and Vinjamuri, Mallinder, Van Ness, and Braithwaite all dovetail pivotally, functioning in tandem with the conversation I have laid out in the preceding paragraphs. Indeed, when we turn to mapping the contexts in which reconciliation and restorative justice efforts, mechanisms, and institutions have been (and are being) actually implemented, an increasingly ramified reality comes into view.

Boesenecker and Vinjamuri sift and parcel a range of empirical cases from across the full spectrum of international justice actors. Their work indicates that presuming an unproblematic complementarity between retributive justice and reconciliation alienates both theorists and practitioners from actual particulars on the ground. They find the same to be true for any simple dichotomous partitioning of categories into which faith-based versus secular, and grassroots versus international might be compartmentalized. If a primarily legal convergence has developed at the level of international organizations— and Boesenecker and Vinjanmuri are persuaded that it has—their remains a deep, cross-cutting diversity among local faith-based and secular actors. Some faith-based and secular actors continue to embrace legal, liberal models of justice and peace while others have innovated with relational features derived from their own traditions.

Despite what many have claimed, there appears to be no simple practical complementarity between individualist and relational conceptions of justice. This facilitates their diagnosis as to why so many of the post-conflict peacebuilding initiatives that are fueled by relational conceptions of justice have operated largely beneath the radar of the global discussions of international justice and peacebuilding. The strategies for transitional peacebuilding that are inspired by relational conceptions of personhood and the models of justice they entail "require longer-term engagement in post-conflict processes" (a point to which Villa-Vicencio's account attests) and often in less visible ways, than has permitted them to actively intervene in the debate at the international level. "In effect, their commitment has minimized their ability to develop and maintain the profile necessary to shape global debates about justice and peacebuilding." This brings to a precise point what is easily one of the most important questions in the present volume.

Processes of reconciliation and restorative justice aim at restored relationships and transformed societies. This drastically expands the time horizon of justice in ways that are foreign to standard varieties of juridical reasoning and retributive expectations. "Justice delayed is justice denied," states the legal maxim thought by many to encapsulate the retributive orientation. Retributive tendencies of the international consensus are liable not to recognize the transformational aims and measures as "justice," in part, because of the expansive time frame they require. Because of this, as Boesenecker and Vinjamuri demonstrate, while the high-profile instances of reconciliation and restorative justice have come to set forth exemplars, the ground-level brims with cross-cutting diversity that remains under-represented (where not altogether *un*represented) at the international level. It is the framing and presuppositions of the debate at the level of international consensus itself that, in effect, obscures the voices at the level of local variety. The need to illuminate and hear these voices—and to account for why they have been occluded—is precisely why the broadly reaching narrative reframing that VanAntwerpen executes and the conversational counterpoint provided by Pope and Villa-Vicencio are so crucial. For the same reasons, the critique and conceptual reframing of amnesty, accountability, and "state-centered" justice conducted by Mallinder and Van Ness prove equally indispensible.

Mallinder interrogates at length a presumption at the heart of the orthodoxy of the international consensus, namely, that amnesty for perpetrators of human rights violations either is (by default), or necessarily contributes to, impunity. She conducts this inquiry, more importantly, by exploring the viability of restorative justice as a comprehensive account of justice, rather than as a *complement* (set of practices necessary for justice in exceptional circumstances), or as a *supplement* ("second-best" justice when "true" justice is not attainable). Positioning amnesty within a comprehensive vision of restorative justice enables Mallinder to, in effect, respond with a bit of conceptual jiu-jitsu to criticisms extending from the dichotomous and oppositional framing of retributive versus restorative justice, namely, to the charge that amnesty fuels impunity.

Impunity emerges when accountability is abandoned. In so far as reconciliation and restorative justice grant perpetrators reprieve from what they justly deserve for their crimes, retributively minded critics argue, they forgo genuine accountability. And yet, on closer inspection, it is far from clear that retributive practices actually supply the forms of accountability that its advocates claim restorative justice cannot. The adversarial orientation of retributive justice contexts (i.e., trial, sentencing, punishment) promotes its own abandonment of accountability. Criminal trials incentivize denying guilt, and often, insistence upon one's innocence (even, and perhaps especially, in the wake of having been tried and convicted). Where guilt is successfully established or ascribed, the retributive framing incentivizes rationalizing one's actions, and appealing to factors that mitigate responsibility. Further, the retributive frame pursues the determination of guilt through isolating the offender as a "defendant" over against the offended party (which, as Van Ness points out, is most likely not the actual victim of the offense, but rather, the state whose laws have been transgressed). These are forms of impunity precisely because they discourage and obstruct, if not prohibit, the substance of accountability—bringing truth to light, recognizing and accepting responsibility, responding to those who have been harmed. The retributive frame marginalizes the importance of identifying and meeting needs of stakeholders in the context of harm and ruptured relationships. As such, it often contributes to dehumanizing all the parties in question. It discourages the possibility of contrition, direct restitution and "tailored repair," apology, forgiveness, all of which have proven to be effective in—if not indispensible for—promoting healing, empowering victims and communities, and transitioning from a violence-torn society to a just and sustainable peace.

Mallinder shows that the appearance of a dichotomous opposition between amnesty and accountability is more a product of the presuppositions that constitute the retributive consensus than logical and practical features of the terms and practices themselves. Clearly, amnesty fuels impunity when it is employed abusively (i.e., to protect violators of human rights from investigation and accountability). However, when one descends to the level of detail and attends to context-specific restorative aims and objectives, it becomes apparent that amnesty provisions have, in fact, mediated the dichotomies projected by the international consensus. When properly framed and applied, amnesty laws can, and have, facilitated recognition of accountability, the acceptance of responsibility, and ensuing efforts at restitution.

The transformational effect of Mallinder's account is most pronounced where she demonstrates that restorative amnesty does not aim to *replace* conceptions of testimony, guilt, and punishment (standard hallmarks of retributive justice). Nor does it seek a hybrid model that holds retributive and restorative conceptions in tandem. Rather, the retributive conceptions get repositioned within a framework oriented by a relational account of justice. Guilt, conceived as that which is determined by a judge or jury in a retributive model, is reconceived, instead, as processes of admission or acknowledgment. Testimony, a species of evidence that provides the basis upon which guilt is determined, becomes not only the act by which accountability through admission and acknowledgment occurs, but is reconfigured as a process of truth-telling positioned within a collaborative and community-encompassing process of truth-seeking. The conception of punishment—typically the compensatory extraction of pain, suffering, and isolation commensurate with the crime—is transposed as offenders' "making amends" through participation in reparative measures. The relational orientation means that all of these features are redirected toward meeting needs, and fulfilling responsibilities, understood to be interwoven in a whole cloth of interrelated victims, offenders, and the encompassing communities implicated therein.

Understood in these ways, amnesties can provide means for moving from what Villa-Vicencio's essay identified as "thin" elements of a comprehensive account of restorative justice and reconciliation (mutual recognition, reciprocal speech, and tolerant coexistence), to "thicker" modes of just relationality. The latter take the form of encounters that aim at truthful speech, truth-seeking through questioning and answerability, and community participation. They aim at "offender-reintegration" to the broader community at the same time that the standard categories of "offender" and "victim" are recognized as politically complex, at times overlapping, and fluid in contexts of dynamic conflict. Reconceived in these ways, amnesty has nothing to do with "letting perpetrators 'off the hook'" vis-à-vis the just deserts for their crimes—one way it frequently gets characterized when juxtaposed dichotomously with retribution. Moreover, neither is amnesty best conceived as a useful *complement* (a means of justice in exceptional circumstances) nor *supplement* ("second-best" justice). The features of amnesty that Mallinder describes are, rather, intrinsic to a relationally derived, comprehensive vision of justice.

Van Ness expands upon the relational reorientation, demonstrating the fundamental deficiency of a simple "victim-offender" conception, in contrast to the kind of comprehensive and integrative account of restorative justice and reconciliation that Mallinder discusses. Relationships ramify outward like the nodal interlacing of relational webs from the point at which relationship has most explicitly been harmed (sometimes conceived as the "victim-offender relation"). And, while a restorative justice vision spares no criticism or effort to reform state-centered justice, neither does it attempt simply to displace the state. Even, perhaps especially, when conceived as a comprehensive vision of justice, this vision does not long for reconstitution of premodern affairs in which the modern state was absent. Nor does its critical stance degenerate into abiding resentment or terminal wistfulness toward the state. It avoids these by drawing the state into its orientational account of justice. In short, the state itself becomes repositioned as a party to the web of relationships, reconceived as agents of responsibility, themselves needing to be held accountable.[22]

If these conceptual reconfigurations appear to suffer the common theoretical temptation of abstraction, Braithwaite's chapter brings this all back to earth, and into real time. Working to balance the aversive tendencies to which a theoretical tilt will often be prone, he introduces an experience-freighted inflection to the praxis-oriented, complex shifting-and-catching-of-balance that integrative and holistic accounts of restorative justice and political reconciliation must sustain. Braithwaite reminds us of how difficult such an undertaking truly is, of the virtuosity it requires, of its indispensability, even if it is something that is never entirely achieved.

Can theorizing restorative justice and reconciliation avoid stultifying categorization, or the tendency of even the most context-sensitive forms of theoretical reflection to abstract and "orientalize"? Braithwaite articulates the challenge of a multi-directional and multi-level discourse between the local and international, theoretical and practical. It is an approach that offers a powerful alternative to the divisions that have emerged between international institutions and local practices (the effects of which are documented and parsed by Boesenecker and Vinjamuri).

Braithwaite proposes no radical departure from the human rights consensus, but rather incorporates and repositions the lessons that consensus has to teach. When human rights discourse imposes itself from outside and above local contexts—however just and right the purposes it serves—it has been met with "ethnic nationalist defiance" and has largely discredited itself. However, in instances where human rights advocates have approached contexts of application with what the anthropologist Clifford Geertz would call thickly descriptive skills and sensibilities, and invested themselves in the painstaking, fine-grained tasks of translation into vernacular terms—and have themselves been open to enrichment, even challenge, from local, traditional justice resources—they have discovered allies and collaborators. This insight is pivotal for the transformational practice that the integrative-holistic accounts of restorative justice and reconciliation pursue. Braithwaite's chapter itself exemplifies these vernacularizing sensibilities in describing the challenges and needs of the kind of intimate, fine-grained conversational framing of retributive and restorative practices that surfaced in the face of the religion/secular challenge above.

A holistic vision of justice need not purport to be a totality. It need not claim to contain all forms of justice without remainder or internal contest. The vision of relationally derived justice that emerges in these pages avoids such a temptation by holding its conception of holism in tandem with that of integration. As conceived here, integration is a continuing process by which disparate elements are brought together, held cohesively, and perpetually woven and re-woven into a unified and ever-expanding whole. As we have seen in the previous essays, such integration requires constant negotiation of apparent oppositions and critical navigation of antinomies. This is one purpose, indeed a necessity, of critical and theoretical reflection in a praxis orientation to reconciliation and restorative justice. The chapters of this book demonstrate that the result is not so much a revolution as the transformation of received conceptions of justice and peacebuilding. Such a process of transformation should not cease to expect its own further enrichment and further transformation.

Notes

1. The philosopher and historian of science, Thomas Kuhn, would make what is arguably the most influential use of this explanatory term ("paradigm shift"), and would most meticulously illuminate the ways that Copernicus exemplified this transformational process, among many others. See his more general, and most broadly influential account, *The Structure of Scientific Revolutions* (Chicago: University of Chicago Press, 1996). For his meticulous exposition of the impact and transformation resulting from Copernicus's work—and, in particular, how its "revolutionary" impact unfolded in fits and starts, and amid great controversy and social and political tumult—see his *The Copernican Revolution* (Cambridge, MA: Harvard University Press, 2003).
2. Kant's case that the good will is the only unconditional good unfolds systematically in his *Groundwork of the Metaphysics of Morals*. For helpful commentary that explicates Kant along these lines see Christine Korsgaard's "Introduction" to Kant's *Groundwork of the Metaphysics of Morals*, trans. Mary Gregor (Cambridge: Cambridge University Press, 1996); see also Korsgaard's *Creating the Kingdom of Ends* (Cambridge: Cambridge University Press, 1996), ch. 1 and 2.
3. Such a society would be characterized by mutual tolerance and non-interference—with "imperfect duties" to aid others in the pursuit of their own rationally chosen ends—under the constraints of constitutionally grounded public law.
4. Immanuel Kant, "Perpetual Peace: A Philosophic Sketch," in *Kant: Political Writings*, ed. Hans Reis (Cambridge: Cambridge University Press, 1991), 93–130. The influence of Kant's essay reaches well into the present era, providing pivotal grounding for John Rawls's *The Law of Peoples*, among many others.
5. Michael Ignatieff identifies three dimensions—juridical, advocacy, and enforcement dimensions—to what he broadly refers to as the "human rights revolution" that began to unfold in the wake of World War II. The "juridical" dimension refers to the emergence and authority of international declarations, treaties, and conventions (the UN charter of 1945, the *Universal Declaration of Human Rights and Genocide Convention* of 1948, revisions to the Geneva Conventions of 1949, among others). "Advocacy" refers to the monitoring activities of NGOs that precipitated from the juridical formulations. The "enforcement" dimension of

the human rights revolution refers to the advent of international criminal tribunals and courts by which violators of human rights and international law can be indicted, tried, and (if found guilty) punished according to the requirements of an international model of justice (primarily as articulated in the documents and agreements that constituted the juridical dimension of the revolution). See Michael Ignatieff, *Human Rights as Politics and Idolatry* (Princeton: Princeton University Press, 2001), ch. 1 (esp. 4–12).

6. Howard Zehr, *Changing Lenses* (Scottsdale, PA: Herald Press, 1990), esp. ch. 5–7 (and perhaps most poignantly, "Afterword to the First Edition").
7. Zehr mapped his account of the "legal revolution," and his case for a paradigm shift to a restorative model of justice, onto Thomas Kuhn's account in *The Structure of Scientific Revolutions* (here p. 193).
8. These debates played out in the essays collected in Howard Zehr and Barb Toews, eds., *Critical Issues in Restorative Justice* (Monsey, NY: Criminal Justice Press, 2004).
9. Zehr, *The Little Book of Restorative Justice* (Intercourse, PA: Good Books, 2002), 60.
10. Michael Sandel, *Liberalism and the Limits of Justice*, 149.
11. For insight into the antecedent debate, see Susan Mendus, "Human Rights in Political Theory," in *Politics and Human Rights*, ed. David Beetham, (Oxford: Blackwell, 1995), 11–25.
12. Desmund Tutu, *No Future without Forgiveness*, 35. For a relational conception of personhood articulated within the broader discussion of restorative justice in North America, see Jarem Sawatsky, *Justpeace Ethics* (Eugene, OR: Wipf and Stock, 2008).
13. See, for example, Judith Butler, *Giving an Account of Oneself* (New York: Fordham University Press, 2005).
14. Sociologist Christian Smith articulates and develops a broadly "personalist" account of personhood that draws upon many of these crucial strands and resources in order to forward an ethically robust counter to the conceptions of "person" that prevail in recent sociology, and across several of the social sciences, through much of the twentieth century. See Smith, *What is a Person? Rethinking Humanity, Social Life, and the Moral Good from the Person Up* (Chicago: Chicago University Press, 2010). For an account of how Christian theological anthropology is analogous (but not reducible) to relational philosophical anthropologies (e.g., those of Martin Buber, Karl Jaspers, Ludwig Feuerbach, John Dewey), see my article "Following at a Distance (Again): Freedom, Equality, and Gender in Karl Barth's Theological Anthropology," *Modern Theology* 28, no. 3 (July 2012): 446–477.
15. Pivotal highlights from the emerging literature on secularism would have to include Jose Cassanova, *Public Religions in the Modern World*; Talal Asad, *Formations of the Secular*; William Connolly, *Why I am Not a Secularist*; William Cavanaugh, *The Myth of Religious Violence*; Elizabeth Shakman-Hurd, *Politics of Secularism in International Relations*; Philpott, Toft, Shah, *God's Century*; Hent deVries and Larry Sullivan, eds., *Political Theologies: Public Religions in a Post-Secular World*; Atalia Omer, "Religion, Conflict, and Conflict Transformation," *Journal of the American Academy of Religion*. Efforts to constructively apply the insights from these conversations include Atalia Omer, *When Peace is Not Enough: How Does the Israeli Peace Camp Think About Religion, Nationalism, and Justice?*, and Saba Mahmood, *The Politics of Piety*. For a critical assessment of respective strengths and weaknesses of this strand of the literature, see Atalia Omer, "Modernists Despite Themselves: The Phenomenology of the Secular and the Limits of Critique as an Instrument of Change," *Journal of the American Academy of Religion*, 2014.
16. Elizabeth M. Bucar and Barbra Barnett, eds., *Does Human Rights Need God?* (Grand Rapids, MI: Eerdmans, 2005); Nicholas Wolterstorff, *Justice: Rights and Wrongs* (Princeton, NJ: Princeton University Press, 2008), David Little, "Ground to Stand On," in *Essays on Religion and Human Rights: Ground to Stand On* (Cambridge: Cambridge University Press, 2014).
17. The language of "pragmatic silence" was Eleanor Roosevelt's. The actual processes and controversies by which this point was settled is detailed by Johannes Morsink's chapter "A Bargain about God and Nature," in *The Universal Declaration of Human Rights: Origins, Drafting, and Intent* (Philadelphia: University of Pennsylvania, 1999), 284–302.
18. Ignatieff, *Human Rights as Politics and Idolatry*, ch. 1 (see note 5 above).

19. For one variation of such an approach see Scott Appleby, "Reconciliation and Realism," in *The Politics of Past Evil: Religion, Reconciliation, and the Dilemmas of Transitional Justice*, ed. Daniel Philpott (Notre Dame, IN: University of Notre Dame Press, 2006), 223–241 (esp. 234–239).
20. In an account that is similar to the framework for restorative justice and political reconciliation that emerges in the pages of the present volume, Amy Gutmann has sketched what she calls an "overlapping consensus" of particularist justifications as a strategy for grounding the nature and basis of human rights (over against the "pragmatic silence" invoked in the drafting of the UDHR). See Gutmann's "Introduction" to Michael Ignatieff's *Human Rights as Politics and Idolatry*, xix. For a critique of the tendency to reduce tradition specific features to an allegedly more basic, shared ontological basis, see William Placher's *Unapologetic Theology: A Christian Voice in a Pluralist Conversation* (Louisville, KY: Westminster/John Knox Press, 1989), ch. 10. For a helpful account of a non-reductionist approach to inter-religious cooperation (that side-steps the violence done to traditions when their differences are construed as surface-level trappings that reduce to shared grounding in "the sacred"), see Mark Heim, *Salvations: Truth and Difference in Religion* (New York: Orbis, 1995). For illuminating reflection on how the distinct particular claims of religious identities and traditions aid in forwarding political reconciliation, see David Burrell's "Interfaith Perspectives on Reconciliation," in *The Politics of Past Evil*, 113–126. Dan Philpott forwards a full-fledged articulation of a theory of "overlapping consensus" between particular, tradition-specific justifications for practices of political reconciliation. See Philpott's *Just and Unjust Peace*, 18–22.
21. The antinomy presented by the two general approaches I am describing here is particularly apparent in juxtaposing the contributions by Alan Torrance and Scott Appleby to *The Politics of Past Evil*, 45–86, 223–240 (esp. 228–231).
22. This transformational point dovetails pivotally with previous conversations. Consistent with this account, states, as has been argued elsewhere, are potentially bearers of forgiveness. Nicholas Wolterstorff, "The Place of Forgiveness in the Actions of the State," in *The Politics of Past Evil*, 87–112.

INDEX

Abel, 184
Abraham, 187
accountability, 10, 41, 56, 59, 139, 253–4
　judicial, 37, 42, 48, 50, 118, 148, 157
　restorative, 1, 5, 27, 32, 58, 149, 157–9
Acholi Religious Leaders Peace Initiative (ARLPI), 1, 45, 46, 62
acknowledgement, 198, 199, 206, 207, 254
　of victims, 27, 31, 147, 159, 207
　of guilt, 27, 39–40, 151, 159, 176–7, 182
Afghanistan, 5, 200
African National Congress (ANC), 202–3, 207, 211
African Union, 200–1
Al-Bashir, Omar Hassan Ahmad, 128, 201
Allende, Salvador, 81
Alywin, Patricio, 179
amnesty, 1, 10, 53–7, 59, 62–3, 83, 106–7, 121, 125, 188–9
　debate surrounding, 42, 98, 104, 246, 252–4
　restorative, 140, 151, 154–5, 160, 199
Amnesty International, 37, 41, 47, 50, 58
Anan, Kofi, 211
Angola, 5
apology, 6, 27, 90, 134, 159–61, 178, 198; *see also* confession
Aquinas, Thomas, 176, 178, 183
Arendt, Hannah, 204
Argentina, 53, 90, 95, 101, 106, 121, 147, 190, 200
Aristotle, 240, 244
Australia, 6, 7, 217, 219, 224

Barth, Karl, 81, 244
Basque Country, 27
Bassiouni, M. Cherif, 122, 130, 131
Bell, Christine –, 149
Belo, Carlos Ximenes, 55–6

Bentham, Jeremy, 129
Blagg, Harry, 218
Boesak, Allan, 86
Boesenecker, Aaron P., 9, 251, 252
Bolivia, 90
Boraine, Alex, 58, 93, 94, 95, 97, 98, 100
Borer, Tristan, 87, 144
Bosnia-Herzegovina, 27, 61, 129, 147
Botha, P.W., 86
Bougainville, 217, 221, 223, 229, 230
Bourdieu, Pierre, 103
Braithwaite, John, 11, 124–5, 151, 199, 225, 251, 255
Braithwaite, Valerie, 228
Brewer, John, 160
Brown, Wendy, 88
Buber, Martin, 244
Burundi, 27, 189, 235

Cain, 184
Call, Charles T., 5
Cambodia, 4
Campaign for Good Governance Sierra Leone, 46, 58
Canada, 2, 6, 7, 217
Catholic Peacebuilding Network, 52, 60
Catholic Relief Services, 46, 52, 61
Cavarero, Adriana, 204
Chad, 90
Charlesworth, Hilary, 222
Chikane, Frank, 86
Chile, 6, 7, 81, 87, 90, 101, 106, 147, 179, 190
Christianity, 24–5, 49–50, 81, 183–90, 217, 223, 250; *see also* religion
Christie, Nils, 120
Civil Society, 37–38, 59, 181; *see also* community
Cohen, Stanley, 157

259

Index

Collier, Paul, 233
Colombia, 61, 189
community, 22–23, 25, 27, 40–4, 124, 153–5, 182
community rituals, *see* local traditions
compensation, 2, 122, 132–3, 198, 230
confession, 104, 125, 134, 180–1, 188, 230
contrition, 182, 188, 253
Copernicus, 240, 241, 245
Courts, *see* trial
Cousens, Elizabeth M., 5
Cristiani, Alfredo, 178

Damas, Artuo Rivera y, 53, 188
De Greiff, Pablo, 93, 100–1, 102, 106, 197, 198
De Gruchy, John, 84, 86, 88, 179, 181
Democratic Republic of Congo, 5, 37, 208
democracy, 31, 78, 121, 124, 151, 204, 209, 211
Descartes, Rene, 84
development, 52, 199, 204, 206–7, 208, 210
Dewey, John, 244
Didcott, John, 208
dignity, 21, 189, 200, 204–5, 211, 228
Donohue, John R., 186
Doxtader, Erik, 83, 87–8
Draku, Moses, 153
Drumbl, Mark A., 148
Du Toit, Andre, 92

East Timor, 7, 41, 51, 53, 55–6, 96, 160, 163
East Timor and Indonesia Action Network, 47, 51
Einstein, Albert, 240
El Salvador, 5, 6, 53, 62, 90, 101, 178, 179, 188, 190, 192
Elias, Robert, 129–30
Enright, Robert, 177
equality, 19–20, 88, 130, 181
European Union, 29

faith based organizations, 9, 39, 42–3, 48–50, 51–8, 60–3, 251
feminism, 17, 21
Feuerbach, Ludwig, 244
Fiji, 220
forgiveness, 27, 40, 43–4, 78, 104, 108, 160–1, 231
 collective, 177–8, 190
 definition, 175–6
 and reconciliation, 9, 78, 104, 107–8, 229
 religious elements, 10–11, 25, 40, 44, 91–2, 107–8, 246
 in South Africa, 9, 89–91

Forsyth, Miranda, 218
Foucault, Michel, 201
Freeman, Mark, 90
Funes, Maurcio, 178

gacaca, 11, 215, 216, 218, 235
Galileo, 240
Gallagher, Susan, 85
Galtung, Johan, 142
Gavrielides, Theo, 149
Geertz, Clifford, 215, 255
Gerardi, Juan, 54
Germany, 5, 6, 123, 225
Ghana, 7
Gobodo-Madikizela, Pumla, 86
Gohar, Ali –, 223
Gonzalez, Eduardo –, 98
Goodman, Tanya –, 89, 90
gotong royong, 11, 215, 222, 224–9
Guatemala, 5, 6, 53, 54, 62
Gutmann, Amy, 181

Haiti, 90, 101, 200
Hardimon, Michael, 80
harm, 3–4, 19, 22–3, 26–7, 32, 118, 123, 126, 145, 152, 154, 161–3
Hayner, Priscilla, 58, 93, 94, 95, 97, 98
Hegel, Georg Wilhem Friedrich, 80–1, 244
Hobbes, Thomas, 30
human rights, 30, 105, 183, 200, 220, 243, 247, 255
 as peacebuilding strategy, 42–3, 79, 93, 103, 183
human rights violations, 26, 123, 139, 144, 146–7, 158, 159, 249
Human Rights Watch, 37, 41, 47, 50, 58, 94, 98
Hurley, Denis, 86
Huyse, Luc, 215, 218

Ignatieff, Michael, 247
immunity, 54, 155, 161, 164
impunity, 10, 51, 56, 138–40, 164, 253
Indonesia, 1, 11, 53, 55–56, 215, 222–3, 224, 225–8, 230,
inequality, 40, 43, 60, 61, 141, 202, 210
institutions, 7, 27, 49, 93, 180, 206, 208, 250
Interfaith Action for Peace in Kenya, 43, 46, 51, 57
International Center for Religion and Diplomacy, 46, 51, 57
International Center for Transitional Justice, 10, 41, 47, 58–9, 78–9, 83, 92–102, 214, 246

Index

International Criminal Court, 1, 4, 29, 37, 42, 48–9, 56, 59, 62, 63, 122, 127, 128, 138, 146, 200–1
International Criminal Tribunal for Rwanda, 121, 125
International Criminal Tribunal for Yugoslavia, 121, 125
international law, 10, 40, 48–51, 103, 118, 121, 127–8, 138–9, 141, 200, 241
Interreligious Council of Bosnia-Herzegovina, 43, 46, 51
Inter-Religious Council of Sierra Leone, 43, 46, 51
Iraq, 5, 27
Islam, 24–5, 40, 57–8, 216, 226, 231
Israel, 27

Japan, 200
Jesus, 25, 183–8
John Paul II, 23, 25, 55, 178, 186, 188–189
Judaism, 24–25, 40, 48–9
justice
  criminal, 17–8, 44, 50–1, 98, 119, 120, 127, 130–1, 145
  debate concerning, 2–5, 6, 7–8, 99–100
  definition of, 16–23, 145–6, 150, 219
  distributive, 89, 232
  relational, 28–34, 40
  retributive, 22, 39, 40, 48, 147, 149, 242

Kairos Document, 81, 87–8, 102–103
Kant, Immanuel, 11, 240–1, 244–5
Karstedt, Susanne, 225
Kenya, 37, 58, 59
Kepler, 240
King, Martin Luther, 177
Koggel, Christine, 19–20
Kony, Joseph, 128
Korey, William, 94–5
Kosovo, 4, 27
Krog, Antjie, 85, 91

Lash, Nicholas, 184, 188
Lebanon, 161
legalism, 6, 38, 42, 48–51, 63, 105, 139
Levinas, Emmanuel, 201, 211, 244
liberal peace, 11, 31, 38, 241–2, 243, 249
liberalism, 16, 20–1, 31, 63, 108, 198, 206
Liberia, 6, 7
Libya, 5, 37
Lira, Elizabeth, 183
Lisan, 42, 56, 154
Llewellyn, Jennifer, 39, 63, 123, 146, 150, 154, 162, 182, 215, 221, 243–4

local traditions, 1, 6, 38, 40, 41, 155–6, 221, 255
Locke, John, 30, 198, 249
Lords Resistance Army, 1, 50, 56, 59, 62, 128, 153
Luna, Erik, 231
Lundy, Patricia, 148
Lyotard, Jean-Francois, 204, 244

McCold, Paul, 123
McCullough, Michael, 175–6, 178, 192
Mack, Andrew, 5
McLuhan, Marshal, 205
Malamud-Goti, Jaime, 101
Malinowski, Bronislaw, 205
Mallinder, Louise, 10, 11, 199, 214, 251, 252, 253–4
Mandela, Nelson, 78, 83, 85, 103, 211
Mani, Rama, 154
Mariezcurrena, Javier, 15
Marshall, Christopher, 186–7, 191, 192
Maruna, Shadd, 228–9
Marx, Karl, 244
Mauritius, 200
Mbeki, Govan, 211
Mbeki, Thabo, 89, 211
Melanesia, 223
Mendez, Juan E., 98, 99–100
Mennonite Central Committee, 38, 41, 45, 46, 52, 60–2
mercy, 24–6, 138, 176
Merry, Sally Engle, 216, 219–221, 223, 233, 234
Meyer, Roelf, 202–3
Mills, C. Wright, 222
Minow, Martha, 83, 121, 133
Mkhatshwa, Smangaliso, 86
Moluccas, 223
Moosa, Ebrahim, 89
Morocco, 7
Mozambique, 5, 42, 56, 57, 224, 235
Museveni, 50, 62

National Association of Evangelicals, 47, 49–50
natural law, 191, 240
Naude, Beyers, 86
Ndebele, Njabulo, 209
Neier, Aryeh, 94–5
Neuman, Justin, 84–5
New Zealand, 6, 217, 219, 224
Nicaragua, 53, 54–5, 61, 62
non-state justice, 215, 216–17
non-truth, 224–225, 227, 229
Northern Ireland, 5, 6
Nussbaum, Martha, 210
Nyerere, Julius, 210

Index

O'Connell, Terry, 229, 231
O'Rourke, Catherine, 149
Obando y Bravo, Miguel, 53, 54–5
Odama, John Baptist, 56
Organization of the Islamic Conference, 43, 46, 51, 57
Ortega, Daniel, 54–5

Pakistan, 223
Palestine, 27
Parmentier, Stephan, 156
participation, 152, 153–155, 158, 201, 225, 254
Paul (Apostle), 226
peace
  negative, 214
  positive, 143, 180, 214
peacebuilding, 4–5, 7, 15–16, 39, 63, 214
Peru, 7, 96, 97
Philippines, 189
Philpott, Daniel, 39, 63, 141, 161, 182, 197, 198, 211, 214, 215, 221, 243
Pigou, Piers, 158
Pinochet, Augusto, 81, 179
Plato, 27
Pope, Stephen J., 10, 11, 250–1, 252
Posel, Deborah, 77, 89, 90
prosecution, 37, 42, 48, 96, 100, 120, 139, 146–8, 149
Ptolemy, 240
punishment, 10, 39, 118, 133, 139, 147, 159–61, 176, 254
  restorative, 134, 186

Quaker Peace and Social Witness, 41, 46, 60

Ramaphosa, Cyril, 203
Rawls, John, 232
rebuilding, 143, 225, 227, 228
reconciliation, 43–4, 58, 160, 214, 227, 232, 248
  debate over, 7–8, 16–17, 80, 93–100, 103–8
  definition of, 23–8, 80–2, 141–4, 176, 178–81, 184–9, 225
  traditional practices, 26, 40, 153
reintegration, 22, 145, 153–4, 155–6, 157, 225, 227, 229
relationship, 3, 16–23, 24–7, 29–34, 39–40, 80, 141–6, 150, 152, 184–7, 189, 205–6, 243–4
religion, 23, 40, 42–4, 60, 156, 191–2, 224, 232, 246–8, 250–1
  in South Africa, 2, 85–6, 88–9, 92, 102–8, 182
remorse, 25, 90, 151, 159–60, 163, 227, 230

reparations, 2, 4, 6, 27, 77–8, 89, 130, 162–3, 197, 249–50; *see also* restitution
repentance, 25, 54, 178, 185, 198
responsibility, 128–130, 133–4, 145, 150, 155, 182, 253
restitution, *see* reparations
restoration, 19, 28, 43–4, 51–9, 130–1, 150, 178, 243
restorative justice, 39–40, 43, 56, 60, 99–101, 118, 123–5, 126, 133, 139–40, 148, 198, 214–6, 231–2, 233
retribution, 58, 122, 152, 182, 207
Revolutionary United Front (RUF), 57
right to truth, 31, 130, 131, 156
rights, 6, 30–1, 130
  victim rights, 123, 134
Roche, Declan, 157
Roht-Arriaza, Naomi, 15
Roman Catholic Church, 29, 38, 41, 43, 46, 51–7, 60, 62, 176, 183
rule of law, 3, 6, 7, 17, 26, 29, 48–50, 79, 121, 138, 139, 142, 143, 144, 146, 180, 188
Ruth-Heffelbower, Duane, 225–6
Rwanada, 4, 5, 11, 27, 53, 94, 200, 216, 218, 235

Salazar, Philippe-Joseph, 87–8
Salter, Mark, 215, 218
Sandinista, 54–5
Sant'Egidio (Community of), 43, 46, 52, 56–7
Schedler, Andreas, 157
Schobesberger, (Colonel), 91
Schreiter, Robert, 185
secular, 6, 42–4, 50–1, 58, 89, 105–8, 245–8
Sen, Amartya, 210
Serbia, 129
Sierra Leone, 4, 96
Slye, Ron, 160
Soares, Aderito, 222
social justice, 52, 61, 181, 198
Solomon Islands, 7, 217
South Africa, 2, 5, 6, 10, 59, 78, 79, 80–92, 93, 98, 99, 101–3, 106, 125, 140, 151, 154, 162, 164, 197, 199, 200–1, 202–3, 206–9, 250
South African Truth and Reconciliation Commission, 2, 77–9, 149, 192, 206,
  and amnesty, 151–2, 155, 157–8, 160, 162
  and religion, 5, 80–92, 101–6, 180, 245–6
  and restorative justice –, 7, 11, 91, 182
Soviet Union, 49
Springs, Jason, 11–12
state justice, 216, 218, 222–4, 231, 255
Strang, Heather, 232
structural injustice, 87, 146, 154, 162, 186, 209
subsidiarity, 23, 29, 124
Sudan, 5, 37, 53, 128, 200, 201
Syria, 5

Index

Taylor, Charles, 79
Tepperman, Jonathan, 80
Thompson, Dennis, 92, 181
Timor-Leste, 5, 10, 140, 152, 153, 154, 155, 158, 160, 161, 163, 164, 217, 222–3
Tojeira, Jose Maria, 179
Tompot, John, 221
Toruno, Rodolfo Quezado, 53, 54
traditional rituals, *see* local traditions
transitional justice, 59, 77–9, 82, 92–102, 104–8, 139–40, 141–2
trials, 39, 48, 51, 53–55, 122, 125, 146–8
tribunals, 4, 121, 138; *see also* trials
trust, 43, 44, 57, 60, 61, 101
truth, 81–82, 90, 133, 152, 157, 188, 201, 226
    commissions, 4, 27, 31, 81–83, 90, 94–99, 133, 138, 154, 180–181
    recovery, 54, 156, 157, 158, 164
    telling, 40, 43–4, 56, 59, 159, 209, 249, 254
Turner, Victor, 89
Tutu, Desmond, 2, 7, 9, 10, 23, 77–8, 79, 81, 84–5, 86, 88–9, 90, 91, 97, 101–4, 182

ubuntu, 81, 83–85, 91, 182, 201, 204
Uganda, 1, 5, 10, 37, 42, 45, 50, 53, 56, 59, 61, 62, 128, 140, 149, 152, 153, 155, 156, 161, 163, 164, 200, 208
United Kingdom, 231
United Nations, 2, 4, 16, 29, 30, 33, 82, 121, 125, 139, 143, 144, 200, 208, 214, 220, 226
UN Peacebuilding Commission, 14–15, 29, 32, 33
United States, 6, 7, 38, 41, 49, 51, 102, 177, 217, 231

U.S. Conference of Catholic Bishops –, 46, 53
Uruguay –, 90

Van Ness, Daniel W., 10, 11, 123, 199, 251, 252, 253, 254
Van Zyl, Paul, 58, 93, 95, 96, 102
VanAntwerpen, Jonathan, 9, 10, 38, 59, 214, 245–7, 251, 252
Vanuatu, 218
Varney, Howard, 98
Verdeja, Ernesto, 198–199, 211
Villa-Vicencio, Charles, 11, 96, 97, 106, 155, 178, 180, 181, 192, 244, 249–51, 252, 254
Vinjamuri, Leslie, 9, 128, 251, 252, 255
Vorster, John, 88

Wajir Peace and Development Committee, 43, 46, 58
Weber, Max, 103
Williams, Bernard, 211
Women to Women, 43, 46, 58
World Jewish Congress, 42, 47, 48
wounds, 26–28, 77, 200, 247, 251; *see also* harm

Yugoslavia, 4, 61

Zacchaeus, 187–8
Zalaquett, Jose, 92, 181
Zehr, Howard, 197, 232, 242–3
Zifcak, Spencer, 158